National Parks, Native Sovereignty

Public Lands History

GENERAL EDITORS

Ruth M. Alexander
Adrian Howkins
Jared Orsi
Sarah Payne

EDITED BY
CHRISTINA GISH HILL
MATTHEW J. HILL
BROOKE NEELY

National Parks, Native Sovereignty

Experiments in Collaboration

UNIVERSITY OF OKLAHOMA PRESS : NORMAN

Publication of this book is made possible through the generosity of Edith Kinney Gaylord.

Library of Congress Cataloging-in-Publication Data

Names: Hill, Christina Gish, 1976– editor. | Hill, Matthew J., 1958– editor. | Neely, Brooke, 1981– editor.
Title: National parks, Native sovereignty : experiments in collaboration / edited by Christina Gish Hill, Matthew J. Hill, and Brooke Neely.
Other titles: Public lands history ; v. 7.
Description: Norman : University of Oklahoma Press, [2024] | Series: Public lands history series ; volume 7 | Includes bibliographical references and index. | Summary: "This volume shares insight into contemporary efforts to address the colonial history of U.S. national parks through research, outreach, and collaborative partnerships with tribal nations"—Provided by publisher.
Identifiers: LCCN 2023040808 | ISBN 978-0-8061-9380-9 (hardcover) | ISBN 978-0-8061-9368-7 (paperback)
Subjects: LCSH: United States. National Park Service—History. | Indians of North America—Government relations. | National parks and reserves—United States.
Classification: LCC E93 .N283 2024 | DDC 363.6/80973—dc23/eng/20230919
LC record available at https://lccn.loc.gov/2023040808

National Parks, Native Sovereignty: Experiments in Collaboration is Volume 7 in the Public Lands History series.

The paper in this book meets the guidelines for permanence and durability of the Committee on Production Guidelines for Book Longevity of the Council on Library Resources, Inc. ∞

Copyright © 2024 by the University of Oklahoma Press, Norman, Publishing Division of the University. Manufactured in the U.S.A.

All rights reserved. No part of this publication may be reproduced, stored in a retrieval system, or transmitted, in any form or by any means, electronic, mechanical, photocopying, recording, or otherwise—except as permitted under Section 107 or 108 of the United States Copyright Act—without the prior written permission of the University of Oklahoma Press. To request permission to reproduce selections from this book, write to Permissions, University of Oklahoma Press, 2800 Venture Drive, Norman OK 73069, or email rights.oupress@ou.edu.

CONTENTS

Acknowledgments | vii

Introduction | 1
Christina Gish Hill, Matthew J. Hill, and Brooke Neely

ONE   Historical Overview | 15
Mark David Spence

PART I   **ENTRY POINTS: EMERGING PARTNERSHIPS, MUTUAL BENEFITS**

INTERVIEW   Max Bear | 35

TWO   Reciprocal Respect: Lessons Learned about Collaboration | 43
Christina Gish Hill

THREE   Indigenous Connections at Rocky Mountain National Park: Notes from a Collaboration in Progress | 61
Brooke Neely and Natasha Myhal

FOUR   Recentering the Middle Ground: A Case Study on Indigenous Nationhood and the Future of National Parks | 77
Mark David Spence

PART II   **HEADWINDS: CHALLENGING CASES, PAINFUL HISTORIES**

INTERVIEW   Gerard Baker   105

FIVE   Historicizing the "Shrine of Democracy": Lakota Perspectives on Mount Rushmore in the Context of the Black Hills | 122
Matthew J. Hill

| SIX | The Lewis and Clark Bicentennial | 142
Jackie Gonzales

| SEVEN | After the Opening: Shared Authority and Multivocality at the Sand Creek Massacre National Historic Site | 164
Ari Kelman

PART III **SUSTAINED COLLABORATIONS: MAINTAINING AGREEMENTS, SUCCESSFUL CO-MANAGEMENT**

| INTERVIEW | Lance Michael Foster   183

| EIGHT | Indigenous Agency and Protected Spaces of Nature: Three Case Studies of Collaboration in North America | 196
Rani-Henrik Andersson

| NINE | Returning to Gather: Cherokee Medicine Keepers, the National Park Service, and the Making of a Plant-Gathering Agreement at Buffalo National River | 216
Richard W. Stoffle, Michael J. Evans, and Clint Carroll

| TEN | Making the Tribal Self-Governance Act Work at Grand Portage | 238
Timothy Cochrane

Epilogue | 262
Christina Gish Hill, Matthew J. Hill, and Brooke Neely

Contributors | 267

Index | 271

ACKNOWLEDGMENTS

WE WISH TO EXPRESS OUR GRATITUDE to the people and institutions whose support made this volume possible. During the long process of researching, writing, and collaborating that culminated in this book, we benefited greatly from the wisdom and generosity of many. While this book has been shaped by all these relationships over the process of its creation, any inaccuracy found within is solely the responsibility of the editors.

The idea for this book grew out of a collaboration that began like any good collaboration: with a National Park Service ethnographic overview and assessment project on Mount Rushmore National Memorial. Matthew was located at the UMass Amherst Center for Heritage & Society when he got the contract. He reached out to Christina and Brooke to join him in writing the ethnographic portion of the EOA because their work intersected with the project goals. Christina worked in the region while researching for Patricia Albers' landmark NPS study of Wind Cave National Park and conducting her own ethnographic work with the Northern Cheyenne. Brooke did ethnographic research in the 2000s on Mount Rushmore and Crazy Horse Memorials during Gerard Baker's tenure as superintendent. She also has family ties to the Black Hills region.

As we worked to create the EOA, we realized that many scholars and other practitioners would benefit from what we had learned in the process. We began to discuss putting together a book that would highlight collaboration building between NPS, Native nations, and scholars. This journey to imagining and co-creating this book has been shaped by interactions with many knowledgeable and generous people. First and foremost, we are all grateful for Gerard Baker's expertise, kindness, openness, and sense of fun amid many very challenging situations. He was successfully collaborating across disparate groups well before we came on the scene. He encouraged us to complicate well-worn narratives about Mount Rushmore and other NPS sites by recognizing Native voices and reconsidering popular understandings about the past. He inspired us in the way he encourages dialogue, faces conflict, and facilitates potential healing. He also tells a mean joke.

Thank you to Joe Watkins, who as Chief of Tribal Relations and American Cultures and Supervisory Cultural Anthropologist for the NPS when we began the EOA, helped us to think about NPS sites as conversation starters about painful histories. We are also thankful for Patricia Albers who suggested that we focus on Native peoples' everyday uses of public lands, rather than just thinking about sacred sites in the Black Hills as has so often been done. Thank you also to Anne Hyde and Jeffrey Ostler at OAH; Craig Howe, Center Director for Native CAIRNS; Lakota elder Basil Brave Heart; Black Hills archaeologist and ethnohistorian Linea Sundstrum; Elaine Marie Nelson at KSU; Lakota writer and activist Charmaine White Face; and Jace DeCory, emeritus professor of Native American Studies at Black Hills State University. We appreciate the knowledge and wisdom each of these people shared in support of the project.

This work would not have been possible without the collaboration of multiple Native communities as well as the communities around various national parks. We want to acknowledge Katie Blindman and the Pine Ridge Cultural Committee for their input and overall support for the project, as well as Teana Limpy, Northern Cheyenne THPO, and the Northern Cheyenne Cultural Committee for their helpful guidance and input on the project. Thank you to Ben Rhodds, Rosebud THPO, and the Rosebud Cultural Committee for their support of the project. We are also grateful to Max Bear, Cheyenne, and Arapaho Tribes THPO and his helpful guidance and support throughout. Thank you also to Betsy Chapoose, Terry Knight, Sr., Alden Naranjo, Hanley Frost, Cassandra Atencio, Garrett Briggs, Devin Oldman, Crystal C'Bearing, and Jordan Dresser.

During this process we were inspired to bring people together in conference panels and other informal convenings to share their experiences collaborating on Indigenous issues within the National Park Service. In doing so, we realized that together we could create a volume that would share these observations with researchers, tribal staff, and park service employees to support collaborative work on public lands. For providing their insight and organizational skills, as well as their role in helping us envision these conversations, we would especially like to thank: Virginia Richie, Jameson Sweet, Ernest House, Jr., Donald Ragona, Tom Thomas, Alexa Roberts, Rich Fedorchak, Kelly Dick, Kim Greenwood, Kathy Brazelton, Kim Swift, and Rising Buffalo Maybee.

One of the biggest challenges of an edited volume is bringing together authors whose work speaks to each other in interesting ways. We are profoundly honored that the authors in this volume were inspired to add their reflections on their experiences collaborating with the park service. They worked patiently with us and each other, balancing the challenges of pandemic life with their commitment to this volume. We shared conversations across fields and specialties, learning from each other as we worked to shape these disparate experiences into a cohesive volume. Thank you doesn't quite cover it: Gerard Baker, Max Bear, Lance Foster,

Rani-Henrik Andersson, Clint Carroll, Tim Cochrane, Mike Evans, Jackie Gonzales, Ari Kelman, Natasha Myhal, Mark Spence, and Rich Stoffle.

This book would not have been possible without our University of Oklahoma Press editor Alessandra Tamulevich and our series editor Jared Orsi. Thank you to Alessandra for believing in the project and for her patience and good humor with our various challenges and shifting requests. Alessandra's insight to place us in Jared Orsi's series made this book what it is. We will always be grateful to Jared for his support. He showed interest and enthusiasm from day one (at a happy hour for public historians), encouraged us at each challenge along the way, and always advocated on our behalf to Alessandra and UOP. His detailed reading of the manuscript was essential to the revision process, providing insight not only on each chapter but also on how they illuminated the wider themes of the volume. We're incredibly grateful for his detailed critique of our scholarship as well as his thoughtful advice about how to complete an edited volume, no small task when organizing texts from such a diverse group of contributors. Jared, your willingness to step up when we needed you and your generosity of management style created a better book. You're a model to us all on how to be a scholar, editor, and collaborator. Especially because you are so darn kind and calm.

We've each been nurtured by colleagues in our respective departments and appreciate the supportive environments they create for our research. We're particularly grateful to colleagues and friends who have read drafts and provided feedback on the manuscript, including: Nell Gabiam, Jonathan Hassid, and Robert Urbatsch at Iowa State University; Elizabeth Chilton, Elizabeth Brabec, and Terry Trudeau (for the help managing the NPS EOA grant) at the University of Massachusetts' Center for Heritage & Society and the Department of Landscape Architecture & Regional Planning; Michelle Samura, Jon Cruz, George Lipsitz, Howard Winant, John Mohr, Avery Gordon, Eve Darian-Smith, and Carolyn Pinedo-Turnovsky from the University of California Santa Barbara; Patty Limerick, Karen Ramirez, Kurt Gutjahr, Roni Ires, Angelica Lawson, Andrew Cowell, Thomas Andrews, Jennifer Shannon, Ashlyn Barnett, Tamar McKee, and Tom Zeiler at the University of Colorado Boulder's Center of the American West and Center for Native American and Indigenous Studies; and the many more folks who discussed or collaborated on the topics and questions covered in this book over many years.

Each of us are continually grateful to the family and friends that support our research in so many ways. Christina would like to thank Alon and Benny for their care, encouragement, and good humor. The process of writing, researching, and travel is often lonely, but the hard work is smoother with them by her side. Also thank you to Jade and others for welcoming her and her family whenever they travel to Northern Cheyenne. Their generosity means more than we have words for.

Matthew would like to thank his partner, the anthropologist Tamara Neuman, for her unwavering support of this project, and for her friendship and intellectual companionship. Thanks as well to his parents, Eugene and Patricia, and to his brother Forrest. A special shout out to his Philadelphia neighbors, the anthropologists Kaushik Ghosh and Sarada Balagopalan, for the wonderful dinners and engaging conversations.

Brooke would like to thank her parents Jamie and Cajer and her sister Meg for creating a lifelong, cozy home for exploring all sorts of ideas and questions; Grandma Marlene and Grandpa Dick for their encouragement and support in the Black Hills; and finally, Nick, Evie, and Hazel for their genuine interest in her work outside the home and for all their love, laughter, and kitchen dance parties.

We are grateful to have been able to come together as a team, managing Zoom meetings across three time zones and through a pandemic to bring the vision of this book to reality. What began as a collaboration between colleagues has grown into a friendship as we planned over drinks at conferences, enjoyed interruptions to our Zoom meetings by children and pets, stayed connected through the darkest moments of the pandemic, and patiently negotiated each other's changing schedules. As is the goal of any research collaboration, we are each richer human beings as the result of this one. We continue to grow in our gratitude to the lands where we live and work, the people who inhabit them, and the complex histories that inspire us to move forward in this work, seeking new avenues for collaboration.

Introduction

CHRISTINA GISH HILL, MATTHEW J. HILL, AND BROOKE NEELY

ON DECEMBER 16, 2021, US Secretary of the Interior Deb Haaland shook hands with the newly sworn-in director of the National Park Service (NPS) Charles "Chuck" Sams III. At first glance, the promotional photo of Haaland and Sams on the steps of the Lincoln Memorial appears to be a swearing in like any other.[1] Of course, as many commentators emphasized at the time, this ceremony also marked a notable historical moment—when the first Native person to head the Department of the Interior officially welcomed the first Native person to head the NPS. Early in her tenure as interior secretary, Haaland had already made significant steps—advocating for tribal land protections, boarding school investigations, and renaming derogatory place names.[2] Many have wondered what precedent the appointment of Haaland and Sams may set for how the federal government engages with Native peoples and tribal nations across the United States, and how their leadership could establish new cultural norms for recognizing Native sovereignty more broadly.

The editors of this volume see this as a moment to celebrate and reflect. When we began this project, as much as we would have hoped for there to be Native people at the helm of these important institutions, we would not have predicted it would happen so soon. We read the news of Haaland's and Sams's appointments with a sense of hope for how they could usher in a new era—one in which Native peoples are more fully seen, and tribal nations engage with the federal government as sovereign nations with deep ties to (and expertise on) the public lands the Department of the Interior oversees. But we also wonder how much Haaland's and Sams's leadership can reshape a federal bureaucracy with a long and troubled legacy in relation to Native peoples. We believe this is a timely historical moment, one largely driven by Native communities, to consider how far the United States has come in understanding the importance of partnering with Native peoples and tribal nations over the management of public lands. At the same time, we acknowledge the constraints Haaland and Sams (and any federal government leaders) face as they attempt to enact change.

We also believe this is a moment for considering how meaningful collaborations between Native peoples and US national parks present a possible route for reckoning with our shared histories and for working to remedy the injuries of the past. This book offers a window into the on-the-ground efforts at a selection of national park sites as they work to more deeply engage with tribal nations. And it highlights how tribal nations strategically navigate their relationships with national parks to advocate for their nation's best interests. Ultimately, Haaland's and Sams's success depends on how widely the NPS (and other federal agencies) adopt and implement Haaland's and Sams's priorities, and how tribal nations continue to put pressure on federal agencies to recognize their sovereign rights to these lands.

National parks have a fraught history in the United States and globally with respect to Indigenous peoples. The creation of US national parks in the late nineteenth and early twentieth centuries was part of a broader project to dispossess Native peoples of their homelands.[3] Furthermore, the early conservation movement that advocated for the creation and protection of national parks ignored or explicitly erased the experience of Native peoples on these lands.[4] In parks such as Yosemite, Yellowstone, and Glacier, park boosters reified these constructed landscapes as original and pristine, arguing that the land was compromised by Native peoples' presence. Mount Rushmore palpably illustrates such exclusion and erasure. The sculptor carved an explicitly Euro-American vision of the nation onto a landscape held sacred by many Native Americans.[5] Though not always quite so dramatically, other parks do the same.

Yet, in response to Native peoples' lobbying over the past fifty years for greater protections of sacred sites and cultural practices, the NPS has worked to address the damage done by this complex colonial history.[6] The NPS now consults with tribal nations on the protection, management, and use of cultural and natural resources located in national parks. Through its Tribal Historic Preservation Officer (THPO) and Ethnography in the Parks programs, the NPS seeks to bring park staff and researchers together with Indigenous resource managers and elders. The projects that emerge from these collaborations explore ways to revitalize, protect, interpret, and potentially co-manage Indigenous landscapes. Tribal nations have also approached the park service to engage with issues ranging from rights of access to co-managing lands. These collaborative projects do not come without obstacles, however. Well-intentioned NPS staff must navigate a challenging bureaucracy and funding shortfalls. Native people also have good reasons to be wary of federal agencies and academic institutions with colonial legacies. As a result, some working relationships are uneasy. Despite the challenges, collaborative projects strive to listen to Native voices, illuminate previously excluded histories, revitalize Native relationships with ancestral lands, and improve access for Native people to perform ceremonies or collect culturally important resources.

In recent years, the US national conversation around Native peoples and national parks has also included calls to return these lands to tribal nations.[7] And some tribal nations have gained increased control over resources and lands managed by national parks and other federal land agencies.[8] We have seen national debates unfold over sites like Bears Ears National Monument, highlighting how much national politics can play into efforts to honor tribal nations' wishes for public lands in the United States. Given all these recent developments within the NPS, as well as the appointment of Deb Haaland and Chuck Sams, we believe this moment is ripe for conversations about new forms of engagement and collaboration among tribal nations, national parks, and scholars.

The existing literature on Native peoples and US national parks is either primarily historical in nature or framed in terms of an environmental studies perspective.[9] More recent studies examine the environmental history of national parks from a transnational perspective, analyzing the origins, ideas, and ideological functions of national parks in comparative perspective.[10] Another body of literature examines national parks, conservation areas, and wildlife refuges from a conservation management perspective, exploring paradigms for the co-management of protected areas.[11] There is also a robust literature on Native peoples and museums, including the NPS's role in the repatriation movement and fulfilling the requirements of the Native American Graves Protection and Repatriation Act (NAGPRA).[12] Building on sponsored research studies of US national parks,[13] with this volume, we highlight ethnographic and ethnohistorical approaches to offer Native perspectives on national parks, while exploring the possibilities and challenges of collaborative work (involving shared interpretation, governance, and management) between the NPS and tribal nations today.

The chapters in the volume come from a variety of perspectives and positionalities: Native scholars and practitioners offer their insights and expertise on the potential for these collaborations. Non-Native park service staff adept at building relationships with Native communities also contributed, along with non-Native scholars who have conducted research that supports these collaborations. By bringing together these diverse perspectives, we seek to contribute to a larger conversation and invite further dialogue.

Coming to the Work

Drawing on case studies from National Park Service sites, this edited volume shares insight into contemporary efforts to address the colonial history of US national parks through research, outreach, and collaborative partnerships with tribal nations. The rise in collaborative work between the NPS and tribal nations over the past two decades is part of a broader wave of engagement and partnerships between tribal nations and federal, state, and non-government institutions. Responding to a backlash from Native people about the management of their lands by the federal government, particularly in national parks, the park service made an official commitment to recognize and consult with Native nations in 1987 with its Native American Relationships Management policy.[14] Native people have been present in most parks since their founding, but their presence had been viewed as either a nuisance by park service staff or as part of the tourist attraction of the park. The 1987 policy recognized the need and provided guidance for more open and formal communication between the park service and tribal nations. Then with a wave of new federal policies in the 1990s that included NAGPRA, National Park Service sites began to view tribal consultation as a required element of their processes and protocols.[15] Native people increasingly worked as interpreters, rangers, and even administrative staff in the NPS. But the road to fully recognizing the sovereignty of tribal nations in relation to federal lands has been a much longer one.

With this volume, we hope to contribute to the conversation about Native peoples' sovereign relationships to federal lands, a conversation that has gained traction in recent years. We seek to create a volume that uses case studies to guide practitioners from Native communities, the park service, and research institutions like universities through the process of partnering to conduct collaborative research. As editors, each of us have experience as scholars conducting research for the NPS. We want to share our own experiences, while bringing together practitioners from each of these groups to relate their experiences with collaborative work as well. Often people involved in this work end up reinventing the wheel because of staff turnover or shifting priorities at parks. When we discussed the challenges we faced in our respective projects, we recognized how much we could learn from each other. We also realized that there are tribal historic preservation officers, park staff, and researchers who have more experience than we do, and we all could benefit from their depth of knowledge. The purpose of this volume is to bring these insights together into one place. Through the case studies presented here, we have seen how establishing ongoing relationships between invested parties can lead to practices and policies within the NPS that uphold Native sovereignty. The volume also highlights how those parks that meaningfully engage with Native peoples have improved and enriched the experience of parks for both tribal partners and the millions of annual park visitors. We recognize Native sovereignty on park service land is inherently limited, but we wish to explore how we can build collaborative partnerships that are more reflective of Indigenous relationships to the land. We ask: how can tribal nations and Native peoples, NPS sites and their employees, and university researchers and other academic practitioners collaborate on mutually beneficial projects and activities?

While this volume has implications beyond the specific NPS sites included and even the National Park Service itself, it is not comprehensive. It does not reflect all the work the NPS and tribal nations are doing together today across all geographic locations. Our focus is methodological instead of location-based. We have structured the volume around case studies that provide examples of different types and styles of collaborative projects to illustrate possible pathways for people interested in engaging in this work. While we do not cover all national parks with their specific locales and the Native communities connected to them, we do recognize that different tribal nations have specific legal relationships with the United States as well as distinct land bases and political circumstances, all of which need to be considered when engaging in consultation and collaboration. While the specificity of collaboration may look different based on locale, history, and politics, we believe the general issues these cases raise offer valuable insight on how best to do this sort of collaborative work. At the least, they can be a starting point for further discussion.

The cases shared in the volume show how some parks have successfully accomplished collaborative relationships, leading to Native-designed exhibits, agreements for utilizing natural resources, and even co-management by tribal nations and the park service. Nevertheless, building such collaborations is complicated, and practitioners often struggle with how best to carry out the work in ways that respect protocols, serve the interests of all stakeholders, and achieve meaningful outcomes. Furthermore, the depth and longevity of this kind of collaborative work often depends on developing strong personal relationships, which can be difficult to maintain over time as people change jobs and retire. Each of the contributors to this volume have worked to build collaborations between the park service, scholars, and Native knowledge holders. This volume describes a three-step process for building collaborative relationships between tribal nations, researchers, and NPS staff: 1) initiating relationships; 2) engaging in difficult conversations; and 3) building sustained collaborations through formal agreements.

While the methodologies discussed in this volume can apply to other public lands and public history sites, we have chosen to focus on national parks in the United States for multiple reasons. We recognize that national parks are by no means unique to the United States. In their national parks, other countries have taken different approaches to developing collaborative relationships with Indigenous peoples.[16] And while a comparative study would be useful, with this volume, we begin the conversation in the United States, where most of our work has taken place.

US national parks have a specific history that is tied to the displacement of Indigenous people from the landscape. In the past, parks not only removed Native peoples from their homelands, preventing them from accessing resources within traditional territories, they also worked to erase Native people from the hegemonic, settler-oriented narratives of the landscape they presented. While other public lands have contributed to these efforts, national parks have a specific mission that includes creating an enjoyable visitor experience and educating the general public. They also have a responsibility to present narratives that are reflective of all citizens of the United States and not just a particular group. Until recently, national parks have largely presented a narrative to visitors that views the nineteenth-century North American landscape as an unpopulated wilderness waiting to be tamed by heroic Euro-Americans. Indigenous peoples have either been erased from the narrative or cast as part of the wilderness. Early conservationists and US federal policymakers saw national park preserves as one method of controlling both the lands and peoples across the continent. Even as park sites have worked to expand their interpretive lens to include Native peoples, they often keep the exhibits that celebrate early conservationists and park founders without considering how the very creation of national parks displaced and dispossessed Native peoples.[17]

US-based Native nations have a specific and somewhat unique legal relationship with the federal government in the United States, and as a part of this relationship, the federal government has a mandate to consult with tribal nations as it manages public lands. The National Park Service, with its own preservation-orientated mission, operates as an important agency and forum for consultation and collaboration with tribal nations. While the methodologies presented here can benefit collaborative work on other public lands as well, the park service's federal status and specific mandate to educate the public create unique opportunities not always found in state parks or Bureau of Land Management and US Forest Service land.

Building collaborative relationships between the park service and tribal nations is one practical way the United States can uphold its responsibility to recognize Native sovereignty. While the United States has acknowledged the sovereignty of tribal nations throughout its history, in practice, the federal government only recognizes tribal sovereignty on a limited basis. The collaborative methods discussed here are designed to bring tribal nations more fully into the conversations happening within the park service. However, collaborations cannot provide full repair for the loss experienced by Native peoples at the hands of the federal government or even the park service. While this collaborative methodology might lead to decolonizing work, it does not fundamentally address the damage done by colonization in North America.[18] For example, building collaborative relationships with NPS will not result in the return of land, as many in the Land Back movement have advocated for more recently.[19] Even with Native people in leadership positions within the park service and with co-management agreements in place at some parks, the park service ultimately has the power to dictate what happens within the park system, revealing the limitations of Native sovereignty in relation to these public lands.

Despite these limitations, we believe the case studies explored in this volume demonstrate that collaboration between the park service and tribal nations can lead to fruitful and lasting accomplishments for park sites and Native communities across the country. Many parks have worked to improve their interpretive programs (e.g., exhibits, ranger talks, media materials) after engaging with tribal representatives about the histories of the parks and Indigenous relationships to the lands. Over the past two decades, Native knowledge holders have increasingly shared their histories at park sites and even helped to create interpretive materials. Within this volume, the Sand Creek Massacre National Historic Site stands out as a notable example of co-created interpretive content at a park site. Often bringing Native voices into the educational materials at a park has involved first reckoning with historical injuries, including removal from a vital landscape and the violence committed against Native people on that land. To begin the collaborative process, park service staff ideally must acknowledge these histories as a part of the process of improving relationships with tribal partners. Ultimately, these collaborations have created opportunities for Native peoples to reconnect with culturally significant landscapes. This may include sharing their knowledge of the land and its cultural and natural history with a wider audience. It may also include accessing the sacred spaces and resources contained within these parks. Such opportunities open up space for tribal nations to reassert the sovereign relationships they have maintained with these landscapes. In some cases, this has even led to co-management of the lands.

Building Collaborations

Collaborations among tribal nations, national parks, and scholars can come about in a variety of ways. One route is through the National Park Service's historical research programs. With historians and ethnographers on staff, as well as contracted researchers, the NPS carries out a range of research initiatives to record the administrative histories and other relevant information about specific parks.[20] They create reports about how parks have been managed as well as how management decisions have reflected social, cultural, political, economic, and environmental trends historically. These histories can also reveal the impacts that parks have had on the multiple populations, both human and non-human, that interact with these landscapes. The NPS encourages parks to conduct oral histories with park service employees to gain more insight into the administrative history of each park.

The NPS has also developed an Ethnography in the Parks program, which conducts ethnographic research with the peoples who have cultural, historical, or economic ties to a specific park site.[21] Some historic sites may call for ethnographers to interview the people that worked in a particular industry, lived in a certain place, or practiced their religious way of life on what is today park service land. Many Indigenous people in the United States have ties to landscapes that today fall under the jurisdiction of the National Park Service. However, the geographic boundaries (i.e., lines on a map) created by the NPS do not reflect the deep and ongoing connections Native people have to these lands. Indeed, for most park sites, Indigenous people of the region have resided on the landscape for generations to gather resources and to assert a culturally defined relationship with the land. Often ethnography conducted by the park service can provide a space for Native people to assert their relationship with these lands, documenting the importance of it and demonstrating the need for it to continue.

Ethnographic and historical research done within the National Park Service works to accomplish many things. It can document the peoples and events represented within a park, capturing multiple perspectives on the past as well as the cultural meanings of the place. It can also enhance the educational materials presented by the park, expanding museum exhibits and making programs more relevant to a wider range of visitors. Finally, it can help to manage cultural and natural resources in ways that are not only appropriate to conservationists, but also to the Indigenous peoples who hold traditional ecological knowledge about the landscape.

While the park service has their own professionals conducting this work, they also contract with outside researchers to complete both ethnographic and historical research. The NPS calls these reports ethnographic overviews and assessments, traditional use studies, and ethnographic landscape studies.[22] This kind of research may or may not involve collaboration. It can entail an archival and ethnographic methodology that does not request participants to help in the design of the research process or the establishment of park management protocols. This research also may or may not involve consultation. Consultation is a formal legal process, through which the park service must share information with different interest groups as it plans new projects on park lands. Consultation requires the NPS to make each group aware of the proposed project and to invite members of each group to meet and consult, including governmental or community leaders as well as members of the community.

Collaboration can (and often does) involve the formal NPS process of consultation with tribal partners, but it does not have to begin with an invitation to consult. Collaborative relationships between park service staff, researchers, and Native peoples have developed organically over time as well. At times, these relationships have been initiated by Native people, as was the case in Tim Cochrane's chapter on Grand Portage National Monument and Mark Spence's chapter on River Raisin National Battlefield Monument. In her chapter, Jackie Gonzales discusses the case of the Lewis and Clark Bicentennial, which was initially driven by the park service, but shifted towards collaboration as Gerard Baker became involved and invited Native peoples to speak candidly about their concerns over the event. As seen in this book, collaboration can be initiated from different positions, and once the relationships are established, they often evolve. Sometimes they develop into long lasting connections that guide the operations of the park, but this usually requires park staff to be open to new models of working with tribal partners.

Strategic Collaboration

The range of case studies in this volume, and the various types of engagement they illustrate, highlight how Native peoples assert agency and sovereignty in reconnecting with homelands and other vital places as they work with the National Park Service. They also show how scholars and park staff can and should play a more modest and supporting role, as they work to assist Native partners in this process. Throughout the volume, we explore the concept of *strategic collaboration* to make sense of the complex process by which project participants come together with sometimes conflicting interests and find ways to strategically engage with one another across these differences. While ethnography is always collaborative to a certain degree because it involves working with people to learn more about their culture and experience, research participants often do not design the research or its protocols. Nevertheless, Native people have used collaborations with park service staff and researchers for their own interests, engaging strategically to motivate change within the National Park Service. The chapters in this volume reveal how tribal nations use these partnerships to assert sovereignty, establish shared governance, accomplish cultural revitalization, and reconnect with ancestral homelands. In many places, Native peoples' strategic collaboration with parks have led these parks to reckon with their relationships with Native communities, rethinking how they interact with both Native people and the broader public on many levels. The volume emphasizes that collaboration is most successful when Native people engage on their own terms.

As a concept and as a framework for practice, strategic collaboration moves beyond the kind of engagement researchers often strive for in collaboration, sometimes with an assumption that all parties are working toward the same goals and with the same intentions. Strategic collaboration recognizes the potential for participants to navigate different sets of interests to accomplish shared or overlapping goals. Native nations, park service staff, and researchers are each seeking their own outcomes from the collaborative process. Sometimes these interests are competing, so integrating them requires openness and flexibility. When it's successful, strategic collaboration can be a process that furthers the sovereign relationships that Native people have with their landscapes. In strategic collaboration, park service staff and researchers assist and support Native people's efforts to access the landscape and to educate the staff and public about their history in a particular place. Ultimately, strategic collaboration is not an equal partnership. Because of its legal status in the United States, the NPS has more power and authority over the spaces they oversee than Native people do. Yet, tribal representatives come to the table and participate on their own terms.

Strategic collaboration is a process that involves developing a reciprocal and respect-based relationship from the start. The volume walks scholars and practitioners through the process of building a collaborative relationship between researchers, Native partners, and public lands representatives. In the case studies that follow, we lay out three general steps for building strategic collaborations. First, staff, researchers, and Native peoples must initiate sustainable relationships. As a result of the history of erasure and assimilation, Native peoples are often wary of developing partnerships with governmental organizations like the park service. But many of the successes presented in this volume are helping to change attitudes on both sides, as is having Native leadership at the top. Once the participants forge trusting relationships, each of the groups are more able to approach the difficult conversations that come with contested understandings of history and the meanings of a specific place. Ultimately, the goal is to gain sustained collaborations that uphold the sovereignty of the tribal nations that are affiliated with a particular landscape.

Volume Overview

The first section of the book provides a *pathway for entering the work*, discussing the steps needed to begin collaborative partnerships, including early tribal consultation, engaging Native collaborators, and framing projects from Native perspectives. Opening with a conversation with Max Bear (THPO for the Cheyenne and Arapaho Tribes) on initiating work with tribal nations, the chapters examine the steps needed to pursue collaborative projects, the range of actors involved, and the potential outcomes. These chapters highlight useful approaches to collaborative work with Native nations, including a discussion of initiating engagement with the Cheyenne and Arapaho nations for NPS sponsored research on Mount Rushmore National Memorial (Christina Gish Hill), expanding the interpretive framework of the nature-focused Rocky Mountain National Park (Brooke Neely and Natasha Myhal), and creating interpretive programs that include Native voices at the urban River Raisin National Battlefield Monument (Mark David Spence).

The second section moves to a discussion of the headwinds that Native communities, NPS staff, and researchers face at sites that explicitly deal with *painfully contested histories*. Opening with a conversation with NPS Superintendent Gerard Baker (Mandan Hidatsa) about his tenure at parks with contested histories (Little Bighorn Battlefield National Monument, Lewis and Clark National Historic Trail, Mount Rushmore National Memorial), this section builds on his thoughts to examine collaborations at sites that erase Native histories, re-narrate Native landscapes, or remember painful and violent events from territorial conquest. The chapters include case studies from Mount Rushmore National Memorial (Matthew J. Hill), the Lewis and Clark National Historic Trail (Jackie Gonzales), and the Sand Creek Massacre National Historic Site (Ari Kelman).

The third section concludes the volume by discussing strategic collaborations that tribal nations have successfully put in place to shape park management. This includes *shared governance arrangements* that open access to harvesting on public land and even create co-management agreements. Introducing the issues with an interview with Lance Foster (THPO for Iowa Tribe of Kansas and Nebraska) on the processes of building collaboration to reassert tribal control over federal lands (at Effigy Mounds, Blood Run National Historic Landmark, and Good Earth Tribal National Park), these chapters go on to explore shared governance arrangements at Wind Cave National Park, Channel Islands National Park, and Gwaii Haanas National Park (Rani Henrik-Andersson), a plant gathering agreement at Buffalo National River (Richard Stoffle, Mike Evans, and Clint Carroll), and a co-management agreement at Grand Portage National Monument (Tim Cochrane).

Overall, the chapters in this volume illuminate the overarching theme of *strategic collaboration*, highlighting how Native peoples assert agency and sovereignty in reconnecting with significant landscapes, and how non-Native scholars and park staff can incrementally assist Native partners in this process. The chapters illustrate how researchers and NPS staff should follow Native nations' protocols to develop meaningful working relationships, to avoid potential stumbling blocks, and to address past injustices. The chapters present Native-NPS partnerships that have attempted to transform parks, park staff, and their interpretative programs, while helping displaced Native communities renew ties to land, strengthen community bonds, and reclaim collective memories. Ultimately, the volume seeks to provide resources for building collaborations that uphold tribal sovereignty. Though uneasy at times, these collaborations have the potential to mutually benefit Native communities, the parks, their visitors, and the broader public.

Notes

1. Department of the Interior, "Charles F. Sams III Sworn In as National Park Service Director," press release (December 16, 2021). https://www.doi.gov/pressreleases/charles-f-sams-iii-sworn-national-park-service-director.
2. Scott Wyland, "Haaland Touts Indigenous, Conservation Work in First Year As Interior Secretary," *Santa Fe New Mexican* (March 16, 2022). https://www.santafenewmexican.com/news/local_news/haaland-touts-indigenous-conservation-work-in-first-year-as-interior-secretary/article_b25c3eee-a549-11ec-8e4f-0f72abc8a8b2.html.
3. See, for example: Theodore Catton, *Inhabited Wilderness: Indians, Eskimos, and National Parks in Alaska* (Albuquerque: University of New Mexico Press, 1997); Robert H. Keller and Michael F. Turek, *American Indians and National Parks* (Tucson: University of Arizona Press, 1998); Mark David Spence, *Dispossessing the Wilderness: Indian Removal and the Making of the National Parks* (Oxford: Oxford University Press, 1999); Philip Burnham, *Indian Country, God's Country: Native Americans and the National Parks* (Washington, DC: Island Press, 2000); Peter Nabokov and Lawrence Loendorf, *Restoring a Presence: American Indians and Yellowstone National Park* (Norman: University of Oklahoma Press, 2004).
4. For more information on the early conservation movement, including its Euro-American ideological framework and the racism of its members and its

approach, see for example: Dorceta E. Taylor, *The Rise of the American Conservation Movement: Power, Privilege, and Environmental Protection* (Durham, NC: Duke University Press, 2016).

5. Albert Boime, "Patriarchy Fixed in Stone: Gutzon Borglum's 'Mount Rushmore,'" *American Art* 5, no. 1/2 (Winter–Spring 1991): 142–67.
6. See, for example: S. Rheagan Alexander, "Tribal Consultation for Large-Scale Projects: The National Historic Preservation Act and Regulatory Review," *Pace Law Review* 32, no. 3 (2012): 895–921; Colette Routel and Jeffrey K. Holth, "Toward Genuine Tribal Consultation in the 21st Century," *University of Michigan Journal of Law Reform* 46, no. 2 (2013): 417–75.
7. See, for example: David Treuer, "Return the National Parks to the Tribes," *The Atlantic* (May 2021) (online April 12, 2021). https://www.theatlantic.com/magazine/archive/2021/05/return-the-national-parks-to-the-tribes/618395/; Jim Robbins, "How Returning Lands to Native Tribes is Helping Protect Nature," *Yale Environmental 360* (June 3, 2021). https://e360.yale.edu/features/how-returning-lands-to-native-tribes-is-helping-protect-nature.
8. In 2000, the Timbisha Shoshone Homeland Act passed as a notable example of land transfer and co-management. See: Theodore Catton, "To Make a Better Nation: An Administrative History of the Timbisha Shoshone Homeland Act," report prepared under Cooperative Agreement with Rocky Mountain Cooperative Ecosystem Studies Unit for Death Valley National Park, California (2009). Since 2019, Yellowstone National Park has transferred bison to the Assiniboine and Sioux Tribes of the Fort Peck Indian Reservation. See: https://www.nps.gov/yell/learn/management/bison-management.htm. In 2021, the National Bison Range was transferred fully to Confederated Salish and Kootenai Tribes. See: Aaron Bolton, "Feds Begin Transfer Of National Bison Range To Confederated Salish and Kootenai Tribes," *Montana Public Radio* (January 15, 2021). https://www.mtpr.org/montana-news/2021-01-15/feds-begin-transfer-of-national-bison-range-to-confederated-salish-and-kootenai-tribes. And in 2022, the Cherokee Nation secured formal permission to gather plans at the Buffalo National River site. See: Alyssa Lukpat, "Cherokee Nation Can Gather Sacred Plants on National Park Land," *New York Times* (April 27, 2022). https://www.nytimes.com/2022/04/27/us/cherokee-plants-national-park.html.
9. See, for example: Catton, *Inhabited Wilderness*; Keller and Turek, *American Indians and National Parks*; Mark David Spence, *Dispossessing the Wilderness: Indian Removal and the Making of the National Parks* (Oxford: Oxford University Press, 1999); Philip Burnham, *Indian Country, God's Country: Native Americans and the National Parks* (Washington, DC: Island Press, 2000); Peter Nabokov and Lawrence Loendorf, *Restoring a Presence: American Indians and Yellowstone National Park* (Norman: University of Oklahoma Press, 2004).
10. See for example: Ian Tyrrell, "America's National Parks: The Transnational Creation of National Space in the Progressive Era." *Journal of American Studies* 46 no.1 (2012):1; Bernhard Gissibl, Sabine Hohler, and Patrick Kupper, *Civilizing Nature: National Parks in Global Historical Perspective* (New York: Berghahn Books, 2012); Patrick Kupper, *Creating Wilderness: A Transnational History of the Swiss National Park* (New York: Berghahn Books, 2014); Adrian

Howkins, Jared Orsi, and Mark Fiege, eds., *National Parks beyond the Nation: Global Perspectives on "America's Best Idea"* (Norman: University of Oklahoma Press, 2016).

11. See for example: Stan Stevens, ed., *Indigenous Peoples, National Parks, and Protected Areas: A New Paradigm Linking Conservation, Culture, and Rights* (Tucson: University of Arizona Press, 2014).
12. See for example: Kathleen Sue Fine-Dare, *Grave Injustice: The American Indian Repatriation Movement and NAGPRA* (Lincoln: University of Nebraska Press, 2002); Mary Lawlor, *Public Native America: Tribal Self-Representation in Casinos, Museums, and Powwows* (New Brunswick, NJ: Rutgers University Press, 2006); Laura Peers, *Playing Ourselves: Interpreting Native Histories at Historic Reconstructions* (Lanham, MD: Altamira Press, 2007); Loriene Roy, Anjali Bhasin, and Sarah K. Arriaga, eds., *Tribal Libraries, Archives, and Museums: Preserving Our Language, Memory, and Lifeways* (Lanham, MD: Scarecrow Press, 2011); Jennifer A. Shannon, *Our Lives: Collaboration, Native Voice, and the Making of the National Museum of the American Indian* (Santa Fe: School for Advanced Research Press, 2014).
13. See for example: Jennifer Talken-Spaulding and Joe Watkins, "Applied Anthropology in the National Park Service's Second Century of Stewardship," *The George Wright Forum*. vol. 35 (2018): 53–64; Michael J. Evans, Alexa Roberts, and Peggy Nelson, "Ethnographic Landscapes." *Cultural Resource Management* no. 5 (2001): 53–57.
14. Keller and Turek, *American Indians and National Parks*.
15. The new policies in the 1990s included the Native American Graves Protection and Repatriation Act in 1990 and a number of President Clinton's Executive Orders in 1994. For more details, see: "Tribal Consultation: Best Practices in Historic Preservation," National Association of Tribal Historic Preservation Officers (May 2005). http://npshistory.com/publications/preservation/tribal-consultation.pdf; Jacilee Wray et al., "Creating Policy for the National Park Service: Addressing Native Americans and Other Traditionally Associated Peoples," Ethnography in the National Park Service, *The George Wright Forum*, vol. 26, no. 3 (2009). http://www.georgewright.org/263wray.pdf.
16. See Howkins, Orsi, and Fiege, eds., *National Parks beyond the Nation*.
17. Taylor, *Rise of the American Conservation Movement*; Spence, *Dispossessing the Wilderness*.
18. See for example: Linda Tuhiwai Smith, *Decolonizing Methodologies: Research and Indigenous Peoples* (New York: St. Martin's Press, 1999).
19. For more information on the Land Back movement, see for example: Nikki A. Pieratos, Sarah S. Manning, and Nick Tilsen, "Land Back: A Meta Narrative to Help Indigenous People Show up as Movement Leaders," *Leadership* 17, no. 1 (2021): 47–61; Kim TallBear, "Beyond Indigenous Performance to Life and Land Back," *Unsettle* (January 26, 2022). https://kimtallbear.substack.com/p/beyond-indigenous-performance-to?s=r; www.landback.org; http://therednation.org/.
20. For more on NPS administrative histories, see Joan Zenzen, "Why Administrative Histories Matter," *The Public Historian* 38, no. 4 (2016): 236–63;

Ann Mitchell Whisnaut et al., "Imperiled Promise: The State of History in the National Park Service," Organization of American Historians (2011).
21. For an overview of this program, see Jennifer Talken-Spaulding and Joe Watkins, "Applied Anthropology in the National Park Service's Second Century of Stewardship," *The George Wright Forum* 35, no. 1 (2018): 53–64.
22. See Talken-Spaulding and Watkins.

ONE | Historical Overview

MARK DAVID SPENCE

IT WAS NOT THAT LONG AGO when the phrase "Native peoples and national parks" raised eyebrows in the National Park Service (NPS) and created a bit of confusion among the visiting public. Visitors might have reflected on the display of rubber tomahawks for sale within a national park information center, or the cheap headbands adorned with dyed chicken feathers in bright tones of green, blue, and red. Or they might have noticed a paragraph in a visitor's pamphlet that briefly noted the long associations that Indigenous peoples have had with places they were evicted from to make way for the development of lands that are now inside the boundaries of a national park. This situation is especially true for parks that are situated among an array of Indigenous nations that still live around the current boundaries of parks like Yellowstone, Yosemite, Mount Rainier, Olympic, Rocky Mountain, Zion, Channel Islands, Everglades National Park, Grand Canyon, and almost all of the national park units in Alaska and Hawaii.

Working from a different perspective, NPS employees tend to reflect on, and take great pride in, the primary symbol of the National Park System; namely, the arrowhead shield with an image of a bison, a lake, a giant Sequoia tree (*Sequoiadendron giganteum*), and a singular mountain peak.

In the 1930s, when park service budgets were greatly augmented by the labor and funding that came through the Civilian Conservation Corps (CCC), the sense of shared heritage and national identity also took on a deeper resonance across the National Park System. This soon resulted in the establishment of eight new park units where the visiting public could access newer and better roads that made travel within a national park a vacationer's pleasure instead of a stressful exercise in dodging pot holes and muddy stretches of unpaved road.[1] As automobile travel and roadbuilding continued to reshape the ways that tourists

15

visited national parks—before and after World War II—the nature of outdoor tourism and recreation was increasingly determined by the condition and quality of park roadways and facilities. The way these engineered features appealed to the aesthetics of drive-by scenery seemed to make roads and automobiles the essential components of every national park vacation.²

Wamaka Og'naka I'Cante: "The Heart of Everything That Is"

Along with roads and automobility, the qualitative aspects of a national park vacation through much of the twentieth century came with expectations of cultural authenticity, vast scenic vistas, hikes, guided horse rides, and a touch of luxury in park hotels and restaurants. Along with such comforts and assumptions, tourists could expect to see a famous array of scenic and historical sights and locales, geological wonders, and Native peoples who imbued a sense of authenticity to the tourist experience. This was particularly true of tourism in *Paha Sapa* (the Black Hills), which the Lakota regard as the heart of everything that is (*Wamaka Og'naka I'Cante*). For tourists, the region is rife with distinctive sites and several national park units that include Badlands National Park (*Mako Sica*), Wind Cave National Park (*Maka Oniye*); Buffalo Gap (*Pte Kinapapi*), Mount Rushmore National Memorial (*Tunkasila Sakpe Paha*), and Devils Tower National Monument (*Mato Tipila*).³ While American tourists and local boosters in the first half of the twentieth century attached their expectations and conceits to various sites in and around Paha Sapa, they also found a kind of cultural salve in tourist-oriented Native pageants. Indigenous people wore their finest regalia and received money from tourists, who were thrilled to experience what they deemed to be profound expressions of historical authenticity and poignancy during their western vacations.⁴

The national parks that American tourists visited in the first half of the twentieth century, and through the present day, have long been sold as dramatic slices of Indigenous and American reality that could augment and appeal to a visitor's craving for a genuine encounter with peoples, landscapes, and popular historical figures like George A. Custer and Crazy Horse (*Thasuŋke Witko*). Despite this seemingly benign fascination that tourists had with Paha Sapa, it was particularly worrisome to Nicholas Black Elk (*Hehaka Sapa*). Paha Sapa was, and remains, a place of ongoing creation, and Black Elk was disconcerted by efforts to expand national park units within the broadly shared homeland of the Great Sioux Nation (*Oceti Sakowin*). Following the establishment of Badlands National Monument in 1939, for instance, Black Elk worried that national parks and reservations would physically divide the various peoples and landscapes of what had become present-day western South Dakota and northeastern Wyoming. As he subsequently noted, the creation of Badlands National Park was nothing more than an American process of making "little islands for us and other little islands for the four-leggeds, and always these islands are becoming smaller, for around them surges the gnawing flood of the Wasichu (white Americans), and it is dirty with lies and greed."[5] In the first years of the twentieth century, Black Elk and his kin had also witnessed the creation of Wind Cave National Park, which involved the transformation of the sacred portal between the surface of the earth and the Underworld from which bison and humans first emerged into the world—long before the site was transformed into a subterranean entertainment zone for tourists.[6]

Native Activism and Federal Recognition

By the 1960s, a new generation of Lakotas in South Dakota felt that their participation in Black Hills tourism no longer served their best interests. For decades, Native participation in tourism had served as a venue that reinforced Native sovereignty and celebrated Native heritage. With the rapid growth of the Red Power Movement, however, new avenues for cultural expression, resistance to settler colonialism, and the fight for self-determination emerged. In fact, Ben Black Elk's funeral on February 28, 1973, shared the spotlight with the first full day of the American Indian Movement's two-month protest and occupation at the village of Wounded Knee on the Pine Ridge Reservation in South Dakota.[7]

Though tribal nations enacted a variety of methods for resisting colonization and assimilationist policies in the early twentieth century, the rise of prominent Indigenous political resistance in the 1960s and 1970s ushered in a new era of Native self-determination and activism. With well-known occupations at Alcatraz and Wounded Knee, the American Indian Movement brought national attention to Native peoples' sovereignty and cultural and religious rights.[8] This political pressure led to a wave of new legislation over the last thirty years of the twentieth century, including the 1974 Indian Self-Determination and Education Assistance Act, the 1978 American Indian Religious Freedom Act (AIRFA), the 1987 National Park Service policy statement to AIRFA, the 1990 Native American Grave Protection and Repatriation Act (NAGPRA), the 1993 Religious Freedom Restoration Act, and the 1994 Native American Free Exercise of Religion Act. These policies, with their emphasis on religious freedoms, cultural rights, and tribal sovereignty, shifted how the federal government and agencies like the National Park Service recognize tribal nations and Native peoples.

In particular, the last decade of the twentieth century ushered in significant changes to how the United States would engage with federally recognized tribal nations. The first of these was the aforementioned NAGPRA of 1990, which "provided for the repatriation and disposition of certain Native American human remains, funerary objects, sacred objects, and objects of cultural patrimony." Four years later, to expand the sovereignty recognized in NAGPRA, President William Jefferson Clinton issued the Presidential Memorandum for the Heads of Executive Departments and Agencies of April 29, 1994, which obligates all "executive departments and agencies [that] undertake activities affecting Native

American tribal rights or trust resources" to function in a "knowledgeable, sensitive manner respectful of tribal sovereignty" in all "interactions with Native American Tribal governments." "The purpose of these principles," Clinton noted, "is to clarify our responsibility to ensure that the Federal government operates within a government-to-government relationship with federally recognized Native American Tribes."[9]

Six months after Clinton's memorandum, Congress passed the Tribal Self-Governance Act (TSGA), which formally recognizes the distinctive government-to-government relationship the US federal government has with tribal nations as well as the autonomy tribal nations should have over their programs and services. The heads of relevant agencies, especially the NPS and various public lands agencies within the Department of the Interior, viewed the programs that resulted from the TSGA as administrative tutelage from which Native nations could develop experience in bureaucratic land management practices—while also compensating for declining budgets across the Department of the Interior. Consequently, the results of the Act are mixed. As Mary Ann King notes, the TSGA has provided "tribes with processes and avenues for interacting, negotiating, and cooperating with the NPS that . . . may lead to greater co-management." However, the NPS has largely "framed and conceptualized" the TSGA in transactional terms that look "more like contracting or procurement than the kinds of relational engagements that inform and underlie co-management."[10]

Clinton subsequently returned to the matter of Native sovereignty near the close of his presidency, when he issued Executive Order 13175 to obligate federal agencies "to establish regular and meaningful consultation and collaboration with tribal officials in the development of Federal policies that have tribal implications."[11] Executive Order 13175 mandated federal agencies to engage in regular and meaningful consultation with tribal governments, not just in activities affecting tribal rights or trust resources but also in the development of federal policies and programs that could impact tribal interests more broadly. In doing so, and in concert with TSGA and NAGPRA, it promoted a stronger government-to-government relationship between the US and tribal governments, with the goal of recognizing and respecting tribal sovereignty.

However effective or incomplete these legislative and presidential actions may have been, some NPS administrators and park superintendents expressed outright contempt for Native peoples and the new layers of bureaucracy that accompanied these new policies. For the most part, critics believed these changes would undermine the agency's authority over park lands and "give back" some portion of the nation's "crown jewels" to people who did not know how to manage the park areas within their homelands. These sentiments were often expressed to the author by NPS employees and park superintendents from the mid-1990s into the mid-2000s, but they have mostly subsided in the past fifteen years or so. Much of this change reflects the successful efforts of tribal nations to exercise their treaty rights more fully in their various dealings with the federal government, but it also stems from a generational change within the NPS. As superintendents and upper-level NPS administrators retired, they were replaced by younger personnel who had risen through the ranks during a period when the agency had suffered through a tempest of internal and external critiques. Among these were charges that the NPS was little more than a "provider of 'drive through' tourism" that had become "extraordinarily deficient" in the management and interpretation of ecological, historical, and cultural resources within national parks.[12] Unlike their older peers, these new employees and future leaders tended to view such criticism as constructive and—unlike their retiring mentors—were willing to question the hallowed notion that the NPS was "the best idea we [Americans] ever had."[13]

A Generational Shift and the Partnership Principle

To the degree that younger NPS employees recognized the validity of some outside criticism, they endeavored to make needed reforms in resource management, cultural and historical interpretation, and the agency's obligations to engage directly with federally recognized tribes. During this generational shift, however, the agency was hampered by a persistent flattening of its annual budget. To compensate for these circumstances, the NPS became increasingly dependent on the support of numerous nonprofit organizations, philanthropical institutions, and countless volunteers. These partnerships became so intrinsic to the functioning of the NPS that they were enshrined in the agency's mission statement, which added the following sentence in 2000: "The Park Service cooperates with partners to extend the benefits of natural and cultural resource conservation and outdoor recreation throughout this country and the world."[14]

Such reliance on outside partners would have been mostly foreign to a previous generation of NPS leaders, but it has since become central to almost everything the NPS undertakes, from resource management to visitor needs. This is even more true of how the NPS addresses the requirements of NAGPRA and Executive Order 13175. As the NPS understands these legal documents, the agency possesses a "unique relationship with Native peoples . . . that is founded in law[,] . . . strengthened by a shared commitment to the stewardship of land and resources, . . . [and] augmented by the historical, cultural, and spiritual relationships that these groups have with park lands, sites, vistas, and resources; they are their ancestral homelands and important resources in maintaining cultural identity . . . . [These groups can also] . . . enhance NPS's understanding of the history and traditional management of places and resources that are now within national parks."[15]

The notion of a partnership wherein Native peoples enhance park interpretation and the visitor experience, and consequently gain permission to temporarily utilize key portions of their ancestral homelands and associated resources, is inherently unequal. Unfortunately, the asymmetry of this relationship is further compounded by the NPS's increasing reliance on contracting or partnering with outside experts to satisfy the requirements of NAGPRA, Executive Order 13175, and the 1994 Tribal Self-Governance Act.[16] More often than not, these partnerships involve contractors who, besides being experts in history, archeology, cultural anthropology, and—on occasion—conflict resolution, have a preexisting relationship with the NPS and are familiar with the legal and programmatic obligations that inform government-to-government relations between the agency and tribes. While a growing dependence on outside experts helps reduce administrative responsibilities and stretches personnel budgets, it also creates some fundamental challenges. In terms of NPS relations with Native nations, it distances the NPS from a fundamental treaty-based obligation, and hands it to professional researchers contracted through universities or cultural resource management firms. The consequences of relying on contractors are essentially threefold: (1) the absence of NPS expertise in these matters contributes to a general ignorance about the significance of park landscapes and resources within the broader homelands of multiple Indigenous groups; (2) the agency relies on tribes and non-NPS consultants to establish the basis for park policies vis-à-vis federally recognized American Indian nations; and (3) it removes park personnel from the kind of person-to-person relationships and negotiations that build lasting trust.[17]

Giving a primary administrative and legal responsibility over to contractors does allow short-handed park staff to focus on other projects and management concerns, but it also brings a peculiar, counterproductive comfort to NPS employees and administrators. As an Organization of American Historians (OAH) study noted in 2011, the NPS is often hampered by a "culture of timidity" that fosters a chronic dread about having to engage and interpret controversial subjects.[18] These can involve matters outside a park, like visitors' interest in the fracking boom around Theodore Roosevelt National Park in western North Dakota, or the racist ideals of that park's namesake, but the most challenging issue for interpretive staff across the National Park System relates to their "efforts to understand and discuss American Indian history," and how it relates to national park units. Such reticence largely stems from a sense that the subject is regarded as inherently "controversial, . . . [and invariably] tied to on-going land claims, bigotry, &c., . . . and thus too hot to handle." As one NPS employee noted, these can be existential concerns, further adding that we tend "to run screaming from any [such] controversy. Period. We have been trained to avoid controversy like the plague."[19]

Though still somewhat common today, the sentiments noted above do not represent a preordained fate within the NPS, or the agency's efforts to engage with tribal nations on a government-to-government basis. As the OAH report noted, a number of employees involved with park interpretation inferred that a dose of humility, coupled with the adoption of current historical analyses and practices, could be empowering for all concerned. As one participant noted, the agency must "stop interpreting from a place of fear. We need to step back from the position of authority and become provokers, facilitators and encourage the public to engage with the material, consider multiple perspectives, and make their own choices."[20] While there is merit in these views, particularly in matters related to interpreting environmental sciences or general notions of what defines "American heritage," there is not a sufficient base of knowledge, understanding, and appreciation of Native histories, cultures, homelands, access to traditional resources, and sovereignty concerns within the NPS. The problem can be ameliorated through Native consultations and the use of outside contractors, but it will not begin to be rectified until the general timidity and misunderstanding within the NPS gives way to a genuine humility about the depth and breadth of many Native nations' ongoing connections to their homelands. The NPS must recognize that park service interpretation and management has been grounded in rudimentary understandings of what park areas have meant—and continue to mean—to various Native peoples since time immemorial.[21]

Partly informed by the ethos of avoiding controversy, and discomfited by rejoinders from Native individuals and tribal representatives who called out the unexamined conceits embedded in the interpretive displays, brochures, exhibits, films, and public talks that shape the visitor experience, the NPS began to make concerted efforts to incorporate Native perspectives into park interpretive programs in the late 1990s. In doing so, however, the agency mostly partnered with non-Native consultants and contractors to create ethnographic, historical, and archeological studies that would serve as the basis for new texts, displays, and films produced by the NPS's Interpretive Design Center in Harper's Ferry. These "partnerships" continue to this day, and increasingly rely on independent scholars, faculty and graduate students within university programs like the Department of American Indian Studies at the University of Minnesota, the Public Lands History Center at Colorado State University, and private firms like Historical Research Associates. While these studies generally foreground Indigenous voices, they are somewhat buffered by the go-between status of the contractor who must also fulfill NPS expectations about addressing specific content, events, and subjects. Once approved by NPS staff, these studies are subsequently used to inform resource management and interpretation programs within a park or administrative region. They also serve as primers for superintendents, new park staff, and district level managers, and inform subsequent reports on some aspect of park management and development. Given the contractor's intermediate position, however, these one-off projects do not necessarily build closer ties or develop more trust between the NPS and tribal nations.[22]

The Sacred, the Profane, and the Trials of Partnership at Mato Tipila

While a growing dependence on outside consultants aligns with the partnership principle that is so evident throughout the NPS, it does not shield individual parks—let alone the park service—from the dreaded effects of controversy. This proved to be the case at Devils Tower National Monument from the mid-1990s through the early 2000s, when park personnel were caught between Native concerns over the growing number of people who were climbing Mato Tipila and the disturbing racist vitriol from some corners of the climbing community.[23] To address these matters, and somehow become all things to all people, then-Superintendent Deborah Liggett engaged ethnologists and historians to develop cross-cultural programs to educate park staff and volunteers, the general public, the rock climbing community, local governmental, and economic development officials about "Devils Tower's historic connections with Native American ceremonial practices and cultural beliefs."[24] These efforts resulted in noticeable improvements to park interpretation of Native communities and their cultural landscapes, and helped guide NPS efforts to consult and collaborate with Native peoples who came to the national monument in the weeks around the summer solstice. However, the studies could not silence the shouted communications of climbers or the occasional ringing of hammer knocking a piton into rock. For Native peoples who had come together for a period of ceremonial and social gathering, the discordant noises emanating from above, along with the crowded and boisterous camps of the climbers, were a near constant annoyance that bordered on willful sacrilege.[25]

In an effort to develop a plan that accommodated the needs of Native ceremonies and the expectations of rock climbers, park officials implemented a Final Climbing Management Plan (FCMP) in 1995 that banned rock climbing during the month of June. Soon after the plan was announced, however, it was challenged in a lawsuit from Andy Petefish, a climbing guide and outfitter based in Colorado. With the assistance of the Mountain States Legal Foundation, Petefish accused the NPS of a host of legal sins that included favoring the spiritual beliefs of Native peoples over Euro-American religions, promoting the religious indoctrination of Euro-American children who were invited to visit Native encampments, discrimination against climbers on the basis of race, and violating the religious freedom of people who insisted they "climb Devils Tower and have spiritual experiences" that make the place "every bit our alter [sic]." Petefish further asserted that Devils Tower National Monument "does not belong to the [I]ndians," and thus it cannot be "their alt[a]r." Petefish also declared that all Native peoples were inherently disposed to "lie, steal, [and] cheat their fellow human beings."[26]

Such vitriol did not prevent the implementation of the new policy in 1995, but the gist of his argument about religious freedom resulted in a sympathetic hearing from the U.S. District Court in Cheyenne, Wyoming, which ultimately decided to rescind the ban on climbing in June because the policy amounted "to [an] impermissible government entanglement with religion" that favored one sense of worship over another.[27] As a consequence of this decision, the NPS altered its policy by implementing guidelines for a voluntary ban on climbing in June. From the Court's perspective, this action sufficiently disentangled the NPS from religion, and resulted in 90 percent compliance with the voluntary ban (as compared to the number of climbers in previous years). In subsequent years, however, the number of climbers has increased fivefold, to about half the number of people who climbed Mato Tipila before the original month-long ban was implemented.[28]

From the NPS perspective, the original temporary ban on rock climbing at Devils Tower National Monument reflected the agency's obligations to uphold the dictates of the American Indian Religious Freedom Act of 1978, the Archeological Resources Protection Act of 1979, NAGPRA, and President Clinton's Presidential Memorandum of April 29, 1994.[29] The climbing ban also corresponded with marked improvements in the relationships between park staff and Native peoples. In her annual report for 1995, Liggett heralded the process of developing the Climbing Management Plan as the beginning of managing Devils Tower "as both a natural and cultural resource." From her perspective, the ban on climbing, and the subsequent NPS response to the *Bear Lodge Multiple Use Association v. Babbitt* decision, represented a highpoint in park staffs' efforts to work with and learn from American Indian communities. Her sense that the trajectory of these developments would continue to rise also proved true, especially during the tenures of Superintendents Dorothy FireCloud (2006–2012) and Reed Robinson (2012–2015), who are both citizens of the Rosebud Sioux Tribe.[30]

Nine-tenths of the Law: *Proprietary Jurisdiction over Sacred Landscapes*

For all the goodwill that informed the effort to craft the climbing ban, the lawsuit inadvertently revealed an intractable and ongoing divide between the NPS and tribal nations in their government-to-government consultations and collaborations. The lawsuit that Petefish's actions engendered was not between his climbing company and the Native peoples who participated in the summer solstice ceremonies at Mato Tipila. Rather, it was between the Bear Lodge Multiple Use Foundation (a nonprofit organization that Petefish created and the Mountain States Legal Foundation represented) and four federal officials: Secretary of the Interior Bruce Babbitt, Director of the National Park Service Roger G. Kennedy, NPS Rocky Mountain Regional Director John E. Cook, and Superintendent Liggett.[31] In terms of liability, the defendants were deemed the legal equivalent of the national monument's owners, and would ultimately be responsible for any changes in policy and visitor access that the court might deem necessary. Put another way, the NPS *owned* a resource (Mato Tipila) that was inherently associated with Indigenous cultures, but was situated within the NPS's long-established ethos of preserving, protecting, and promoting parks "for the benefit of the people."[32] Even though Superintendent Liggett and other park personnel genuinely fostered a collaborative relationship with Native peoples, and vice versa, these relations occurred within an inherent imbalance. Namely, one that recognizes Native concerns but necessarily addresses them within the agency's recognized "proprietary jurisdiction" over the management of park areas, associated resources, and the regulation of permissible activity.[33]

Such a conception of ownership or possession undermines the sense that Mato Tipila is a shared or co-managed "cultural resource." Moreover, it removes the national park unit from its broader cultural contexts. Though it seems to stand alone, like a singular "irruption of the sacred into the world," Mato Tipila is situated within a constellation of sacred and materially significant places on the Northern Plains that include Bear Butte (Mato Paha), Paha Sapa, Wind Cave (Maka Oniye), Cave Hills (Buffalo Home Buttes), and the Missouri River (Mnisose).[34] Through a process that Linea Sundstrom refers to as "cross-cultural transference," the names, stories, and understandings associated with these places were adopted by countless generations of allies, migrants, and interlopers who incorporated these locales within their own sacred geographies. This process of cross-cultural transference remains an ongoing process that moves across generations and among different Native communities, and invariably reflects the life-sustaining vitality of particular places, their interconnections with other locales, and the intrinsic sacredness that defines them. Put another way, the holy attributes of Mato Tipila, and the larger sacred geography in which it is situated, reflects the ongoing processes of creation that connects the present and the coming future with all life since Creation.[35]

Much of the sacred geography noted above has also become part of the National Park System. Along with Devils Tower National Monument, the park service manages locales of deep cultural and spiritual significance within the Black Hills region and adjoining areas of the Northern and Central Plains. Among these are: Mount Rushmore National Monument (which defaces *Tunkasila Sakpe,* or the "Six Grandfathers of Creation" who represent the six directions of North, South, East, West, Above/Sky, and Below/Earth); Wind Cave National Park, Fort Union Trading Post National Historic Site (Confluence of the Missouri and Yellowstone rivers); Knife River Indian Villages National Historic Site (near the main channel of the Missouri River); Fort Robinson and Red Cloud Agency National Landmark (in the Western Pine Ridge); Agate Fossil Beds National Monument (at the headwaters of the Niobrara River in northwestern Nebraska); Scotts Bluff National Monument (on the upper North Platte River); Bighorn Canyon National Recreation Area, which is especially sacred to the Apsáalooke (Crow people); and Badlands National Park.

Paradigm Shifts

In the past few years, Indigenous peoples' efforts to live and travel within their traditional homelands, on their own terms, have involved an inspiring array of cultural journeys that involve fellowship with other Indigenous individuals, places, animals, plants, trees, rivers, etc. These include a group of women who started hiking together during the late 2010s in the Southern Sierra Nevada Mountains. In the process they shared the stories they knew about specific locales they passed or stayed at along the John Muir Trail—which they renamed the *Nüümü Poyo* (The People's Trail).[36] The first major hike they took came with reminders of historical traumas, primarily in the form of trail signs that identified "Squaw Lake," and various trail markers that simply referenced stretches like Muir Pass, but which offered no insights on the cultural significance of particular places. As Nüümü attorney Anna Hohag noted, "Our ancestors used the trail to trade, travel and manage the landscape as stewards of the land. . . . When our people were removed, our places and routes were replaced with outsiders, and our histories and identities erased from the trail." One of many places they made sure to name was Mount Whitney (*Tumanguya*). They also served as ambassadors to non-Indigenous hikers on the trail—some of whom had been following the Nüümü women's social media as they traveled along the Nüümü Poyo.[37]

Coinciding with the cultural reclamation that occurred on the Nüümü Poyo, the Save the Redwoods League (in partnership with Redwood National and State Parks) has recently embarked on a new approach to environmental protection and cultural land management known as Redwoods Rising. Since the dawn of the twentieth century, the Save the Redwoods League (SRL) has been singularly devoted to purchasing uncut groves of redwood trees from logging companies, with an eye toward incorporating them into the replanting and restoration of adjoining parcels. By the late 1960s, when the NPS acquired vast swaths of cutover lands and chewed up riparian areas, the SRL made a new push to acquire groves of large trees as monuments to the League's major benefactors. While this practice resulted in lovely monuments to donors who were acknowledged on bronze plaques mounted to large boulders, fewer and fewer old-growth trees and groves remained for such an approach to forest restoration. Instead, the SRL (beginning in 2018) partnered with California State Parks and the National Park Service to restore swaths of still viable forest lands. In the process, the SRL (which had long accused Native peoples of causing damage to forest lands) began to partner with NPS projects that were co-managed with federally recognized tribal nations.

In the process, they have extended that partnership toward two federally recognized Indigenous nations whose lands abut the national and state parks complex—*Tolowa Dee-ni'* Nation, located near the California and Oregon border, and the *Olekwo'l* (Yurok), situated at the mouth of the Klamath River. While both nations are committed to restoring the health and ecological integrity of their lands, they differ in their approaches to using grant money for forest restoration and to reintroducing endangered animal populations, including the Humboldt marten (*Martes caurina*) and the fisher (*Pekania pennanti*). Condor introduction, on the other hand, has proved very successful. For the most part, however, Native peoples of the Coast Redwoods in northernmost California are especially interested in restoring and protecting roots, plants, mushrooms, berries, and other traditional food plants that they can sustainably tend and harvest.

In this regard, they are particularly committed to maintaining the diets and resource bases that their ancestors maintained for future generations—who in turn will commit themselves to providing for future generations in an unbroken cord of reciprocity to past, present, and future iterations of their communities. The Tolowa Dee-ni' Nation, located near the California and Oregon border, and the Olekwo'l (Yurok), located at the mouth of the Klamath River, are particularly focused on the chain of ancestors and new generations who will sustain the food rituals and diets that weave through the generations like unbroken strands of knowledge and fellowship.

Conclusion

Over the past century, the NPS has undergone a dramatic transformation in recognizing the natural and cultural significance that the lands occupied by prominent western parks hold for Native peoples—who were displaced in the process of creating these parks. Native peoples have never ceased to make their claims to these lands known to park officials and the general public. In the first part of the twentieth century, those claims included Native participation in the Anglo tourism economy, whether through participation in park dedications, the staging of pageants, or the presence of Native interpreters like Ben Black Elk at Mount Rushmore.[38] In the context of the civil rights movement, these harmonization efforts gave way to more active forms of Native protest. This helped to precipitate legislation under the Clinton administration requiring the NPS to engage with tribal nations on a government-to-government basis regarding the management of tribally significant cultural and natural resources on public lands. While such consultation is evident in the mediation of the dispute over climbing at Mato Tipila/Devils Tower, the NPS still had the upper hand as the manager of park lands, resources, and as the final arbiter of permissible uses. In this respect, there remains a tension between mandates requiring federal agencies to consult and collaborate with tribal nations about the interpretation and use of federal lands, and the TSGA, which called for a transition to Native communities managing their own lands (see Cochrane, this volume).

The case of Native communities reclaiming sacred places such as the Nüümü Poyo/John Muir Trail in the Southern Sierra Nevada Mountains, and the SRL partnership with NPS-tribal co-managed projects suggests promising new developments. The SRL-NPS partnership with the Tolowa Dee-ni' Nation and the Olekwo'l is particularly auspicious, as these Native communities are playing a larger role in managing the traditional plant and animal species inextricably tied to the maintenance of tribal identity and sovereignty (see Stoffle, Evans, and Carroll, this volume). Such partnerships portend a future in which tribal nations increasingly play an active role not only in interpreting but managing tribal resources on federal lands.

Notes

1. See Laura E. Soulliere, "Early Park Road Development," in *Historic Roads in the National Park System: Special History Study* (October 1995). http://npshistory.com/publications/transportation/historic-roads.pdf. See also Paul S. Sutter, *Driven Wild: How the Fight against Automobiles Launched the Modern Wilderness Movement* (Seattle: University of Washington Press, 2005), and David Louter, *Windshield Wilderness: Cars, Roads, and Nature in Washington's National Parks* (Seattle: University of Washington Press, 2006). On NPS expansion in the 1930s, see Harlan D. Unrau and G. Frank D. Williss, *Administrative History: Expansion of the National Park Service in the 1930s* (Washington, DC: National Park Service, 1983), chapters 2 and 3.
2. For national park developments in the mid-twentieth century, see Alfred Runte, *National Parks: The American Experience*, 2nd ed. (Lincoln: University of Nebraska Press, 1997), 209–35. On expansion in the 1950s and 1960s, see Ethan Carr and Sarah Allaback, *Mission 66 Visitor Centers: The History of a Building Type* (Washington, DC: National Park Service, 2013), 63–123.
3. The national park sites noted in this paragraph also correspond to an array of sacred locales related to the creation of the earth, all life, and a number of sacred portals that lead to extensive cave systems that include the Cave Hills to the northeast of Paha Sapa.
4. Suzanne Barta Julin, "Building a Vacationland: Tourism Development in the Black Hills during the Great Depression," *South Dakota History* 35, no. 4 (Winter 2005): 291–314.
5. John G. Neihardt, *Black Elk Speaks: Being the Life Story of a Holy Man of the Oglala Sioux* (Lincoln: University of Nebraska Press, 1988), 8–9.
6. See Adam Rossi, "Where the Earth Breathes Inside: The Attitudes of Lakota People Toward Wind Cave National Park (MA thesis, West Virginia University, Morgantown, 2017), 44–56. See also Mark David Spence, *Passages Through Many Worlds: A Historic Resource Study of Wind Cave National Park* (US National Park Service, 2011). Niitsitapii (Blackfeet People, or "the Real People") is a term that encompasses the distinct and collective elements of the Blackfeet Nation. Given the polylingual nature of communication between distinct tribal nations and multiple language families, the term also has resonance among the Lakota (Lakota) and the Očhéthi Šakówiŋ (aka the Seven Council Fires of the Great Sioux Nation).
7. Matthew J. Hill, "Reinterpreting Mount Rushmore's Heritage: Native Engagements with a National Memorial in the Context of the Black Hills," Report for a Cooperative Ecosystems Study Unit Task Agreement P15AC01108 (2019), 136.
8. For more details on the rise of activism for Native self-determination and new US federal policies in the late twentieth century, see, for example, Paul Chaat Smith and Robert Allen Warrior, *Like a Hurricane: The Indian Movement from Alcatraz to Wounded Knee* (New York: The New Press, 1996); Lee Irwin, "Freedom, Law, and Prophecy: A Brief History of Native American Religious Resistance," *American Indian Quarterly* 21, no. 1 (1997): 35–55.

9. Quotations are from NAGPRA. https://www.nps.gov/subjects/nagpra/index.htm (accessed September 3, 2020); "Presidential Memorandum: Government-to-Government Relations with Native American Tribal Governments" (April 29, 1994); *Federal Register*, vol. 63, no. 96 (Tuesday, May 4, 2000): 27655–57.
10. Mary Ann King, "Co-management or Contracting? Agreements between Native American Tribes and the US National Park Service Pursuant to the 1994 Tribal Self-Governance Act," *Harvard Environmental Law Review* 31: 2 (2007): 475–530. Tim Cochran's chapter presents a superb and inspiring example of how sustained relationships between NPS personnel and tribal members can lead to lasting collaborations that are able to respond to new developments within a park unit while also adapting to corresponding changes within the NPS and tribal governance as conditions and expectations change over time.
11. "Tribal Self-Governance Act," Pub. L. 103-413, title II, §204, Oct. 25, 1994, 108 Stat. 4271; and Executive Order 13175, "Consultation and Coordination with Indian Tribal Governments," *Federal Register*, vol. 65, no. 218 (Thursday, November 9, 2000): 67249–52. The term "federally recognized Native American tribes" broadly applies to all tribal nations that have entered into a treaty relationship with the United States of America or have completed the formal process of federal acknowledgement and recognition that was established in the 1930s. For background, see Gerald Carr, "Origins and Development of the Mandatory Criteria within the Federal Acknowledgement Process," *Rutgers Race & the Law Review* 14 (2013): 1–23; at present, there are 574 federally recognized tribes in the United States.
12. Quotations are from the "Vail Agenda," as cited in Richard West Sellars, *Preserving Nature in the National Parks: A History* (New Haven, CT: Yale University Press, 1997), 276–77. For a fuller context on this criticism, and the NPS response, see pp. 277–81.
13. Stegner quotation from Wallace Stegner, "The Best Idea We Ever Had," in Page Stegner, ed., *Marking the Sparrow's Fall: The Making of the American West* (New York: Henry Holt, 1988), 137.
14. National Park Service, "NPS Entering the 21st Century." https://www.nps.gov/articles/npshistory-entering-21st-century.htm. See also Janet A. McDonnell, "Reassessing the National Park Service and the National Park System," *George Wright Forum* 25, no. 2 (2008): 9–12.
15. Quotations are from the National Park Service, "Connecting with American Indians, Alaska Natives and Native Hawaiians." https://www.nps.gov/history/tribes. It is worth noting that that NPS budgets have remained stagnant over the past decade, which has resulted in a number of partnerships with non-profit organizations, state agencies, tribal nations, universities, professional societies, and conservation groups. On budgets, see Congressional Research Service, "National Park Service Appropriations: Ten-Year Trends," updated July 2, 2019. https://fas.org/sgp/crs/misc/R42757.pdf. On the proliferation and necessity of partner organizations, see Potrero Group, *National Park Partners: Status and Trends* (Washington, DC: National Park Foundation, 2019).
16. The Tribal Self-Governance Act (1994).

17. The growing reliance on contractors within NPS Cultural Resource Management programs is noted in Anne Mitchell Whisnant et al., "Imperiled Promise: The State of History in the National Park Service," Organization of American Historians (2011), 55–57. On conflict resolution, see *Cultural Anthropology*, "Building Tribal and NPS Relationships." https://www.nps.gov/orgs/1209/building-relationships.htm. This critique cannot be universally applied across the NPS. Park units with superintendents and high-level staff who are also members of federally recognized tribes are generally more cognizant of the need to maintain ongoing relationships. The same is true for non-Native personnel who have a long history with a particular park unit and the peoples who were dispossessed by its establishment. This is particularly true of Michael Reynolds, who briefly served as the superintendent of Yosemite National Park in 2019.
18. Anne Mitchell Whisnant et al., "Imperiled Promise: The State of History in the National Park Service," Organization of American Historians (2011), 55–57.
19. Quotations and general observations are from the section entitled "Fixed and Fearful Interpretation" in Whisnant et al., "Imperiled Promise," 111–13. On fracking near Theodore Roosevelt National Park, see Mark Fiege, Janet Ore, and Jared Orsi, *Theodore Roosevelt National Park, North Dakota Historic Resource Study* (Fort Collins: Colorado State University—Public Lands History Center, 2017), 170–79. Roosevelt's writings on race are legion, but see James Bradley, *The Imperial Cruise: A Secret History of Empire and War* (New York: Little, Brown, 2009).
20. Quotation from Whisnant et al., "Imperiled Promise," 111.
21. For clear examples of these weaknesses and strengths, see *Collaboration and Conservation: Lessons Learned from National Park Service Partnership Areas in the Western United States* (Woodstock, Vermont: National Park Service and the Conservation and Study Institute, 2004), which presents the issue of partnership within the context of natural resource management programs makes just a few passing references to "Native peoples," "local and Indigenous" communities, and two nods to the Quechuan Indian Nation; also see a more recent study entitled "Planning for American Indian Interpretation" (2018), which focuses on the Potomac River corridor and notes that "American Indian history and culture is very popular, especially with the heritage tourists and families with children, and interpretation at many places throughout the [Potomac Heritage Corridor] enhances recreation experiences. . . . Living history presentations are a powerful way to connect with audiences, and other forms of programming, including . . . special events, such as American Indian Day (Friday after Thanksgiving); and cultural landscape interpretation can help to communicate the relevance of the culture and history associated with the site in the present."
22. For examples of such reports, see Jeffery R. Hanson and Sally Chirinos, *Ethnographic Overview and Assessment of Devils Tower National Monument, Wyoming* (Denver: US Department of the Interior—National Park Service—Intermountain Region, 1997); Patricia C. Albers et al., The Home of the Bison: An Ethnographic and Ethnohistorical Study of Traditional Cultural Affiliations to Wind Cave National Park (submitted in fulfillment of Cooperative Agreement

#CA606899103 between the US National Park Service & the Department of American Indian Studies, University of Minnesota, 2003); Maria Nieves Zedeño et al., "Cultural Affiliation Statement and Ethnographic Resource Assessment Study for Knife River Indian Villages National Historic Site, Fort Union Trading Post National Historic Site, and Theodore Roosevelt National Park: Final Report—December 8, 2006" (Task Agreement No. J606804112, DSCESU Cooperative Agreement CA-1248-00-002); Peter Nabokov and Lawrence Loendorf, "American Indians and Yellowstone National Park: A Documentary Overview" (Yellowstone National Park, 2002); Douglas Deur, *In the Footsteps of Gmukamps: A Traditional Use Study of Crater Lake National Park and Lava Beds National Monument* (National Park Service—Pacific West Region, 2008).

23. See Wendy Anne Felese, "No Common Ground: Competing Worldviews at Mato Tipila" (PhD diss., University of Denver, 2018), 210–16. Use of the term Mato Tipila in this essay corresponds to the orthography of the *New Lakota Dictionary* [online]. https://www.lakotadictionary.org/phpBB3/nldo.php (accessed September 14, 2020).

24. Quotation from Raymond Cross and Elizabeth Brenneman, "Devils Tower at the Crossroads: The National Park Service and the Preservation of Native American Cultural Resources in the 21st Century," *Public Land and Resources Law Review* 18: 5 (1997), 24. Mato Tipila is the Lakota term for the site. The author of this essay also served as a consultant for the revision of interpretive materials and texts at the park unit in 2001–2002.

25. See Heath A. Fire, "Cultural Encounters of the Controversial Kind," *High Plains Applied Anthropologist*, 19 (Spring, 1999), 40–41. The climbers did not recognize their actions as intrusive or sacrilegious, in large part because they viewed the park as a scenic and inspiring playground that had been established for their "benefit and enjoyment." Critics of the climbers often described their actions as akin to climbing the tower of a cathedral. A more fulsome metaphor might describe climbers as a group of recreationalists who crash a monastery to climb its walls and swim in its fountains in the midst of an annual religious pilgrimage.

26. Andy Petefish quoted in Fire, "Cultural Encounters of the Controversial Kind," 42. References to "Euro-American" follows Petefish's terminology.

27. *Bear Lodge Multiple Use Association v. Babbitt et al.*, 2 F. 2d 1448 (US Dist. 1998).

28. For a fuller discussion of *Bear Lodge Multiple Use Association v. Babbitt*, see Erik B. Bluemel, "Prioritizing Multiple Uses on Public Lands After Bear Lodge," *Environmental Affairs Law Review* 32:2 (2005): 365–94. On climbing numbers, see Chris Kalman, "It's Time to Rethink Climbing on Devils Tower," *Outside*, July 25, 2018. https://www.outsideonline.com/2329411/why-its-time-rethink-climbing-ban-devils-tower. It is important to note that Native leaders preferred a voluntary ban on climbing because they believed it result in people making willful decisions based on understanding and respect.

29. Partly in response to the decision in the Bear Lodge Multiple Use Foundation case. President Clinton also issued Executive Order 1307, Indian Sacred

Sites, issued on May 24, 1996. The Order stipulated that each "executive branch agency with statutory or administrative responsibility for the management of Federal lands shall . . . accommodate access to and ceremonial use of Indian sacred sites by Indian religious practitioners and avoid adversely affecting the physical integrity of such sacred sites." For a fuller discussion of these issues, see Bruce Babbitt, "Memorandum to Members of the Working Group on American Indians and Alaska Natives," Clinton Digital Library (September 27, 1996). https://clinton.presidentiallibraries.us/items/show/17487 Clinton Digital Library (accessed October 5, 2020).

30. FireCloud and Robinson continue to work in the National Park Service, with FireCloud currently serving as the Native American affairs liaison and assistant to the director of the NPS, and Robinson serving as the tribal relations manager in the Midwest Region of the NPS. Both FireCloud and Robinson are Sicangu Lakota (Brulé).

31. The named defendants in this trial were also supported by multiple tribal nations, Native individuals, religious groups, and scholars.

32. The clause "for the benefit of the people" comes from the Yellowstone National Park Protection Act of 1872.

33. The NPS describes this authority as *proprietary jurisdiction*, in which "the NPS exercises all the rights of a property owner" and, unlike a private individual, has also been "delegated authority [by Congress] . . . to make and enforce regulations" on its property.

34. Quotation is from Mircea Eliade, *The Sacred and the Profane* (New York: Harcourt, Brace, 1959), 45. Place names not rendered in English are presented in the following languages, by order: Noahá-vose (Tsėhésenėstsestȯtse, Cheyenne), Awaxaawi Shiibisha (Hiráaca, Hidatsa), Makȟá Oníya (Dakȟótiyapi, Dakota language). "Buffalo Home Buttes," or "Buffalo Emerging Caves," are English translations of the Nueta (Mandan) and Hiráaca (Hidatsa) names for the locale in what is now northwestern South Dakota.

35. The notion of an ongoing process of creation is embodied in the Nakoda (Assiniboine) term for the Creator: dáguwaką šká šká, which can be literally translated as "Great Mystery—To Move." The term and its translation suggest the sense of an entire landscape that is alive and in motion, both in the moment and across a great expanse of time. See also Gerard Baker, "The Missouri River: The Backbone to Survival," in Kimball M. Banks and Jon Czaplicki, eds., *Dam Projects and the Growth of American Archeology: The River Basin Surveys and the Interagency Archaeological Salvage Program* (London: Routledge, 2016), 202–13; Linea Sundstrom, "Sacred Islands: An Exploration of Religion and Landscape in the Northern Great Plains," in Marcel Kornfeld and Alan J. Osborn, eds., *Islands on the Plains: Ecological, Social, and Ritual Use of Landscapes* (Salt Lake City: University of Utah Press, 2003), 258–300, quotation from p. 260; Sundstrom and Richard Bradley, "Mirror of Heaven: Cross-Cultural Transference of the Sacred Geography of the Black Hills," *World Archaeology* 28, no. 2 (October 1996): 177–89. Other tribal nations with long-lived associations with these locales include Lakota, Tsétsêhéstâhese (Northern and Southern Cheyenne), Só'taeo'o, Hinono'eino (Northern and Southern Arapaho), Sahnish (Arikara),

Chaticks si Chaticks (Pawnee), Umo^n'ho^n' (Omaha), Pa^{n}ka (Ponca), Na'isha (Plains Apache, or Kiowa Apache), Ka'igwu (Kiowa), N~~umunuu~~ (Comanche).

36. Nüümü refers to Paiute peoples and the broader language they speak.
37. The bulk of this information comes from personal engagement with some of the women who founded and constitute Indigenous Women Hike and their website at https://www.facebook.com/indigenouswomenhike.
38. See Elaine Marie Nelson, "The Legacy of Black Hills Tourism and Native American Performers," in Matthew J. Hill, ed., *Reinterpreting Mount Rushmore's Heritage: Native Engagements with a National Memorial in the Context of the Black Hills* (Cooperative Agreement #P14AC00888, Washington, DC: US National Park Service and University of Massachusetts–Amherst, 2019).

PART ONE | **ENTRY POINTS**
Emerging Partnerships, Mutual Benefits

Interview: Max Bear

MAX BEAR IS THE TRIBAL HISTORIC PRESERVATION OFFICER for the Cheyenne and Arapaho Tribes in Oklahoma. He has been in his current position since 2018, and has overseen the culture and language program for the tribe since 2015. In these roles, Bear has worked with numerous national parks and other public land agencies. The following is adapted from an interview with Brooke Neely on April 6, 2022. This interview reflects on the process of initiating collaborative work with tribal nations. Bear describes some of the approaches taken to begin collaborating with researchers or park service officials. He considers the challenges of the consultation process and the potential outcomes of successfully developing a collaborative working relationship with Native nations.

Brooke Neely (BN): For people who may not know about the Tribal Historic Preservation Program (THPO), what do you do in that role?

Max Bear (MB): We preserve our historical footprint in the landscape of our historical lands, which is all of North and South America. That's Cheyenne and Arapaho land. As far as recorded history goes, you can trace that back to pre-treaty lands. We have stories about different areas amongst our people. It's kind of like a library you can access, and the stories are already told. I try to preserve everything I can in my work. I've been here quite a while and I plan to stay as long as I can.

When a national park decides to build structures, they have to consult with the tribes that were historically in the area. Section 106 from the National Historic Preservation Act says that they need to consult with the tribes on top of everything else they do for the project. A prime example is cell phone towers. They'll call on us to ask if there are any significant historical sites in the area. I use historical documents and surveys and other information to determine the historic properties that might be affected and make recommendations to make sure that they're not going to disturb anything, or if anything is found, we have a good idea of what we're going to do to proceed.

And then there are national parks where we work on programmatic agreements that help them educate the staff at a park. For example, we're creating a programmatic agreement with the Little Bighorn Battlefield National Monument site that can be a good reference for park staff and can help answer questions about the Cheyenne and Arapaho perspectives on the site and its history. Because our ultimate goal is to educate everybody about where the Cheyenne and Arapaho people have been.

BN: So you work with a lot of park sites. How do you share information with all of these parks with the limited time you have?

MB: We talk about that amongst ourselves—that we don't want to reinvent the wheel [with all the different people and sites who request our input]. We want to keep general information that we can share broadly, and then we can go more in depth at times with some sites. But we want to be able to put out general information about our people from our narrative.

BN: Yeah. So, could we go into a little bit about how these projects come about? How do they usually get started? How do you initiate them or how do national park sites initiate the work?

MB: Typically, we don't really have a lot of say on what projects the parks have. Most work I do with the National Park Service starts with a formal request to consult, often in the form of a letter. We have [a] say on: did they do their due diligence on researching the project, on the site it's going to be on? We just got to make sure that once they're digging the ground, my office handles everything that's historic sites and stuff like that. And in case historical human remains are found, we have the NAGPRA program (Native American Graves Protection and Repatriation Act). There's a whole protocol system that goes along with that as well.

BN: It seems like you're talking primarily about formal consultation mandated by the National Park Service. I'm curious if there are other examples when you are pulled in for something other than managing the landscape or making sure historical sites aren't disturbed. Are there different ways that you interact with these park sites?

MB: Yes. A prime example of that is Rocky Mountain National Park. The large size of Rocky Mountain National Park means we can't cross all our Ts in one shot. We have to go through things as they come up with projects overtime. Let's say something has to be done in a certain area [e.g., a building remodel, a trail or road, etc.]. We get the survey, we review the survey, and we take a look at the site because there's nearly always things that a trained archaeologist or anthropologist may not see or may not know. But we do know because we know what to look for. And that's stuff that's not taught in school. It's the way we pray and the tools we use to pray and things like that. So as a project comes at Rocky Mountain, I just try to deal with them as they come up because there's no way to survey the entire park.

BN: I'm hearing from you that there is a process and a set of protocols for how you interact in your formal role as THPO to make sure that park sites are doing their due diligence and that they're accounting for the impact on the landscape, and that you all are able to come in and use your tools. Are there times where you feel like you're pushing them to think in new ways? Do you push them in order to advocate for your nation's needs?

MB: Oh, yeah. It can get . . . I'm not going to say tense, because it's not at that level usually, but there are times when we have to sit here and just say "you don't understand what you're doing" to people who have PhDs. Because sometimes they don't know. They can give you a brief history report on a site. And they can go out there and do their grid searches and everything like that, but they miss something, they always miss something, because they're not trained [to see what we see]. So, when we're able to consult, we sit down with folks and explain what we need to look for, what has happened, or what we think is on that property. We're going to see something totally different. And we have to explain why we see things differently. Because our sciences and our trial and error through the landscape—we've already had that solved years and years ago. So, when they miss something, we make sure that they see it, and then that they can be familiar with that thing that they may have missed. And it can be something as simple as a rock circle, or a rock that doesn't belong there. We have to teach them what to look for. That way it makes them a better person and a better archaeologist.

BN: It seems that in your work, you have to have patience, not just for educating people who don't understand your peoples' ways of knowing the land. You also need to have patience for all the protocols, policies, and classifications that the federal government creates that then you and your office have to navigate. For example, NPS makes a distinction between "natural resources" and "cultural resources." How do you approach this sort of terminology and management within NPS?

MB: Yeah, they're all resources to us. Like I said, it can be the rocks. It can be a rock that we can turn into an arrowhead, a rock that we can use for burial sites. It's easier for them to say what that is—is that a natural resource or a cultural resource? To us it's all the same. All water is sacred. Our plants and everything, everything we use, they're all tools. We've always had to give tobacco to these things, because they have spirits in them. So, that's culture. That's natural. To us, it's a different meaning to us—all this stuff. We look at animals, you know, we call them relatives. When we go hunting, we hunt for food versus just for sport. We offer tobacco when we take that life. We have to be respectful when we go out to hunt, because we don't want anything bad to happen to us. We have to be respectful in every facet. So that's natural, cultural, spiritual resources that we have. So that's all under one umbrella to us. But NPS folks have to break it up to understand. So, on my side, you can't just stick somebody in the Tribal Historic Preservation Office; they have to know something, or they had to grow up in our traditions to understand these things. And I think that's why I was put in here, because I knew a little bit about something. And I'm learning more and more every day. I'm never gonna quit learning 'til the day I die. [chuckle]

BN: Yep. [chuckle]

MB: My patience has to grow, has to be better, day to day. That's where the THPO job, I think, lies.

BN: Yeah, I think about how in the context of our interpretive project at Rocky Mountain National Park, we've had meetings with THPOs where they ask about hunting and plant gathering as a part of possible educational programming. They don't necessarily make a distinction between education and resource gathering.

MB: Yeah, it goes back to teaching them that all this is under the same umbrella and that's what we got to explain to [NPS staff]. When we're talking about them renovating something on a national park site, that park has stuff that we need, stuff that we use at the same time. Let's open us up to being able to come up there and harvest an elk. I don't know if you know how elk hunting is nowadays. You got to pay for it just to go hunt elk. And that is really good meat. You know, there's a lot of things on that elk that we use. And teeth, there's only two teeth that you can get out of one elk. And if you've ever seen one of those elk tooth dresses, the entire shirt is covered in all those teeth. And that's a symbolic kind of a status. When you see those dresses, that person was a good hunter, was a well-off person or something. Because it took time to get those and time to make that dress. So yeah, we have to tie that stuff in together when we're trying to get a consultation. We have to make that open for us. Because we think differently, we react differently. If we're going to be doing something in a park, we've got to be able to do everything in that park. If you can open it up to saying, "Is this a cultural resource or a natural resource?" okay, but all of that is under the same umbrella to us.

BN: Well, yeah. My next question is about the possibilities and challenges of this sort of work. I'm curious: why does this work feel important? Why does this work with national parks feel like it's worth your time?

MB: I mean, I think Rocky Mountain National Park specifically has shown a lot that you all wanted to follow up [referring to NPS staff at the park and faculty and students at the University of Colorado Boulder working on a collaborative project]. A lot of parks, you know, they'll keep their consultation to the minimum required. From this page to this page, and that's it. Maybe they'll follow up, something like that. But we've been working together at Rocky Mountain National Park for a few years now. They've opened up the conversation to keep on going . . . because it has to be an ongoing consultation, we can't close it out. And that's the ultimate goal. I think just to make sure our people know what we're doing. Make sure that we're doing good, meaningful work with these national parks. And making sure they understand our point of view in our narrative. And that's where the patience comes in. Because I've dealt with some parks (or other entities) where they draw their consultations at just the letter, and they get a phone call from us, and it is kind of surprising to them.

BN: Okay, so actually engaging in a long-term conversation is something in and of itself. We also need to do something with that conversation. But that even the ongoing conversation is important.

MB: Exactly. And I think that should be with, you know, all the other entities, national parks, and the federal departments that we deal with. It should be an ongoing consultation. So, we want them to know that we're always here to answer questions or help them through whatever they need to do.

BN: Boy, it's a whole lot more fruitful and meaningful work when you actually can engage it in in a more ongoing way. But it is interesting, when you think of the range of possibilities, that you have a lot of parks and people within the federal government system where the consultation is a very short, discrete part of their work. And they don't feel like they can invest the time to engage in a longer-term conversation, which is too bad.

MB: Yeah. But then it goes back to [the fact that] they don't know what they should be doing. That's why it's up to us to educate them.

BN: So, you're giving non-Native people a lot of patience and understanding for what they don't know. And what they don't even know they don't know.

MB: Yep. [chuckle]

BN: So, do you have to somehow find common ground, find ways to communicate across different ways of knowing or interacting with the land, and advocate for your nation's needs?

MB: Yeah, I think it's kind of where me as a person got the advantage on that as well. Because when I was in the military, I was on the ship. And I was one of the most qualified people in my division. So, I knew the ins and outs of my job and everything I did. So, when we went to shipyards, we had to rewrite some technical manuals. And you have to use certain language and basically be the technical writer. I was part of a small group of the people who worked in these things in our division, and we had to use a certain language, so I got used to that. And we had to talk to certain people, so I got used to that, too. That's why I guess I sound a little more diplomatic.

BN: Is it kind of like speaking multiple languages?

MB: Yeah, exactly.

BN: Okay, I have one more question. I'm curious: what do you hope to see in the future in terms of how national parks engage with tribal nations and Native peoples?

MB: In the past few years, from dealing with [government and non-government] agencies, I've seen that there's a more in tune checkpoint with our consultations. I try not to let our consultation stop at just the letter. I asked questions that follow up and then proceed and whatnot. And then we can move forward. I hope that the Department of Interior now can establish a framework. While they have their positions, Deb Halaand and the national park director, they can do a framework for us. Because I think a lot of us are on the same level as far as THPOS or anybody in this field are in the same mindset of how we want consultation to be conducted. Some can be overwhelming, some can be as simple as keeping the consultation open-ended. So, I hope that framework is there in the future and hope we can go by that. And that it helps the National Park Service and Department of Interior to think differently in all their agencies, subagencies. Because things are different nationwide, and things are different at the local levels.

BN: What would feel like signs of it heading in the right direction? What might that be for you?

MB: Well, we just got a notification from the tribes that Deb Halaand herself has set up a consultation process to make things a little better. That's going to include a whole lot more, not just the THPO office, but it includes our governor and all our folks here in the administration. And I think it's going to start with how to consult with tribes better. And their research on boarding schools, and that's part of the big meeting, but I want to be able to be in there and tell them how they should be consulting.

BN: So better consulting. I'm hearing both that you would like to reliably get that consultation letter in the first place. But then you would also like a process for having ongoing communication, and not just checking off a consultation letter or one meeting, that having something more long term would feel better? Or is it case by case?

MB: Kind of case by case, but there is something that should be on the table for a long time. That's what I'm saying, that framework—I hope they establish that. That way we're always here, they're always reaching out to THPOs for anything and everything. And our side, it can be simple. We're looking at the same goal to get the projects taken care of to do what they need to do, but we want to make sure that the due diligence was done as far as moving the earth and not erasing our historical footprint of Cheyenne and Arapaho people or any other tribes.

BN: So, it seems like you're wanting a better framework for consultation and communication and relationship building between national parks and tribes. Does that tie into recognizing sovereignty? And the role that tribal nations should play in managing these lands that are their historical, ancestral territories?

MB: Yeah, it's another example of government-to-government relations. You know, that's the important part, it has to be decision-maker and decision-maker meeting at the table. And like I said, consultations on the government side are sometimes interpreted as just sending a letter. I don't think a lot of them are prepared when they get a reply to the letters. Because I've been down that road plenty of times. I sent a letter asking questions. Because all I got was a letter saying that they're going to do a project. And at the bottom of the letter it says most of the times, our findings indicate that there's no potential effect to the area. And I'm saying, well, how did you come up with that determination that you're not showing me? So, at that point, I should go talk to the person making these decisions, because I'm the person that can make the letter saying, okay, this is good to go. You're clear. That's my representation of all our tribal members, our people, and our history and whatnot. So that's my responsibility. So that's what we call government-to-government consultation and relations. Because when you do that, you're able to make decisions right then and there and then you can follow up with paperwork later. Sometimes we don't get that opportunity for that kind of consultation.

BN: It feels like just sort of an exchange of letters. But it is about so much more than just that letter. I think it's interesting to hear all this from you, Max, because, you know, we work together, and we haven't often had the time to pause and reflect. It makes me appreciate more of what you face on a daily basis in your job. You're really generous.

MB: And that's what it takes. Yeah, we want to offer and spread those good feelings. That's what we call them. Good thoughts and good feelings.

TWO | # Reciprocal Respect
Lessons Learned about Collaboration

CHRISTINA GISH HILL

I ARRIVED ON THE NORTHERN CHEYENNE RESERVATION feeling prepared. I had accepted an offer from the National Park Service (NPS) to conduct an ethnographic overview and assessment (EOA) with Cheyenne and Arapaho people to learn about their perspectives on Mount Rushmore. The project leader, Matthew J. Hill (see Chapter 5), had brought together several scholars to develop an assessment that covered the entire history of Mount Rushmore, from the monument's creation to the changing role it had in the tourism of the Black Hills. I had been asked to write the section about Cheyenne and Arapaho relationships with the Black Hills and the impact of Mount Rushmore on those relationships.

I had extensive archival knowledge of Cheyenne and Arapaho history and had previously spent several years conducting ethnographic research on the Northern Cheyenne reservation. Also, in the early 2000s, I had conducted research for a similar NPS-sponsored project on Wind Cave National Monument.[1] During my first visit to discuss the Mount Rushmore assessment, I was staying with the Cheyenne family that had taken me in years ago as a young student, and I had been communicating with the president of Dull Knife College about the project. The college had begun working with their oral history project to set up interviews in preparation for my visit. I knew this subject would be difficult to broach because I would ask people to speak about such a painful place. Mount Rushmore not only desecrated a sacred landscape with statues of presidents who had championed policies meant to destroy Native nations; underlying the monument is the trauma of the theft of the Black Hills.

I was a little nervous because the tribal historic preservation officer (THPO) had not yet responded to my inquiry. Nevertheless, I had a meeting with the vice president lined up. I figured he could help me navigate the THPO's office. I did not want to circumvent the tribal government, even though I was working with the college. My instincts on this were correct, but I had made a critical error. I had the wrong email address for the THPO, and I never called. I came to the reservation ready to conduct interviews, but in my meeting with the vice president, I learned that I had not gone through the proper channels. Permission from the college was not enough. The nation had implemented a process to approve research in the time since I started actively conducting my dissertation research. I needed to speak to the THPO, and once I received a go ahead from her, I needed to present the project to the cultural committee. I had traveled all that way only to put the project on hold. I had not followed proper protocol. In fact, I had not even figured out proper protocol, despite my years of experience working with this community. I had failed to abide by one of the earliest lessons I learned as an outside researcher—emailing and calling only goes so far. Your collaboration is not really solidified until you go for a visit. I suspect I would have struggled to discover my error if I had not been able to sit down with people face to face. Developing collaboration requires meeting people where they are.

The park service had not required that we conduct ethnography with Plains nations, but we believed it was essential to creating a well-rounded document despite the difficulty. Hill and I created a list of interview questions we would present to Cheyenne, Arapaho, and Lakota people. We asked about the meaning of the Black Hills in each culture, why people travel to the Hills, and how they feel about Mount Rushmore, as well as questions about how the NPS could reach out to their communities to collaborate on incorporating Native perspectives at the monument. At that time, the park service staff had no explicit plans to partner with Plains nations connected to the Black Hills. Ultimately, however, we hoped that this EOA could be a first step to building a collaborative relationship between Plains nations with ties to the Black Hills and Mount Rushmore. Because the park service often contracts scholars to conduct research for them, it is not unusual for a scholar to find him or herself in this position—as a bridge between Native stakeholders and the NPS. This provides independent researchers with a powerful opportunity to utilize reciprocity to develop mutual respect with the goal of paving the way for cooperation between park service staff and Native nations.

During the ethnographic work I conducted among Cheyenne and Arapaho people, everyone interviewed discussed the pain Mount Rushmore continued to cause, yet each participant also provided advice for how the park service could build a reciprocal, respectful relationship with Native peoples. By asking for thoughts and suggestions about the impact that the monument has on Native peoples, the park service has opened the conversation about collaboration, but building this relationship will require much more effort. Several interviewees related that they were not aware of a time when Mount Rushmore personnel had reached out to Cheyenne and Arapaho people, and most people I spoke with were happy that their communities were invited. Ms. MS, who was working in the Northern Cheyenne land office at the time of the conversation, set the tone when she noted, "Honestly, we're all in this together."[2]

Collaborative work between Mount Rushmore and the Cheyenne and Arapaho nations is in the earliest stages. Throughout the interviews, four requirements emerged for building a collaborative relationship between the park service and these Native nations. First, opening the door for this type of relationship requires the NPS to take responsibility for how Native people have been excluded from the research process, leading to inaccurate or even offensive representation at parks. Second, the park service must acknowledge the shameful moments in US history, including the erasure of many Plains nations from the history of the Black Hills, alongside the laudable ones. Third, building this type of relationship involves listening deeply to Native perspectives, a style of listening not common among non-Native researchers. Fourth, it necessitates surrendering power to Native people to guide the process toward achieving the agreed upon outcomes. Surrendering power requires a commitment to honor the wishes of those who share their knowledge concerning the use and publication of that knowledge. This step also requires that participants are compensated for their time and publicly acknowledged for their contributions.

To reach these goals, researchers and staff must work towards the kind of reciprocity expected in many Native communities that honors the humanity of all collaborators and recognizes their interrelatedness. Building a partnership between the park service and Native nations depends on a commitment from the park service to privilege Native perspectives as they work to develop new park spaces, activities, and management practices. While not comprehensive, these four steps create a foundation that parks can use to design protocol for reaching out to Native nations. Collaboration involves building lasting human relationships between individual actors, the kind that cannot be scripted by an institution.[3] Depending solely on individuals to maintain this type of collaboration, however, can lead to a revolving door effect. When individuals who built the relationships move on to new jobs in the park service or tribal government, without some institutionalized mechanisms, these partnerships can fall apart.[4] Therefore, it would behoove the NPS to consider establishing procedures and even offices that could sustain collaboration with Native nations. While the commitment of time and resources required from a collaborative approach can be taxing for a small monument like Mount Rushmore, which has a limited supply of both, the cooperation that could result from it has the potential to be transformative for park service staff, Native people, and visitors alike. This chapter describes some methods vital to building a collaborative relationship. Ultimately the park service will need to shift its framework for Mount Rushmore in order to build meaningful relationships with Plains nations and incorporate their needs and perspectives at the monument.

The Black Hills as a Vital Cultural Landscape

For many park service officials, collaborating with Native peoples has become an important part of their agenda, but there is still much to be done. For Native nations across the United States, this is certainly true of Mount Rushmore. Because it is carved into a sacred landscape that US courts have determined was unlawfully taken from Lakota, Cheyenne, and Arapaho people, it represents the most hypocritical and colonial elements of the relationship between Native nations and the United States government. Mount Rushmore creates a twofold problem for Native people with ties to the Black Hills. As a statue carved into the rock, it is a desecration of a sacred landscape. As a representation of US presidents, this statue honors people who championed policies destructive toward Native nations. For Native people, the desecration of this sacred place is exacerbated by the symbolic content of the patriotic monument, which leads to overwhelmingly negative connotations associated with Mount Rushmore.

It would be hard to overestimate the importance of the Black Hills complex for Cheyenne and Arapaho people. Wallace Bear Chum underscored this when he stated, "Being a Cheyenne, you're always taught that it's a sacred [place] and there's a lot of history to it. People used to live around there and did ceremonies around there, especially at Bear Butte."[5] Ms. MS emphasized the power of the place when she related that, from an Indigenous perspective, one does not visit the Black Hills as a tourist attraction separate from the wider landscape. She explained, "You go there, and you surrender yourself to those relationships and you ask yourself, 'How can I be in this place responsibly?' There's renewal in that [action]. The Black Hills give us so much life. It's a reciprocal relationship, so we have a responsibility to be there. The Black Hills, in turn, share a responsibility to renew who we are as Cheyenne people and to renew our stories."[6]

Virginia Ritchie, a Southern Cheyenne and Arapaho nation member with relatives from both nations, stated that her Arapaho grandparents talked about Sun Dances and other ceremonial gatherings that took place in the Black Hills because it was such a sacred place.[7] The Black Hills are an appropriate location for such gatherings because of the emphasis the Sun Dance has on renewal and healing, both for the world and for people.

Cheyenne and Arapaho people travel to the Black Hills to conduct ceremonies, fulfill spiritual obligations, and gather culturally necessary resources, but also for personal renewal. Dr. Richard Little Bear, president of Dull Knife College on the Northern Cheyenne reservation, stated that regardless of the hardship, "I do know that a lot of people go out there and camp out there for a week or even two weeks, during the summertime, and most of the time those resources have been gathered for the past year. The food, the money, the arrangements going down there, those resources gathered, like tents and all that have been either borrowed or bought so that it's a comfortable experience to go down there. And, people revere that experience very highly, they plan for it all year to go down there."⁸ While traveling to the Black Hills for ceremonial reasons is a priority, Northern Cheyenne people reported traveling to the Black Hills at least occasionally just for recreation. Cheyenne and Arapaho people in Oklahoma, on the other hand, related that their trips to the Hills were almost always taken for ceremonial reasons because it was so far and expensive to go. While Cheyenne and Arapaho people traveling to the Black Hills sometimes choose to make visiting tourist sites a part of their trip, they are very concerned about the development taking place and the increased influx of visitors. Ms. LN, a Southern Cheyenne and Arapaho nation member and veteran, noted that she comes to the Hills first as a Native person. She reflected thoughts I heard from many people when she explained that she cannot be a tourist in the Hills because they are her home.⁹ Ms. Ritchie reiterated this idea, stating that she is not a tourist because this is her land.¹⁰

As a national monument with a patriotic message, Mount Rushmore is meant for all Americans, but it alienates Native visitors and erases Native American perspectives. Some Native people visit Mount Rushmore during their trips to the Hills, including Native students on school fieldtrips. Native citizens understandably have a different experience of the space than most other Americans. The park service has attempted to bring Native people into the conversations about how they should be represented at the site, most notably by hiring Gerard Baker (Mandan Hidatsa) as superintendent from 2004 to 2010. For more insight on Baker's efforts at the memorial, see an interview with him in the next section of the volume. Yet Cheyenne and Arapaho people still feel deeply wounded by Mount Rushmore.

Taking Responsibility

Building a collaborative relationship between researchers and Native peoples first requires taking responsibility. For over a century, researchers representing universities, private institutions, and the US government have often fueled their own agendas by conducting biased studies about Native people. Vine Deloria Jr. first brought attention to the issue in 1969.¹¹ Thirty years later, Linda Tuhiwai Smith demonstrated that gathering knowledge from Indigenous peoples remained a mostly colonial project.¹² In response to these critiques, many scholars have provided methodological direction for collaborative work between researchers and Indigenous peoples.¹³ Taking responsibility requires researchers to not only acknowledge shameful moments in the history of relationships between Natives and settlers, but also a shameful history of appropriating and misusing Indigenous knowledge. Because these practices continue today, each individual must recognize colonial research practices and be prepared to develop his or her own practices in a manner that departs from this misuse. Taking responsibility as a researcher involves designing research methods and protocol with input from Indigenous collaborators.

Yet, knowing how to begin can be incredibly challenging. Reaching out is the first step. Most Native nations have the contact information for their government offices posted online: mailing addresses, email addresses, and phone numbers of tribal government officials and heads of tribal offices, including the THPO. Some nations are also affiliated with tribal colleges that have faculty and students who might be interested in collaborating with researchers. Often the THPO is a good person to start with, but the president of the tribal college or college faculty may also be helpful. Regardless, to take responsibility, it is essential to disclose your research and ask about the process involved to conduct further research with a particular Native nation.

Many Native nations have set up their own review boards in order to assess proposals made by researchers who wish to conduct studies in the community. Some have specific IRB processes, including forms to fill out, while others require a researcher to present his or her work in front of the tribal council or a separate cultural committee. The THPO will know the requirements. Every community has its own process, and the procedures vary from place to place. Native nations regularly deal with hundreds of requests and often have a small staff to handle them. Researchers need to be sensitive to this fact and plan their timeline accordingly. It can take months to complete the process or schedule the needed meetings. Furthermore, communicating by email only goes so far. Making phone calls is essential. It is often more efficient to discuss issues than to write about them. Also, talking is more personal than writing and goes a long way to demonstrating a collegial attitude and sensitivity to Indigenous protocol.

When presenting work to a Native nation, researchers need to discuss the scope of the work, describe their research methods, state the benefits of the research to the nation, and provide a plan for sharing the results of the research. The scope of work describes the general objectives and purpose of the research and provides enough background information for the board or THPO to understand the proposal. Describing the proposed research methods is vital because the nation needs to be able to determine if the practices are appropriate. The researcher should also leave space for the community to alter the research methods. It is important to make suggestions but also clearly indicate that the methods can be changed to fit the needs of the community. Sometimes the board or THPO will also suggest alterations to the research subject, noting that some information is too sensitive to be shared or is proprietary in nature.

Stating the benefits to the community indicates to the nation that the researcher is not simply extracting knowledge for his or her own benefit but has considered the impacts of the research. When possible, the researcher should listen to the needs of the community in relation to the project and seek to match the benefits with these needs. Finally, it is important that the researcher shares the results with the community and incorporates the board or THPO's requirements for data protection. Native nations often request that researchers notify them of their publications and sometimes require the right to comment on materials before they are published. Communicating the full research plan and providing space for the board or THPO to make alterations is the foundation of collaborative work. While studies on specific topics using particular methods are often requested or required by institutions like the park service, there is plenty of space to allow knowledgeable Native people to shape the research plan before it is enacted.

In our own work with the Northern Cheyenne, Southern Cheyenne, and Arapaho nations, we encountered different expectations. We worked with the Southern Cheyenne THPO, Max Bear, in Oklahoma, who grounded me, as the one conducting the interviews, in the process of conducting research there. He worked with me to recruit participants and provided me with a background on the relationship between the people and the Hills before I began chatting with others. At Northern Cheyenne, I met with the THPO during my first visit and discovered that I needed to go before the cultural committee and then reschedule the interviews I had set up with the tribal college so that they could be done with approval from the committee. We were given permission to attend this meeting over the phone, since we needed to schedule it about a month in advance and had limited travel funds. Many tribal governments prefer in-person meetings, however, so being prepared to travel and present can be valuable. That said, since the Covid-19 pandemic, many tribal offices have shifted to virtual meetings, so this could warrant a conversation about preferred venue.

The Northern Cheyenne have a tribal research review board in place called the cultural committee that reviews proposals to conduct research on the reservation. It is made up of elders and other tribal officials. Bringing our research proposal before the committee resulted in a powerful conversation that helped my supervisor and me tweak the project before conducting interviews. When describing the project, my supervisor stated that we planned to focus on "everyday relationships" with the Black Hills, and one of the committee members asked, if that was so, why did we use the term "ceremonial activities" in our proposal? This was useful because our research was not intended to explore ceremonial activities but rather the reasons people visited the Hills and their feelings about Mount Rushmore's presence in such an important landscape. By acknowledging the ceremonial importance of the Hills, we had unwittingly given the idea that we were researching ceremonies, so we edited the proposal and removed the language of sacred sites and ceremonial activities.

The committee also asked how we planned to manage the intellectual property from the project. I replied that we would gain informed consent from each participant and would keep the interviews confidential if that was the individual's wish, but that we would also acknowledge people who wished to be acknowledged for their thoughts in any publications. We would return transcripts to interviewees for comment when possible. We would also seek feedback on any publications before going to press. Finally, we would provide participants copies of their own interviews if requested. The committee also asked where the interviews would take place. We said that we were happy to meet wherever the participants felt most comfortable—at their homes, at the college, in their offices, or even outside. And I ended up conducting interviews in all these settings.

The committee also wanted to know if we would offer an honorarium. They felt it was appropriate to compensate participants for their time. We decided to offer a small gift card and a braid of sweetgrass at Northern Cheyenne and the same gift card and a pouch of tobacco at Southern Cheyenne and Arapaho. In a truly collaborative relationship, the Cheyenne and Arapaho THPOs and knowledgeable culture keepers would work together to design the research project from the beginning. But this project was a first step towards creating a bridge with the park service in the hope that these entities could work towards achieving truly collaborative relationships.

Nevertheless, the role of researchers as intermediaries between the NPS and Native nations reveals multiple complications. Researchers might be tempted to act as neutral third parties, but this approach runs the risk of discouraging full engagement between the park service and Native communities. An essential component of taking responsibility, however, is presenting your role as a researcher and your positionality in that role clearly. Researchers conducting an EOA are not in a government-to-government relationship and must not represent themselves as spokespeople for the NPS. Researchers must be careful of the language they use. For example, if a researcher states he or she is consulting for the park service, this might lead tribal officials to believe the park service needs to initiate the process of consultation, but this is a formal government-to-government process undertaken using specific protocol. Confusion and even anger can erupt if tribal leaders feel that this process should be taking place but is not.

The Northern Cheyenne vice chairman at the time, Conrad Fisher, noted that our letter of consultation was not adequate because tribal officials, including the THPO, had not been consulted in the design of the scope of work for this project. He expressed that as third-party contractors, we were not adequately positioned to discuss these concerns with the nation—that the NPS should be contacting the Northern Cheyenne government directly. By pulling Mike Evans, the head of the division overseeing our work, into the conversation, we were able to foster a discussion between park service officials and Northern Cheyenne officials about the scope of work and the direction the research should take. This helped to avoid conflict by demonstrating that we were not attempting to wiggle out of obligations or conduct research without permission from each of the different offices in the community. Researchers working for the park service need to be prepared to take responsibility for the research process and know exactly what their position is in relation to the park service. Often, they have little power to facilitate change at the park service itself, but they can pave the way for conversations between park service staff and Native peoples.

Acknowledging Shameful Histories

The creation of state and federal lands has been a part of the historical process of removing and erasing Native people from their lands, and while the parks have intentionally begun to shift these dynamics, Native people still struggle to regain their reciprocal relationships with the land.[14] Chester White Man noted, "It's pretty hard for our folks to say anything about things like this." He followed this statement with a comment that reflected how important starting a conversation around the painful topic of Mount Rushmore has been when he said, "It's always good to air it out."[15] In this comment, White Man reiterated the sentiment that many others shared, expressing the importance of NPS's willingness to acknowledge the pain the monument has caused for Plains peoples.

Most people felt alienated both by the presence of the monument as well as its honorific narrative about US history. They also expressed that Native people have been erased from this narrative entirely. Ms. MS explained, "A lot of these places don't get contextualized or narrated from an Indigenous perspective, for Indigenous children, much less for non-Indigenous, and I think that that's incredibly dangerous because it erases and supplants Indigenous narratives and indigeneity to place with settler narratives. I'm not saying that settlers can't have their own narratives and stories to place. They can, but they shouldn't have to come at the cost of erasing and supplanting the Indigenous ones. And that's what Mount Rushmore does." As a result, Ms. MS commented that she does not see herself or her Cheyenne people reflected in Mount Rushmore.[16]

Wallace Bear Chum was specific in his critique. He felt that the museum was lacking in representations of Cheyenne history and perspectives. White Man reflected on the impact of this when he stated,

> We want our children to understand the history of this country, but we also want them to understand their history. And that's not being taught anywhere, except for maybe reservation schools. It really needs to be brought to everybody's attention, what struggles we went through. They say, "this is the biggest mass murder in the US," but they forget about Wounded Knee, Washita, Sand Creek.
>
> I would like to add that the US government or NPS needs to get these stories right not because of money but because of truth. Like at Sand Creek, Washita, Wounded Knee, and the breakout at Fort Robinson—correct it. It doesn't take much, they have to swallow their pride, be grown up about it. Our government is still in its adolescence because they can't accept what they did to our people. Not just to Cheyennes and Arapahos but to all nations.[17]

White Man explicitly called on the park service to acknowledge its role in the shameful history of the United States.

Ms. Hamilton got very emotional when she spoke with me about the impact Mount Rushmore has had on her people. When asked for her thoughts on the monument, she explained that since Mount Rushmore is already there, "we do not have to accept it, but we have to adapt." Then she began to tell me about the time she drove past the monument with her son in the car. She related that her son was in his thirties at the time and as they approached, he told his mom that he did not want to stop. As she told the story, Ms. Hamilton began to cry softly, and through her tears, she told me that her son said, "Mom, I know what this place has done to our people." She continued, "That's how deep this pain is for us. I shed tears because it's a big loss. I'm glad my children recognize that."[18]

On the one hand, interviewees suggested that Mount Rushmore's very existence is alienating, which could lead to a sense that there is no room for discussion. Yet almost everyone wanted the conversation to move forward. Many interviewees noted how different Indigenous perspectives on land, development, and experiencing place are from Western ones. While Indigenous perspectives center on respectful reciprocity, the dominant Euro-American perspectives express authority over the land. This research is evidence that the NPS wants to work towards collaboration with Native people, but true collaboration requires that the worldviews of Native Plains nations guide the process at least in part. While this would go a long way towards building a reciprocal collaboration, the question remains: what could this process look like?

Deep Listening

Many whom I spoke with noted that the first step to the collaborative process is listening. Wallace Bear Chum stated that even though the economy surrounding Mount Rushmore is already there, the park service still needs to be aware of the Native perspective and pay attention to all the nations concerned, including the Lakota, Arapaho, and Cheyenne, among other Plains nations. Teanna Limpy, the Northern Cheyenne THPO, emphasized how important it was to contact Native nations, work with their THPOs, and consult with elders to create interpretation and understand the site. Several others noted that when approaching issues dealing with a powerful place like the Black Hills, the people embarking on this work need to first approach the ceremonial sector of Native populations. Mr. BC suggested that bringing these knowledgeable elders together for a meal would be a positive way to begin the conversation. He strongly emphasized that this kind of collaborative work must begin with the ceremonial sector instead of the political offices of the nation because politics should be separate from ceremonial activities. His emphasis on a meal reflects the importance of maintaining reciprocal relationships through generosity.[19] Reciprocity is not simply about making sure all voices are heard and reflected in any action the park service might take, but also about building relationships through caring for each other. This includes things like providing a meal and taking the time to eat together and become acquainted.

Ms. MS expanded on the appropriate attitude to take when approaching the ceremonial sector. She noted that Indigenous pedagogy and understandings of human development emphasize becoming apprenticed by your elders. While the learner can ask questions, the elders are the ones who speak, not because they are placed above others in a hierarchy, but because they are so deeply respected. This respect encourages the learner to exercise a humility that allows him or her to absorb what is going on. This requires the learner to build an active relationship with elders. Ms. MS used her relationship with me as an example, noting that if we had only communicated over email, we would not have been able to share the depth of conversation that we did. Since we had met more than once, we began to build a relationship. She stated, "Listening and talking and being a good relative is critical because it allows people to make these connections and to live in that active relationship with each other." Then she made explicit the connection about relatedness to the land and relatedness to people when she said, "That's the same active relationship that happens when you are out on the land, whether you are hunting or gathering plants or implementing Indigenous fire as a technology for land management; just being there implies a responsibility." She concluded her thoughts, saying, "I think it keeps you human." In his article for this volume, Tim Cochrane notes that collaboration at Grand Portage National Monument has been successful because people took the time to develop interpersonal relationships. He argues that these relationships can't be scripted by an institution. While this is true, these relationships are so essential to collaborative work that they should be cultivated within the park service. If we are to take seriously the idea that collaboration involves following Indigenous protocols, researchers and staff need to take the time to form the relationships.

Perhaps one reason that following Cheyenne protocol (or that of any Native nation) has been a challenge for the NPS is that it involves committing to opening oneself up to a very non-Western way of knowing. Several interviewees had advice for non-Natives attempting collaborative work with Native nations. Ms. MS suggested that a person try to be authentic and humble. She followed that by saying, "My biggest piece of advice would be: don't speak." And she laughed, continuing, "Just listen for a while. You don't need to speak." Mr. SD, a Northern Cheyenne ceremonial leader, reflected that people need to spend some time in a place. He said, "It is important to stay for the whole ceremony." With our busy lives, he was posing a challenge to slow down and really pay attention. Ms. MS was a little more pointed in her critique, suggesting that non-Native people struggle to open themselves up to Native ways of knowing and being with the landscape because they are afraid to surrender power. She encouraged people to ask questions to gain a sense of the protocols and taboos that are required when seeking Indigenous knowledge. But the first step is "to build those relations by approaching people with an authentic and genuine heart." She reminded me that regardless of one's fear, letting go is vital to understanding the relationship between Cheyenne people and their known landscape.

Ms. MS described this letting go very effectively, invoking the power of words and the importance of listening from a Cheyenne perspective:

> Cheyenne people hold words [to be] really sacred and so I think that's part of where the humility comes in. I wish more people would practice this—not just Cheyennes but everyone. Your words are really powerful and they can definitely set up human reality, including human relationships to land and how we practice in land. They construct our reality. And so we know that as Cheyenne people, your words are really powerful and you only say something when you know it. But you also say it in a good way, and that's why you know you're not supposed to talk down to anybody. Your words are going to have an impact whether you know it or not, so you have to think and feel deeply before you speak. And so my best piece of advice would be to think and reflect internally and listen. Don't even ask questions for a while. Just let the place and the stories come to you and fill you. Because by asking questions, you're already trying to put it into a particular way without seeing the whole thing. It's kind of a reductionist move, even if people don't intend it that way. You need to see the whole, and the only way you can see the whole is by just sitting and listening.

This is more difficult than we may realize because, as Wendy Hui Kyong Chun points out, "more often than not, we assume we know how to listen."[20] Taiaiake Alfred argues that listening is essential to the process of decolonizing Native relationships with their landscapes, stating that if non-Native people are willing to listen, they will discover "an alternative to the settler society by inviting them to share our vision of respect and peaceful co-existence."[21] Letting go in the way that Ms. MS describes can be incredibly difficult for non-Native people, particularly because for many it involves allowing for a dramatically different worldview. Because NPS employees have been entrusted with the responsibility to maintain landscapes of national importance, shifting away from the established protocols could be challenging. At the same time, because the balance of power has been so one-sided for so long, collaborative work with Native peoples must privilege Native protocols and ways of knowing. For Mount Rushmore personnel to learn and follow Lakota, Cheyenne, and Arapaho protocol would be a meaningful sign that the park service is serious about incorporating the perspectives of Plains nations.

Surrendering Power

After speaking with several Cheyenne and Arapaho elders, it became clear that Mount Rushmore staff had not fully acknowledged its shameful history, creating deep-seated problems. As a result, building a collaboration between park service staff at the monument and Plains nations has been challenging. Neither the Northern Cheyenne nor the Cheyenne and Arapaho nations of Oklahoma have had much say in what happens at Mount Rushmore. As a result, building a collaboration requires tipping the scales of power back to these nations. Approaching Native people with humility and acknowledging the historical injustices they have suffered is essential. Surrendering power requires not only that Native people have a seat at the table, but a commitment to incorporating their ideas into both the design and the management of the monument.

Ensuring that Native people have control over the collaboration at all stages must occur even in preliminary research. While ethnography has long established protocols for ensuring that the researcher respects collaborators' power over their own knowledge, it is worth discussing how to accomplish this. I do this in two ways. First, I always acquire informed consent for conducting an interview, and to digitally record it or simply take notes. Acquiring information without going through this process places power in the hands of the researcher. While conducting research about Mount Rushmore, there were elders who did not provide consent to record but did request that I take notes. One elder did not want his words to be recorded at all but did want to share his thoughts with me. When approaching a participant, I also used consent forms. Researchers have been skeptical of consent forms, feeling that they might, as Alex Golub has stated, create a "bureaucratization of the relations [we] have with informants."[22] Instead, Golub discovered that the form did not actually diminish the rapport he had established with his participants. He points out that all interviews are negotiated social events, and not "genuine" social events like we might wish to imagine. He argues that the consent form is part of "the process by which you and your informant build up the interview as a social event."[23]

I would argue that such a form goes beyond establishing the value of the interview. When used ethically, the form demonstrates to participants that as a researcher, you will respect their time, their privacy, and their wishes for the knowledge they share with you. My consent forms always make clear that the participants can share as much or as little as they want, and that the content of their interview belongs to them. During my research, I listened to complaints about requests made to other researchers for interview recordings. These participants were told that they were not allowed to receive these recordings because they were now the property of the researcher. Reciprocity demands the return of recordings and transcriptions when requested. It also allows for space for a participant to reassess what they have shared. Respect demands that researchers acknowledge those who share their knowledge as they would any other valuable source. My consent form also ensures that those who wish to be acknowledged in publications will be. Understanding the shared knowledge as belonging to the knowledge holder, the researcher surrenders power over that knowledge. In that way, we acknowledge the people we work with as scholarly sources instead of human subjects.

Another component of acknowledging participants is to compensate them for their time and honor the value of the knowledge they share. Providing some form of renumeration is a respectful way to compensate a person for their time and knowledge. I also offer a culturally appropriate gift to demonstrate that I understand that receiving knowledge is an honor. As mentioned before, sometimes I offer a sweetgrass braid or a pouch of tobacco, but different Native nations will value different gifts. I work with knowledgeable members in the community to determine what appropriate compensation would be and what kinds of gifts would be most appreciated. If a researcher is not familiar with the cultural expectations around gifting in a community, it is important to ask. Knowing how to present a gift can prevent accidentally inappropriate behavior. For example, giving tobacco to an elder might obligate that person to share knowledge with you. At Southern Cheyenne and Arapaho, I spent several days at one of the community centers waiting with the THPO and his assistant for people to show up for an interview. We had advertised around the nation asking people to join us, but not mentioning that there would be any compensation. Over the course of the day, many people came to share their knowledge or to ask about the project. Late in the afternoon, a younger woman came to share her feelings about the monument. Once we had discussed the consent form and she had agreed to the interview, this woman watched me slide a pouch of tobacco across the long table we were sitting at. She turned to Max Bear and said something like, "Well, she's doing this the traditional way, isn't she?" Mr. Bear smiled in a way I could not read, but I had the feeling that demonstrating my respect for her knowledge in a culturally appropriate way was appreciated. Asking for knowledge in a culturally respectful way is an important way to surrender power, demonstrating that collaborators are in control of what they share during the project.

Surrendering power also necessitates that Native peoples connected to each park guide the process of determining the actions needed to reach mutually beneficial outcomes. Many people suggested that the NPS hold meetings with the Cheyenne and Arapaho nations to discuss access, to identify culturally important locations and resources, to revamp Mount Rushmore's educational component, and to design collaborative practices. The reasons that Cheyenne and Arapaho people have often been left out of the conversation surrounding Mount Rushmore also point to the historic erasure of Native presence in the Black Hills generally and the Lakota connection to the Hills specifically. Because Euro-American understandings of space, until recently, have associated each ethnic group with a distinct, bounded geographic space, Cheyenne and Arapaho presence, not to mention that of Kiowa, Apache, and other Native nations, has been erased from the Black Hills. By reaching out to multiple groups who have historically associated with the region, the NPS can begin the work of reversing this erasure. To fully commit to surrendering power involves ensuring that the voices of Lakota, Cheyenne, Arapaho, and other Plains peoples are incorporated into the decision-making process at Mount Rushmore.

Conclusions

Most tourist sites in the Black Hills, including Mount Rushmore, have emphasized narratives that glorify Euro-American expansion, resource extraction, and economic development. Building a collaborative relationship with Plains nations can help park service staff to implement a different narrative at the monument. When building collaborative relationships with the Northern Cheyenne nation and the Southern Cheyenne and Arapaho nation, staff at the site do not need to be timid. Cheyenne and Arapaho people may be very emotional about the site, but they are also willing to have the difficult conversations that could lead to a richer, deeper interpretation of the place, as well as a renewal of the relationship between Cheyenne and Arapaho people and that section of the Black Hills. Park service staff, however, must commit to a reciprocal relationship built on respect. This requires taking responsibility, acknowledging painful histories, deep listening, and, most importantly, surrendering power.

Mr. SD stated, "It is good for the park service to dip their toe, but they need to put their whole foot in and then go in with both feet."[24] Several people commented that they wanted this EOA to lead to more interaction and collaboration with Mount Rushmore. They were very positive about the potential despite the monumental nature of the challenge. People recognized that the park service was opening the door for collaboration by conducting interviews. Chester White Man stated, "I appreciate what you are doing here today, recording our thoughts and feelings." Wallace Bear Chum also noted that "it's good to see Mount Rushmore reaching out and trying to gather information." He finished his statement with the "hope that they continue to work with the tribe directly and get them more involved, especially because it relates to the Black Hills."

In his final statements to me, Mr. BC said, "I think it's about time that we need to start healing."[25] In listening to the many people I interviewed over the course of my time at both the northern and southern reservations, the overarching message seemed to be that reciprocal, respectful collaboration was a vital first step to begin the healing process. Ms. Ritchie noted that being able to access land through the NPS and conduct ceremonies would go a long way to helping Native people heal. In my own ruminations over the suggestions offered by Cheyenne and Arapaho people, I started to understand that healing needs to take place on both sides, and it must include reclaiming landscapes and retelling histories. But this is not work that Native people can do alone. Non-Native people need to also be brave enough to rename moments in their own history in a way that acknowledges multiple perspectives. They need to allow that their claim to a landscape is simply one of many and be open to the legitimacy of other types of claims. Dr. Little Bear noted that Mount Rushmore "celebrates the taking of Native American lands. The westward movement caused a lot of Native Americans to die, a lot of families were disrupted, and we lost a lot of land without compensation, and yet it is an iconic movement in American history."

Non-Native people can participate in this renaming by acknowledging the loss created by westward expansion and can recognize the reclaiming that is taking place as Native peoples continue to maintain their relationships with the sacred Black Hills. By creating space at Mount Rushmore for Native narratives, the park service can create a model for collaboration that acknowledges renaming and reclaiming.

Dr. Little Bear reflected, "I don't mean to be so gloomy about this whole thing because there is a good side to life too." He talked about how much he enjoyed living on the Northern Cheyenne reservation because he can speak his language with other Cheyenne people on their own land, land he noted "that a lot of our people died for." There are positive sides of Cheyenne history that should be shared, especially when so many Americans see Native people as victims. As we were concluding our interview, he stated that it seems to be the privilege of the victors to write history, and they slant it their way. He paused and noted, "If we had been the winners, we would have slanted it our way too." And then he looked at me with a twinkle in his eye and said, "But it would have been a better slant." He laughed and said, "just kidding," but I got the feeling that he was not totally kidding.

As reflected in Dr. Little Bear's comments, there is a compassion in Cheyenne and Arapaho statements about Mount Rushmore. This compassion is inspiring. It opens an avenue for presenting "a better slant." Among the people I spoke with, the process of reclaiming and renaming meant opening up the dialogue and presenting multiple narratives, not only about Mount Rushmore and Cheyennes and Arapahos, or even Euro-Americans and Natives, but wider narratives about the Black Hills, these four presidents, and all the people who have come together, in conflict and collaboration, to make the United States what it is now. Ms. MS's final thoughts reflected powerfully on the braveness of the commitment I saw among Cheyennes and Arapahos to begin a conversation about Mount Rushmore. She stated, "That's why I agreed to this interview because it's not just about me. It's about making sure I'm responsible in keeping stories and belongings to this particular place alive and well." I want to put forward Ms. MS's final statement as a challenge to all of us. She stated, "Now that we know better; we have to do better." By reaching out to Cheyenne, Arapaho, and Lakota peoples for their perspectives on the site through sponsored research, the NPS has taken a difficult first step toward potentially building a collaboration. Nevertheless, if they want to continue to move forward with a relationship, they need to approach the process with care, being thoughtful about the next steps they take to work with Cheyenne and Arapaho peoples and by extension other Plains nations. Through taking responsibility, acknowledging its own painful past, listening deeply, and surrendering power to Native collaborators, Mount Rushmore can build a collaboration that benefits the park, the Native peoples who call the Black Hills home, and the visitors who come to learn about this incredible place. By acknowledging alternative worldviews embodied in Native communities that recognize the sacredness of the entire Black Hills, Mount Rushmore can become part of constructing a more inclusive narrative of American history, one that recognizes the historical and contemporary impacts of Native Plains peoples.

Notes

1. Patricia Albers et al., "The Home of the Bison: An Ethnographic and Ethnohistorical Study of Traditional Cultural Affiliations to Wind Cave National Park," US National Park Service Publications and Papers (National Park Service, 2003).
2. While most people I interviewed requested that I use their names in the manuscript to acknowledge them for their knowledge, some wished to remain anonymous. For those that did, I use the initials of a pseudonym I created.
3. Tim Cochrane's piece, this volume; Lance Foster's interview, this volume.
4. Brooke Neely and Natasha Myhal's chapter, this volume.
5. Wallace Bear Chum, interview with the author, Lame Deer, MT, 2017.
6. MS, interview with the author, Lame Deer, MT, 2017.
7. Virginia Ritchie, interview with the author, El Reno, OK, 2018.
8. Richard Little Bear, interview with the author, Lame Deer, MT, 2017.
9. LN, interview with the author, El Reno, OK, 2018.
10. Ritchie, 2018.
11. Vine Deloria Jr., *Custer Died for Your Sins: An Indian Manifesto* (New York: Macmillan, 1969).
12. Linda Tuhiwai Smith, *Decolonizing Methodologies: Research and Indigenous Peoples* (London: Zed Books, 2013).
13. Marie Battiste, "Research Ethics for Protecting Indigenous Knowledge and Heritage: Institutional and Researcher Responsibilities," in *Handbook of Critical and Indigenous Methodologies*, ed. Norman K. Denzin, Yvonne S. Lincoln, and Linda Tuhiwai Smith (Los Angeles: Sage, 2008): 497–510; Bagele Chilisa, *Indigenous Research Methodologies* (Thousand Oaks, CA: Sage Publications, 2011); Deloria, *Custer Died for Your Sins*; Jason Brent Ellis and Mark A. Earley, "Reciprocity and Constructions of Informed Consent: Researching with Indigenous Populations," *International Journal of Qualitative Methods* 5, no. 4 (2006): 1–13; Jay T. Johnson et al., "Creating Anti-colonial Geographies: Embracing Indigenous Peoples' Knowledges and Rights," *Geographical Research* 45, no. 2 (2007): 117–20; Margaret Kovach, *Indigenous Methodologies: Characteristics, Conversations, and Contexts* (Toronto: University of Toronto Press, 2010); Renee Pualani Louis, "Can You Hear Us Now? Voices from the Margin: Using Indigenous Methodologies in Geographic Research," *Geographical Research* 45, no. 2 (2007): 130–39; David Ruppert, "Building Partnerships between American Indian Tribes and the National Park Service," *Ecological Restoration* 21, no. 4 (2003): 261–63; Linda Tuhiwai Smith, *Decolonizing Methodologies: Research and Indigenous Peoples* (London: Zed Books Ltd., 2013); Joshua K. Tobias, Chantelle AM Richmond, and Isaac Luginaah, "Community-based Participatory Research (CBPR) with Indigenous Communities: Producing

Respectful and Reciprocal Research," *Journal of Empirical Research on Human Research Ethics* 8, no. 2 (2013): 129–40.

14. Philip Burnham, *Indian Country, God's Country: Native Americans and the National Parks* (Washington, DC: Island Press, 2000); Robert Poirier and David Ostergren, "Evicting People from Nature: Indigenous Land Rights and National Parks in Australia, Russia, and the United States," *Natural Resources Journal* (2002): 331–51; and Mark David Spence, *Dispossessing the Wilderness: Indian Removal and the Making of the National Parks* (Oxford: Oxford University Press, 1999).
15. Chester White Man, interview with the author, El Reno, OK, 2018.
16. MS, 2017.
17. White Man, 2018.
18. Bobbi Hamilton, interview with the author, El Reno, OK, 2018.
19. BC, interview with the author, Lame Deer, MT, 2017.
20. Wendy Hui Kyong Chun, "Unbearable Witness: Toward a Politics of Listening," *Differences: A Journal of Feminist Cultural Studies* 11, no. 1 (June 1, 1999): 114.
21. Alfred Taiaiake, *Wasáse: Indigenous Pathways of Freedom and Action* (Peterborough, Ontario: Broadview Press, 2005), 35.
22. Alex Golub, "Using Informed Consent Forms in Fieldwork," *Savage Minds* (blog), August 10, 2007, https://savageminds.org/2007/08/10/using-informed-consent-forms-in-fieldwork.
23. Golub, "Using Informed Consent Forms in Fieldwork."
24. SD, interview with the author, Lame Deer, MT, 2017.
25. BC, interview with the author, Lame Deer, MT, 2017.

THREE | Indigenous Connections at Rocky Mountain National Park
Notes from a Collaboration in Progress

BROOKE NEELY AND NATASHA MYHAL

ON A FOGGY AND DRIZZLY SEPTEMBER AFTERNOON, a group of tribal members, National Park Service (NPS) staff, and university faculty and students walked carefully down a pine-filled hill in Rocky Mountain National Park (RMNP) into a wide, open meadow. A park archaeologist led us through the clearing to a rocky hillside, pointing the way to two pine and aspen pole structures—one still intact, the other sliding imperceptibly down the hill. Hundreds of these sorts of structures have been found throughout the park, and they provide physical evidence for what the tribal members already knew: this place had been home for people for thousands of years before it was ever a national park.

The collection of people in the meadow came together for a two-day meeting in 2017 to discuss ways the park could better include and reach out to Native peoples—both to expand the interpretive program the park creates for its 4.5 million annual visitors and to support tribal members' connections to the Rocky Mountain region. The meeting launched a long-term collaborative project that is now known as "Indigenous Connections at Rocky Mountain National Park." The collaboration includes the NPS (specifically RMNP and the Intermountain Region cultural anthropology program), representatives from six tribal nations with connections to the region (Northern Arapaho Tribe, Cheyenne and Arapaho Tribes, Northern Cheyenne Tribe, Southern Ute Indian Tribe, Ute Indian Tribe of Uintah and Ouray, and Ute Mountain Ute Tribe), and two academic centers at the University of Colorado (CU) Boulder (the Center of the American West and the Center for Native American and Indigenous Studies).[1] The authors of this chapter are a faculty member at CU Boulder (Brooke Neely) and a PhD student at CU Boulder (Natasha Myhal). We have served as project leads and facilitators at the university since 2017, with Myhal moving on in 2021 to complete her dissertation.

In this chapter, we share the origins and development of the "Indigenous Connections" project, focusing in particular on what it means to enter into this sort of work as well as the possibilities of a collaboration between a federal agency, an academic institution, and multiple tribal nations. Drawing on scholarship about Native peoples and public history, we consider the following questions: How do we build a collaborative partnership among tribal nations, a federal agency, and an academic institution; what opportunities and challenges arise in this sort of project; and how does the history of colonization shape contemporary efforts to reckon with past injustices?[2]

We highlight the potential of collaborations between the NPS, tribal nations, and academics. The "Indigenous Connections" project has the potential to disrupt existing, entrenched narratives and practices around US national park sites generally and at RMNP in particular. It could offer a broader, more complex and accurate set of stories to the general public, and could foreground Indigenous ways of knowing and using park lands, particularly in "nature-focused" parks like RMNP, Yellowstone National Park, and Yosemite National Park. And it could provide space for tribal nations to set the terms of engagement with federal agencies and academic institutions. However, these possibilities are emergent and contingent upon several variables. NPS staff must relinquish considerable control and authority over the stories they tell and the ways they do business. Academic researchers must continually rethink what sources of knowledge they privilege and take cues from tribal partners along the way. Tribal members must work in the face of considerable wariness and distrust of the US government and academic institutions, and they must balance the interests of non-tribal entities with what they see as the pressing needs of their own communities.

Even with its limitations and challenges, we see promise in this project. The project team hopes to move beyond merely reinterpreting the official history of a national park for visitors. We also seek to support tribal nations in their efforts to connect with park lands and to educate their communities about their ties to this place. Whether we fully achieve this vision remains to be seen. Over the past fifteen years, parks across the country have increasingly collaborated with tribal nations to develop new interpretive programs and exhibits (e.g., Sand Creek Massacre National Historic Site, Glacier National Park, Grand Canyon National Park, Little Bighorn Battlefield National Monument).[3] This edited volume reflects the growth of this sort of work, in particular in Ari Kelman's discussion of shared authority at the Sand Creek Massacre site and Gerard Baker's work expanding the stories told at Mount Rushmore and elsewhere. We hope the "Indigenous Connections" project contributes to a broader conversation about how tribal nations and national parks can best engage with one another to: 1) uphold tribal sovereignty; 2) better educate the general public about Native peoples; 3) consider new ways of understanding and interpreting the peoples (Native and non-Native) connected to national park lands; and 4) recognize alternative ways of knowing and using park lands based on Native peoples' expertise. In sharing more about the "Indigenous Connections" project, we also emphasize the value of approaching this work through the lens of *strategic collaboration* and the need for park staff and scholars to assume the role of supportive assistant in any project that seeks to meaningfully engage with tribal nations.

Laying the Groundwork

While some collaborations between national parks and university faculty start with a formal call for proposal, this project began with informal conversations. In 2016, interpretive and cultural resources staff from RMNP sat around a conference table with faculty from the Center of the American West (CAW) and the Center for Native American and Indigenous Studies (CNAIS) at CU Boulder (including the authors of this chapter) to discuss possible areas of collaboration and shared interests, in particular how national parks consult and work with tribal nations. The park staff explained they were struggling to engage with tribal nations that have connections to the Rocky Mountain region, including Ute, Arapaho, and Cheyenne peoples. The park was working on a new interpretive plan, and they needed to better include Native peoples in the process. While they had invited tribes to consult on the interpretive plans and they had a history of consulting and working with Ute, Arapaho, and Cheyenne tribes, they had not yet managed to hold a meeting with tribal representatives for the interpretive planning effort.

Park staff wondered if, as a starting point, the CU Boulder team could facilitate a workshop with tribal members at the park to assess and discuss possible changes to the current interpretive program at the park. The CAW convenes events and workshops around many contemporary (often contentious) issues facing residents of the western United States. The CNAIS conducts research and applied work on pressing concerns for Indigenous peoples in North America and beyond. And both university centers share a long-standing interest in the ways tribal nations work with US federal agencies. The entire university team, including the authors of this chapter, thought this would be a valuable way to get involved in the efforts to address the NPS's role in dispossessing Native peoples of their lands across the western United States.[4] The NPS staff and university faculty left this discussion with a plan to engage the cultural anthropology program at the NPS regional office, so we could be sure we were following NPS protocols for inviting tribal nations to consult on and participate in the project. The CU Boulder team committed to explore funding opportunities that could support the planning and hosting of the workshop.

The project that emerged out of these early discussions and the subsequent workshops has the following goals: (1) to encourage park visitors to see RMNP not just as a beautiful natural setting but also as a place where Native people hold strong historical and contemporary connections; (2) to support tribal connections at the park (e.g., facilitating tribal member visits to the park and encouraging the park to consider Indigenous knowledge as they manage the park lands); and (3) to build better relationships among tribal nations, NPS, and the University of Colorado.

The broader "Indigenous Connections" team (tribal representatives, NPS staff, and university faculty and students) has sought to develop a collaborative partnership that respects the knowledge of and connections to this region that tribal nations have, and recognizes the legacy of dispossession and displacement of Native peoples that was part of the creation of the national parks. The Ute, Arapaho, and Cheyenne nations that have connections to the RMNP region reside quite far from the park boundaries, with reservations in southwestern Colorado, Utah, Wyoming, Montana, and Oklahoma. In the mid- to late nineteenth century, as US settlers streamed into the Rocky Mountain region in search of gold and other resources, the Ute, Arapaho, and Cheyenne peoples fought to maintain their territories.[5] But eventually, through a series of treaties and US government coercion and force, the now six federally recognized tribal nations ended up on reservations far removed from what is now RMNP. Of course, the Ute, Arapaho, and Cheyenne (and their various bands) have distinct and specific historical experiences, which must be considered in any contemporary efforts to wrestle with the past. In all cases, however, each tribe's geographic distance from the park site and the history of their forced removal from the Rocky Mountain region inform and shape the "Indigenous Connections" project.

In this work, we are attempting to move beyond the federally mandated government-to-government consultation model for work between federal agencies and tribal nations. Although tribal consultation is an important legal framework that recognizes sovereignty, it often becomes a box to check rather than a meaningful and ongoing relationship to forge.[6] In our minds, creating a collaborative partnership helps to build more lasting relationships and prioritizes Native peoples' perspectives and interests as they relate to public lands and education at national park sites. Collaborative partnerships also provide further opportunities for tribes to assert their connections to park lands—by supporting tribal members visiting the park and/or encouraging youth to learn about their ancestral homelands. In other words, tribal representatives can and do advocate for their communities through this sort of collaboration, even as the park staff work to expand public education and awareness.

The Early Road to Building a Collaboration

The more organic and informal framework that initially shaped the "Indigenous Connections" project has meant that to some degree, we have had to figure out the process as we go. For example, we don't have a formal task agreement with the NPS, a common model for NPS-university engagement. After the initial exploratory meeting in 2016, with the help of the cultural anthropologist from the NPS Intermountain regional office, the park staff initiated a formal consultation process to launch the "Indigenous Connections" project. They sent formal letters to ten tribal nations, specifically to the Tribal Historic Preservation Officers (THPOs), or other designated cultural offices, and the chairperson or president. The park followed up with phone calls and emails to tribal representatives and initiated additional conversations about the project. From these efforts, six tribes expressed a desire to consult. They included the Northern Arapaho Tribe, the Cheyenne and Arapaho Tribes, the Northern Cheyenne Tribe, the Southern Ute Indian Tribe, the Ute Indian Tribe of Uintah and Ouray, and the Ute Mountain Ute Tribe. These tribes had all consulted with the park in the past and their connections to the region are well-known and documented.[7] NPS staff held initial meetings (some in-person and some via phone) with tribal representatives to explain the project, to let them know about the plan to hold a workshop to discuss the project further, and to gather input and suggestions from the tribes as early in the process as possible. Once NPS staff carried out the formal consultation phase, we entered the "collaboration" phase of the project, during which the CU Boulder team could play a more active role in planning and facilitating the workshops and some of the subsequent project activities. The university team then engaged more directly with the points of contact for each tribe, including THPOs, Native American Graves Protection and Repatriation Act (NAGPRA) coordinators, and/or cultural office directors. The team invited them to the workshops and requested their thoughts on what they saw as the most important considerations as the park made changes to its interpretive program. Some tribal representatives expressed skepticism that the park (and the university) would make any meaningful improvements given their spotty track record, but all six tribes sent representatives to the workshops to engage in a discussion about possible next steps.

The workshops, first in September 2017 and then in January 2018, offered an opportunity for NPS staff to share the current exhibits and programs at the park, and for the tribal representatives to share their views on the changes they would like to see at the park. Some key takeaways from the discussions included: 1) the need for tribes to tell their own stories and histories, with NPS staff only sharing information each tribe has vetted; 2) a strong desire to support tribes' efforts to connect with the landscape and educate their youth; 3) the importance of showing non-Native visitors (with color photos and vibrant programs) that Native peoples continue to connect with this landscape and are alive and well despite all the sepia-toned photos that make them seem relegated to the past; and 4) the need for NPS to recognize Native peoples' ways of utilizing and connecting with the landscape, which may differ from the frameworks NPS uses to manage the lands. The workshop discussions also established a shared set of goals for the interpretive program at the park, including new permanent exhibits, videos with tribal members, summer visitor programs presented by tribal members, tribal youth visits to the park, and new website content. We also committed to regular communication and collaboration on the next steps for the project.

The first step toward these goals involved gathering existing research on tribal histories in the park region and documenting the information in a way that would be useful for park staff, namely through a content summary document on each tribe that would go in new interpretive ranger packets and be available to all park staff. The workshop discussions highlighted the value of creating a set of content documents that park rangers could draw upon to develop new exhibits and programs. Participants discussed how much prior research had already been done with Ute and Arapaho representatives at the park, but that because of staff turnover and unclear institutional processes for using the information, the existing research was not being fully utilized by the current park staff.[8] Tribal representatives expressed concerns about reinventing the wheel at the park, causing new NPS staff members to ask the same sorts of questions over and over again, and they shared that they hoped the work their tribes had already done with RMNP could be better integrated at the park. Each spring, new seasonal rangers are hired at RMNP and are tasked with creating their own ranger talks and other programs. The Lead of Interpretation at the park saw these ranger trainings as a prime moment for expanding the programs' interpretive scope—for example, by using the content documents as a route to synthesizing information about Native peoples and better integrating it into the park's regular practices and processes for training staff and developing new programs.

With this plan taking shape, the university team and park staff secured additional funding to travel to tribal offices, provide stipends to tribal partners, and hire a graduate student to work on the project. Through regular emails and phone conversations, and then with trips to visit the Northern Arapaho, Cheyenne and Arapaho, Southern Ute, and Ute Mountain Ute offices, the CU Boulder team and RMNP staff engaged in conversations with each THPO (or equivalent tribal representatives). We discussed how best to co-create the content documents and ensure we included the information each tribe saw as most important and omitted any information the tribes did not wish to share with the public. Some tribal partners wished for the university team to draft outlines and other documents for them to review, comment on, and revise. The Northern Arapaho THPO decided to write their own documents to ensure they shared the information on their own terms. The CU Boulder team checked in regularly with this THPO office to offer support when they asked for it—for example, by locating and sharing archival and secondary research materials from the university library. From 2018–21, we worked on these documents, trading drafts with tribal partners and revising the content through ongoing conversations.

The road to creating the documents took considerable time and persistence, especially during a global pandemic that shut down the park and tribal offices. But by the spring of 2022, documents for four of the tribes were in the final stages of formal review and approval by tribal governments.

These documents share historical and contemporary information on each tribe, including an overview of the dispossession and removal period and the continuous efforts by the tribes to maintain their cultural traditions and care for their people. The documents also include information on the seasonal migrations and uses of the landscapes in and around RMNP as well as answers to the top six visitor questions interpretive rangers field every year, which include: where are the Native people who lived on this land living today; why did they leave; and do they still live in tipis? These content documents are already helping to shape the development of new exhibits at the various park visitor centers around RMNP. They are also feeding into other interpretive projects, including creating ArcGIS StoryMaps for each tribe. This web-based educational tool allows tribes to more easily co-create content and will provide visitors with an engaging platform for learning more about Native peoples at the park. As of early 2023, the project team is exploring next steps for "Indigenous Connections," with a desire to maintain these relationships for years to come. More specifically, we are exploring cultural and art programs run by tribal members, podcasts featuring Native voices, web-based content that builds upon the exhibits, social media engagement, and job pipelines for Native park staff. In the future, the project team also hopes to broaden the reach of "Indigenous Connections" to other park units and tribal nations.

While the "Indigenous Connections" project carries great promise and has accomplished modest yet meaningful goals so far, the path to building this collaborative project has not always been smooth—we have had plenty of hiccups and mistakes along the way. The tribal representatives have offered their precious time and resources and have had to assert their nations' interests to outside organizations—a US federal land agency and a public university—that they have little reason to trust given their collective histories. The NPS staff has had to navigate their own institutional protocols and budget constraints while trying to make changes they saw as valuable and aligned with the educational mission of their organization. The university team has had to figure out its role and how best to engage with both a federal agency with sometimes confusing bureaucratic processes and busy tribal nations with good reason to be wary of universities and federal agencies.

The interview with Max Bear, THPO for the Cheyenne and Arapaho Tribes and "Indigenous Connections" partner, earlier in this volume highlights the value of reflecting on and learning through these sorts of collaborations. During the years of relationship building in the "Indigenous Connections" project, we have come to believe successful collaborative partnerships include several key tenets, which come from our experience and a few key resources we have regularly consulted on how best to work with Native communities:[9]

> Listen: We strive to really listen to our tribal partners and put them at the forefront of the project. This includes communicating regularly throughout the year and as project needs arise.
>
> Follow through: We do our best to incorporate tribal partners' ideas and suggestions into the activities of the project, to move from discussions to tangible actions.
>
> Follow tribal and federal government policies and protocols: We have followed the protocols both of tribal nations and the National Park Service for research and government-to-government consultation and other initiatives.
>
> Create collaborative goals: We have worked to create project goals and figure out the process collaboratively with all the project partners.
>
> Build in reciprocity: Our project aims must be mutually beneficial and recognize that the goals of various partners may be different. Traveling to visit tribal offices is a good first gesture of reciprocity, but it is only the beginning.
>
> Be flexible: The project team must adapt to the different and changing needs and interests of the partners. Flexibility should be built into the process.
>
> Take time and be patient: We have devoted considerable time to this collaboration. It has involved coordinating multiple partners, holding many meetings and phone calls, and sending countless emails.
>
> Communicate clearly: We strive to maintain open and ongoing lines of communication and encourage honest dialogue.
>
> Be inclusive: We have worked to welcome all tribal nations with an interest and connection to the park region.
>
> Be historically and socially aware: We try to recognize the ways historical and social factors shape the working relationships. This includes considering contemporary tribal policies and issues that matter most to their communities today.

While these tenets may seem simple or obvious, we have found they can be trickier to apply consistently in practice. They also echo a similar list in Gish Hill's chapter in this volume. The "Indigenous Connections" team aspires to all these collaborative goals, but we often stumble and experience the work as an ongoing learning process. Indeed, thinking critically about the elements of a collaborative partnership has helped us reimagine how NPS sites, tribal nations, and universities can work together to better include Indigenous peoples in national parks, and ideally uphold tribal sovereignty and support cultural connections to the landscapes in the process.

Possibilities

We believe the "Indigenous Connections" project is filled with possibilities. It offers an opportunity to educate the general public and encourage them to see RMNP not just as a beautiful "wilderness" area, but also as a place with deep and long-standing human presence and connections. Settler-colonial narratives remain firmly entrenched in RMNP's interpretive program (similar to most other national park sites). Any visitor who sits down to watch the orientation film at the Beaver Meadows Visitor Center will only briefly hear about Native peoples. The film moves quickly from a general discussion of the people who called the park lands home before Euro-American settlement to the history of the creation of the park in the early twentieth century. The stories in this film and throughout the park are largely about white Americans' arrival to the region and the value of preserving the natural landscape. The interpretive exhibits and programs largely ignore the violence and trauma of the dispossession era for Native peoples. The Fall River and Kawuneeche visitor centers, two key stops for visitors entering from the west and east sides of the park, largely ignore Native peoples. In the Alpine Visitor Center at the top of Trail Ridge Road, the park does include a wall of exhibit panels that describes the Ute peoples who inhabited the region, but this exhibit wall is one of four in a room otherwise devoted to flora and fauna within the park. Overall, the prevalent messages at the park reflect larger discourses in the United States that relegate Native peoples to the past, tie them in essentializing ways to nature, and erase their histories and contemporary experiences. As of early 2023, RMNP installed new freestanding exhibits in all the visitor centers at the park based on the content created through "Indigenous Connections," and the park is developing a new permanent exhibit with tribal representatives at the Kawuneeche Visitor Center.

During the "Indigenous Connections" project, tribal partners have expressed the pain and frustration of visiting sites like RMNP and not seeing their people represented there in a meaningful and accurate way. They have also conveyed frustration that representatives from their tribes have worked with the park for years without them seeing meaningful changes. At the same time, many of the project's tribal partners see value in educating the general public, and they have explicitly communicated that they see national park sites as particularly important spaces for educating non-Natives because of the high numbers of annual visitors. They have said they think more people learn about Native people through national parks (and museums) than they do through schools. Tribal partners also view this interpretation- and education-focused project as a vehicle to advocate for their nation's needs, especially by supporting their peoples' connections to the park region and asserting their rights to access and use these lands. This approach on the part of tribal members echoes the thoughts of Cheyenne and Arapaho people in Gish Hill's chapter earlier in this volume, where they explain that they see value for their communities in re-envisioning national park sites.

In RMNP, park staff have been quite open to recognizing the limits of their current interpretive program, and they are actively engaged in thinking about how the park can better share information with visitors about the Native peoples who have long been connected to this region. This process of recognition involves a collective reckoning with the past and its contemporary effects. Ideally, the work of "Indigenous Connections" will help disrupt the entrenched narratives that paint RMNP as a pristine natural setting and a place born primarily out of the imagination of white conservationists.

By working with tribal partners, park staff are striving to broaden and complicate the stories the park tells visitors, especially the emphasis they place on the natural landscape, preservation, beauty, and recreation. Ideally, an expanded interpretive framework recognizes the role of the US national parks in Native dispossession and offers a more truthful account of Native peoples' experiences, both in terms of historical trauma and erasure, but also in terms of resilience, sovereignty, and ongoing connections to this land. Through these efforts, park staff are trying to improve and enrich the park's relationship with Native peoples.

We also strive to follow the lead of tribal partners when they set their terms of engagement with federal agencies and academic institutions. In the process of co-creating the content documents, tribal partners challenged the project team to reconsider the information we share and the wording we use to better reflect the value we place in Native peoples' knowledge and oral traditions. For example, in a discussion of the length of Ute peoples' presence in the Rocky Mountain region, a Ute partner suggested we change the phrase "Ute believe" to "Ute know." This semantic shift better recognizes and legitimates Ute knowledge of their history. Similarly, the THPO from the Cheyenne and Arapaho Tribes reviewed a draft of their content summary and noticed we were relying too heavily on academic texts. He recommended that we work to directly incorporate more Cheyenne and Arapaho voices, both historical and contemporary. This co-creation process better allows for tribal partners to steer the work and foreground their knowledge.

The co-creation process has also allowed for tribal partners to have their voices heard regarding the logistics of the project itself. Early in the process, the park staff and university team heard that tribal representatives travel often and far for meetings with a host of non-tribal institutions, and that they would like the park staff and CU team to share the travel load. In an effort to better accommodate tribal partners and recognize their critical role in this project, we worked to budget time and money for these trips, and park staff and CU faculty and students have visited Ute, Arapaho, and Cheyenne partners at their offices in southwestern Colorado, Wyoming, and Oklahoma. These trips have been valuable for forging working relationships and for a more substantive and meaningful exchange of ideas. This is a somewhat simple example of relinquishing some control over the process and establishing reciprocity, but it can be a way to illustrate commitment and respect.

The "Indigenous Connections" project has the potential to foreground Indigenous connections to the lands that are now part of RMNP, and to recognize and support their ways of knowing and using the land. The project is working to revise and improve the current park narratives about Indigenous peoples and the park's history more generally, and it is trying to encourage and support Indigenous peoples as they return to the park and reconnect with their ancestral lands. However, all of this requires that we navigate limitations and dilemmas along the way.

Challenges

During a conference call with a Ute tribal partner, as we discussed next steps for the "Indigenous Connections" project, she shared that she gets "heartburn" doing this sort of work. She explained that working with federal agencies and academics can be tiring and painful—because she has to continually explain and assert her peoples' sovereignty and their knowledge and connection to the landscapes across the Rocky Mountain region. She said she may forge ahead on these projects, but they are not easy for her. Indeed, several challenges complicate this sort of collaborative project. The legacy of colonial violence and injustice shapes even micro-interactions of the project team. A large, collaborative network of project partners and a variety of bureaucracies make the work slow and unpredictable at times. And expanding and improving interpretive content at a national park site may raise the awareness of the general public, but it does not necessarily improve the lives of Native peoples in fundamental ways.

On a visit to a Ute Tribal Historic Preservation Office in 2018, the director shared his concerns about the university and NPS participants' motives. He explained that it can be frustrating how outsiders come in with a lot of requests for tribes and do not necessarily listen and follow tribal members' guidance, nor do they properly compensate or provide benefits for tribal nations in the process. Indeed, distrust is present in any collaboration between tribal nations, the US federal government, and an academic institution. With a long history of broken treaties, violence, and trauma, tribal members have every reason to be wary of partnering with the NPS and a team of university faculty. The US federal government—through the treaty-making period, forced removal and assimilation, and the damaging practices of the Bureau of Indian Affairs—has a terrible track record in its policies regarding tribal nations. And academics have an equally troubling track record conducting research "on" Indigenous peoples; much of early anthropology research was more extractive and exploitative, with most of it benefitting settlers rather than Indigenous peoples.

Given this baggage, it is remarkable to create any sort of collaborative relationship. With "Indigenous Connections," we have tried to recognize this historical legacy as we negotiate our collaboration, taking extra time to listen to and recognize Native peoples' ongoing frustration and pain and trying wherever possible to shift the project to account for tribal partners' interests and preferences. We also see value in exploring the discomfort of these histories. It can be tempting to seek a simple remedy for the uneasiness that comes when the weight of history bears down on us. However, it can be more fruitful to avoid the impulse to fix or control, and instead engage fully in the difficult conversations and reflections that come along the way.

The logistics of relationship building and collaborative work with multiple partners can become tricky. Working with the NPS, like any federal agency, comes with a host of challenges, including navigating the nebulous nature of their planning and budget cycles and the frequency with which park staff move around to other positions/parks. It is challenging and takes considerable time to make concrete changes to an underfunded federal bureaucracy. The park staff we work with are committed to the project, but they are increasingly stretched thin as federal funding gets tighter and the activities of the parks continue to grow. NPS staff across the United States must abide by a host of federal policies and practices that do not necessarily align with the priorities and preferences of tribal nations.

For example, we heard from NPS staff early on in the process that our project was strictly about education and interpretation, not about natural or cultural resource management and definitely not about treaty rights. However, over and over again, we have sat down with tribal partners to discuss the information they would like the park to share with visitors, and the conversation has often shifted to a discussion of plant gathering or hunting rights or even the theft of Native lands by the US government. Tribal partners have repeatedly reminded us how interconnected the education piece is with their desires (and rights) to access and use their ancestral lands. At the same time, while park staff have worked hard to listen and follow the suggestions of tribal partners, they have had a tough time implementing this interconnectedness, in part because the federal bureaucracy they inhabit so firmly separates public education, cultural resources, and natural resources. We are optimistic that long-term relationships and engagement with tribal nations will help move the needle a bit more within the NPS. But for now, this is a challenge without an easy remedy.

Working with multiple tribal nations (in this case, three Ute tribes and three Cheyenne and Arapaho tribes) means adapting to varying expectations and desires. We have had to recognize and work around the limited bandwidth that Tribal Historic Preservation Offices and other cultural offices have for this project, since they are asked to consult on many federal, state, and local projects. On a more practical note, to foreground Native peoples' expertise, we have modified the work process and approach based on the preferences of each tribal partner. For example, one tribal partner wished to write most of the content for our project, while others wished to have conversations through which the CU team drafted the documents and shared them for regular review. In another instance, we started by creating separate content summaries for each tribe, but over time, the three Ute tribes suggested we combine their summaries and collaborate with them simultaneously. We have modified the direction of the project through ongoing conversations with all partners.

Tribal partners have been engaged in a variety of ways during this project, illustrating strategic engagement in action. Some tribal partners have expressed more concerns than others, about the project generally or the specifics of the process. Some have expressed concerns that the park and the university team are the ones benefitting most from this project, and they have wondered how the project will also serve the interests of their tribe. Other tribal partners have expressed concern about how park staff will share the information they provide them, and how the visitors will learn about and understand what they read and hear. Park rangers have considerable autonomy in creating programs, and visitors may interpret the information in a range of ways. So, some tribal partners are wary of how their knowledge and information will be circulated and used. Keeping these lines of dialogue open is one avenue for Indigenous people to assert their sovereignty and authority over their communities and histories. Also, because we are working with multiple tribal nations, we encounter discussions about which tribes or specific historical bands have the best claim to the park region. At the same time, some tribal partners focus more on the positive potential of engaging with the national parks and of educating the general public, and they see this project as a valuable venue for asserting the needs of their nations. Through all these discussions with tribal partners, we work to listen and take all their concerns seriously. We also strive to maintain the same level of commitment to the rockier relationships as we do with the smoother ones.

The challenges we have encountered in the "Indigenous Connections" project may look different from various vantage points. In other words, the various stakeholders for this project may see and interpret the challenges differently. What might look like a challenge of time and productivity for the park staff or the university team (e.g., what are the deliverables and when will they be delivered?) may be a challenge of cultural and community protection for tribal members (e.g., how do we defend our people and culture from the encroachment of outsiders?). The project team has had to recognize that the interests of tribal partners may not be the same as the interests of the non-tribal partners. When the various project partners engage strategically, however, they nonetheless find common ground and room for collaboration.

Paths Forward

This project highlights the potential for US "nature" parks to consider (and possibly address) their role in erasing Native peoples from the landscape, both in terms of physical displacement and in terms of the narratives the park disseminates to visitors. And collaborative partnerships among tribal nations, national parks, and academic institutions have the potential to foreground Native peoples' interests and educate the wider public in beneficial ways. But we are tempered in our assessment of whether a project like ours has the capacity to enact meaningful change in the lives of Native peoples in the United States.

Indigenous social movements have worked for decades to assert tribal sovereignty, to reclaim their lands, and to care for their people. Much of these efforts revolve around regaining control over their communities and homelands. The recent protests at Standing Rock and the #LandBack movement are part of long-standing efforts to empower and support Native peoples. Such recent protests and initiatives have roots in the mid-twentieth century American Indian Movement occupations and other direct actions, but also in Native resistance efforts since the start of Euro-American colonization.[10] Drawing upon global decolonial thought and activism, Indigenous peoples have long advocated for upholding sovereignty and dismantling the control colonial nation-states have over Indigenous peoples.[11] Recently, the NDN Collective, an organization leading the Land Back efforts, described their goals on their website: "Together, we decolonize and transform systems while providing tools and strategies for Indigenous self-determination and movement-building."[12]

With these ideas and efforts in mind, we find it valuable to consider how the "Indigenous Connections" project fits into this broader picture and potentially supports larger Indigenous social movements. We do not think this project serves to decolonize national parks. We work within the framework of a federal institution, and even though we collaborate with open-minded and well-intentioned federal employees and academics, we can never fully rid ourselves of the NPS's institutional power and legacy. While we believe the "Indigenous Connections" project could help to broaden and boost education and awareness-raising efforts, we also wonder if projects like this could be used by the US federal government to justify not honoring treaty rights or other requests from tribal nations. It may be a way for the NPS to nod to Native peoples' sovereignty, while ignoring Indigenous social movements and other calls for the United States to return public lands to Native peoples.[13]

Ultimately, we understand the "Indigenous Connections" project more as a process of reckoning and strategic collaboration (similar to other cases highlighted in this volume), one through which tribal nations can work to assert their sovereignty as well as their deep and lasting connections with their lands. We see promise in making even small and incremental changes to public spaces in the United States. Better representing Indigenous peoples in the national parks has immense value in terms of redefining our collective understanding of the United States as a nation with multiple and complicated historical narratives. In the long run, NPS interpretation and education may help to change non-Natives' appreciation and knowledge of Indigenous peoples and *slowly* help to dismantle colonial legacies in the United States. Representation is just one step toward addressing the damage done. But we see potential power in educating the general public, disrupting prevalent narratives of Native peoples, and supporting tribal nations as they work to connect with their lands and care for their communities.

Notes

1. Given the in-progress nature of this project and collaboration, we have opted to omit the names of participants in this chapter.
2. See, for example, Mary Lawlor, *Public Native America: Tribal Self-Representation in Casinos, Museums, and Powwows* (New Brunswick, NJ: Rutgers University Press, 2006); Laura Peers, *Playing Ourselves: Interpreting Native Histories at Historic Reconstructions* (Lanham, MD: Altamira Press, 2007); Loriene Roy, Anjali Bhasin, and Sarah K. Arriaga, eds., *Tribal Libraries, Archives, and Museums: Preserving Our Language, Memory, and Lifeways* (Lanham, MD: Scarecrow Press, 2011); Jennifer A. Shannon, *Our Lives: Collaboration, Native Voice, and the Making of the National Museum of the American Indian* (Santa Fe: School for Advanced Research Press, 2014).
3. See, for example: Ari Kelman, *A Misplaced Massacre: Struggling Over the Memory of Sand Creek* (Cambridge, MA: Harvard University Press, 2015); https://www.nps.gov/glac/learn/historyculture/tribes.htm; https://www.nps.gov/grca/learn/historyculture/associated-tribes.htm; "New Visitor Center at Little Bighorn Battlefield National Monument," National Park Service press release (October 10, 2020). https://www.nps.gov/libi/learn/news/new-visitors-center.htm.
4. See, for example: Robert H. Keller and Michael F. Turek, *American Indians and National Parks* (Tucson: University of Arizona Press, 1998); Mark David Spence, *Dispossessing the Wilderness: Indian Removal and the Making of the National Parks* (Oxford: Oxford University Press, 1999); Philip Burnham, *Indian Country, God's Country: Native Americans and the National Parks* (Washington, DC: Island Press, 2000); Peter Nabokov and Lawrence Loendorf, *Restoring a Presence: American Indians and Yellowstone National Park* (Norman: University of Oklahoma Press, 2004).
5. For more on the Euro-American settlement and Native resistance in the nineteenth century in the Rocky Mountain region and beyond, see for example: Ned Blackhawk, *Violence Over the Land: Indians and Empires in the Early American West* (Cambridge, MA: Harvard University Press, 2006); Elliott West, *The Contested Plains: Indians, Goldseekers, and the Rush to Colorado* (Lawrence: University of Kansas Press, 1998); Thomas Andrews, *Coyote Valley: Deep History in the High Rockies* (Cambridge, MA: Harvard University Press, 2015); David Treuer, *The Heartbeat of Wounded Knee: Native America from 1890 to the Present* (New York: Riverhead Books, 2019).
6. For more information on the history of federally mandated tribal consultation, see the introduction and the historical overview in this volume. See also: "Tribal Consultation: Best Practices In Historic Preservation," National Association of Tribal Historic Preservation Officers (May 2005). http://npshistory.com/publications/preservation/tribal-consultation.pdf; Jacilee Wray et al., "Creating Policy for the National Park Service: Addressing Native Americans

and Other Traditionally Associated Peoples," *The George Wright Forum*, vol. 26, no. 3 (2009). http://www.georgewright.org/263wray.pdf.
7. See John Brett, *Ethnographic Assessment and Documentation of Rocky Mountain National Park* (Scotts Valley, CA: CreateSpace, 2013).
8. See, for example: Brett; Sally McBeth, *Native American Oral History and Cultural Interpretation in Rocky Mountain National Park* (Scotts Valley, CA: CreateSpace, 2013); Thomas Andrews, *Coyote Valley: Deep History in the High Rockies* (Cambridge, MA: Harvard University Press, 2015). Considerable archeological research has also been conducted at the park; we do not cite most of this work in order to help keep the sites better protected.
9. See, for example: Guidelines for Collaboration (website), facilitated by Landis Smith, Cynthia Chavez Lamar, and Brian Vallo, Indian Arts Research Center (Santa Fe: School for Advanced Research, 2019), https://guidelinesforcollaboration.info; Chantalle Hanschu, *State-Tribal Consultation Guide: An Introduction for Colorado State Agencies to Conducting Formal Consultations with Federally Recognized American Indian Tribes*, Colorado Commission of Indian Affairs (2014), https://ccia.colorado.gov/sites/ccia/files/documents/CO%20State-Tribal%20Consultation%20Guide_0_0.pdf; Linda Tuhiawi Smith, *Decolonizing Methodologies: Research and Indigenous Peoples* (New York: Zed Books, 2013 [1999]).
10. For more information on the Land Back movement, see also: Nikki A. Pieratos, Sarah S. Manning, and Nick Tilsen, "Land Back: A Meta Narrative to Help Indigenous People Show up as Movement Leaders," *Leadership* 17(1) (2021): 47–61; Kim TallBear, "Beyond Indigenous Performance to Life and Land Back," *Unsettle* (January 26, 2022). https://kimtallbear.substack.com/p/beyond-indigenous-performance-to?s=r (accessed May 4, 2022); www.landback.org; http://therednation.org. And for more information on Native activism and social movements, see: Paul Chaat Smith and Robert Allen Warrior, *Like a Hurricane: The Indian Movement from Alcatraz to Wounded Knee* (New York: The New Press, 1996).
11. See, for example, Smith, *Decolonizing Methodologies*; Eve Tuck and K. Wayne Yang, "Decolonization Is Not a Metaphor," *Decolonization: Indigeneity, Education, and Society* 1(1) (2012): 1–40.
12. See: https://ndncollective.org/.
13. See, for example: David Treuer, "Return the National Parks to the Tribes," *The Atlantic* (May 2021) (available online April 12, 2021). https://www.theatlantic.com/magazine/archive/2021/05/return-the-national-parks-to-the-tribes/618395 (accessed April 27, 2022); Jim Robbins, "How Returning Lands to Native Tribes Is Helping Protect Nature," *Yale Environmental 360* (June 3, 2021). https://e360.yale.edu/features/how-returning-lands-to-native-tribes-is-helping-protect-nature (accessed April 27, 2022).

FOUR | # Recentering the Middle Ground
A Case Study on Indigenous Nationhood and the Future of National Parks

MARK DAVID SPENCE

THIS CHAPTER OFFERS southeastern Michigan's River Raisin National Battlefield Park (NBP) as a remarkable but highly unexpected model of mutual collaboration and assistance. Though it is still one of the newest and smallest units of the national park system, the close relationships that have developed between park staff and the Wyandotte of Anderdon Nation present a model for mutual exchange and collaboration that is grounded in two overlapping dynamics: the endurance and tenacity of the Wyandotte of Anderdon Nation, and the blend of humility, respect, and helpfulness that River Raisin staff bring to their relations with Indigenous nations (whether federally recognized or not) associated with the park area. At the time of its establishment, nothing signaled that the new park unit would have much to contribute to broader debates or necessary reforms within the National Park Service (NPS) regarding interpretation, administration, or relations with tribal nations. Centered on the site of a former papermill and paperboard factory that lasted from 1910 until 1995, the core area of the national park unit sits atop a toxic brownfield. Nevertheless, efforts by both the Wyandotte of Anderdon and park staff showcase the mutually beneficial possibilities of cross-cultural collaboration at national parks.

First designated as a unit of the NPS in 2009, the River Raisin NBP was originally conceived as a place to preserve, commemorate, and interpret the locations of a pair of War of 1812 battlefields, with a particular emphasis on "the significance of the American sacrifice on the hallowed grounds of the battlefield."[1] Along with these stated purposes, the new park unit also reflected "park barrel" politics, which, in the case of River Raisin NBP, were championed by an interlocking set of federal, state, and municipal agencies, chambers of commerce, and local historical societies. All these stakeholders viewed the park unit as a catalyst for community renewal and development in the economically battered city of Monroe and the broader "Downriver" region of southeastern Michigan where it is situated. With high expectations that the upcoming bicentennial of the War of 1812 (2012–15) would bring large numbers of tourists to the area, local and regional government agencies envisioned a new future in which hospitality, outdoor recreation, and heritage tourism would contribute to a diverse and lasting economic recovery. In concert with these expectations, the NPS put together an extensive land acquisition and development plan for the national battlefield park that would assist the region's hoped for recovery.[2]

The two battles that define the boundaries and historical significance of the national park took place along both sides of the River Raisin (aka *la Rivière Aux Raisins*) in January 1813. While the first battle ended in a draw, the second engagement resulted in an absolute rout of the American forces, which included approximately one thousand US soldiers, six hundred Kentucky militiamen, and a much smaller contingent of one hundred Francophone militiamen. The victors were primarily composed of Bodéwadmi (Potawatomi), Wyandotte, and Algonquian-speaking warriors from across the Great Lakes and the Middle Ohio Valley, along with a contingent of British regulars and several dozen *Canadien* militiamen who lived in the vicinity of Fort Malden on the eastern side of the Detroit River in what is now present-day Amherstburg, Ontario. All told, US forces lost more than four hundred men within the battlefield area, along with hundreds of militia and US Regulars (professional soldiers of the federal United States Army) who fled pell-mell to the south, where they were quickly intercepted by Indigenous warriors on horseback. Of the captured, somewhere between thirty and one hundred US soldiers and militia died of their wounds or were killed outright before the rest of the survivors were taken across the frozen Detroit River for imprisonment at Fort Malden. The battle and its aftermath proved to be one of the worst defeats of US forces during the entire war; it also marked a highpoint for the confederacy of Native nations that had allied with the British and fought under the leadership of two highly respected Wyandotte war leaders, Myeerah (Walk-in-the-Water) and Stayeghtha (Bark Carrier, aka Roundhead). In doing so, this confederacy compensated for previous defeats in present-day Indiana and Ohio and rolled back decades of US civilian encroachments into their territories. In addition to the American casualties, the Francophone hamlet along the *Riviere aux Raisins* was utterly destroyed.[3]

A Multi-unit Park for a Postindustrial Future

The initial efforts to establish the national park unit focused on commemorating the loss of American life that occurred at Frenchtown in January 1813.

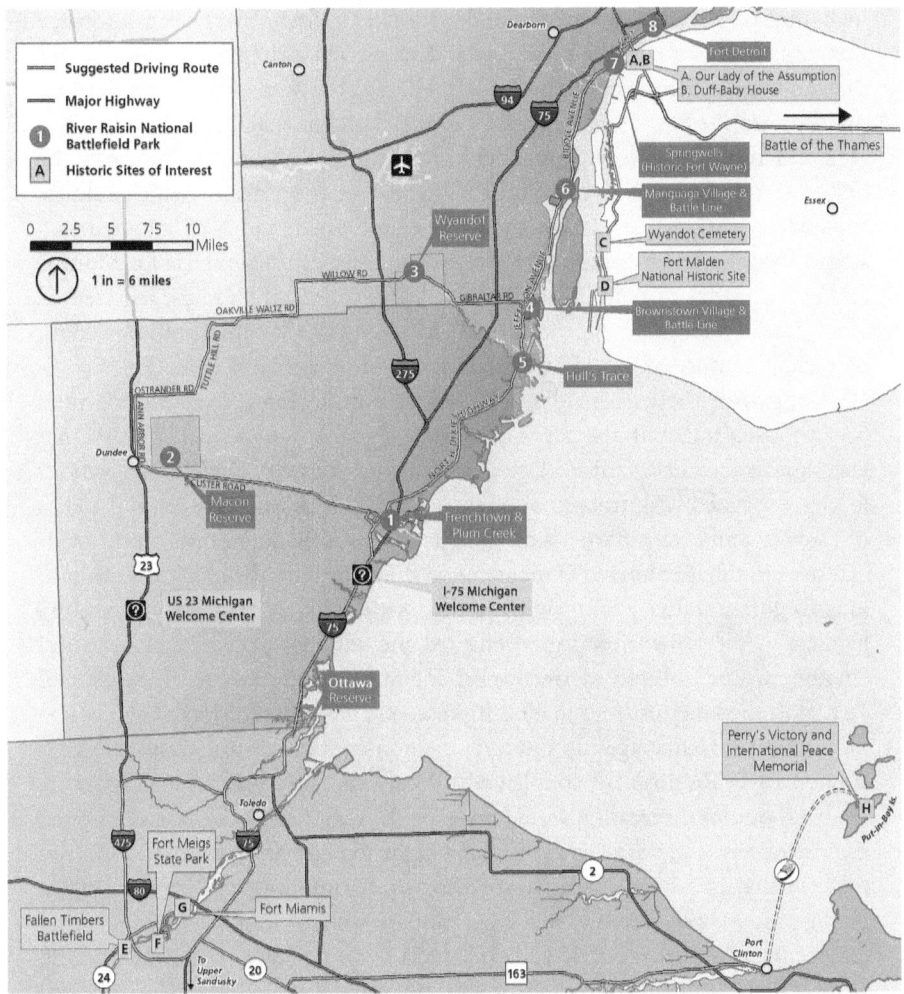

River Raisin National Battlefield Park, related historical sites, population centers, and present-day transportation corridors. Courtesy of the National Park Service, River Raisin National Battlefield Park.

Downriver communities in Monroe and surrounding counties also identified with the *habitants* (i.e., *Canadien* residents, agriculturalists, and fur traders) who lost their homes, properties, and community during the battles and their aftermath. Like the residents of Frenchtown, the people of Monroe and the Downriver region were collectively faced with the prospect of rebuilding their lives and community in a ruined landscape. Through most of the twentieth century, Monroe was home to several large and small companies associated with the Detroit-based auto industry. These included Monroe Shocks, Bendix Brakes, steel and aluminum mills, a Ford manufacturing plant, a vast packaging plant on the battlefield site, and a wide array of light-industrial manufacturers including La-Z-Boy furniture. By the early twenty-first century, the landscape was composed of abandoned factories and an endless variety of industrial toxins that polluted the soils and air and leached into the wetlands and creeks that drained into the River Raisin, Lake Erie, and shoreline marshes.

Local history, however, did offer a rallying cry for how to resurrect the hollowed out Downriver economies: "Remember the Raisin!" which soldiers shouted at the start of subsequent battles, and which the NPS adopted as a slogan for the new park unit, also served as an inspirational phrase for Monroe and other nearby communities. A national park unit in their midst represented a new kind of development that would allow Downriver communities to move past a half-century of industrial decline and environmental degradation.[4]

Along with the battlefield site in Monroe, other Downriver communities became associated with the national battlefield park through: ancillary sites that encompassed former Native village areas; a historic cemetery in Monroe; various locales associated with troop movements; related historical sites within the City of Detroit; and extant portions of Hulls Trace, an early nineteenth-century federal roadway that conveyed combatants to the encounter. Bringing attention to long-forgotten military campaigns, battles, Native villages, and French-speaking hamlets in the Downriver region ensured the national park and its historical environs would collectively draw more attention to the events of the War of 1812 and the long histories that both preceded and followed the conflict.

NPS plans to manage and interpret the non-contiguous properties that constituted River Raisin NBP, coupled with local expectations that "heritage tourism" and outdoor recreation would diversify the regional economy, also fostered the rise of new civic organizations that sought to cultivate a sense of pride and purpose that had been absent from Downriver communities since the 1970s. In the process, several towns and regional park systems took note of their own connections to the War of 1812, while local antiquarians dug up references to ancient and historical Indigenous towns, ceremonial sites, and extensive burial grounds. These "rediscoveries" led to the development of interpretive signage in some Downriver Metroparks that helped reinscribe Native placenames and historical personalities into the landscape. The same was true for sites within the expanding holdings of the Detroit River International Wildlife Refuge, which included extensive parcels adjacent to the battlefield site.[5]

Remembering the Raisin: *The Wyandotte of Anderdon Nation*

Some peoples had not forgotten the conflicts and locales that were being folded into the developing national battlefield park. These included the clusters of Wyandotte communities in the Greater Detroit area who still lived near the sites of their former villages and towns on the Canadian and US sides of the Detroit River, including Maguaga (aka River View), Gibraltar (aka Big Rock), Brownstown (also Big Rock), Atieeronnon (Bob-Lo, aka Bois Blanc Island), downtown

Detroit, including the neighborhood of Corktown, Windsor, Ontario, and locales near Amherstburg, Ontario. Though unknown to NPS officials and residents of Monroe at the time, the establishment of the River Raisin NBP coincided with an ongoing cultural and political revitalization within the Wyandotte of Anderdon Nation, whose members had become increasingly focused on realizing a long-deferred dream of securing their own lands in the Downriver region. This bolstered their multigenerational effort to gain federal recognition and establish a nation-to-nation relationship with the United States of America.[6]

The Wyandotte of Anderdon is a small tribal nation, but it retains a persistent and ongoing association with locales on both sides of the Detroit River, as well as every unit of River Raisin. Their association with the region precedes the arrival of Europeans in the early sixteenth century. After contact, disease and multiple conflicts among the Wyandotte, other Indigenous groups, and European colonizers splintered the Wyandotte Confederacy. These intermittent wars, which led to a great deal of violence, death, and exile, finally subsided in 1701 with the Great Peace of Montréal.[7] The Great Peace also coincided with the establishment of Detroit. Along with serving as a French regional administrative center, Detroit also concentrated the products and proceeds of the fur trade, the parceling out of farms to *habitants,* and the establishment of Indigenous villages. The Wyandotte, who had wide ranging connections to the north, east, and west of Detroit, also played a significant role in these activities.[8] Through the second half of the eighteenth century and the early decades of the nineteenth, Wyandotte leaders in the Detroit River region brought together multiple Indigenous communities on matters of war, peace, trade, and alliance. As the traditional Keepers of the Council Fire for these alliances, caretakers of the Great Calumet (ceremonial, or peace, pipe) that opened important councils, and holders of the great wampum belts that embodied the intents of past alliances, the Wyandotte provided an essential forum for engagement among allied Native communities.[9]

After the War of 1812

In the decade that followed the War of 1812, the Wyandotte lived in four different locales: the Wyandotte Reserve on the Huron River, about seven miles west of Big Rock (Brownstown), the Upper Sandusky Reservation in present-day Wyandotte County, Ohio, the Big Spring Reserve about fifteen miles north of Upper Sandusky, and the Anderdon Reserve just to the north of Amherstburg, Ontario, and directly across the Detroit River from Gibraltar, Michigan. The boundaries of the reserves/reservations were established in two treaties in 1818.

Between the War of 1812 and the 1818 treaties, a few Wyandotte left present-day Ohio to live with the "Canadian Wyandotte" on the Anderdon Reserve near Amherstburg. By the late 1830s and 1840s, when Wyandotte removal from Ohio to present-day Kansas was imminent, some Ohio Wyandotte moved to Anderdon.[10] While their number is unrecorded, it is very likely that more would

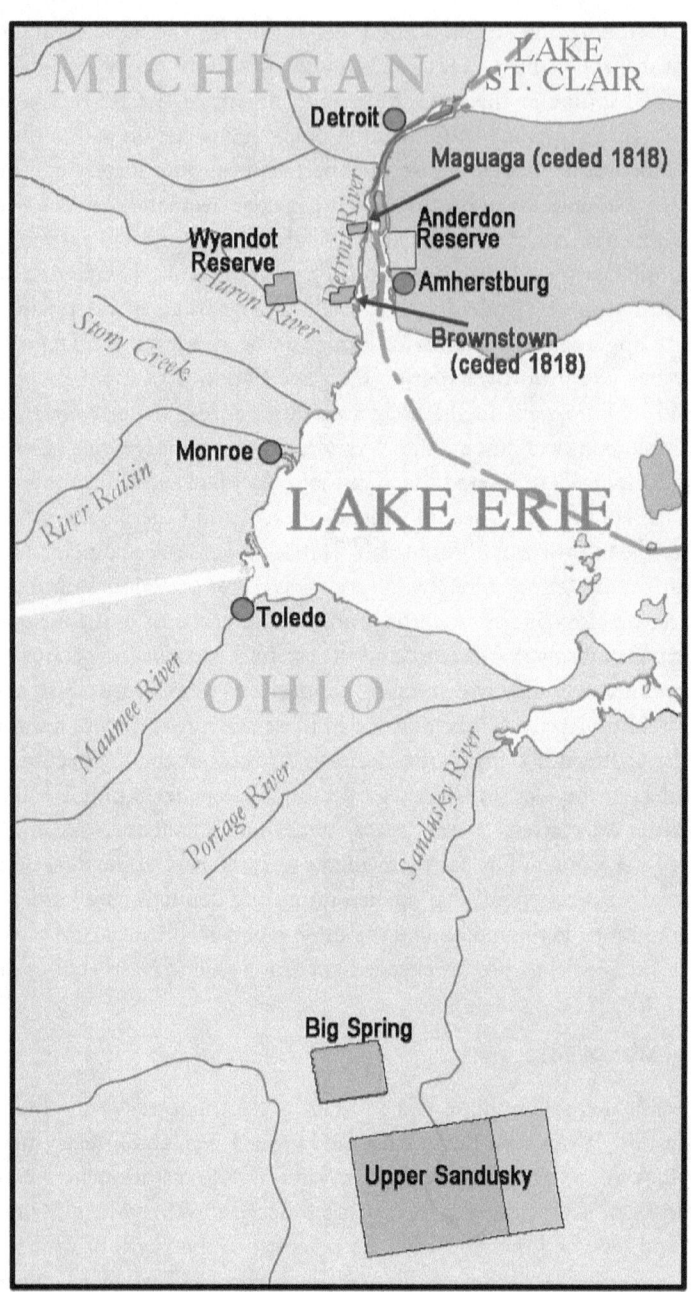

Wyandot reservations, ca. 1836. Courtesy of the National Park Service, River Raisin National Battlefield Park.

have come if not for a significant reduction of the Anderdon reserve in 1836 from 23,000 acres to 7,700 acres.[11] Consequently, the Wyandotte population at Anderdon never grew much beyond about 200 people. In 1878, nearly all the people who constituted what was then referred to as the "Wyandotte Tribe" in Canada applied for citizenship under the auspices of the Indian Act of 1876, and most of the reserve was surveyed and patented as the private property of Wyandotte residents, with the remainder sold off to Anglo-Canadians.[12]

"There My Lineage Would Form a Group, Surrounding Me"[13]

Descendants of the "Wyandotte Tribe" and the "Wyandotte of Anderdon" remained in the Detroit River region and sustained family ties and enduring associations with relatives on both sides of the river. In the second half of the twentieth century, archives held by churches, public libraries, and universities attracted scholars interested in Wyandotte history and language. One such scholar was Charles Oscar Warrow, a direct descendant of three Wyandotte chiefs who led the Wyandotte community at Amherstburg from the end of the War of 1812 until 1835. Along with others, he conducted research in local historical records, consulted with scholars on Wyandotte history, worked on genealogies, poured over local historical records, and used extensive personal contacts to identify other Wyandotte descendants in the Detroit River area. Warrow's son, Ted Warrow, joined with other Wyandotte descendants to further this cause in the 1990s. Their efforts revitalized the region's Wyandotte community, with an eye toward ensuring its future viability on both sides of the Detroit River.[14]

Two Ways About It: *Parallel Futures Rooted in Different Pasts*

Nearly two centuries after the Battles of the River Raisin, the Wyandotte of Anderdon continue to draw on their long history in the Detroit River region and pursue a multigenerational endeavor to strengthen their community and exercise sovereignty within their historical homeland. Regarding the latter concern, the Wyandotte recognized that collaboration with the NPS would ensure that Native perspectives became embedded into the park landscape and interpretive programs. Moreover, a collaborative relationship with a federal agency (NPS) and a new national park unit could boost their long-standing efforts to gain status as a federally recognized American Indian tribe.

Somewhat similarly, non-Native park boosters and regional history groups also saw an opportunity to revitalize their communities while showcasing the historical significance of Monroe and the Downriver area. Plans to establish a national park unit within the city limits also brought hopeful visions of new economic opportunities that would attract tourists and foster a civic rebirth. Smaller communities throughout the Downriver region also saw a once-in-a-lifetime chance to access a new infusion of federal and state money for environmental

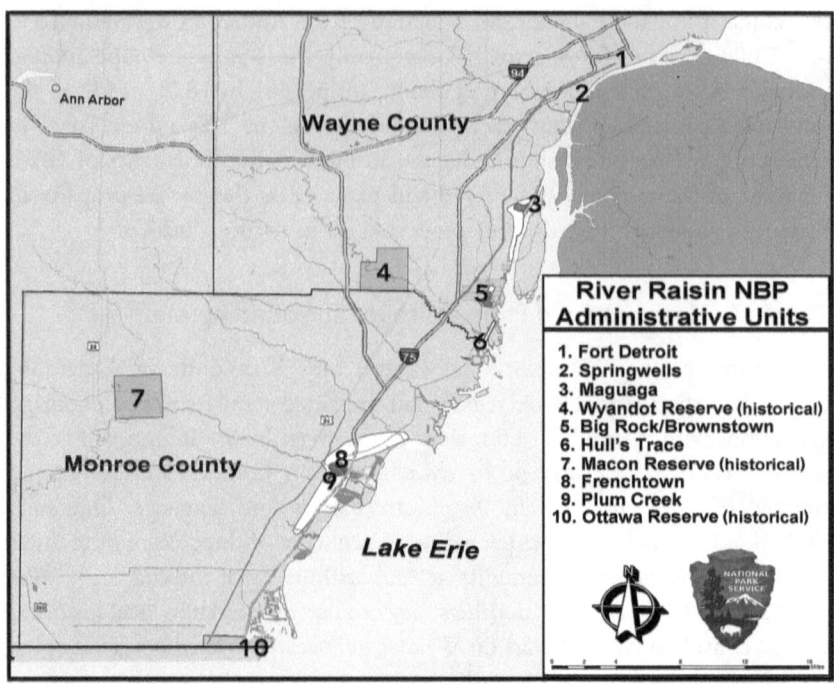

Ancillary sites associated with the administration of River Raisin National Battlefield Park. Courtesy of the National Park Service, River Raisin National Battlefield Park.

mitigation and remediation projects that would employ significant numbers of people, remove blight, and create usable building sites for future development. Initial expenditures for developing the national battlefield park were also directed toward similar purposes, which involved cleaning up and transforming heavily polluted industrial sites within the statutory boundaries of the park unit, restoring them to the more bucolic conditions of the early nineteenth century. In concert with these projects along the River Raisin, federal and state monies also supported an extensive revitalization of Monroe's historic downtown area (just a few blocks west of the battlefield site), where future tourists would dine, shop, take in the town, and spend the night.[15]

While there was some public unease about unearthing a killing field and the charred remnants of *habitant* homes, this was tempered by the sense that the national battlefield park would provide a fitting honor to "the significance of the American sacrifice on the hallowed grounds of the battlefield." Guided by historical records and archeological investigations, the general contours of the historical battlefield were reconstituted in a gently rolling expanse of grass and scattered groves of softwood trees, interlaced with a path leading visitors to interpretive signs that describe the homes and properties of Frenchtown, the positions and movements of combatants, and routes of retreat. In addition to the battlefield site, the statutory boundaries of the River Raisin NBP also include discontinuous parcels that are located within state and county park systems, as well as non-contiguous sites listed on the National Register of Historic Places that are associated with the eighteenth and early nineteenth century history of the Downriver region. Many of these properties, including the battlefield, are adjacent to or very close to sites along Lake Erie and the Detroit River that are managed by the US Fish and Wildlife Service.[16]

Like their non-Indigenous neighbors, the Wyandotte of Anderdon also foresaw important opportunities in the suite of federal and state programs. Because members of the Wyandotte of Anderdon Nation had also worked in the same industries as their non-Indigenous neighbors, they also welcomed the federal "economic rescue plans" that were directed toward saving the faltering industries that had long been the backbone of the Downriver region.[17] Regarding the development of the national battlefield park, however, the Wyandotte of Anderdon Nation were both concerned and strategic in its initial engagements with NPS staff. Because their forebears had been the Keepers of the Great Council Fire for the Native confederacies that variously resisted or engaged with European empires and the United States, the Wyandotte were also concerned that their central role in the War of 1812 and the battles at the River Raisin would raise old prejudices. These fears were bolstered by historical studies and statements from early park proponents that the Wyandotte and their allies were brutal and dishonorable fighters who killed out of wanton bloodlust. As the principal victors at the River Raisin, they could potentially be cast as the unholy agents of a massacre committed against US soldiers and state militiamen.[18]

Playing War

The Wyandotte and other Native nations were right to be wary of how the Battle of Frenchtown would be reenacted. In the five years that preceded the 2010 opening of River Raisin NBP, and the years since, the Battles of River Raisin have been annually commemorated the third week of January in a sort of lightly scripted pageant with Black Powder demonstrations that feature male combatants dressed in period military dress who march, gather in formations, shout, and fire muskets in unison. Women and children also don period costumes that variously approximate the clothes and personal accessories that were common among the French-*Canadien habitants*. In short, commemoration was something of an outdoor costume party with a decidedly marshal tilt that celebrated the heroism and drama of warfare, while portraying the innocence of the US soldiers and Kentucky militia. Present-day Indigenous people have declined the indignity of joining these affairs directly.[19] Consequently, the commemorative Battles of River Raisin mostly overlook the original Native participants. While the absence of Native re-enactors is understandable, there is something peculiar about reenacting (against an invisible but victorious enemy) the largest and most complete defeat of US forces during the entirety of the war.

Battlefield commemorations have a long history in the United States, but they invariably function as noisy public spectacles that dramatize warfare as entertainment, where participants ("combatants") perform specific battle formations, give Black Powder demonstrations, and storm their "enemies" on the other side of the field of battle. In the process, the events manage to become celebrations of a vaguely defined American ethos of heroic sacrifice, hard-won victory, and national progress. In short, cosplay as history is less about understanding historical context than it is about giving new life to old tropes about right and wrong, victim and victor, and us and them. Given the popularity of two annual battle commemorations at Fort Meigs (near Toledo, Ohio) and the annual "Mississinewa 1812" festival and battle reenactment in La Fontaine, Indiana, the Wyandotte of Anderdon Nation were concerned that an important part of their history could be subsumed and perverted by the creation of the new national park in Monroe. They worried about the possibility that non-Native sentiments and histories would overwhelm interpretation and learning at River Raisin Battlefield National Park. These fears were confirmed in January 2011, when the new national park unit hosted its first battle reenactment—which featured reenactors who were descendants of Kentucky militiamen who died at the River Raisin.

Every year, for the last twelve years or so, the Wyandotte of Anderdon Nation have recognized the annual battle reenactment by sending a representative to offer prayers that honor all the Indigenous peoples who have lived along the lower River Raisin since time immemorial.[20] While the brief ceremony provides a meaningful way for the Wyandotte to be present at the River Raisin battlefield on the day of the annual reenactments, their presence in no way condones the way that Native peoples are depicted, omitted, or forgotten altogether during the annual "battles." Despite their ambivalence toward the battle reenactments, the Wyandotte are playing a long game, in hopes of creating a renaissance for their people and the many generations to come. It is this ethic, ultimately, that inspires perseverance and neighborly collaboration between the NPS, civic organizations, the Wyandotte of Anderdon, and other Indigenous nations in Oklahoma, Michigan, and the Great Lakes region.

Friends and Teachers

Perhaps the best illustration of how the Wyandotte of Anderdon think of the Battles of River Raisin and their historical significance stems from honest exercises in self-representation, commitments to public education, the compilation of genealogies, informed interpretation of North American history, and frequent interaction with park sites, park staff, and regional educators. Wyandotte relations with the NPS at the River Raisin NBP have been cordial and extensive since the park was first established in 2009. In the intervening years, Ted Roll,

Grand Chief of the Wyandotte of Anderdon Nation, has served as an ambassador for his people and an active participant in acquiring exhibit materials for the national park unit. He helped to convert a multi-sports complex into a vast exhibit space that now possesses a partial reconstruction of a traditional Wyandotte Long House, hand-built watercraft, and a variety of tools, plant materials, and foods that reflect the daily life of the Wyandotte and other Native nations over the course of countless generations. Roll also maintains a close and wide-ranging interest in the ongoing development of the River Raisin NBP. He is an executive board member of the River Raisin National Battlefield Park Foundation—which cooperates with and assists the NPS in management and public outreach programs. He frequently contributes to park interpretation and, along with other members of the Wyandotte of Anderdon Nation, has been a frequent contributor to public presentations, educational programs, and ceremonies at various units within the national battlefield park. Because the Wyandotte of Anderdon Nation are still not a federally recognized tribal nation, some of this work also involves a close association with the federally recognized Wyandotte Nation of Oklahoma, which has a formal, nation-to-nation, treaty-based relationship with the United States, and an array of federal agencies.

Wyandotte Journey Towards Understanding

By far the most noteworthy phase of the relationship among the Wyandotte of Anderdon Nation, the NPS, and the Wyandotte Nation of Oklahoma occurred in the summer of 2015, when leaders from the Wyandotte Nation of Oklahoma and the Wyandotte of Anderdon Nation came together at the River Raisin NBP headquarters to embark on a program entitled the "Wyandotte Journey Towards Understanding." The program brought together tribal elders and youth, non-Native educators, and NPS staff to learn about Wyandotte history and develop curriculum and interpretation to spread that understanding widely. The Journey received glowing reviews from participants, who took in several presentations that involved wide-ranging discussions about places and events that were important in both US and Wyandotte history and identity. NPS staff and educators were deeply moved by the multiday experience, and all noted how their historical understanding of the region had been enlarged and transformed by Native perspectives.[21]

The significance of the Journey is captured in the comments of Wyandotte participants, who included members of the Wyandotte of Anderdon Nation and the Wyandotte Nation of Oklahoma. All reflected on a deepened sense of homeland, struggle, return, and understanding the significance of the Journey and the way that places, relatives, and perseverance can restore a once divided community. The best way to convey these sentiments, and their centrality to Wyandotte/Wyandotte peoples in Michigan, Oklahoma, and other places in North America, is to present the responses of participants.[22]

*Deryl Wright, Wyandotte National Cultural Committee
and Tribal Elder (Oklahoma)*

The Journey gave the tribe and the cultural committee the bigger picture. Specifically, the Michigan and Ohio part of our history, which previously was not well understood. The cultural committee now passes on what we have learned to other tribal members. It made us, as a Nation, more informed. Now the Chief [Billy Friend] even takes this information to Wyandottes around the country. It has raised awareness within the tribe of where we came from and what we are all about. We are better able to understand and communicate tribal history. I think the original purpose of the Journey was to educate educators, but in the process, it educated us too. You will never know how much you have helped us, the Wyandotte as a Nation. Culture doesn't just happen. It is built, and it is built continually.[23]

Debbie Dry, Wyandotte Nation Cultural Committee (Oklahoma)

I had been to some of the places in Michigan and Ohio before, but this was the first time with the Cultural Committee and some of the elders. The entire Journey was a connection for me to the past. Being there in person is a totally different experience. Being there feels spiritual. You don't get that from reading about it. The Journey increased my respect for my ancestors, because what they suffered allowed us to be where we are today as a Tribe. . . . Every year we have summer interns. I can now share my Journey experience with them, how it made me feel. Passing on the experience to the next generation in preparation for them to go, or in case they cannot go, on the Journey themselves. . . . Everyone who goes on a Journey might not get all of it, but they will get something. Something will stand out and grab their heart. . . .

A Historian's Journey

My first visit to Monroe and the various sites that were designated to become part of the River Raisin NBP occurred before the "Journey of Understanding." At the time, the recently established national park unit represented a rough template for an array of federal, state, regional, and civic interests that sought to use historical tourism and park development to reverse economic and environmental degradation in the region. Because I live in a city and county in the State of Oregon that was also in the midst of a similar revitalization, I felt that I had a handle on the pulse of the place as I began my research in the local historical society and took my initial tours of the battlefield area and associated sites. However, I was not prepared for some of the better known (though unknown to me) ways that generations of city leaders had celebrated and defined Monroe's history. Foremost among these was the large equestrian monument to George Armstrong Custer.

I was also introduced to Black Powder displays and became aware of the large amount of time that volunteers gave to describing their replica fire arms, expensive military uniforms, the reasons for the different types of marching formations they conducted, and the steps needed to load and fire a small canon. While I enjoyed these explanations and the people I met in Monroe, the Battle of the River Raisin was not going to be the central topic of my study. Rather, my primary interests were directed toward the vast array of contexts in which the battle occurred and the broader histories that preceded and followed the events of January 1813. As a contract historian, I was charged with writing what the NPS calls a Historic Resource Study—a book-length history of the area prior to its establishment as a unit of the National Park System and ending with the park's early development. Because I opted to start my study at the advent of the Pleistocene, when the imprint of human history became increasingly more visible in the landscape, my narrative would cover much of eastern North America and encompass five centuries of historical change that were marked by displacement, persistence, and continuity. Consequently, it would take some time before I would begin to explore the martial aspects of the site's history.[24]

Before I left Monroe to begin researching in archives and special collections in Detroit and Ann Arbor, Superintendent Scott Bentley informed me that a group from the Wyandotte of Anderdon wanted to meet me for dinner. Their purpose was threefold: to convey their long-standing connections to the Downriver area, to reveal their intimate association with the sites and events that the NPS would be managing and interpreting, and to ensure that Native peoples would be at the center of the new park's historical narrative. We hit it off during that first meeting, in part because we shared intersecting family histories in Quebec and the Great Lakes region. This history started with the advent of the French-Canadian fur trade in the early seventeenth century and extended into the first half of the nineteenth century, when our forebears were enveloped by the United States in the decades that followed the War of 1812 via the ensuing treaties that drew straight lines across multiple homelands.

Despite a good meeting of the minds, I was not always able to keep up with an array of conversations that were largely driven by the presentation of genealogical charts, references to Downriver locales that I had yet to visit, and the broad geography of Wyandotte movements throughout the Great Lakes and the St. Lawrence River Basin—a vast region the French called the *Pays d'en Haut*, and the historian Richard White referred to as "the Middle Ground." Over the course of the project, however, the riddles embedded in this first meeting would become clearer with subsequent visits to the region, the growing size of my research files, further conversations with Wyandotte and other Native peoples in Michigan, Indiana, and Ohio, and the ongoing process of writing and revising. In time, cultural geography, family lineages, the formation and maintenance of broad Native confederacies, and strategic alliances with different imperial powers became the familiar foreground of a complex history. Eventually, I came to realize that Superintendent Bentley's little exercise in matchmaking would prove foundational to my larger study and continues to echo in this essay.[25]

Remaining, Remaking, and Remembering

When compared to battlefields like Gettysburg, or heavily visited national parks in the West, the River Raisin NBP does not have a "wow" factor. However, what it lacks in scenery, acreage, and crowds, it more than makes up for with an abundance of relationships. These include municipal, state, and federal agencies and the associated properties they manage, Chambers of Commerce, Friends groups, and volunteers. What truly singles out River Raisin NBP and its administration is the lasting, deferential relationship it has maintained with the Wyandotte of Anderdon Nation and the descendants of other Indigenous nations that fought against US troops and state militias at the River Raisin. This unique relationship illustrates the benefits of what few national parks have ever fully considered; namely, how the NPS can best recognize and promote the exercise and application of Native sovereignty within a people's readily acknowledged homelands, as opposed to regulating Native access and use? What conceits underlie the proprietary nature of the NPS, its management of Indigenous lands, and the restrictions it places on how and when Native peoples can and cannot use or tend the resources that countless generations have shared with their ancestors and descendants? At the River Raisin NBP, the answer is fairly simple and suggests that the best future for the NPS lies in working towards becoming a less proprietary public lands agency, and a strong advocate for Indigenous communities and tribal nations that are working to restore and strengthen their communities and homelands on terms that past and future generations would understand and bless.

Restoring and Renewing

Since the 1990s, the Wyandotte of Anderdon Nation has taken an active interest both in efforts to revitalize their political and cultural institutions and in projects related to environmental restoration and historical interpretation in the Detroit River region. For example, in 1999, the nation came together with other peoples of the Wyandotte diaspora to celebrate the Feast of Souls, a centuries-old ceremony that drew upon "the power, traditions, and culture of [their] Confederacy before its dispersal."[26] The multiday event spawned a joint statement among groups vowing to work together to preserve their culture. Similarly, in the early 2000s, the Wyandotte of Anderdon cooperated with the US Fish and Wildlife Service to protect and restore Humbug Marsh and make it a centerpiece of the Detroit River International Wildlife Refuge.

Relations with the NPS and staff at the River Raisin NBP have been even more extensive. In addition to Grand Chief Ted Roll's formal and informal engagement with the park, other members of the Wyandotte of Anderdon Nation have also

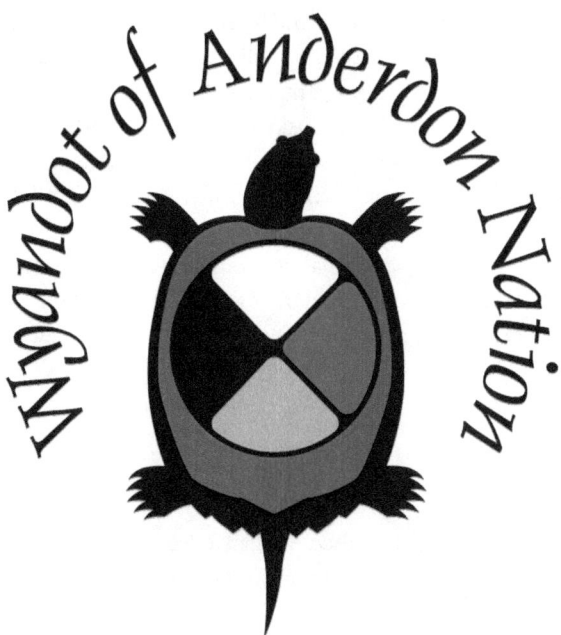

Symbol of the Wyandot of Anderdon Nation. Courtesy of Brett English, facility operations specialist at River Raisin Battlefield Park.

participated in public presentations, educational programs, and ceremonies at various park sites, including the 2015 "Wyandotte Journey Towards Understanding." The program, which included site visits to multiple units of River Raisin NBP, as well as to Fallen Timbers Battlefield and Fort Miami's National Historic Site in Maumee, Ohio, received glowing reviews from participants—nearly all of whom noted how their historical understanding of the region had been enlarged and transformed by Native perspectives. The "Wyandotte Journey Towards Understanding" also served as the basis of a program and tour in mid-September 2016 for attendees of the annual meeting of the American Association of State and Local History that was held in Detroit. Entitled "War and Peace: Following in the Footsteps of the Huron-Wyandotte," the program was also well-received by this group of academics and professional historians.[27]

In September 2018, representatives from the Wyandotte of Anderdon Nation and the Wyandotte Nation of Oklahoma came together for the bicentennial of the treaty that resulted in the cession of Big Rock and Maguaga, and the relocation of the "Michigan Wyandotte" to the Huron Reserve. To mark the treaty, the two nations jointly hosted a gathering at Six Points, a fifteen-acre parcel that the Wyandotte of Anderdon Nation envision as their future home, including sites for gatherings, ceremonial use, tribal offices, and the public presentation of Wyandotte history, culture, and environmental stewardship. Staff from River Raisin NBP assisted with a second event at a nearby park in Gibraltar, which was also attended by Susan White, the Refuge Manager for the Detroit River International Wildlife Refuge.

The ceremony was centered on the presentation and blessing of three wampum belts. The first commemorated the 1818 treaty, the resilience of the Wyandotte of Anderdon, and their 2018 return to Big Rock. The second belt focused on the 1843 removal of the Wyandotte from Upper Sandusky (in Ohio) to present-day Kansas, and the subsequent persistence and growth of their descendants across 175 years. The third belt honored the Wyandotte/Wyandotte/Wendat Confederacy, from the time its members lived in their ancient homelands, through the many travails and separations that followed initial encounters with Europeans, to the enduring bonds that recently brought them together at Ossossané in Ontario, and the commitments they made to collectively work for the benefit of future generations.

Commemorating the Two Hundredth Anniversary of the Wyandotte Force Migration

The significance of these three belts is described well in comments made by River Raisin NBP Superintendent Scott Bentley during the presentation of the first belt:

> The 200th commemorative wampum belt was woven by over 400 Southeast Michigan youth in a purple field emphasizing the horror and tragedies of losing the villages of Brownstown and Monguagon after an intense 33-year struggle to retain them. On each end of the belt, fragmented pieces of the Treaty of Greenville wampum belt (ca. 1795) are [depicted] to illustrate the broken treaties and worthless words that were inscribed in it. The two squares represent the two villages and the nearly 1,200 Wyandotte that lived in the villages when they were taken from the Wyandotte in 1818 by the United States under the leadership of Territorial Governor Lewis Cass. The six-sided star [near the center of the belt] symbolizes the Six Points development and the return of the Wyandotte to this site of the Confederated Council Fire at Big Rock (aka Brownstown) 200 years after the Treaty of St. Mary's. The six points [of the star] represent the traditional Wyandotte prayer to the North, South, East, West, Heaven, and Mother Earth as a thank you to the Great Creator for protecting the Wyandotte people and keeping them strong during the 200-year journey since leaving their villages.
>
> In the middle of the [white] six points design is one purple bead representing the heart and soul of the Wyandotte as one people . . . , protected by the Great Creator. [Two broad rows of white beads running across the center portion of the belt show] the open lines of understanding and healing [that are required] as together we journey to understand and share for the benefit of future generations. Between each symbol on the belt there are seven beads representing the seven generations who came

Gathering of Wyandots and other dignitaries at River Raisin National Battlefield Park, 2015. From left to right: Scott Bentley (Superintendent (NPS-River Raisin N.B.P.), the Honorable Tim Walberg (U.S. Congressional Representative), Clyde Pidgeon (Wyandot of Anderdon Nation), the Honorable Second Chief Norman Hildebrand, Jr. (Wyandotte Nation), the Honorable Chief Jan English (Wyandot of Kansas), the Honorable Grand Chief Konrad Sioui (Huron-Wendat First Nation), Douglas Chaffin (River Raisin National Battlefield Park Foundation), the Honorable Grand Chief Ted Roll (Wyandot of Anderdon Nation), the Honorable Robert Clark (Mayor of Monroe, Michigan), the Honorable Dale Zorn (Michigan State Representative). Photo credit: the National Park Service, River Raisin National Battlefield Park.

before us making our journey possible and the seven generations to come, reminding us to be good stewards of Mother Earth and to remember the lasting impacts of decisions we make today on the future generations.[28]

The place, timing, and tone of this commemorative event powerfully illustrates the enduring significance of the Battles of Frenchtown and the broader contexts in which they occurred. For the Wyandotte, those contexts include their status as the Keeper of the Council Fire for large Native confederacies before and during what has been called the Sixty Years' War for the Great Lakes (1754–1814). The Wyandotte were also deeply involved with the battles along the River Raisin; their villages of Big Rock and Maguaga were sites of conflict, and Big Rock was central to the strategic concerns of the British, the United States, and the Native confederacy through most of 1812 and 1813. In short, the Wyandotte were one of the most engaged and affected groups in the Northwest Theater of the War of 1812. The seventh-generation references that were made during the wampum belt ceremony in Gibraltar also serve as reminders that such concerns long preceded the War of 1812 and continued long after. Native peoples in the early nineteenth century, regardless of how they chose to engage with or avoid war, invariably considered their deep obligations to past and future generations—as did their forebears and descendants. Such concerns also guided their approaches to the profound challenges that came with subsequent land cession and removal treaties.[29]

For the Wyandotte and other Native peoples, the War of 1812 was the culmination of a sixty-year struggle to ensure the ancient past would carry through to future generations. As the events and memories embedded in the 1818–2018 bicentennial wampum belt attest, this struggle resulted in horror, profound loss, displacement, and dispossession. While these post-war traumas resulted from US policies toward American Indians and—to a somewhat lesser degree—British and Canadian policies toward First Nations peoples, they were greatly exacerbated by widespread prejudices against Native peoples, the duplicity of government officials, and the constant push to convert reservation lands into private property. Like other Native groups in North America, the Wyandotte in the Detroit River region sometimes became invisible to their non-Indigenous neighbors in order to survive these multiple threats. Yet even as they "hid in plain sight," they sustained a persistent attachment to their home territory and to their former role as Keepers of the Great Council Fire.[30]

The 2018 wampum belt ceremony and the recent acquisition of the Six Points property are the fruits of this tenacity, and bear testimony to the multigenerational effort to shape a viable future within the Wyandotte homeland. This process remains ongoing and is also evident in the Wyandotte of Anderdon Nation's collaborations with the US Fish and Wildlife Service and the NPS: two agencies that are committed to restoring and managing the environmental, cultural, and historical legacies that define the Detroit River region. Because the Wyandotte are so embedded in the landscapes and histories of the area and are so connected to past and future generations, they "Remember the Raisin!" like no other people. Through two centuries of horror and healing, they have come to embody the significance of the battles and their historical legacies. This is not to suggest that the Wyandotte represent the past in a way that echoes William Faulkner's oft-quoted observation that the "past is never dead. It's not even past." Rather, it is to suggest something more significant and more lasting. While Faulkner alluded to the ways the past continually haunts the present, the Wyandottes' concern for the next seven generations implies that the present is a commitment to an ever-living future. In other words, the degree to which the Wyandotte embody the historical significance of the Battles of Frenchtown coincides with the impacts that their present-day decisions will have on their homeland and their descendants over the next seven generations.[31]

Notes

1. National Park Service, "The Journey to Becoming a National Park." River Raisin National Battlefield Park Michigan, 2021. Retrieved July 20, 2023 (https://www.nps.gov/rira/learn/management/index.htm).

2. S.22—Omnibus Public Land Management Act of 2009, 111th Congress (2009–2010). https://www.congress.gov/bill/111th-congress/senate-bill/22; "Management" section of the River Raisin National Battlefield Park's NPS website. https://www.nps.gov/rira/learn/management/index.htm (both sites accessed on January 24, 2021); Lary M. Dilsaver, *America's National Park System: The Critical Documents*, 2nd ed. (Lanham, MD: Rowman & Littlefield, 2016), 331–38.
3. David M. Stothers, Timothy J. Abel, and Andrew M. Schneider, "Archaic Perspectives in the Western Lake Erie Basin," in *Archaic Transitions in Ohio and Kentucky Prehistory*, eds. Olaf Prufer et al. (Kent, OH: Kent State University Press, 2001), 242.
4. Ahmed White, *The Last Great Strike: Little Steel, the CIO, and the Struggle for Labor Rights in New Deal America* (Berkeley: University of California Press, 2016), 101–2, 147–50; Steven C. High, *Industrial Sunset: The Making of North America's Rust Belt, 1969–1984* (Toronto: University of Toronto Press, 2003), 92–121; Joel Kotkin, Mark Schill, and Ryan Streeter, *Clues From The Past: The Midwest as an Aspirational Region* (Indianapolis: Sagamore Institute, February 2012), 4–13; National Park Service, *Foundation Document: River Raisin National Battlefield Park, Michigan* (National Park Service, December 2012), 6–13. http://npshistory.com/publications/foundation-documents/rira-fd-2012.pdf (accessed September 9, 2021); Community Foundation for Southeast Michigan, "America's Newest National Battlefield Park," *Report* 30: 2 (September 7, 2016): 10–12. https://cfsem.org/story/americas-newest-national-battlefield-park (accessed September 16, 2021). It is worth noting that "resurrect" and "resurrection" are often used to describe efforts to restore and renew Downriver communities, environmental conditions, and infrastructures; see, for instance, Kathy Warnes, "The Renaissance of the Winding River Raisin," *Meandering Michigan History* (blog). https://meanderingmichiganhistory.weebly.com/monroe-memories-and-more.html (accessed September 21, 2021).
5. For a good example of how a new-found pride and purpose was expressed in the region, see City of Monroe, Monroe Charter Township and Frenchtown Charter Township, *Resilient! Monroe: Resource Atlas* (October 15, 2003; updated March 2, 2020). http://www.resilientmichigan.org/monroe.asp.
6. The term "Wyandotte," which is used throughout this essay, serves as shorthand for an association of First Nations/American Indian peoples in Canada and the United States. The people who are a key focus of this essay are primarily descended from Iroquoian-speaking peoples who identified as Tiontonati, and other communities the French called "Huron." These peoples were closely related to the Wendat, who moved to the east to escape the violence of the Beaver Wars and receive assistance from Jesuit missionaries. Today, the elements of the broader Wyandotte Confederacy are located in Oklahoma—where most of the Wyandotte Nation (which is mostly composed of peoples who resided on, and were removed from, reservations in northwestern Ohio during the 1830s. The Wendat (Huron-Wendat First Nation) primarily reside at Wendake, Quebec—which is within the broader boundaries of Quebec City. The Wyandotte of Anderdon Nation is primarily composed of peoples

who avoided removal to "Indian Country" (i.e., Oklahoma) in the 1830s and continued to live on both sides of the Detroit River.

7. Gilles Havard, *The Great Peace of Montreal of 1701: French-Native Diplomacy in the Seventeenth Century*, trans. Phyllis Aronoff and Howard Scott (Montreal: McGill-Queen's University Press, 2001), 79–90; Richard White, *The Middle Ground: Indians, Empires, and Republics in the Great Lakes Region, 1650–1815* (Cambridge: Cambridge University Press, 1991), 34; Michael J. Witgen, *An Infinity of Nations: How Indians, Empires, and Western Migration Shaped National Identity in North America* (Philadelphia: University of Pennsylvania Press, 2004), 246–53. Algonquin and Nippising peoples are Algonquian speakers who lived to the northeast of the Tionontati prior to the displacements of the Beaver Wars.

8. Translated quotation in Edgar Andrew Collard, *Montreal: The Days That Are No More* (Toronto: Doubleday Canada, 1976), 18.

9. David Curtis Skaggs, "The Sixty Years' War for the Great Lakes, 1754–1814: An Overview," in Skaggs and Larry Lee Nelson, eds., *The Sixty Years' War for the Great Lakes, 1754–1814* (East Lansing: Michigan State University Press, 2010), and Helen Hornbeck Tanner, *Atlas of Great Lakes Indian History* (Norman: Published for the Newberry Library by the University of Oklahoma Press, 1987), 92–95; Sandy Antal, *A Wampum Denied: Procter's War of 1812*, 2nd ed. (Kingston, Ontario: McGill-Queen's University Press, 2011), 221–23; Richard White, *The Middle Ground: Indians, Empires, and Republics in the Great Lakes Region, 1650–1815* (Cambridge: Cambridge University Press, 1991), 514–15; John Sugden, *Tecumseh: A Life* (New York: Henry Holt, 1999), 209, 284–85, 437; Trevor T. Johnson, "The Wyandotte Village of Maguaga: Vital Ground in the Michigan Territory during the War of 1812," prepared for the National Park Service, River Raisin National Battlefield Park (June 2016), 18–19, 21–23.

10. Charles Garrad, *Petun to Wyandotte: The Ontario Petun from the Sixteenth Century* (Ottawa: Canadian Museum of History and the University of Ottawa Press, 2014), 515–16. Note: in referencing a specific "reserve" or "Reserve," this paragraph follows the capitalization that is used in government documents.

11. Laurie Leclair, "The Huron-Wyandottes of Anderdon Township: A Case Study in Native Adaption, 1701–1914," master's thesis (University of Windsor, 1988), 42–44; Rhonda Telford, "How the West Was Won: Land Transactions Between the Anishinabe, the Huron and the Crown in Southwestern Ontario," in David H. Pentland, ed., *Papers of the Twenty-Ninth Algonquian Conference* (Winnipeg: University of Manitoba Press, 1998), 328–42; Michel Ducharme, "Closing the Last Chapter of the Atlantic Revolution: The 1837–38 Rebellions in Upper and Lower Canada," *Proceedings of the American Antiquarian Society* 116 (October 2006): 413–30; Theodore Binnema and Kevin Hutchings, "The Emigrant and the Noble Savage: Sir Francis Bond Head's Romantic Approach to Aboriginal Policy in Upper Canada, 1836–1838," *Journal of Canadian Studies* 39 (Winter 2004): 115–38.

12. This and the following paragraph are based on Leclair, "The Huron-Wyandottes of Anderdon," 72–82; Garrad, *Petun to Wyandotte*, 118–19,

122–24, 516; Horatio Hale, "Huron Folk-Lore. I. Cosmogonic Myths. The Good and Evil Minds," *Journal of American Folklore* 1 (October–December 1888): 177–80; and Hale, "The Fall of Hochelaga: A Study of Popular Tradition," *Journal of American Folklore*, 7 (January–March 1894): 4–6. The last few Wyandotte to forego their "Indian" (aka First Nations) status and become Canadian citizens did so in 1914.

13. John L. Steckley, *De Religione: Telling the Seventeenth-Century Jesuit Story in Huron to the Iroquois* (Norman: University of Oklahoma Press, 2004), 179. Quotation comes from a translation of a seventeenth-century Jesuit text on Baptism that was originally rendered in the Wendat (i.e., Wyandotte) language.

14. Scholars who worked with these materials and consulted with Wyandotte/Wyandotte in the Detroit River region, Kansas, and Oklahoma include Charles Aubrey Buser, Patricia Anderson Buser, John L. Steckley, and Charles Garrad. Correspondence between the Buser's and the people named in this paragraph can be found in the Charles and Patricia Buser Collection in the Ohio State University Rare Books and Manuscripts Library.

15. *City of Monroe Parks and Recreation Master Plan* (Prepared by Beckett & Raeder, 2014); and *Resilient! Monroe: Resource Atlas* (October 15, 2003).

16. *City of Monroe Parks and Recreation Master Plan*, prepared by Beckett & Raeder (2014); and *Resilient! Monroe: Resource Atlas*; and *City of Monroe Parks and Recreation Master* Plan, prepared by Beckett & Raeder (2014); Roy Goethie et al, "Watershed Management Planning for the River Raisin: Perspectives on Changing Land Use, Dams, Water Quality and Best Management Practices," Master's thesis (University of Michigan, 2007).

17. David Kiley, "As Obama Takes Victory Lap Over Auto Industry Rescue, Here are the Lessons of the Bailout," *Forbes* (January 20, 2016). http://www.forbes.com/sites/davidkiley5/3016/01/20/obamas-takes-victory-lap-over-auto-industry-rescue/#49ea4f775497 (accessed February 2, 2020).

18. NPS, "Management: The Journey to Becoming a National Park." https://www.nps.gov/rira/learn/management/index.htm (accessed February 3, 2021).

19. Videos, written notices, and descriptions of these events are readily found online. Gregory Evans Dowd, *A Spirited Resistance: The North American Indian Struggle for Unity, 1745–1815* (Baltimore: Johns Hopkins University Press, 1992); David Curtis Skaggs, "The Sixty Years' War for the Great Lakes, 1754–1814: An Overview," in Skaggs and Larry Lee Nelson, eds., *The Sixty Years' War for the Great Lakes, 1754–1814* (East Lansing: Michigan State University Press, 2010); Robert Allen, *His Majesty's Indian Allies: British Indian Policy in the Defence of Canada, 1774–1815* (Toronto: Dundurn Press, 1996); Timothy J. Shannon, "The Native American Way of War in the Age of Revolutions, 1754–1814," in Roger Chickering and Stig Förster, eds., *War in an Age of Revolution, 1775–1815* (Washington, DC: German Historical Institute, 2013), 137–58. The Confederacy comprised individuals, families and communities from several distinct cultural groups that included Wyandotte (aka Wyandotte or Huron), Shawnee, Bodéwadmi (Potawatomi), Odawa (Ottawa), Ojibwe (Chippewa), Lunaapeew (Lenape, or Delaware), Myaamia (Miami), Waayaahtanwa (Wea), Hoocąągra (Ho-Chunk, aka Winnebago), Kiikaapoi

(Kickapoo), Muscogee (Creek), Ökwe'öwé (Seneca-Cayuga; aka, "Mingo"), OΘaakiiwaki (Sauk, or Sac), and Meskwaki (Fox).
20. Dean Cousino, "Tribe Blesses Battlefield at Ceremony," *Monroe News* (October 28, 2015).
21. "Wyandotte Journey Towards Understanding: Project Evaluation," *Self Governance Communication & Education Consortium*, https://www.tribalselfgov.org/wp-content/uploads/2018/07/Wyandotte.pdf (accessed September 16, 2018).
22. Additional excerpts here:

> **Tom Lowler, Wyandotte of Anderdon Nation (Michigan)**: [O]ne thing I noticed was that a lot of people, who were along for the ride, began to learn the historical significance of our area and specifically the Anderdon role in that. The trip also solidified relationships between the Anderdon and National Park Service. The Journey helped the Anderdon understand our own ancestors and what they did in this area. Our own history. The main significance is that the Wyandotte of Anderdon members are gaining knowledge of their real past and history. . . . We will help present history in detail, accurately, for future generations. This will help the Anderdon. Personally, I saw things on the Journey that I knew and understood, but I had not seen it. I had only read about it. . . . When you actually see you understand the significance of a specific place more. I think this was important and helped the Wyandotte of Anderdon have greater pride in their ancestry and position here. We now understand our own tribal history.
>
> **Brenda Roll, Wyandotte of Anderdon Nation (Michigan)**: After hearing people on the Journey speak, I realized there was more interest from others about the Journey than I had realized. I did not realize there were so many people interested in the history of the Wyandotte. It is important because sparking the interest potentially means more people becoming involved and learning about their ancestry. The project will raise the involvement of the members of the tribe. It was interesting to see other people's reaction to learning about their ancestors' involvement in history, and how it affected them. Some were hearing their history accurately for the first time. It was different than what the history books tell.
>
> **D'Arcy Tammaro, Wyandotte of Anderdon Nation (Michigan)**: Because of the outreach that is happening through the Journey, it is strengthening relationships and awareness in our community of what happened here and the significance of how that affects today. People are not generally aware of the historical things that happened here. I think they should know. I am glad word is getting out. If the Wyandotte parents have the knowledge base they will pass it on to their children and to the children that come to visit Six Points. It is all about carrying things forward. There is a lot of excitement contributed to the Journey. It does nothing but help the future. Everything around the program is helping.
>
> **David Culver, Wyandotte National Cultural Committee (Oklahoma)**: The most significant change from the Journey was in myself. I got a real

awareness of ties to the land in Michigan and elsewhere. I enjoyed the partnership with the National Park Service, educators and all of the specialists. It brought history to life and tied [the] present to roots. As a tribal citizen, I learned more who we are as a people and now share that with future generations. It is a partnership to protect history. Prior to the Journey, most of the people in the tribe did not realize their history. The Journey developed an interest in where we came from. It was very important psychologically, because now we know where we came from. . . . As a former federal employee, it was good to see government agencies have come full circle from trying to hide the history of what was done to Native Americans now telling the story. It is important to show how far we have come as a country. It is a change in the mindset of the people.

Danielle Lowler, Wyandotte of Anderdon Nation (Michigan): I felt like the trip triggered my own personal journey. It inspired me to learn, grow, and research more and more of my own story. I have become involved with other National Nations now as well. I have even traveled to Montana to help with efforts there. I have been learning my own identity along the way. . . . The Wyandotte were unknown, went into hiding, and did not go to Oklahoma or Canada. We are here, have always been here and near here. I want to educate our area about the Wyandotte. I want our area to recognize that we are here and who we are.

Judy Kukpwski, Wyandotte of Anderdon Nation (Michigan): The significance of the Journey was not just seeing the change within the Wyandotte of Anderdon, but seeing that others realize we are here! Many people did not realize the Wyandotte of Anderdon people are still here. The Journey was important for a lot of people, because it dispels the myth they had been fed that we were destroyed and did not exist anymore. It is significant because people are realizing that we exist and aren't gone, we are here. We are having many more inquiries and new members because of the Journey. As a Wyandotte of Anderdon historian the Journey opened new avenues of information for me. I now have new sources of information to add to what I know.

Chief Billy Friend, Wyandotte Nation (Oklahoma): The Journey has enabled us as a Nation to understand our own Journey as a tribe. We have taken the concept of the Journey to apply to individuals and families. We challenge citizens to research or find their own Journey. One of the most significant things is the title "Journey Towards Understanding." This Journey was a seed that started the process of many Wyandotte on their personal Journey. The Journey is growing each tribal citizen into understanding their own personal Journey, whether they are early or late in their Journey. We want to expand on the original Journey, it is now an even more personal matter. The Journey was very educational and enlightening. It was important to be able to further our own knowledge of our ancestors, to see what they went through, and see how they persevered to enable us to be where we are as a Nation today. For those of us who participated on the Journey, we now fully embrace that part of our history. Although we had seen pieces of our history before, we got to put all of the pieces together on this Journey. It laid a foundation for the tribe that we can continue to build upon.

23. "Wyandotte Journey Towards Understanding Project Evaluation"; Matt Thompson, "Wyandotte Chiefs Offer Their Perspective," *The Blade* (June 25, 2015); "Battlefield Presentation Provokes Discussion about War," *Monroe News* (May 29, 2017). https://www.monroenews.com/story/news/2017/05/29/battlefield-presentation-provokes-discussion-about/20770986007 (accessed September 16, 2018).

24. Mark David Spence, *Native Ground, Middle Ground, Battle Ground: The River Raisin, the War of 1812, and the Course of North American History* (n.p.: privately printed, 2019).

25. Richard White, *The Middle Ground: Indians, Empires, and Republics in the Great Lakes Region, 1650–1815* (Cambridge: Cambridge University Press, 1991).

26. Erik R. Seeman, *The Huron-Wendat Feast of the Dead: Indian-European Encounters in early North America* (Baltimore: Johns Hopkins University Press, 2011) 59–79; Kathryn Magee, "Dispersed, But Not Destroyed: Leadership, Women, and Power within the Wendat Diaspora, 1600–1701," PhD diss. (Ohio State University, 2011), 93–101.

27. Thompson, "Wyandotte Chiefs Offer Their Perspective"; "Wyandotte Journey Towards Understanding: Project Evaluation"; "Battlefield Presentation Provokes Discussion about War."

28. Jim Kasuba, "200th Anniversary of Wyandotte Forced Migration to Be Observed in Gibraltar with Special Activities," *News-Herald* (September 20, 2018). https://businessdirectory.thenewsherald.com/news/200th-anniversary-of-wyandot-forced-migration-to-be-observed-in-gibraltar-with-special-activities/article_46210b50-bd31-11e8-84bc-a7f311195ba0.html (accessed June 9, 2023). Quoted text as read by Scott Bentley, Superintendent of River Raisin National Battlefield Park. Video of the ceremony posted at "Wyandotte of Anderdon Nation Wampum Belt Ceremony." https://www.youtube.com/watch?v=3nNcA6WfHGk (accessed October 2, 2018).

29. David Curtis Skaggs, "The Sixty Years' War for the Great Lakes, 1754–1814: An Overview," in Skaggs and Larry Lee Nelson, eds. *The Sixty Years' War for the Great Lakes, 1754–1814* (East Lansing: Michigan State University Press, 2010), 1–20.

30. Kay Givens-McGowan, "The Wyandot and the River," in John Hartig, ed., *Honoring our Detroit River: Caring for Our Home* (Bloomfield Hills, MI: Cranbrook Institute of Science, 2003), 31.

31. It is important to note that the Wyandotte of Anderdon Nation's ongoing process of community revitalization parallels recent historical trends toward greater self-determination since the late 1960s in the Great Lakes region and across the country. The 1990s also witnessed the restoration and recognition of nation-to-nation relations with a number of American Indian communities through the process of federal recognition. Stephen Cornell, *The Return of the*

Native: American Indian Political Resurgence (New York: Oxford University Press, 1990); Joane Nagel, *American Indian Ethnic Renewal: Red Power and the Resurgence of Identity and Culture* (New York: Oxford University Press, 1996); Joanne Barker, *Native Acts: Law, Recognition, and Cultural* Authenticity (Durham, NC: Duke University Press, 2011); Dennis F. Kelley, *Tradition, Performance, and Religion in Native America: Ancestral Ways, Modern Selves* (New York: Routledge, 2014). The five tribal nations in Michigan that gained federal recognition in the 1990s are the Little River Band of Ottawa Indians, the Little Traverse Bay Bands of Odawa Indians, the Match-e-be-nash-she-wish Band of Pottawatomi Indians of Michigan, the Nottawaseppi Huron Band of the Potawatomi, and the Pokagon Band of Potawatomi Indians (Michigan and Indiana). The seven groups with a longer established federal recognition are the Bay Mills Indian Community, the Grand Traverse Band of Ottawa and Chippewa Indians, the Hannahville Indian Community, the Keweenaw Bay Indian Community, the Lac Vieux Desert Band of Lake Superior Chippewa Indians, the Saginaw Chippewa Indian Tribe of Michigan, and the Sault Ste. Marie Tribe of Chippewa Indians.

PART TWO | **HEADWINDS**
Challenging Cases, Painful Histories

Interview: Gerard Baker

GERARD BAKER IS MANDAN-HIDATSA, and he grew up on the Fort Berthold Reservation in North Dakota (home of the Mandan, Hidatsa, and Arikara Nation). Baker worked in the National Park Service (NPS) for thirty-six years, serving as superintendent of Little Bighorn National Monument, Chickasaw National Recreation Area, Lewis and Clark National Historic Trail, and Mount Rushmore National Memorial. From April 2010 until his retirement later that year, he served as the assistant director of American Indian Relations at NPS headquarters in Washington, DC. The following is adapted from an interview with Matthew J. Hill and Brooke Neely on November 10, 2021. This interview highlights this section's theme of painfully contested histories, with Baker discussing the controversies he encountered as he worked to introduce stories of American Indians at national parks like Theodore Roosevelt, Little Bighorn, and Mount Rushmore.

Matthew J. Hill (MH): You had a long eventful career in the National Park Service. And we wondered what you find most satisfying about the work that you did?

Gerard Baker (GB): When I look back at my past, with my career at the National Park Service, I look at it in two different phases. The first phase I find very unique, because I came in when they still had the National Park Service technician series. And that technician series was, you did everything. Now we're pretty specialized, but in those days, we did everything from cleaning the bathrooms, to cutting grass, to interpretation, to a little bit of security. Not law enforcement, but security. So, the first phase of my career was as a field ranger, which to me is what the parks was [sic] all about. When I first joined, I had no idea in fact, I thought I was applying for a North Dakota construction job. Didn't read the application very good [sic]. It said seasonal Park Service job. And so they said come to Medora. So, I did, I went to Medora. That's where my first job in the National Park Service was—cleaning toilets. I worked my way down to management from there.

It was interesting. I got to do a little bit of everything, from working at [Theodore] Roosevelt [National Park], which was a fairly typical national park with a visitor's center and campgrounds and backcountry and buffalo and elk and all that business. So, I got to do a lot of different things. But it was a learning phase obviously. And I was still going to school at Southern Oregon University. I graduated in 1979 and joined the park service from there.

I actually go back to my early years, as far as what I tried to accomplish in the park service, which was getting the park service to open that door for the American Indians. In the early years, it was learning from elders especially before we had electricity and running water. When I was first growing up on the reservation—the Fort Berthold reservation—it was listening to a lot of old people talking. The correlation, for me, between that time and the park service was their philosophy about saving the land, the spirits of land, the animals, and taking care of the land for the future generations. Which was basically what the park service in the early years bragged about.

So, when I was at Theodore Roosevelt National Park, it was there that I realized there were things missing from the park. Not in a negative way but some information was just missing. That was the story of the American Indians, no matter what park I was at. In this case, at Theodore Roosevelt, we had great interpreters. We had great seasonal [interpreters] that told the story of the cottonwood trees and the Little Missouri River, the topography and the visual landscapes, including the animals and then of course, about Theodore Roosevelt. If I was on patrol, I'd stop and listen to them. But continuously, I would realize that one thing was missing, and that was the story of the American Indian. And looking back now, as I observed the park service individuals that worked there—seasonals and permanents—I realized that, for one thing, they didn't know how to talk about the tribes. They didn't know how to communicate about what happened with the tribes and the land that now [is the] park service.

This got me thinking [about] how to influence that. One of the first programs that I ever did at Theodore Roosevelt, I volunteered for. By then I had graduated, if you will, from being a maintenance guy that cleaned bathrooms and cut grass and picked up trash. I went to the ranger series and became a law enforcement ranger. I drove a patrol car which I was pretty proud of. But like I said, I would always watch these folks. And I started realizing that we didn't know how to communicate.

One of my first permanent jobs was at Knife River Indian Villages. This was a place that we called in my language *Awa-Di-ghick-hoo*, The Five Villages. It was the traditional home of the Mandan-Hidatsa. I'm Mandan-Hidatsa, and so that was a special treat. Still being in that first phase of my career, which was a little bit of maintenance, but I was also involved in developing interpretation and school programs. This was my first taste of trying to get the story of the tribes across.

The second phase is my management phase. I came into a superintendency right away, actually. I think that was why I went with the Forest Service for a little while, because I was at a GS-9 (federal general schedule pay scale), as a lot of us were in the park service. And I couldn't get out. It was just tough to get jobs. I have a family and that fit well. I got offered by the Forest Service to go to a GS-11 for more pay. So, I went to Red Lodge, Montana. I went there for a couple of years.

Then Little Big Horn opened up. That was the start of my second phase—management. I threw myself into Little Big Horn at the time when it was on the edge of being very controversial for some. The reason I say for some is that after thinking about it, there was a group across the United States that was in favor of the story of George Custer. But not much [for] the story of the triumphs [of Native people] or even why that battle took place and all the history behind it. And only the Crow tribe was there because it's within the Crow Indian Reservation. They had a full staff of Crow help, including maintenance, administration, and rangers. They were well-defined there. But what they didn't have is the story of the other tribes. I'll go back to that later. At that time, I sort of broke away from the park service, I think, in a way—I didn't follow the regime. I was consciously aware that the park service was set up in a militaristic style from day one. It's changing now. But in my early years, that's how it was. So, my second phase is my management years.

MH: Cool. So, I'm just curious, how was your attempt to introduce the [Native American side of the] story received? For example, at Little Bighorn. I don't know if you tried to do the same at Knife River. But how was your effort to introduce that story received?

GB: I think it was received very well by the Native community. It wasn't received as positively by a lot of members of the white community, especially the ones who were specifically involved in either the Custer society or the Mount Rushmore Society. These were two organizations that were supposed to help manage the parks and make it easier, supposedly, in many different ways, including fiscally. With the tribes, it was cautious at first because, from what the tribes would tell me later on, the park service had never really invited them to come on board for meetings, or if they did, it was very uptight. But as I became a superintendent in different places, I always would take my management team.

They knew that and communication was wide open at that time. So, what I would do is I would take these folks, no matter where I went. I would call up every tribe that was within the vicinity of that park. Let's look at Little Bighorn. What I did there is not only call up the Crows, obviously, because they were right there, and the Northern Cheyennes, but [I] also called up all the bands of the Lakota that fought against George Custer in that historic battle. I introduced myself and then also talked to my staff, telling them that we put ourselves on the agenda of the tribal councils in different places. We would go there; they wouldn't come to us.

When I was very young, before we had cars on the rez, sometimes the government would come to us, but they just stopped. After that, if you wanted to do deals with the government, you had to go to them. Remembering that, I told my staff, we're going to go to the councils, and we're gonna present ourselves. The first thing I believe, when you create the relationship, is you have to create it with a good heart and good open mind. I had people that didn't like to go, and that's just the way it was. But you had to understand how they were players within your organization. I would tell my staff that when we go there, we would definitely wear uniforms. That was something new. Because when the agency sometimes went to tribal governments, or tribal areas, they were scared to wear the uniforms. I, for one, was extremely proud of my park service uniform, especially that damn brown hat. I wore that all the time, no matter where I went.

I would tell my staff is—when they introduced us, they would introduce me, and then I would introduce them to the council. What we were doing is humanizing ourselves. We're not governmentizing ourselves, we're humanizing ourselves. So, I told my staff, tell them who you are. Tell them where you came from. Even talk about your folks, talk about your kid, talk about sports, talk about yourself as a human being first. And you could almost see that some of the tribal people's eyes were going, "Wow, these folks live like me in a way. They go to basketball games and volleyball games. You know, they do this, they do that." And then [I present] the invitation in a political way [to] the tribal council first of all, to invite them to come back to their homeland. I would never say, "You're invited to come back to Little Bighorn battlefield or invited to come to Mount Rushmore." I would say, "You're most welcome to come back to your homeland. And we need to know who to work with in order to make that happen." Immediately, they would come with their different organizations within the tribe—the cultural group or the elder group. And if not, I would usually ask for those groups. I would say we'd like to talk to your elders . . . because the elders never change.

One thing I told the staff that we have to remember as we go through the political arena of dialogue with the parks and the tribes, is that the park service is just like the tribal council. And the tribal council is just like park service. We don't stay. Everybody moves. Sometimes you have to deal with a brand-new tribal council every four years. Sometimes every two years. Sometimes they have to deal with a new superintendent at the park service every three [or] four years, depending on the goals of that person and how long they stay. Some of those parks that are in Indian Country, unfortunately, are stepping-stone parks.

I hate that idea. I'll say that right now. Knife River is a stepping-stone park, Fort Union Trading post is a stepping-stone park. What that means is they usually get first time superintendents. That [park] is where they learn the first basics and then go on from there. So, they're not expected to stay there. If you don't stay someplace, you create no sustainability when it comes to dialogue with the tribe, and vice versa. No matter where I was, I knew I'd be going sometime. And so, it was very important to me to establish a bond between my staff and the tribes. The first thing you do after [visiting] was to invite them to come and tell their story. Without interruption by the way. That was most important.

One of the best times I've ever had and one of the best learning experiences I've had [was] from the Lakota for example. I talked with a bunch of old guys and put them in the park service van and took them for a ride on the [Little Big Horn] battlefield and didn't say a word. You should have heard the stories. It was incredible! So, the first thing I thought about as the superintendent is, how do you bring these stories to the general public? Because [the tellers], they're on fire with excitement talking about warriors and everything you can imagine.

Here's the other problem with some of these places, including Mount Rushmore and Little Bighorn—educating the public on how to listen to Indians tell their stories. We don't know how to do that. We used to train park service rangers to give their strict interpretive stories. That's what we're used to in the parks. So, when I started bringing American Indians into the role of interpreters, we had this group called The Custer Battlefield Associates, or something to that effect. They got so upset because we weren't talking primarily about Custer or about the battle just from the Army standpoint anymore. These Indian people were talking about the battles from the American Indian standpoint, finally. That was a big conflict.

Now I'm sure you guys both understand, I had the advantage of being an Indian. There's stuff I could say that you guys couldn't say and not get them mad. And I tell you, I, I took advantage of that advantage. The lesson there is we need to give more American Indians management roles. Instead of teaching the white guys how to handle Indians, let's just hire Indians, to put it bluntly. I think we're coming a long ways, now we have more and more in [the park service]. The trust was always there. It was on the other side, where the trust was lacking. It was the Custer groups [that] wanted nothing to do with Indians. They wanted nothing to do with the Indian stories. In fact, I'm sure you heard the Custer group complained so much about our American Indian interpreters that they went straight to DC. DC sent in a huge training corps of top-notch NPS interpreters, from Harpers Ferry and from other areas. And they taught my crew how to talk. I got really upset about that because they were young. Most of them had gone to my house [after work]. And they would say, "What should we do? They don't know how to do this." I would tell them, just listen to them. Play the damn game, I said, but you know that the reason I hired you was to take your stories that you heard from your grandpa, that fought in this damn battle, and to educate these white people. That was my role.

Now you have to understand [the regular] visitors coming in, a lot of them, loved the stories by the Indian kids. They loved the way we interpreted that. But it was the other side. They decide what they're going to do is try to find fault. What they kept telling DC about me as superintendent is I was trying to change the story. In fact, the story wasn't being changed; the story was being added onto by the tribes in such a way that the average visitor had never heard before. They've heard from the Crow side. But the Crow were with the army; they were the scouts. A lot of the tribes didn't like that. And so that became part of our interpretation too. Why did the Crows become scouts? Why were the Arikaras scouts? They were enemies against the Cheyenne and Sioux. That was hard from a tribal standpoint.

The first time I got the tribal leaders together, that was a real challenging meeting. Because we were talking about NAGPRA repatriation [of] the bodies that we were finding—pieces of bones and so forth. Because that whole area was a battlefield, how do we interpret that? So that was an area that I utilized to bring the tribes together. Because you have to find some point where you all agree or disagree. The agreement that everybody made—I don't care if there were so called enemy tribes or not—in that meeting in my office, is that we have to do something respectfully, for the bones of the deceased in that battle.

So, we all got together in this case, and we went away from NPS protocol. I hope that doesn't sound negative. They brought their pipes with them. And myself, I'm a pipe holder. And so, I took my pipe as well. At certain times when things would get so hot and heavy, so heated, we would stop and take the pipes and use them. And we would pray. And you're not going to find any park service meeting that does that. I'm hoping now you do. Because more and more tribes are involved. So that really helped us out because we still had disagreements. We will always have disagreements because, number one, we're enemy tribes. Number two, we're human beings. But I would be extremely honest with them and lay it on the line. If I didn't understand something, I would say that. I would even get a little upset with them sometimes. But I could do that as an Indian male. They understood that. I also had a sweat lodge down there. I wouldn't use that to bribe anybody, but I used it for my own prayer. But they would be invited down there. I had the holder of the Sacred Hat from Cheyenne down there one night. The next night I had a [NPS] regional director down there.

So that was used, and I think it brought us all together as well. All of these things helped. I think what helped the most was really frank communication. I had a very good relationship with the president of Pine Ridge, with the Northern Cheyenne Chairman, with the Assiniboines. It was really good. There's a give and take. And as an Indian Superintendent, you have to have the ability to say no to some of these folks, too. Because we're all human; we like to take advantage. If they don't respect you then, they'll respect you a little more in the future. It happened a couple times. We just couldn't do things. But that was that relationship that we started in the park service—the back and forth.

MH: Just listening to what you were sharing. It sounded like the focus was on listening in the beginning. You talked about inviting people in once trust was established, presumably to the parks and then to share their stories. Does that seem like the right sequence: listening, building trust, and then inviting folks in?

GB: Yeah, of course, they're almost simultaneous. Because you don't want to wait too long. As soon as I got there [to a park], I would invite people in. If I saw an Indian family out there, I was one of the first ones to go greet them. I remember at Mount Rushmore, I was the first American Indian superintendent there. The first Indian family I saw there, I went out and I was all excited to greet them. Because some people told me, especially some of the relatives, they would say you're never gonna see Indians up there. So, the first Indians I saw there was this family. I went over there shook hands with them and we were visiting and visiting away. All the sudden, this older man—must have been the grandfather—he looked at me and he said, "So what do you do here?"

I said "I'm the boss. I'm the superintendent." Oh, they all started laughing. They just bust out laughing. The old guy said, "No, really. What do you do here?" (laughter)

MH: (laughter)

GB: Oh, I had a fun time. That was my usual reaction. I actually took those folks to my office to prove it. Which was great. But anyway, they still have some kind of feelings towards that park. Little Bighorn, we all know that the truth there is simple. It was a simple battle. Mount Rushmore is a little bit different. Mount Rushmore is extremely philosophical.

MH: Right.

GB: And extremely heart wrenching as to what happened.

MH: Right.

GB: And so for a long time, I didn't blame the tribes if they didn't want to come back. But I'm gonna leave the door open for them. When they did start coming back, we had more and more families coming in there. I would sit out on the front area, and I would watch, especially some of the old ladies. Nobody around hardly. Just their family. And they would look up at those four presidents and they would cry. I would watch them, discreetly of course.

And later on, I would walk around them and I'd finally see them. Of course, they'd be fine by that time, looking at the other things. A lot of times I've managed to get these ladies sitting down and I would start visiting with them in my uniform, obviously. And it got to a point where I could actually say, I saw you here a while ago. Why did you cry? And the answer was really astonishing.

I thought, they're gonna say because they lost land. Understandably. Because they lost a freedom of the land, understandably. What they told me was interesting. Nine out of ten would say, because they lost somebody in Vietnam or the Gulf War. Because Mount Rushmore is associated with the military, that's what they saw.[1] When I thought about a point of agreement, that was one for Mount Rushmore. That was one that could get people back. Because we've always been warriors, Indian people, Indian men, and Indian women now too. Rather than fight the enemy here, we had to join the military and fight the enemy abroad. And we still earn credit that way. We still earn feathers and earn horses. It's a very deep-seated emotion.

MH: Right.

GB: So, when tribes come there, that is what they see. Especially the women because they lost husbands. They lost sons. They lost grandsons. That's how they look at Mount Rushmore. The other way, of course, is that they don't like it because they were kicked out basically. My first activity there to try to get the Indian tribes back in was to put up a teepee right in front of the Mount Rushmore. Didn't say a thing. I told my staff, "Hey, let's put up a teepee." I had a really good staff. So, we put up a teepee. In fact, I was up there one day, and I was raising heck with it, trying to adjust some poles. I had a couple people come by pretty soon. About 10 minutes later I had about 15 people there. About 20 minutes later I had over 150 people there.

So, I gave them a program about teepees and the Black Hills and the tribes and what it stood for. They loved it. So, I went from there to actually getting some folks from Pine Ridge. I hired two of the Okichita members. Okichita is a traditional policeman's society for the Lakota Sioux. These guys were AIMers.[2] Do you know what AIMers are?

MH: Yeah, yeah.

GB: These guys were AIMers. I had dealt with them one night at Fort Union. I was there preventing them from cutting fences and so forth. But I knew these guys, so I hired them. In the end, it was really good. We put up four teepees right by the faces. And we used to keep track [of] how many people visited there. We had over a million visits in those teepees.

MH: Wow.

GB: So, it was very popular. When I left, they took the damn things down—excuse my language . . . Anyway, they changed it. People don't understand. I had Akichita members speaking at Mount Rushmore. These were the old AIMers. They were mean looking sons of a gun, I can tell you that. (laughter)

MH: (laughter)

GB: It was so funny because they were so nice. They'd answer your questions and always wear the uniform. I told them, you guys got to wear this uniform. And they were really good. Really, really good. In fact, if you ever look at Ken Burns, his National Park series, his section on Rushmore, they have one of the boys giving a program. I think it's really good.

I guess the bottom line is when you hire qualified people and when their people see them, they're going to say, "Hey, look at this!" So, people want to go see their relatives and it goes from there. I was always very open with people. I would tell them, don't be afraid to tell what you want to tell. It's history. It's fact. And then I told the same thing at Little Big Horn. No matter where I went, especially with Lewis and Clark. Because I think, they were so used to having the government tell them, "Well, you can't go negative or you can't say this, you can't say that." For years, we were regulated like that. So, we're used to that. I tried to open that door. And I'm hoping they're still opening that door to open interpretation.

MH: Cool. That's good. Brooke, do you have a follow up question?

Brooke Neely (BN): You mentioned that educating the public on how to listen was challenging, because we don't know how to do that. And the NPS rangers, in many ways, they're just trained to speak, right? So how do you flip that? I was curious what you think, how do you get rangers to listen?

GB: Two different ways. One of the ways is Native employment. The other way is to bring in tribes as teachers. So why is the park service still having white teachers trained, especially about Native things? You want to start infiltrating your teaching cadre, if you will, with qualified American Indian speakers and teachers. You tell those teachers, you need to teach my staff how to tell the story. That's very important, because there's some things that we believe that the non-Indian should not be saying. As an example, I got upset one time because I saw a young non-Indian lady speaking about the pipe and she was holding a pipe. Traditionally, the women are not supposed to do that. And so, the only realistic way to do it is to bring Indian speakers. That means you have to convince the park service higher ups to do that. Where's your best interpretive training, supposedly? That's Harpers Ferry interpretive center. I've been there many times getting trained on how to interpret. [What] I told my staff one time at the Little Big Horn is that they're teaching you how to speak white. What we have to do is go in and teach them how to speak Indian, in the interpretive sense because of the multiracial audiences nowadays. And to tell the story correctly. But that's improbable because that's got to come from the higher-ups. I don't think the park service is going to do that yet. I wish they would but there's nobody on staff, even in the Washington office. And that has not been pushed yet because we're scared to, I think.

BN: It'd be nice if Deb Haaland and Charles F. Sams, the new director, had some sway.

GB: I'm hoping that makes a difference. Because they're gonna be busy putting out fires. Especially Deb Haaland. That was a big conversation when she first [got appointed]. We were so excited in Indian country. "Oh, now she can do this. And this and this." Somebody finally wrote, "Hey, folks, wait a minute. She's got all these fires to put out. She can't work miracles." It's got to start in multiple locations, including your park, including the regional offices, including Washington. It's going to take a long time. Unless we get people hired in some of those positions.

BN: Well, that's helpful. Thank you. And it would be great to ask a little bit about what you were suggesting, Matthew, in terms of the kind of the opportunities and benefits from doing this kind of work.

MH: That's a good question. What, from your perspective, do you see as the biggest opportunities or benefits to working with tribal partners?

GB: I think that obviously, the benefits are many—learning the history of the park, adding in stories that have not been done before, or correcting the stories you've done. For example, if from an interpretation standpoint, they can add stories, like creation stories. But [they must] understand when they can tell those stories, understand the protocol. Another obvious advantage is natural resources. I think a lot of tribes have a very strong natural resource program that they can bring into the parks and [provide] that view. For example, in Montana here, Yellowstone has been giving buffalo out to some of the tribes. But I hear grumblings about that here in Miles City, about how those Indians are getting free things again. And so, again, that means to me that the interpretation hasn't been up to par. We haven't sat down and said, "Okay, folks, this is what's going on." The advantage of open communication as that fellow said, and bringing in the tribal perspective to your park, which maybe was their land at one time. Maybe they had a village there. Maybe they had other things they could share. To me, the advantage of that is in management, including youth organizations. Getting a tribe involved to educate their youth, and maybe getting them talking about future employment. That's all possibilities.

MH: Right. So, it sounds like part of it is educating visitors, white visitors, maybe who weren't familiar with Native history of parks and correcting erroneous stories. And also bringing in the tribal perspective.

GB: I think that's very important. Because I think as human beings, if we're going to hear a story, we expect to hear one story. Well, if you have multiple perspectives, which is a common theme nowadays, you hold multiple stories. That doesn't mean they're incorrect or that one is above the other. That means they're all correct. We as the public and national parks sometimes have a really hard time understanding that. That's what I mean as far as how to understand and how to listen. One thing I always think about when I see Indian seasonal [workers] is their sense of humor. People aren't used to that. Especially for rangers. We're kind of stoic. So, I think the humor is really important, really important. Anyway, there's a whole educational process that needs to happen in order for all this stuff to be successful. And it's gonna take a long time.

BN: You invested yourself in this sort of work from the inside. So, my assumption is, you see it as very valuable. But have you met with folks from tribal nations, when you went to council meetings, who said, it's just not worth it to us to work with national parks?

GB: Oh yeah, I think almost everybody says that, Brooke. I think almost everybody feels it when you come in, but you don't stop. You have to convince them of who you are, meaning who the park is and what the park is. Especially [if] there's history there. If somebody says, "No, I don't wanna mess with you guys. You guys are too big. And you have your own story." What I emphasize at that point, is I open that door and challenge them. If you have another story, come and tell it. Let's educate these people. Otherwise, they're going to go away with the same attitude and incorrect answers. So, you challenge that committee if they say go away. Challenge them to come and see what they know about that place. It may be they don't know much.

Again, Knife River. Our people were there forever. And then we left in 1837 because of smallpox. We hadn't been back since. When I first got to Knife River, there was hardly any Indian people coming to visit there. In fact, I heard about Knife River all my early life on the reservation. And we never went to see it. I was the only one to work at Knife River from the tribe. I realized after a while why we never had Indian people visit. Number one, we never invited them. And number two, because of the strength of oral history and the incredible devastation that we experienced in 1837. There was still a fear of getting smallpox. Now think about that one.

MH: Hmm . . .

GB: To me, that's incredible. Because of what oral history recorded. That's incredible. I started working there in 1977, a brand-new national park. Our people were scared to go because they thought . . . The old ladies, when I first went home, they smudged me and they prayed and they gave me hell. They said,

"Don't you ever pick anything up from Knife River and bring it home. You're going to bring smallpox to us." This was in 1977, guys. Think about the power of those words. Think about the power of that interpretation. Nowadays if we hear that, who's gonna understand that. Those are the kinds of stories, the feelings, the philosophies, if you will, that I want to get into the park service from American Indian people. To have non-Indians understand because that just adds to the story.

BN: Yeah, thank you.

MH: You talked about the squeaky wheel of groups like the Custer society and the Mount Rushmore society. How did you deal with the squeaky wheel? Because that seems to be related to the benefits and also some of the challenges of telling these kinds of stories.

GB: I think that was definitely a challenge. In both places I dealt with it head on. And in some cases, I probably shouldn't have because that squeaky wheel included some of the leaders from the park service in DC. Maybe they didn't understand what I was trying to do as I look back on it now. Maybe that's where I didn't approach it correctly. I should have approached more from an understanding [position] rather than, "Okay sucker, let's fight." Sometimes I won; sometimes I didn't win. But the fight went way beyond the borders of that park.

Let's look again at Rushmore. That fight included most of South Dakota because there's a deep split there I believe between Indians and whites in South Dakota. I could handle that battle inside the park boundaries. That's no problem. I had a good staff that could handle that. It was on the outside. Both sides needed to come together, and they did not. They did not. How do you get two races talking after hundreds of years of non-communication, hundreds of years of broken treaties. That makes a difference. That makes a big difference in how we communicate on both sides.

MH: Right.

GB: I have people come to me and tell me in different locations, including Rushmore, and put their finger almost on my chest. Because I wouldn't allow them to test me. But they would say, "I gotta tell you that you have too damn many Indians here." How do you handle that from a management standpoint? How do you handle that individual because that is part of your management? [You have to] understand that this guy is not going to change. That person is always going to have that theory. And all you can do is make your programs the best you can make them. That's all you can do.

At first, I had people come in and talk to me in my office. They would say, "Well, we know that you don't have an education. We know that you only went to high school. We know you got this job because you're an Indian." I got that a lot of times. Now, you have two choices. First choice is that you get madder than hell, and act like that. Second choice is I would educate them. I would sit down and explain my degrees. I have three degrees. I would explain what they're in and what schools I went to. So, for me as American Indian superintendent, that was part of my management. That's the negative part, but it's part of management. It's something you can't avoid as an American Indian superintendent. Because you get questioned no matter where you're at.

MH: Yeah.

GB: But there's a lot of challenges when you start thinking about that. Even among your staff because you still have to communicate to your staff. As an American Indian superintendent, I had to know twice as much as my staff in their own individual areas.

MH: I think this leads naturally into our next question. What's the best way to engage people in difficult conversations? Could [you] talk a little bit more from your perspective on these kind of really challenging problem at parks with pragmatic histories, like Mount Rushmore, the Little Bighorn Battlefield, and the Lewis and Clark trail?

GB: The best way to engage I found is obviously don't get personal but get real. Don't hem-haw around. That's one thing I learned early on. And if you make a mistake, you make a mistake. And as a government official, do not be afraid to say I'm sorry. [To say] I didn't do this right. I'll do this right next time. We'll do it together. But the biggest issue there is to not try to save face. Show them you're human but not weak. That was [true] for me on both sides of the fence—the Indian and the white side. I'll say this as a manager, the white folks can be pretty blunt. I'm not being negative here. Indians can be the most blunt. Indians can be wide open. They can put you down immediately. And you can't let them do that. You've got to come right back. The first time I met Russell Means, for example, him and I looked like two roosters trying to fight. (laughter)

MH: (laughter)

GB: And we turned out to be good friends. You know, we're both sitting there squared off at each other. He was gonna throw a punch and I was gonna throw a punch. I told myself, man, I grew up on the rez. I grew up fighting. Let's go for it. And he wouldn't do it. I'm not recommending superintendents do that. (laughter)

MH: (laughter)

GB: But I'm just saying that worked for me at that time. But I did grow up on the rez. Once he knew that, we became damn good friends. We really did. He called me a couple of times. And we talked about parks. He would get really mad. And I'd say, "Well, you can get mad all you want. This is what's going on." But he was really good that way. Anyway, it's open communication and that's hard. I talk like it's easy. That's damn hard to do. Especially if you've got somebody so damn mad that they're sitting in front of you crying.

BN: Yeah . . . Well, at some point I had a meeting where a tribal representative said, "I just have heartburn working with the park service." And it was such a meaningful way of describing it. Does engaging with difficult conversations also involve trying to get more comfortable with being uncomfortable? Or being with people who are angry?

GB: Not at all. That's one of the most honest emotions you can have. That's a truthful emotion. There's no BS about that. You need to learn how to work with it for the benefit of both. The first thing you want to do is find out why. Maybe there's heartburn because there's too many policies. There's too much regulation. Then you ask, what will make it better? And if they say, we got to get rid of ARPA (The Archaeological Resources Protection Act)—well, we can't do that. That's just the way it's gonna be. We're gonna have ARPA, so you're gonna have heartburn when you deal with us. (laughter)

BN: (laughter)

GB: I've had that happen. And I'm sure they were mad at me, but I couldn't change it. That's why you need to know more than the average person because then you have to go into why that particular law or policy is important to the park service. Sometimes even if you don't believe it. I've been at meetings saying, "I don't even believe this you guys. I wouldn't want this to happen, but we have it in law. We have no choice." And we all go into it with a negative feeling. But how will we make it work for us?

BN: Yeah, I think you used the term sticking with it.

GB: Yeah.

BN: Sometimes for non-Native folks trying to do this work, there can be an impulse to try to fix it. Because you're in an uncomfortable situation and you want to get out of it.

GB: One thing we're doing that we have to get out of completely, is we're taking it personally. We can't take it personally. That's Park Service policy. That's not

Brooke's policy, or Gerard's policy. I understand that we [can] take it personally because that's the job we have, and we love the job. But again, you have to understand how to manage. And once you find that out, a lot of your heartache goes away. That's one thing I didn't find out for a long time. I didn't find that out until I had my first stroke. Then I finally found it out and thought, what the hell am I doing. I should approach it differently.

BN: Hmm . . . And differently meaning?

GB: Differently, meaning understanding where that person was coming from. Understanding where I was coming from with laws and policies. And where I was coming from as [an] individual and how to make that all work. which I didn't do.

BN: Boy, you did a lot of amazing things. Just listening to you . . . Oh my goodness.

GB: It was fun. It was interesting.

BN: Yeah. You began your superintendency in an era where a lot of people put a lot of expectations on you. Like you would have the power to make so many changes. But then the national politics changed.

GB: I think so. Everybody hit me at Rushmore. The first one to talk about me in the paper was an American Indian woman. She didn't know what I was like, but she called me the first Indian Santa Claus.[3] That's how I was described at Mount Rushmore. Because I was the first one. How do you take that? That's what was positive for me, because both sides were giving me hell, not just one side. Which means I was doing a good job.

BN: Yeah, and you harnessed it, right?

GB: I think so. I hope so. But there's a lot more to learn. And the generations are getting more open now. I noticed with my own kids in college, they're getting wide open. Which means that they're not scared. They're speaking the truth and they're not caring. Whereas, we had too much care back in the old days. We didn't want to hurt anybody.

BN: It's like a hunger like with my students. When I start sharing information related to this, they want to know why they aren't getting more of this information.

GB: Right. Look at the park service. It has not changed, when it comes to the park service in DC. They're trying to change in parks. For example, Knife River has had the first Indians superintendent. They're trying to change in places, which is really good. But DC, Harpers Ferry, FLETC (Federal Law Enforcement Training Center), and I went to all those places, they have to change. Because the top interpretive centers or training centers in the park service haven't changed. When I went to FLETC, it was fun. You learned little things like how to get speeders and arrest [people] and fight. But nowadays those guys come out of there and they are cops. I mean cops. And that's not how rangers are supposed to be.

It's the time. It's the community. I really stress that because that's what's happening in the community. If we had rangers like me from the old days, shit, we wouldn't survive right now. There's too many bad guys out there. It's the community runs the park, primarily. It [creates] the whole atmosphere. And if the community doesn't like what you're doing, you have a fight on your hands. But you still got to run the park. You still got to tell those stories. At the same time, you fight. So, you have two different arenas—the political and the park.

BN: It's a lot to take on. There's the whole weight of history and this larger social climate. It must wear on you.

GB: Oh hell, yeah. It wears on you. In many different ways. But you can't let your staff or the public know that. So, you gotta deal with that too, personally. There's that part of the management in these tough areas that we need to consider too. Because if you're tough, your [health] is not going to last. But if you're weak, you're not going to last either.

BN: It must feel good to be in Montana now?

GB: Oh, it feels great. But I'm still involved. My brother Paige, who has also [retired from] the park service, and I just got hired by the tribe to put together a park at home. They bought a three-thousand-acre unit of an old ranch that we're going to turn into a primitive park. We're putting the emphasis on natural resources. [We're creating] a foundation for kids almost like the Black Canyon in Crow. I want to establish a kid-based program for natural resources and culture. So, I've still got my hands in here, there. But it's great. It's great to be out of it. Especially, since they've been getting me to do different things. I just finished up a program with the park service on Native American month. And I was the narrator for a panel. But I just found that once they know you're available, boy, you start getting called. (laughter)

MH: (laughter) You gotta have an unlisted phone number.

GB: (laughter) Gotta learn how to say no, gracefully. You want to give them the best thing. But you can't always do it.

BN: Well, thank you for saying yes to us.

MH: Thank you, Gerard. We so much appreciate your time. It's always really enjoyable to speak with you.

GB: Alright, guys. Thank you.

Notes

1. Mount Rushmore National Memorial's patriotic qualities make it a popular destination for military families. Given the high rate of military service among American Indians in the United States, Mount Rushmore is a destination for Native veterans and their families.
2. Members of the American Indian Movement also known as AIM.
3. Santa Claus is a derogatory reference to Gerard Baker's role as the Superintendent of Mount Rushmore—seen by many Natives as primarily a destination for white Americans. By taking on this role, Baker sought to add complexity to the predominantly Euro-American narratives about the site.

FIVE | Historicizing the "Shrine of Democracy"
Lakota Perspectives on Mount Rushmore in
the Context of the Black Hills

MATTHEW J. HILL

IN 2015, THE NATIONAL PARK SERVICE (NPS) kicked off the Mount Rushmore ethnographic overview and assessment (EOA) as part of an extended effort to provide greater historical context to the monument. The NPS EOA followed in the wake of a 2013 Organization of American Historians–sponsored consultation at the memorial with the western historians Jeffrey Ostler and Anne Hyde. The latter emphasized the need for the NPS to historicize Mount Rushmore National Memorial by giving the monument's own history and politics more serious attention. Along these lines, the EOA sought to provide Native perspectives on Mount Rushmore by consulting directly with tribal nations affiliated with Mount Rushmore and the Black Hills. This was in keeping with the purpose of an EOA, which is to document the Native perspectives and cultural meanings that are associated with a site where a "traditional" community has had a longstanding presence.[1] Yet, this proved difficult in the sense that Mount Rushmore represents a form of "negative heritage" for the Lakota, Cheyenne, and Arapaho communities, a contested site that becomes the repository of a "negative memory" in the collective imagination.[2] Specifically, as described in this chapter, Native peoples associate Mount Rushmore with a legacy of Euro-American conquest, genocide, and broken treaties (specifically, the Fort Laramie Treaties of 1851 and 1868). These negative associations made it difficult for Euro-American researchers to conduct the ethnographic portion of this study.

The Lakota Holy Man Lame Deer captured the painful memory that Mount Rushmore represents to the Lakota and other Native people. In the wake of the American Indian Movement's 1970 protest at Mount Rushmore, he noted, "This [Mount Rushmore] is what conquering means. They could have just as well carved this mountain into a huge cavalry boot standing on a dead Indian."[3] One western historian underlined this perspective, describing the purpose of Mount Rushmore as to "erase and replace."[4] With its carvings of the four presidents, Mount Rushmore engages in processes of Indigenous erasure by desecrating a sacred landscape and refocusing the tourist gaze on the heroic exploits of Gutzon Borglum and his crew of miners. In this respect, it is a monument to the "American Way" and a "can do" attitude in a "somatological, visual, and consumable form."[5] Yet in a deeper sense, Mount Rushmore is a celebration of the "pioneer spirit" of the early miners who invaded the Black Hills seeking gold in the aftermath of General George Custer's 1874 Black Hills expedition. Acknowledging this larger purpose, Borglum referred to Mount Rushmore as a shrine to western expansion. In doing so, he mythologized the four presidents as "empire builders" who played important roles in the "founding, preservation, and expansion" of the United States.[6]

Given this history of erasure, I consulted with a variety of Native and non-Native historians and anthropologists on how to frame the ethnographic research required for the project in ways that would be sensitive to Native concerns. At the suggestion of the Plains anthropologist Patricia C. Albers, who authored a magisterial study of Wind Cave National Park (2003), I (together with my ethnographic collaborator, Christina Gish Hill) decided to focus the ethnographic portion of the study on Natives' "sociocultural connections" to the Black Hills. This entailed steering conversations away from sacred sites. Instead, we focused on the types of ongoing activities that gave rise to a sense of present-day connectedness or attachment to the Black Hills. We began conversations with Native collaborators by soliciting their views about the Black Hills, the associations that they held with them, and the types of activities (e.g., working in tourism, recreational visits, family memories, foraging activities) that formed the basis of those associations. Only after these initial conversations did we turn to the more painful topic of tourism development and its impacts on the Black Hills, including at sites like Mount Rushmore. We concluded by seeking Native collaborators' input on how they would like the interpretation of Mount Rushmore to change, whether through improved access, tribal involvement in educational programs, or other efforts to create more inclusive or historically accurate narratives.

To acknowledge the legacy of this difficult past, we also followed the advice that was given to us by Joe Watkins (Choctaw Nation of Oklahoma), the former head of the NPS Park Ethnography Program. Rather than skirt the problematic history of Mount Rushmore, he recommended that we "use the monument as a conversation starter" to discuss "what happened in the past," and how the creation of Mount Rushmore was "perceived by Native Americans."[7] We also followed the advice of former Native superintendent of Mount Rushmore

Gerard Baker (Mandan-Hidatsa), who had ignited controversy when he established the Lakota, Nakota, and Dakota Heritage Village, a site of three teepees where Native interpreters told the pre-carving history of the lands that would become Mount Rushmore. Like Watkins, he advised us to not steer away from controversy. "Controversy," as he put it, "isn't negative. It changes things." Having frank conversations about troubling histories, as he had promoted during his tenure, helps to "challenge official narratives, historicize the past, and not leave Indians standing on the sidelines."[8]

In addition to receiving Institutional Review Board (IRB) approval at our home universities, we also solicited the input of Lakota, Northern Cheyenne, and Southern Cheyenne & Arapaho tribal review boards on how best to conduct the research among tribal members. Before the meetings, we submitted a copy of our research proposal, outlining the purpose of the project, the principal research questions, and the proposed project outcomes. As previously noted, we emphasized that we planned to focus on the everyday uses of and general views about Mount Rushmore and the Black Hills so as not to interfere with secret or ceremonial knowledge. At Pine Ridge, the research review board approved the Mount Rushmore ethnography project and regarded it positively. The review board members liked the fact that we sought to conduct interviews with knowledgeable elders about the Black Hills, and to make their views known at Mount Rushmore. The cultural committees at the Southern Cheyenne and Arapaho tribes were similarly supportive. A staff reporter from the Southern Cheyenne and Arapaho Tribal Tribune even published an article about Christina Gish Hill's research in Indianz.com, noting that one of the goals of the project was to gain "perspectives from the Tribes to present to the NPS for resource management."[9]

Due to the broad scope of the research, I focused on Lakota perspectives on Mount Rushmore while Christina Gish Hill (this volume) concentrated on Cheyenne and Arapaho points of view. This chapter represents a first step in recognizing Native perspectives, laying the foundation for subsequent conversations. It shows how Native participants both historicized the site and reasserted Lakota perspectives as part of a broader sacred landscape that encompassed the entirety of the Black Hills. First, it describes three painful aspects of Mount Rushmore: the fact that the memorial desecrated the sacred ground of the Black Hills, glorified four presidents whose policies were detrimental toward Natives, and limited Indigenous peoples' access to the sacred landscape surrounding Mount Rushmore. The chapter, then, turns to the way in which Lakota collaborators reasserted Lakota understandings of Mount Rushmore in the context of the Black Hills, by highlighting how the Hills formed the heart or center of the universe, served as a ceremonial complex, and provided a storied landscape, encoding important moral lessons. The chapter ends with a discussion of repair work, exploring Lakota perspectives on how the problem of Indigenous erasure might be addressed at Mount Rushmore—by making the site more reflective about its own history and providing much needed historical context about its creation.

Lakota Views of Mount Rushmore

Lakota perspectives on Mount Rushmore do the important work of disrupting the memory landscape that exists for white visitors. They critically challenge its construction amid the sacred Black Hills—the heart of Sioux territory—and the highly symbolic view (propagated at the site) of the presidents as benign "founding fathers" of the nation. They also take issue with its interpretative focus, on the carving of the mountain and the four presidents, by highlighting the violence involved in the taking of the Black Hills. In this respect, the Lakota commentary on Mount Rushmore disrupts the site's sculptor's (Gutzon Borglum) narrative of the memorial as a "Shrine of Democracy" by invoking the forms of official forgetting that the site sanctions. These unquestioned assumptions about Mount Rushmore were challenged through a threefold focus on: the creation of the site as a desecration of sacred ground, the genocidal policies of the presidents towards Native peoples and their lands, and the regulated nature of the environment at the monument itself.[10]

Mount Rushmore as Desecration

Lakota participants repeatedly described Mount Rushmore as a desecration of sacred ground. The Lakota environmental activist Charmaine White Face captured the painful, traumatic sentiments that many Lakota feel about Mount Rushmore when she noted that creating the site in the center of the Black Hills was like carving "a monument to Hitler right in the middle of Jerusalem."[11] The great grandson of the Lakota chief Sitting Bull, Ernie La Pointe, similarly compared the carving of Mount Rushmore to "someone going into a Catholic church or synagogue or Mormon temple with a can of spray paint and spraying images on it."[12] Reflecting a concern that park managers at Mount Rushmore were not truly interested in hearing Native perspectives about the site, the Lakota educator Jace DeCory suggested that I interview people from the Mount Rushmore Society about their point of view.[13]

Jace Decory went on to recount her recollection of an editorial in the *Rapid City Journal* published during Mount Rushmore Superintendent Gerard Baker's tenure, in which some Society members stated what they understood to be the purpose of Mount Rushmore: "We're not here to tell the Native Story but the American story about what made America great."[14] Similarly, Karen Little Thunder (Rosebud Sioux) viewed Mount Rushmore as a place that propagates a lot of "racial hatred."[15] Given the fact that many tribal educators take field trips of elementary school children there, she wondered how they could incorporate it into their curriculums, since it might be difficult for Lakota youth to see themselves represented in the site. She then added, "As much as we hate it, we are stuck with it, the presidential quotes and all." Ernie La Pointe summarized the painful past that Mount Rushmore represents for many Lakota when he pointed out that "the guy [Gutzon Borglum] who carved Mount Rushmore was a grand wizard of the Ku Klux Klan," adding, "I think he did it [the carving] just to spite the Natives."[16]

Lakota participants also expressed concern about the impact that Mount Rushmore's creation, and ongoing development activities, had on degrading the environment. Commenting on the creation of Mount Rushmore, Jace DeCory stated: "You don't blow up relatives," referring to Gutzon Borglum's use of dynamite to carve the presidents out of the granite cliffs at Mount Rushmore. "The Six Grandfathers [the Lakota name for the mountain] were already beautiful." DeCory distinguished, in this regard, between the Lakota relationship to the environment as a "living being" or "relative," and that of settlers, who viewed the environment as a resource that could be exploited for human consumption. Sandra Woodard (Oglala Lakota), an educator and environmental activist, described Mount Rushmore's negative environmental impact, stating: "A lot of us don't like it because there's too much cement, asphalt. We don't believe in covering up Mother Earth with that kind of substance. It just kind of destroys her.... We see it as a desecration of the environment." The use of cement, together with the lax attitude towards drilling leases in the Black Hills, resulted in "the destruction of a delicate ecosystem" that contained healing plants and herbs used by the Lakota for traditional medicines.[17]

Lakota people also emphasized the spiritual nature of Mount Rushmore before it was carved. Charlotte Black Elk (the great-granddaughter of the Lakota holy man Nicholas Black Elk) connected the sacredness of Mount Rushmore to Lakota cosmology and its location in the peaks of the Harney Range.[18] When I asked her how the Lakota perceived sites like Mount Rushmore, she stated: "When you look at our cosmology, we have a site called Tayamnipa. And it is the Pleiades, six principal stars with a seventh one in the middle. And that middle one is Harney Peak. Rushmore was built on one of those peaks of that circle. So, we view that as a desecration."

In invoking Tayamnipa, the head star of the seven stars that form the Pleiades constellation, Charlotte Black Elk refers to the belief that those seven stars mirror seven peaks in the Harney Range, the highest of which is Black Elk Peak (previously Harney Peak), and one of which is Mount Rushmore (known to many Lakota as Six Grandfathers Mountain, Tunkasila Sakpe Paha). In commenting on the correspondence between the stars and peaks in the Harney Range, she wrote: "When the Sun is aligned with the Tayamnipa, Principles of the Three Bodies, we are among the Grandfathers [the Black Elk Range]. The leaves of the shielding tree that whispers, the aspen, are now the size of a thumbnail. We travel to *Opaha Ta I*, Mountain at the Center Where He Comes, and welcome the thunders back for another season of renewal."[19]

When the sun aligns with Tayamnipa during the spring solstice, the Lakota travel to Black Elk Peak, in the Black Elk Range, for the "Welcoming Back the

Thunders" ceremony. This celebration greets the Wakinyan, powerful creator/destroyer figures that manifest themselves through thunder and lightning, preparing all creation for the welcoming back of new life.[20] The fact that Mount Rushmore is one of the peaks that correspond to the seven stars of the Pleiades constellation places it in a location that has sacred significance for the Lakota.[21]

Shortcomings of the Four Presidents

A second set of concerns that Lakota collaborators raised had to do with the narratives about the four presidents immortalized at the site—George Washington, Thomas Jefferson, Abraham Lincoln, and Theodore Roosevelt. Lakota challenged one-sided narratives about the presidents, which overlooked the impact that their policies had on Native peoples. In doing so, they countered celebrations of westward expansion. Rather than mythologize the four presidents as "empire builders," who, in sculptor Gutzon Borglum's words, played important roles in the "founding, preservation, and expansion" of the United States, they pointed to the presidents' involvement in the genocide of Native peoples. Specific critiques targeted each of the four presidents, undermining Borglum's rationale for including them in the so-called "Shrine of Democracy": Washington's contribution as the nation's "founder" and "first statesman"; Jefferson's efforts, as the "first expansionist," to incorporate the Central West into the United States through the Louisiana purchase; Lincoln's designation as the "nation's savior" for eliminating slavery and saving the Union; and Roosevelt's movement onto "the western plains," and securing "commercial control" over the Panama Canal through military intervention.[22]

Lakota raised the general concern that Mount Rushmore paid insufficient attention to the fact that these four presidents participated in the genocide of Native peoples. The Oglala Lakota elder, storyteller, and Red Cloud Indian School language instructor, Philomene Lakota, lamented that visitors to Mount Rushmore wore blinders with respect to the human rights violations perpetuated by these presidents.[23] She talked about how they focused on "the resources they could get" from Indian lands and how they relied on claims of entitlement, encapsulated in the "Doctrine of Discovery," to dispute the Native rights to the soil in the United States. The Lakota elder Sandra Woodard discussed the implications of their land grab: "We feel that those people [the four presidents] who are immortalized in those stones up there were people who were trying to exterminate our people, so we don't view them very respectfully." Mirroring Sandra Woodard's views, Lakota elder Basil Brave Heart referred to Mount Rushmore as a "Shrine of Hypocrisy," playing on Gutzon Borglum's vision of it as a "Shrine of Democracy."[24]

Lakota also emphasized the shortcomings of the four presidents with respect to Native peoples. As Jace Decory commented: "Some people see it [Mount

Rushmore] as affirmative, others see it as ugly art, and still others get political and view the four men up there [the presidents] as all that is dehumanizing. Two of them owned slaves [Washington and Jefferson] and Lincoln hung thirty-eight Dakotas [at Mankato, Minnesota]. Some people talk about those men and the defacing of the rock." Jace DeCory highlighted the specific contradictions of George Washington and Thomas Jefferson, who continued to own slaves while espousing the principles of liberty and equality.[25] Meanwhile, Abraham Lincoln approved the largest one-day, mass execution in US history during the 1862 US-Dakota War, resulting in the hanging of thirty-eight Dakota men at Mankato, Minnesota.[26] Scholarship on the execution has shown that Lincoln acted more out of a concern to stem the discontent of rebellious Minnesotans than to dole out justice to the Dakota who were rendered guilty at a war trial plagued by irregularities.[27] The Lakota educator Victor Douville expanded on concerns relating to the other three presidents, noting that in addition to holding slaves, George Washington also illicitly secured Native lands west of the Appalachian Mountains to which he was not entitled, had them illegally surveyed, and took advantage of his fellow comrades-in-arms.[28] Moreover, Thomas Jefferson seized millions of acres of Native lands west of the Mississippi through the Louisiana Purchase without consulting Indigenous people. Finally, while Theodore Roosevelt set aside land for national forests and national parks, he also authorized the taking of many tribal lands in the process.[29]

Access to Mount Rushmore

Lakota elders expressed frustration at the lack of access to Mount Rushmore and other public lands in the Black Hills for the purposes of gathering plants and herbs or performing sacred ceremonies. One of the most frequently voiced complaints was the high cost of parking at Mount Rushmore. The Oglala Sioux Tribal Council member Mike Her Many Horses found it ludicrous that the Lakota had been illegally kicked out of the Black Hills by the federal government and now were expected to pay the exorbitant entrance fees to visit the park at Mount Rushmore.[30] Jace DeCory similarly noted that the primary reason that the majority of Lakota do not visit Mount Rushmore is that "you have to pay a huge fee to park there." "If you have a big family," she added, "you have to pay for two vehicles."[31] Doug Bissonette, an administrator with the Oglala Sioux Tribe at Pine Ridge, commented that there was a "different feeling" at Crazy Horse Memorial in comparison with Mount Rushmore, especially for the Lakota.[32] Expanding on this, he stated, "You can go to Crazy Horse for free if you are Indian," adding, "You can get a bowl of buffalo stew or an Indian taco, so it is oriented towards the tribes." Free parking and admission, as well as amenities geared towards Native people—food, crafts, books—made a visit to Crazy Horse more welcoming for Lakota people.

Another access issue related to the challenges that tourism posed for harvesting sacred herbs and plants. Jace DeCory talked about how her grandfather, Frank Fools Crow, used to send her to collect bee balm (bergamot or *wahpe wastemna*, sweet-smelling leaf) in the Black Hills for the Sun Dance at Kyle, South Dakota, and to make medicine for their ceremonies. She would also collect the inner bark of the red osier dogwood (or *cansasa* in Lakota) in the springtime when it had more sap in its branches for use as tobacco in pipe ceremonies and smudge offerings.[33] Typically, she would go to NPS or state land to collect these medicines so as "not to get shot" on private lands. Yet even though such plants still grew at Mount Rushmore, she would never go there now to collect them because of the tourists "traipsing through the area."[34] This differed from the cooperative relationship that the Lakota had with the superintendent at Bear Butte State Park, Jim Jandreau, who didn't have a problem with them collecting Native plants, so long as they only took what they needed and didn't pull up the plants. Sandra Woodard similarly discussed how few Lakota harvested plants for ceremonial purposes at Mount Rushmore because of the high levels of security at the site. As she put it: "We certainly don't have much access to Mount Rushmore. . . . It's so guarded, federal and state, that you can't really go up there in freedom and do what you want and participate. . . . So, a lot of our people don't go up there."[35] In other words, the multiple layers of security used to manage the crowds at Mount Rushmore restricted Lakota freedom of movement and discouraged access.

Acquiring the required permits for harvesting traditional plants and performing sacred ceremonies posed another access barrier. Charlotte Black Elk described some of the general challenges that Lakota face in accessing national forest and park lands because of the way legitimate uses have been defined by the federal government. She explained that the US Forest Service "has recreational, preservation, commercial, and resource use as their four missions," but nothing "about cultural use."[36] As a result, when the Lakota seek permission to "go and pray and do a hanbleceya or vision quest near Harney Peak," they have to request a permit.[37] While the Forest Service will try to "slot" such cultural uses into their existing categories, sometimes the Lakota must pay for the permit. Charlotte Black Elk gave the humorous example of a time that she had to pay the Forest Service forty dollars for a permit to conduct a vision quest near Harney Peak, while they let the Hells Angels motorcycle gang conduct a gathering for free. It was only recently that the Lakota were legally allowed go to the Black Hills to pick wild fruit or get medicine. Prior to that time, she noted, one had to "pose as a tourist and sneak in so you could go pray." The development of roads in the Black Hills has also enabled the Lakota to take advantage of what she called the "right of way" to pick choke cherries on Forest Service land, to harvest a piece of sage, or to pick acorn caps at the Council Oak Tree (in Hermosa), which the Lakota believe is the descendent of the first oak tree that grew upon the earth.

Lakota Relationship to the Black Hills

In these discussions about Mount Rushmore, Lakota collaborators reasserted its place in the broader context of the Black Hills. They emphasized that Mount Rushmore wasn't a discrete site, but part of an integrated cultural landscape that formed the center of the Lakota universe. This special relationship to the Black Hills emerged from what anthropologist Tim Ingold refers to as a "dwelling relationship" in which a landscape is defined through an "ontological engagement with the material environment."[38] From this perspective, landscape is not an area embodied in a quantity of acres so much as a "quality of feeling" or "emotional investment."[39] To express this investment, the Lakota used the metaphor of the heart. They also referred to the Black Hills as a sacred altar or ceremonial center, an axis mundi in which ceremonies performed at specific sites create a portal, facilitating transmission between the human and spirit worlds. Finally, they described the Black Hills as a unique memory landscape, in which social and moral values and wisdom are embodied in legends and metaphors associated with specific geographic places.

The Heart of Everything That Is

The metaphor of the heart figured prominently in Lakota discussions of the Black Hills. As Sandra Woodard noted: "The Black Hills have always been important. It's the heart of everything that is. It's a sacred place." Basil Brave Heart echoed this sentiment by referring to the Black Hills as a "hocoka within a hocoka," an altar (hocoka) located in a region that was sacred to the Lakota.[40] Charlotte Black Elk referred to the Black Hills in a similar way, stating: "It's the center of the whole universe and of the earth. And it's a place that from a satellite photograph appears as a heart. And the highest point of that is Harney Peak, now Black Elk Peak." As previously noted, the Lakota name for the Black Hills (Paha Sapa), "the heart of everything that is (Wamaka Og'naka I'Cante)," derives from the Lakota's story of their origins in the Hills. This idea is underscored by a sacred map on a buffalo hide in which the center of the Black Hills appears as a buffalo heart—the heart of the earth-being Maka. More than merely a metaphor, the actual geography of the Black Hills corresponds to this idea, being shaped in the form of a human heart. As Charlotte Black Elk explained, "We always think of a heart as a valentine heart. But if you look at a human or a mammal heart, it has a different shape. And that's how the Black Hills is shaped." In discussing the sacred names of the Black Hills, including Wamaka Og'naka I'Cante (the heart of everything), Hocoka yapi (The Center), or Otiwita (The Sanctuary), Patricia Albers suggests that these terms convey "an intimacy born out of a deep knowledge and experience of the Hills" on the part of a people who had "lived there and been nourished by their presence."[41]

As the "heart of everything that is," the Black Hills emerged as the "penultimate center" of Lakota ritual. As New Holy argues, all Lakota ceremonies,

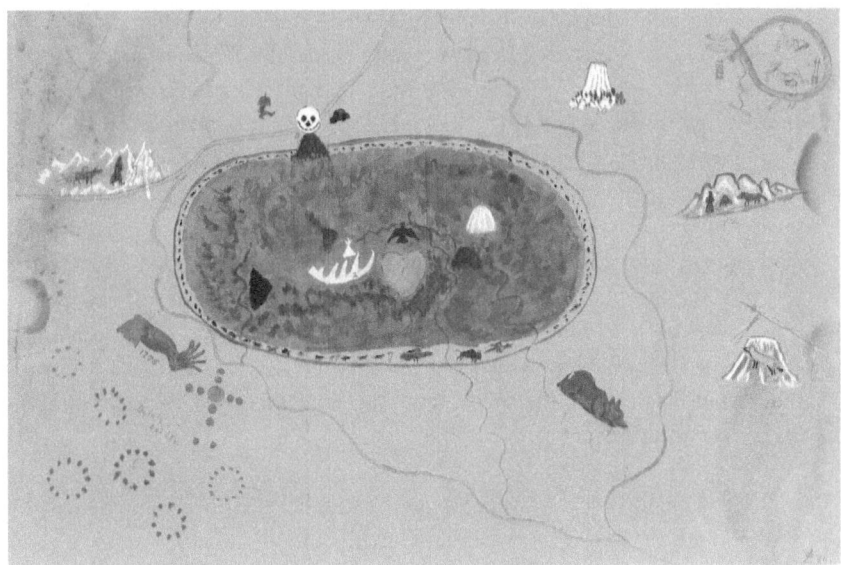

1940s map of the Black Hills. Courtesy of Deadwood History, Inc.

whether the Sun Dance, the sweat lodge, or the sacred pipe, seek to unify the Lakota nation by taking the ritual practitioner on a journey, both spiritually and physically, back to the Black Hills.[42] Lakota representatives were to make such pilgrimages to the Black Hills at least once every seven years to perform ceremonies that would renew and regenerate both the world and the Lakota people.[43]

An Integrated Ceremonial Complex

Lakota elders emphasized the importance of the Black Hills as an integrated ceremonial center. Victor Douville succinctly captured this notion by referring to the Black Hills as a "giant temple with all of the important shrines of worship within."[44] Similarly, Sandra Woodard, in discussing the ceremonial significance of the Black Hills, stated, "We [the Lakota] didn't live in the Black Hills. It's a place where we went and worshipped. . . . People would come from long distances to this area."[45]

Victor Douville further elaborated on how the Lakota participated in this ceremonial complex by going on a pilgrimage taking place between the first day of spring and the summer solstice. He described this pilgrimage in an interview:

> When the sun enters Cansasa Ipusye, the Dried Willow constellation, which is made up of [the constellations] Aires and Triangulum . . . we drag the inner bark of the [red] willow and make tobacco and load the pipes and smoke [during] the ceremony of the vernal equinox. And then thirty days later, we travel to the Black Hills, where the sun enters . . .

[the] Pleiades [constellation]. It's represented on earth by what is called Black Elk Peak, which is where we gather to do the Welcome Back the Thunders Ceremony. And then we wait, and in thirty days, we travel and next go to the center of the Black Hills, [to a site] which is called Pe Sla . . . [or] the 'Bald Spot.' And above the earth, would be the circle, the center of the Red Racetrack, where it forms a giant medicine wheel in the sky, which matches where [the Racetrack is] in the Black Hills below. And then we do the Welcome Back all Life ceremony. And the fourth and last one is when the sun reaches the Gemini [constellation], which is what we call the Mato Tipila ceremony, which is . . . [at] Mato Tipila, Where the Bear's Reside, which is also called Devil's Tower. That's when the Vernal Equinox or the sun enters that. And then we begin the Sun Dance ceremonies.

By synchronizing their movements and ceremonies with the movement of the sun through the spring constellations, the Lakota became partners with the celestial powers (Wakan Wasta) in renewing life on earth. In this respect, the importance of sites like Black Elk Peak, Pe Sla, and Mato Tipila is not as single landmarks but their relationship to one another and the wider area of the Black Hills of which they form one part.[46]

A Storied Landscape

Lakota participants reasserted Mount Rushmore's/Six Grandfathers' relationship to the Black Hills by tying certain geomorphic features of the Hills to legends and metaphors that in turn carry a moral resonance about how the Lakota should live as a people.[47] In Charlotte Black Elk's telling of the race between the two-leggeds and the four-leggeds, it takes place after a great cleansing of the earth in which the Earth being Maka eliminates most of the nations of humans for becoming selfish and greedy. In response, the four-leggeds and moving and growing things, led by the buffalo (tatanka), band together and vow to destroy the two-leggeds for not living properly and bringing destruction on all of creation. Then winged creatures, overhearing the plans of the four-leggeds, hold a council, and decide (at the urging of the owl) to side with the two-leggeds (humans and birds). The four-leggeds and the winged, then, hold a council and agree to a contest of endurance, in which they agree to run a race four times, clockwise around the Black Hills, the Heart of Everything that Is. The story concludes with the victory of the Magpie, which in this case allows the two-leggeds (including humans) to continue their existence. Maka, then, decides to leave the red trail left by the bloodied footprints of the racers on the Racetrack as a reminder to the two-leggeds of their responsibility to everything else in creation.[48] In sum, the red clay valley surrounding the Black Hills comes to serve as a reminder of the race, and the obligations of the two-leggeds to care for the four relations. These four relations include the growing and moving things, the winged, the four-legged, and the two-legged.

In addition to creation stories that reference Inyan Kara Mountain (stone creator) on the Wyoming side of the Black Hills, where the lonely Inyan desires a mate and creates Earth (Maka), elders frequently mentioned the genesis of the Lakota people from the subterranean caverns at Wind Cave in the southern Black Hills.[49] In commenting on this genesis legend, Charlotte Black Elk describes how the Pte people, upon entering the surface of the earth from the caverns of Wind Cave, had to relearn survival practices. The transformation of the Pte Oyate into common people, Ikce Oyate, meant that they weren't above anything else in creation. This humbling transformation suggests the responsibility of the Lakota towards all creation implied by the concept of *mitakuye oyasin*, which translates to "we are all related" or "all my relatives."[50] The moral principle, then, of the genesis legend is that while the Ikce may take their food and survival resources where they find it, they must do so in a respectful manner, and take only what they need.[51] In terms of the Lakota principle of mitakuye oyatsin, the Lakota as common people must honor the reciprocal obligations and mutual responsibilities that derive from being related to all life forms, both human and nonhuman.[52]

Repairing Indigenous Erasure

Lakota also suggested ways in which the relationship between Mount Rushmore and Lakota peoples could be improved or repaired. The first concern was the issue of Indigenous erasure at Mount Rushmore and in the Black Hills. As Albers notes, tourism development in the Black Hills took place, particularly beginning in the 1920s, with the advent of automobile travel, as tourism promoters sought to capture tourists en route to Yellowstone, Glacier National Park, and the Tetons. As tourism development shifted from the southern to the northern Black Hills, it did so in a way that emphasized the trials and tribulations of Euro-American pioneers and the battles between the United States military and tribal nations in the region. These Euro-American cultural narratives focused on the "adventures, exploits, and hardships associated with the taking and settlement of the Hills," with Mount Rushmore standing as the "quintessential expression" of these exploits.[53] In addition to the frontier history celebrated in northern Black Hills towns like Custer, Deadwood, and Rapid City, another variant of tourism development emphasized Victorian scenic landscapes through the construction of picturesque roads, lakes, and vistas at places like Custer State Park.[54]

Sandra Woodard succinctly summarized the problem of Lakota invisibility at Mount Rushmore and within the tourism economy of South Dakota in general: "You talk about tourism in this state. They said, 'Well, we're a tourist state.' But they don't emphasize the Indigenous people who are here, the Lakota peoples who are here, that are rightfully here, and own this land. We didn't sell our land. We're still here. Tourism is promoted, but it's not promoted in a positive way for us."[55]

Woodard also mentioned that she had met a lot of tourists "who want to come and learn from us [the Lakota]," but lack the opportunity, because Natives are not "looked positively upon" in tourism pamphlets. When I asked if there was anything that the NPS could do at sites like Mount Rushmore or Wind Cave to promote Lakota history, she replied, "Some of these tourist attractions kind of probably have like snippets of our history. How this used to be, how we'd lived here. But that's about it. *We're in the past.* The Lakota used to live here, and they did this, and they did that."[56]

Basil Brave Heart invoked the example of Wind Cave to talk about the problem of Indigenous erasure in the Black Hills. He talked about how the Lakota emergence story at Wind Cave was replaced by a settler story in which tourists were told that a cowboy was purportedly "riding horseback and the wind came, and his hat blew off." So, as he put it, "that's how they nationalized it," which was "very sad" for Native people.[57] In fact, the story of the discovery of Wind Cave by a cowboy whose hat blew off fits within the "legend-making tradition" associated with the Hills and the mythological drama of the American Frontier West, with its "discoveries, challenges, and conflicts over its riches."[58]

In contrast to the Native invisibility at Mount Rushmore, Jace DeCory described how the Crazy Horse Memorial attempted to address the continuous presence of Native communities. In discussing the variety of Native artifacts that can be found in the Crazy Horse exhibit hall, she stated: "It's a hodgepodge, but at least you can see Native stuff from all over the US, and the diversity of Native people." These handicrafts, as she put it, showed visitors that "all these Native people are still here," even if the operators of Crazy Horse could do more to educate the public. Jace DeCory thought that Mount Rushmore staff should do something similar. She also thought that tourists who visited Mount Rushmore from other countries would be open to a more inclusive experience. To supplement the focus on the presidents, she suggested that the Park Service could use the walking trail around Mount Rushmore to educate visitors about the Native relationship to the landscape. Despite its Euro-American orientation, Charmaine White Face also emphasized the benefit of exposing people who visit Mount Rushmore to an Indigenous perspective, particularly given the fact that it is one of the few encounters that many tourists have with the Black Hills. Commenting on the Lakota, Nakota, and Dakota Heritage Village, she added, "OK, we don't like what has happened here [at Mount Rushmore], but how else are we going to get our story out? How else do we tell people this is desecration, except sitting, being right there? Yes, this is desecration. And this is treaty territory, and this is a sacred place."

Lakota participants also discussed the lack of economic benefit that they have derived from tourism at Mount Rushmore and the rest of the Black Hills. Victor Douville noted, with respect to tourist sites in the Black Hills, "I think they say it [the Black Hills] makes about one to three billion [dollars] a year in tourism attractions, while our reservations around there are in . . . poverty. As they grow rich telling the story of those various [presidents] . . . we get nothing. We sink more into poverty, and we sink into poverty because we're not utilizing those spiritual centers anymore."[59]

He added that while tourism in the Black Hills draws millions of dollars in revenue, the Lakota's Black Hills Land Claim against the federal government ironically remains unresolved.[60] He viewed the tourism economy, then, as having few if any real benefits for the Lakota given that the profits are retained exclusively by tourism operators. Moreover, the descendants of pioneers have captured control of the Black Hills, restricting Lakota access to their main spiritual and ceremonial centers. Because they have been banned from those centers, the Lakota can't keep the correct balance with the world and fulfill their responsibilities to the plants and animals they depend on for sustenance. As a result, they sink into poverty, both spiritual and economic.[61]

To enhance Native economic benefit, Victor Douville proposed incorporating more of a Native voice at Mount Rushmore while providing a balance between pioneer and Native histories at the site. Offering what he considered a "more authentic" narrative about the Black Hills, one that incorporated a Native as well as pioneer perspective, would help "alleviate the tensions between Native Americans and non-natives."[62] He gave the example of interpretative work that he and other Lakota educators had done at Mount Rushmore, at the invitation of Superintendent Gerard Baker, where they talked about what Mount Rushmore and the Black Hills meant to them spiritually. A more balanced narrative "gained strength under [Gerard] Baker, but lost momentum after he left: We haven't [since] been invited up there."[63] He added that tourists at Mount Rushmore responded positively to their message, and that they even invited some non-natives to the reservation to do sweat ceremonies. Oglala Lakota Tribal member Daphne Richards Cook, who heads the Alliance of Tribal Tourism Advocates (ATTA), an initiative to increase tourism on the reservations,[64] similarly discussed Lakota efforts to "tell their story," while "protecting their own resources, language, and culture."[65] She talked about the challenges of instituting an educational component at places like Mount Rushmore and Badlands National Park, while helping Native youth "take pride in their aboriginal lands in the Black Hills." She believed that cultural tourism could play a role in "protecting the seventh generation"—by ensuring the transmission of Lakota cultural knowledge and helping Native youth become "stewards of their land, language, and culture."

The cultural education initiative that many Lakota educators mentioned favorably was that of the Mountains of History Teachers Institute. A collaborative initiative between Mount Rushmore, Crazy Horse, Black Hills State University (BHSU), and Technology and Innovations in Education (TIE), the Institute, funded by a US Department of Education Grant, offered graduate level professional training for history teachers from across the state.[66] The Cheyenne River

Sioux Tribe educator and historian Donovin Sprague talked about how he and the other educators worked to design an inclusive curriculum for the program, drawing on both sides (settler and Native) of the legacy of the four presidents at Mount Rushmore, including "policies that were detrimental to American Indians."[67] They taught both Native and non-Native graduate students in the program and incorporated visits to Mount Rushmore for several weekends per year. In the context of these visits, Sprague would emphasize that Mount Rushmore is in the Black Elk Wilderness area, discuss books like Black Elk Speaks, and explain how Black Elk's son, Ben Black Elk, had a continuous presence at Mount Rushmore for many years. Sprague also drew on landmarks near Mount Rushmore, like Black Elk Peak, describing how it was a sacred Lakota site for the vision quest, and how the Lakota Welcoming Back the Thunders ceremony took place there every year. The program also provided historical context for Mount Rushmore and the Black Hills, covering events like the Fort Laramie Treaty of 1868 and the Battle of Little Big Horn.

Conclusion

The Mount Rushmore EOA generated several insights about ways the park staff might further engage with the Lakota and Native peoples. For starters, they could juxtapose the story about Gutzon Borglum and his heroic exploits with Native perspectives on the carving of a sacred mountain as a desecration. Even Gutzon Borglum seemed sensitive to the potential injustice involved in his carving, given the Lakota land claim United States v. Sioux Nation of Indians, No. 79–639, which ran for over sixty years (from 1920 to 1980), including during the period of Mount Rushmore's carving (1927–41).[68] Perhaps aware of the claim, Borglum proposed to the Pine Ridge Historical Society in 1930 to create a "Sioux Indian memorial" from the granite removed from Mount Rushmore. He proposed to locate the memorial one hundred miles south in the Pine Hills foothills near Chadron, Nebraska.[69] Explaining to visitors why Mount Rushmore is such a painful site for the Lakota would represent a first step in the healing process. Improving Native access to Mount Rushmore, including offering free parking for Native people and making the site available for the harvesting of Native plants, would further demonstrate a desire to make the memorial more receptive to Native visitors.

In addition to situating the creation of Mount Rushmore in the broader history of westward expansion, settlement, and dispossession of Native people, park staff could also present Native cosmologies that locate the site of Mount Rushmore in the ceremonial context of the Black Elk Range and the Black Hills. In doing so, they could show how sites like Black Elk Peak, Pe Sla (the Bald Spot), and Mato Tipila (Bear's Lodge or Devil's Tower) are all part of an integrated ceremonial complex. Moreover, they could highlight the importance of these sites, and the accompanying ceremonial cycle they support, to the survival and renewal of the Lakota people. Such pedagogy could be further accompanied by instructional materials on the Black Hills as a moral landscape and the teachings associated with sites such as the Racetrack (the red clay valley surrounding the hills), emphasizing the responsibility of humans (the two-leggeds) to take care of the environment. Such a pedagogical orientation could further be connected to the Lakota idea of mitakuye oyasin, the inter-relatedness of all things.

While not replicating the experience of the Native artisans in the Crazy Horse exhibit hall, park staff could seek to find additional ways to support the living presence of Native peoples in the Black Hills, whether by highlighting the work of Native artisans, educators, or environmental activists. They could build on the work started by Superintendent Gerard Baker by strengthening the Native programming at the Lakota, Nakota, and Dakota Heritage Village, and incorporating Native storytellers, like Darrell Red Cloud (who works at the park during the summer months), into the interpretative division of the park. Continuing the tradition of the Mount Rushmore tribal summit, initiated by Gerard Baker in 2008, would be a way to continue the dialogue about Native concerns. The park could also follow the lead of Jim Jandreau at Bear Butte State Park, expanding the interpretative focus and Native access to make it more inclusive for Native peoples. Building on the work of the Mountains of History Teachers Institute, park staff could also work with local colleges like Black Hills State University (BHSU) and their tribal counterparts (Oglala Lakota College and Sinte Gleska University) to offer programs for educators and training for Lakota and other Native peoples interested in working as interpreters.

Mount Rushmore National Memorial is a part of the public lands that comprise the Black Hills National Forest. In this respect, it is a public commons, like the lands that surround it.[70] As a result, park staff have a responsibility to all of the constituencies that have a stake in the Black Hills. What differentiates the Native relationship to this landscape is that it is both economic and spiritual. While the Lakota who I interviewed hope to derive some economic benefit from Black Hills tourism, their relationship to the Black Hills is necessary for their ongoing survival as a distinct people. While some visitors would prefer to forget the Indigenous plight and the history of broken treaties, the legacy of those treaty violations, including the seizure of the Black Hills and the creation of Mount Rushmore, continues to negatively impact Lakota communities.

Mount Rushmore has made great strides in addressing the complex legacy of its creation through the strategic collaborations with tribal elders initiated by Superintendent Gerard Baker, the creation of the Heritage Village, and the seasonal hiring of Lakota storytellers like Darrell Red Cloud. Further work will hopefully build on this legacy by engaging Native collaborators in moving beyond the narrow story of Gutzon Borglum and his heroic conquest of nature as an expression of the "American Way." To expand this story, the park could engage Native historians and elders in telling the story of westward expansion, the 1851 and 1868 treaties, and the 1860s gold rush resulting in the illegal taking of the Hills. Many of the Lakota (as well as Northern Cheyenne and Southern Cheyenne and Arapaho) that we spoke to were excited about this prospect. As the Lakota elder Basil Brave Heart noted in response to a question about whether it would be possible to shift to a more inclusive and healing narrative at Mount Rushmore, "I think it needs to be done with spiritual prudency, spiritual patience," adding that such a proposal had to come "not from a cerebral spirituality, but from a heart spirituality."

Notes

1. Michael J. Evans, Alexa Roberts, and Peggy Nelson, "Ethnographic Landscapes," *Cultural Resource Management*, no. 5 (2001): 53–57.
2. Lynn Meskell, "Negative Heritage and Past Mastering in Archaeology," *Anthropological Quarterly* 75(3) (2002): 557–74.
3. John Fire Lame Deer and Richard Erdoes, *Lame Deer, Seeker of Visions: The Life of a Sioux Medicine Man* (New York: Simon and Schuster, 1972), 91.
4. Conversation with historian Mark David Spence, May 9, 2016.
5. Michael Pretes, "Tourism and Nationalism," *Annals of Tourism Research* 30 (2003): 133–34.
6. John Taliaferro, *Great White Fathers: The True Story of Gutzon Borglum and His Obsessive Quest to Create the Mt. Rushmore National Monument* (New York: Public Affairs, 2004), 208.
7. Conversation with Joe Watkins, November 15, 2015.
8. Interview with Gerard Baker, September 24, 2015.
9. Layota Lonelodge, "'Our Home Place': Tribes Look to Protect Black Hills," *Cheyenne and Arapaho Tribal Tribune* (August 21, 2018). https://www.indianz.com/News/2018/08/21/our-home-place-tribes-look-to-protect-bl.asp.
10. In the context of our research, we discovered that these perspectives on Mount Rushmore were held by other Native participants that we spoke with, including the Northern Cheyenne.
11. Charmaine White Face, interview with author (Rapid City, SD, October 9, 2018).
12. Ernie La Pointe, interview with author (Bear Butte State Park, Sturgis, SD, September 30, 2018).
13. Jace Decory, interview with author (Spearfish, SD, 2018).
14. Decory, 2018.
15. Karen Little Thunder, interview with author (Rapid City, SD, 2018).
16. La Pointe, 2018.
17. Sandra Woodard, interview with author (Rapid City, SD, October 6, 2018).
18. Charlotte Black Elk, interview with author (Manderson, SD, October 9, 2018).
19. Ronald Goodman, *Lakota Star Knowledge: Studies in Lakota Stellar Theology*, ed. A. Seeger (Mission, SD: SGU, 2017), 50–51.
20. The seven stars of the Pleiades constellation are also important in Lakota cosmology because they are correlated with the story of the seven little girls, in which Fallen Star, a supernatural hero, shoots an eagle, and places the spirits of

seven girls (who the eagle has killed atop Black Elk Peak) in the sky as the Pleiades constellation (*wicincala sakowin*—seven little girls) (see Goodman, *Lakota Star Knowledge*, 50–51). See also Patricia Albers et al., "The Home of the Bison: An Ethnographic and Ethnohistorical Study of Traditional Cultural Affiliations to Wind Cave National Park," US National Park Service Publications and Papers (National Park Service, 2003), 507–508; Raymond J. DeMallie, *The Sixth Grandfather: Black Elk's Teachings Given to John G Neihardt* (Lincoln: University of Nebraska Press, 1984), 401–408; Alexandra New Holy, "The Significance of Place: The Lakota and Paha Sapa," PhD dissertation (Berkeley: University of California at Berkeley, 1997), 153; David C. Posthumus, *All My Relatives: Exploring Lakota Ontology, Belief, and Ritual* (Lincoln: University of Nebraska Press, 2018), 130.

21. The Rosebud Sioux educator, Victor Douville, also emphasized the spiritual nature of Mount Rushmore, connecting it both to an earlier Lakota name and cosmology. As Douville noted: "When they carved Mount Rushmore, it destroyed the sacredness of it. Because it used to be called, the Mountain Lion Hill or Mount. And it was changed to Mount Rushmore." Mount Rushmore, then, was first called Cougar Mountain or Mountain Lion Hill (*Igmu Tanka Paha*) on account of the many mountain lions or cougars that lived in the vicinity. (See Albers, "Home of the Bison," 312). Moreover, he viewed the changing of the name "Cougar Mountain" to "Mount Rushmore" as part of the sites' conversion to a non-Indian structure, noting that the carving of the monuments "insulted the integrity of our tribe."
22. Taliaferro, *Great White Fathers*, 208, 239–40.
23. Philomene Lakota, interview with author (Whiteclay, NE, June 20, 2018).
24. Basil Brave Heart, interview with author (Pine Ridge, SD, October 7, 2018).
25. Albert Boime, "Patriarchy Fixed in Stone: Gutzon Borglum's 'Mount Rushmore,'" *American Art* 5 (1991): 143–67.
26. As Martínez notes, citing Miles A. Browne's essay "Abraham Lincoln and the Great Sioux Uprising of 1862," "Lincoln admitted that he was poorly informed regarding Indian policies. He paid little attention to the Office of Indian Affairs." David Martínez, "Remembering the Thirty-Eight: Abraham Lincoln, the Dakota, and the US War on Barbarism," *Wicazo Sa Review* 28(2) (2013): 19.
27. Carol Chomsky, "The United States-Dakota War Trials: A Study in Military Injustice," *Stan. L. Rev.* 43: 13 (1990); Martínez, "Remembering the Thirty-Eight," 5.
28. Victor Douville, phone interview with author (May 9, 2019). In acquiring these lands, Washington violated both Dinwiddie's proclamation and the Royal Proclamation of 1763. The latter expressly prohibited colonial governments or subjects from: 1) surveying or granting any unceded Native land; 2) permitting settlement on Native land (defined as all land west of the Proclamation's settlement boundary line); and 3) arranging private purchases of land. Instead, an official system of public purchases would provide the vehicle for the extinction of Native title. See Matthew J. Hill and Jon Parmenter, "The Fort Stanwix

Treaties. An Ethnohistory of Iroquois Diplomacy and Dispossession," National Park Service #P15AC01320 (Amherst: University of Massachusetts, 2018), 62. See also Colin G. Calloway, *The Indian World of George Washington: The First President, the First Americans, and the Birth of the Nation* (New York: Oxford University Press, 2018), 218.
29. See Mark David Spence, *Dispossessing the Wilderness: Indian Removal and the Making of the National Parks* (New York: Oxford University Press, 1999).
30. Mike Her Many Horses, interview with author (Pine Ridge, SD, 2018).
31. DeCory, 2018.
32. Doug Bissonette, interview with author (Pine Ridge, SD, October 5, 2018).
33. The red osier dogwood also goes by the name of red willow.
34. DeCory, 2018.
35. Woodard interview, 2018.
36. See Martha Geores, *Common Ground: The Struggle for Ownership of the Black Hills National Forest* (Lanham, MD: Rowman & Littlefield, 1996)
37. Charlotte Black Elk interview, 2018.
38. See John Wylie, *Landscape* (New York and London: Routledge, 2007), 158.
39. Wylie, 159.
40. New Holy, citing Powers, notes that when used ritually, a *hocoka* refers to "a sacred space, the center of the universe, within which a supplicant prays, sings, or otherwise communicates with the spirits." William Powers, *Yuwipi: Vision and Experience in Oglala Ritual* (Lincoln: University of Nebraska Press, 1982), 14; cited by New Holy, "Significance of Place," 137–78.
41. Albers, "Home of the Bison," 15.
42. New Holy, "Significance of Place," 155.
43. New Holy, 151.
44. Douville interview, 2019.
45. Woodard refers here to the post-reservation period. Archaeological evidence presented by Linea Sundstrom and Pat Albers shows that multiple Indigenous groups with different adaptive strategies and settlement patterns used the region for many millennia; see Albers, "Home of the Bison," 2. Linea Sundstrom, "Rock Art of the Southern Black Hills: A Contextual Approach," PhD dissertation (University of Kansas, Lawrence, 1989); Linea Sundstrom, "Mirror of Heaven: Cross-Cultural Transference of the Sacred Geography of the Black Hills," *World Archaeology* 28(2) (1996):177–89.
46. Pat Albers notes a similar relationship between Wind Cave, the Race Track, the Buffalo Gap, and the Hot Springs, which also form what she calls an "integrated landscape." See Albers, "Home of the Bison," xiv.
47. Keith H. Basso, *Wisdom Sits in Places: Landscape and Language Among the Western Apache*, 1st edition (Albuquerque: University of New Mexico Press, 1996), 63.
48. Goodman, *Lakota Star Knowledge*, 67–69.
49. For a discussion of the *Inyan* creation legend, see New Holy "Significance of Place," 121–24.
50. Posthumus, *All My Relatives*, 14.

51. Charlotte Black Elk, "Story of the Big Race," in Goodman, *Lakota Star Knowledge*, 67–69.
52. Posthumus, *All My Relatives*.
53. Albers, "Home of the Bison," 169.
54. Albers, 170. See also Suzanne Barta Julin, *A Marvelous Hundred Square Miles: Black Hills Tourism, 1880–1941* (Pierre: South Dakota State Historical Society, 2009); Elaine Marie Nelson, "Dreams and Dust in the Black Hills: Race, Place, and National Identity in America's 'Land of Promise,'" PhD Diss. (University of New Mexico, Albuquerque, 2011).
55. Woodard interview, 2018.
56. Woodard interview, 2018.
57. Brave Heart interview, 2018.
58. Albers, "Home of the Bison," 170.
59. Mearhoff notes that tourists spent $1.6 billion on lodging, food, recreation, and transportation in the Black Hills in 2018, accounting for 39 percent of the state's total tourism industry sales of $4 billion in 2018. See Sarah Mearhoff, "Tourism Spending Rises in Black Hills-Badlands Region, State Says," *Rapid City Journal Media Group*. https://rapidcityjournal.com/news/local/tourism-spending-rises-in-black-hills-badlands-region-state-says/article_1eeba95a-c286-5cf2-a7e8-c77ca8443914.html (accessed June 17, 2019).
60. Douville interview, 2019; Edward Lazarus, *Black Hills White Justice: The Sioux Nation Versus the United States, 1775 to the Present* (Lincoln: University of Nebraska Press, 1999).
61. I am indebted to Christina Gish Hill for this insight.
62. Douville interview, 2019.
63. Douville interview, 2019.
64. Jomay Steen, "Tribal Group Boosts Reservation Tourism," Rapid City Journal Media Group (2005). https://rapidcityjournal.com/news/local/tribal-group-boosts-reservation-tourism/article_4d5ca77b-e1bc-59f1-a440-9b54d672382e.html (accessed June 18, 2019).
65. Daphne Richards Cook, phone interview with author (September 29, 2018).
66. See "Monumental Education," Milken Educator Awards (2009). http://www.milkeneducatorawards.org/connections/articles/view/monumental-education (accessed June 16, 2019).
67. Donovan Sprague, phone interview with author (February 10, 2017).
68. The Lakota land claim sought monetary compensation from the federal government for the illegal seizure of the Black Hills. See Lazarus, *Black Hills, White Justice*; Albers, "Home of the Bison," 179–81.
69. See "Sioux Memorial Issue," *Nebraska History* XXII (January–March, 1941).
70. Albers, "Home of the Bison," xiii.

SIX | # The Lewis and Clark Bicentennial

JACKIE GONZALES

IN THE 1990s, the National Park Service (NPS) saw enormous tourism and media potential in the upcoming two hundredth anniversary of the Lewis and Clark expedition, also known as the Corps of Discovery expedition. The agency planned an elaborate mobile exhibit and correlated events to retrace the journey two hundred years after it occurred. Agency officials hoped the three-year event would celebrate the accomplishments of these men, who explored vast, previously unknown stretches of the North American continent.

But obviously the vast continent was unknown only to the Americans of European descent who funded Lewis and Clark's expedition as a journey of conquest, meant to lay groundwork for later substantiation of land claims against Britain, France, and Spain. People had long flourished in complex civilizations from the Mississippi River to the Pacific Ocean. Meriwether Lewis, William Clark, and their party were visitors on these peoples' lands, and they were only able to survive thanks to the generosity and hospitality of the people they met along the way. Descendants of these many communities were not only wary of celebrating the bicentennial—they were deeply offended by the notion of celebrating an event that represented the "beginning of the end" for so many people and cultures.

When NPS officials initially reached out to tribes, they did so out of fear that Indigenous opposition to the event would ruin the prospects of the bicentennial celebrations, not out of any official need for a consultation process. This early outreach offended so many tribes that the agency ended up completely changing its approach to the event.

The revamped approach of the Lewis and Clark Bicentennial handed control of narratives and events over to tribes, allowing many people to discuss a painful history and its legacy. This led to an event that allowed different groups of people to tell their own stories and emphasize what was meaningful to them. Tribes who did not want to talk about Lewis and Clark but instead wanted to discuss the pain that American expansion had wreaked on their communities over the past two hundred years could now do that. Native people who chose to participate did so because they could use the bicentennial and the funding that came with it to accomplish their own agendas and fulfill their own needs, rather than support those of the NPS.

The Lewis and Clark Bicentennial represented a novel coming together of federal agencies, Native nations, and local communities to commemorate, rather than celebrate, an event that fundamentally changed the North American continent. But while the model used in the bicentennial was successful in forging collaboration for this one traveling event, it did not change long-term collaborations between the NPS and Native people at place-based parks. One issue with applying lessons learned during this event lies in how the Lewis and Clark NHT differs from most other NPS sites in that it connects other sites without managing land directly. The NPS owns land as part of other NPS sites along the trail, such as Knife River Indian Villages National Historic Site and Lewis and Clark National Historical Park (formerly Fort Clatsop National Memorial), but the Lewis and Clark National Historic Trail itself manages no land. Bicentennial commemorations spanned the nation, but the exhibit also only spent a finite time in each place. Despite these shortcomings, the seeds its organizers planted, and the lessons learned from this approach, contain insights that can inform future collaboration between the NPS and Indigenous nations.

I came into this project in 2016, as a consulting historian tasked with the administrative history of the Lewis and Clark National Historic Trail (NHT) for the NPS. This work was performed through a contract between the NPS and the company I work for, Historical Research Associates, Inc. The pages that follow tell, in retrospect, the story of how Native people and the NPS collectively planned the bicentennial. I am an historian telling the story after it played out, not a participant in the events of the bicentennial. As part of this project, my colleague Emily Greenwald and I interviewed twenty-three individuals who had worked for or partnered with the Lewis and Clark NHT. The excerpts from oral histories in this chapter are from those interviews and are used with permission from the interviewees and the NPS. The full administrative history of the trail is available online at npshistory.com/publications/lecl/adhi.pdf.

NPS Planning for the Lewis and Clark Bicentennial

The NPS approached the Lewis and Clark Bicentennial on the heels of a major failure: the 1992 Columbus Quincentennial.[1] Although the NPS had grand plans for that anniversary, Indigenous groups across the Americas had little interest in celebrating an event that led to the devastation of their civilizations. As Richard Williams, an NPS employee at the Lewis and Clark National Historic Trail, described the debacle, "And then all of a sudden, they [the NPS] found out that . . . there's Indians still out here, [and] they just weren't crazy about Columbus at all . . . And the park service said oh, shoot, maybe we should have talked to them."[2] In response to widespread boycotts by Indigenous people across the Americas, the NPS abandoned its Columbus Quincentennial plans.[3] Williams realized that American Indian involvement in the Lewis and Clark Bicentennial would be "imperative, if we are to avoid the kind of backlash that occurred with the Quincentennial of Columbus discovery of America."[4]

NPS employees built their early bicentennial plans on those developed by the Lewis and Clark Trail Heritage Foundation (LCTHF), the Lewis and Clark NHT's primary nonprofit partner.[5] In 1986, LCTHF members created a Bicentennial Committee (which they also called the Bicentennial Celebration Committee), with the goal of stimulating interest in the history of the Corps of Discovery and promoting tourism around it.[6] At the center of the bicentennial, the LCTHF envisioned a "traveling theater and traveling museum" that would traverse the route Lewis and Clark had taken.[7] Harry Hubbard, the founder of the Bicentennial Committee, hoped that Congress might fund the Lewis and Clark Bicentennial as generously as it had funded the Bicentennial of the US Constitution.[8] The LCTHF board spun off the Bicentennial Committee into a separate nonprofit organization, the Bicentennial Council, to create capacity for a national event.[9]

In May 1994, the NPS convened partners to plan for the bicentennial and discuss the traveling exhibit idea.[10] In attendance at the meeting were NPS employees from the Lewis and Clark NHT, regional offices, Washington, Fort Clatsop National Memorial, Knife River Indian Villages National Historic Site, the Niobrara National Scenic Riverway, Nez Perce National Historical Park, and Jefferson National Expansion Memorial. Gerard Baker, Superintendent of Little Bighorn Battlefield National Monument, was also invited, but he was unable to attend.[11] No representatives of tribes were invited to the meeting.[12]

Later in 1994, the Bicentennial Council elected its first three Indigenous board members, Lawrence Wetsit (Assiniboine), Jeanne Eder (Dakota), and Allen V. Pinkham, Sr. (Nez Perce).[13] Having tribal representatives on the board did not erase the difficulties of commemorating a painful history. Pinkham, a US Forest Service employee at Clearwater National Forest, recalled friction over the use of the word "celebration" at the first Bicentennial Council meeting he and Eder attended:

> So, I and Jeanne show up at this Fort Leavenworth meeting. And one of the first things they said [was], "Well, we've got to do a preamble for the bicentennial committee so it will kind of give us guidance on what we're going to do and how we're going to do it." And the purpose, of course.

And they went through, and then it says, "We will celebrate Lewis and Clark Bicentennial."

And Jeanne kind of blew up and says, "You will not put no celebration in this preamble because we will not celebrate Lewis and Clark and what they did. We Indian people will not do that." And I agreed with her. And we argued a little bit, probably about an hour or so, about that one word.

And we took a break and we came back again. And they said, "Well, why don't we find another word instead of 'celebrate?'" They finally got the message, you know? [laughs] And somebody said, "Well, why don't we say 'commemorate' Lewis and Clark?" You know, that's kind of an inclusive word about other people. I says, "Well, that sounds a little bit better."

So, we changed that one word and we became a little bit more satisfied. But this was the attitude of these scholars and historians and educators.[14]

In response to Pinkham and Eder's resistance, the Bicentennial Council struck the word celebration from its mission statement, but this change did not erase many council leaders' celebratory approach.[15] The way the NPS and the Bicentennial Council approached Lewis and Clark was similar to how the agency told celebratory stories of conquest without considering Indigenous peoples' pain arising from those same stories at sites like Grand Portage National Monument (see chapter by Tim Cochrane).

Indigenous board members disliked how the Bicentennial Council and the NPS presented fully formed ideas and then asked tribes for a rubber stamp of approval.[16] Tensions reached a breaking point in April 1996, as Pinkham later recalled:

And then we had another meeting in Skamania, Washington, down on the Columbia. Down there by Cascades. And there again, Harry Hubbard had his ideas . . .

". . . then we'll call in the Indians to do their thing, you know, pow wows or horse parades."

Jeanne blew up again. "You will not do this! We're not your damn Indians!"

And Harry Hubbard didn't know what to do. So, he called for a recess. And then Jeanne Eder, [and] . . . a couple other Indian women . . . Dark Rain Thom was there [and] . . . Gail Chehak, I think . . . And they said, "Allen, you've got to do something. You've got to make things right."

I says, "Yeah, I'll do it. What do you want me to do?"

She says, "Well, you go up there and smudge the people. I've got some sweet grass here. You can use this."

So, we go back to the assembly. . . . there was about a little over a hundred people. So, I told them, "Get in a circle around this room and

Allen Pinkham (left), member of the Bicentennial Council, member of the Nez Perce Tribe, and a Forest Service employee, speaking to Matt Buckner, an NPS employee, during the bicentennial, 2004. Courtesy of the Lewis and Clark NHT.

I'm going to do something for you to make things right. I realize there were harsh words spoken and we want to try to make things right so we can continue on with what we need to do."

So, I went around to each one of them and smudged them with this sweet grass. You know, it's an old ceremony among Indian people to do these kinds of things. So, I went around and did that for everyone. And I tried to explain to them, harsh words were spoken but now we want to soften these words so that we can get together and solve our problems. And everybody became a little more relaxed about this. . . .

From that day on, things got better. When we raised an issue, they listened. And we're not here to be showcase Indians. We're here to do what's best for our people. And we want to tell you what our issues are. Nationwide. We're not these people over on a reservation that are taken care of by the United States government. We are people, too.[17]

Pinkham's healing ceremony eased tensions at a critical point in bicentennial planning, but the tensions remained between those who wanted to celebrate Lewis and Clark and those who saw their journey as the beginning of the end.[18]

Lewis and Clark Fever

Meanwhile, national interest in Lewis and Clark exploded, elevating the two men to pop culture icons.[19] This was primarily due to Stephen Ambrose's 1996 book, *Undaunted Courage*, which glorified the two leading men, and Ken Burns's and

Senator Byron Dorgan (D-ND, *left*) at a bicentennial event in Bismarck, North Dakota, 2004. To his right are Lewis and Clark NHT Superintendent Gerard Baker and Tex Hall, who was then President of the National Congress of American Indians and Chairman of the Mandan-Hidatsa-Arikara Nation. Courtesy of the National Park Service.

Dayton Duncan's 1997 PBS miniseries, *Lewis & Clark: The Journey of the Corps of Discovery*, which over twenty million people tuned into on its first airing.[20] The resulting surge in interest in Lewis and Clark led to estimates that twenty to thirty million people might travel in their footsteps during the bicentennial. Federal officials used these numbers to justify spending on the bicentennial, but the same numbers caused alarm for tribal managers, concerned for the health of the natural and cultural resources in their communities.[21]

Congress hopped aboard the Lewis and Clark train, especially members from states along the trail that might benefit from an increase in tourism. In 1997, Senator Byron L. Dorgan (D-ND) introduced a resolution to "support the commemoration of the Bicentennial of the Lewis and Clark Expedition."[22] In 1998, members of Congress formed a Lewis and Clark Bicentennial Congressional Caucus, whose members coordinated with federal agencies and the Bicentennial Council to bring Lewis and Clark–related tourism to their states.[23]

As plans gathered steam, the US Army Corps of Engineers argued that it should manage commemorations, since it controlled most of the Missouri and Columbia Rivers on which the Corps of Discovery traveled for the bulk of their journey. But the Army Corps had poor relationships with most tribes, since dam construction in the mid-1900s had flooded land on many reservations without the consent of Indigenous people.[24] Baker later pointed to these contentious relationships as the reason that the NPS took the lead on bicentennial commemorations, even if the NPS relationships with tribes was far from perfect.[25]

With Congressional funds pouring in, plans for bicentennial commemorations grew ever grander.[26] A 1998 plan called the traveling classroom the "Lewis and Clark Corps of Discovery II: 200 Years to the Future" and described it as "a combination of mobile museum exhibits, live interpretation, use of the internet, distance learning video, and spectacular laser light shows" that would "reach millions of people."[27] And, as late as 1998, NPS plans for the bicentennial referred to "celebrations" of the history.[28]

"Listening Sessions"

As bicentennial plans ballooned, the NPS appointed Francis Calabrese interim superintendent of the Lewis and Clark NHT.[29] Calabrese, an archeologist, had overseen a decades-long NPS-funded archeological excavation at Knife River Indian Villages in North Dakota, a former Hidatsa village site.[30] Under Calabrese's direction, the NPS held four regional "listening sessions" with tribes in 1999: in Lewistown, Idaho (co-hosted by the Nez Perce Tribe); Great Falls, Montana (co-hosted by the Montana Tribal Association); New Town, North Dakota (co-hosted by the Mandan, Hidatsa, and Arikara Nation); and Wichita, Kansas (co-hosted by the Otoe-Missouri Tribe).[31] The NPS declared the purpose of the meetings was to "provide tribes the opportunity to share their views and recommendations surrounding the upcoming bicentennial."[32]

Many Indigenous individuals present at these meetings saw these listening sessions as ineffective, offensive, and absent of meaningful attempts at collaboration.[33] Attendees characterized this as typical of the NPS: make plans first and conduct token tribal consultation after the fact. Attendees were sensitive to how tribes had been historically used by the park service—asked to dance and pose for pictures, but never afforded the leadership, power, or monetary benefits that the NPS obtained from their services.[34] Bobbie Conner (Cayuse-Umatilla-Nez Perce), director of the Tamástslikt Cultural Institution on the Confederated Tribes of the Umatilla Reservation, remembered

> . . . being at a restaurant, a couple of tables away from the National Park Service staff. And he was an archeologist, this gentleman who'd worked many years for the park service, [and he] had this really overwhelming desire, uncontrollable desire, to talk about handling human remains. And we kept saying in meetings, "We have a protocol for talking about that. We pray before we talk about that. I mean, this isn't something we casually bring up in conversation." And he would just not shut up.
>
> And so, one night we're around dinner and it was tribal people around one table. And he joined us. He pulled up a chair and joined us. And then he started talking about exhuming the remains of a child on some project. And he didn't realize that everyone stopped eating. Everybody put down

their silverware. That no one was really engaging his storytelling. But he just—I mean, if there was a trail of faux pas, it was all his.[35]

In addition to these extreme instances of cultural insensitivity, tribes simply had more important things to worry about than the bicentennial. Conner elaborated,

> So, my tribe is worried about a new ambulance. They're worried about money for the language program. They're worried about how we're going to keep the native plant nursery running. They're wondering how we're going to build a new school building for the new charter school. We have healthcare needs that are much more paramount. We have floods, and bridges, and handicap ramps to build. This doesn't compare. Porta Potties for people on the Lewis and Clark Trail wearing old buckskin reenactment outfits was low on every single tribe's priority. Nobody made a priority of that. And it never became a priority for us.[36]

The park service's listening sessions did not change the reality that asking tribes to use their time and money to celebrate two white men who represented the "beginning of the end" for every tribe they encountered was financially unrealistic and deeply insulting to many American Indians.[37]

Gerard Baker Becomes Superintendent of Lewis and Clark National Historic Trail

After the listening sessions debacle, the NPS hired Gerard Baker as superintendent of the Lewis and Clark NHT. Baker, a career NPS employee and a member of the Mandan, Hidatsa, and Arikara Nation, had grown up on the Fort Berthold Indian Reservation and began his career at Knife River Indian Villages National Historic Site. He had served as superintendent of the Little Bighorn Battlefield National Monument in the early 1990s and shepherded the site through the contentious aftermath of a name change from Custer Battlefield National Monument.[38] He also later served as superintendent of Mount Rushmore National Memorial (discussed further in Matthew J. Hill's chapter).

Unlike previous superintendents, Baker understood that Lewis and Clark were a painful topic for many people. He explained,

> It's a tough subject, you know. Everybody looked at it as a cheery subject, win/win. It's not. There's some tough subject matter when you start talking about that. Especially with tribes, a way of life. A lot of tribes saw Lewis and Clark as the beginning of the end. Which I think is true.
> As the superintendent of that particular project, it was tough for me to have to sit there quietly a lot of times, and not respond. Not saying,

Gerard Baker speaks at a Lewis and Clark Bicentennial event, 2003. Courtesy of the Lewis and Clark NHT.

"Hell, yeah, I agree with you." You know, growing up on a reservation and seeing all this bullshit happen to us as Indian people, I agree. As a superintendent, you've got to stay in the middle. And you've got to be the leader. And show that leadership in different things. Be it quietness or whatever, you know. But at the same time, you have to show that you're supportive of various groups so they come on board and do in fact tell their story.[39]

When Baker asked tribes to participate in the bicentennial, he promised that they would be able to tell their stories without censorship, edits, or curation. The NPS had a long history of making such promises to tribes that it later broke. Baker, by contrast, had followed through on a similar pledge at Little Bighorn to avoid censorship of tribal perspectives.[40] Baker's approach, along with his natural charisma and deep connections in Indian country, changed how some tribes felt about participating in the bicentennial. As Conner put it, "Tribes got completely coopted when they made Gerard the superintendent. It was just like all right, yes, we'll play ball with you. Yes, . . . we'll do programs."[41]

Not all Indigenous people were persuaded by Baker, as Baker later recounted:

And in my being naïve about everything, I thought man, the tribes are going to want to come onboard! It's going to be an opportunity. They're going to meet me with open arms. They're going to say, "Oh, you're the best thing that ever happened to the park service! The best thing that ever happened to Indian country. We just can't wait now."

And it was just the opposite. I think a lot of them pretty much disliked me. Called me a traitor as an Indian, being with the government. Coming to steal their stories like the old days, like anthropologists would. . . .

Baker's roots made these sorts of conflicts extremely personal for him. He remembered an encounter at an early meeting:

I asked them if they had any questions. And this one lady raised her hand. And the first thing she says, she looked at me and she said, "I don't trust you." She said, "You're nothing but a government bureaucrat with braids." And there was at least, maybe four hundred people there at this meeting.

And so, I looked at her and I said, "Ma'am, you're absolutely right." I said, "I am a government bureaucrat with braids." And I said, "Because I'm a bureaucrat with braids, I will give you a government answer for your question." I said, "You have alternatives here. The alternative that you're choosing right now, is to stick your head in the sand and let all these white people come by and not give them an opportunity to learn about you. To keep perceiving misconceptions that they have about Indian people, about how we're all drunks. And how we're uneducated. How we're all stupid. And how we're all less than them—white people. As Indian people, that we're less than them. . . . You can let all that go by us. And then when they go . . . you pull your head out of the sand and keep doing what you're doing. . . ."

"The preferred alternative is to not put your head in the sand," I said. "Get mad, if you're going to get mad. Stay mad. And educate these white people that come through here that we're not drunk, dirty, stupid Indians. That we're very intelligent. We can teach as much as they can, if not more. That we have a culture we're proud of."[42]

Baker prioritized hiring Native staff. In 2001, he hired Otis Halfmoon as an American Indian Liaison, the site's first. Halfmoon met with tribes and shared the tension that he felt between his own concerns about the bicentennial versus the "opportunity to tell our side of the story."[43] Baker later hired as additional American Indian Liaisons Darrell Martin, who was Gros Ventre and a leader of the Fort Belknap Indian Community in Montana, and Dick Basch, a member of the Clatsop-Nehalem Confederated Tribes in Oregon.[44]

Otis Halfmoon, pictured here giving a presentation during the bicentennial, was hired by Gerard Baker as the Lewis and Clark NHT's first American Indian Liaison. Courtesy of the Lewis and Clark NHT.

Tent of Many Voices

Baker also prioritized broadening the discussion of the bicentennial beyond the perspectives of Lewis and Clark. He established four questions to guide dialogue:

1. What life was like before Lewis and Clark?
2. What was life like during Lewis and Clark's journey?
3. What has life been like in the last two hundred years?
4. What does the next two hundred years look like?[45]

This inclusive model allowed for many people to share differing, even conflicting, interpretations of the Lewis and Clark story. By considering both the present and the future, Baker opened the door to programming that addressed tribes' concerns—promoting economic development, improving life on reservations, protecting cultural and natural resources, and preserving language—while still allowing for other non-Indigenous content.

Baker called this space the "Tent of Many Voices."[46] Anyone who wanted to speak simply filled out a proposal and sent it to NPS staff, who then placed that person or organization on the schedule (for other examples of the NPS handing narrative control to Native people, see Ari Kelman's chapter in this volume).[47]

Conner recalled that the Tent of Many Voices changed the equation for tribes wary of participating: "Gerard was, on behalf of the park service promising some accountability. . . . you can choose not to be videotaped. You can choose not to sign a release. You can come to the Tent of Many Voices and you'll be uncensored. And we felt confident that his representations of how the Tent of Many Voices would be run was a much safer proposition than what we'd been hearing before."[48]

Karen Goering of the Missouri Historical Society recalled that the Tent of Many Voices provided "a level of respect . . . to the divergent views that I don't think most people had ever seen before in the Lewis and Clark story."[49]

Baker received pushback against this approach from the highest levels of government. He explained:

> And there was a section there [in the exhibits] about the treaties. I think it was either that or Wounded Knee, or something that was really vivid about what happened. Really, really vivid, about massacres of Indians and killing Indian babies. . . .
>
> I approved it . . . . And I got word that the White House got a hold of it. . . . And they said they weren't going to approve that, because of the language in there. And I got mad and I said, "Bullshit. We're going to do it. I don't care what the White House says. . . ."
>
> And I remember getting off the plane in Portland. I . . . got this call on my cell phone. Said, "This is Karl Rove."
>
> I said, "Bullshit!"
>
> "No," he said, "this is Mr. Karl Rove, from the White House."
>
> I said, "Really?"
>
> He said, "I want to talk to you, Mr. Baker, about your text on your narration on your Lewis and Clark exhibit."
>
> I said, "Really?!"
>
> He said, "Yeah. It's a little bit too strong, we feel, that you can't do this this and this."
>
> So I said, "Ah, I disagree with you. I'm not going to change it." I said, "I'm the superintendent. You guys hired me. So, I'm going to keep it the way it is."
>
> He said, "You can't do that."
>
> I said, "Bullshit. I'm not going to do that. Leave it the way it is."
>
> He said, "Mr. Baker, people that disagree with our administration usually have to find a different job. Or they sometimes don't have a job at all."
>
> I said, "Are you threatening me? Are you threatening me?"
>
> "Oh, no. I'm just telling you what happens."
>
> I said, "Bullshit! You're threatening me, you son of a bitch!" That's what I said on the phone. There was kind of a pause.

Performers prepare to enter the Tent of Many Voices in Missoula, Montana, 2006. Courtesy of the Lewis and Clark NHT.

He said . . . "We're going to change it."

I said, "Tell you what. You can change it. Go ahead and change the damn thing. You change it and I'm going to call all my Indian contacts." Excuse my language, now, but this is what I told him. I said, "I'm going to call all my Indian contacts. We'll get off it. And you ain't got a fucking program."

"I'll get back to you," he said. That was it.

I said whoa, I think I just blew it. I don't have a job anymore. So I kept going and I said oh, shit, oh, shit, oh, shit, oh, shit. Driving, driving.

Phone rings about an hour later . . . rings, I pull over. He says, "This is Mr. Karl Rove from the White House."

I said, "All right."

He said, "Mr. Baker, after thorough discussion, we decided that you can do what you want to do." Then he gave me the old White House verbiage. "But be careful," he said, "we'll be watching you."

(Baker laughs) I said, all right, man. . . .

Wow! So, that's politics. That's politics. I think people can't understand, maybe won't realize, that's a White House people don't see.[50]

Baker's insistence that tribes be allowed to tell their own uncensored stories kept tribal partners on board.

Circle of Tribal Advisors (COTA)

While the NPS reached out to Indigenous nations and developed educational exhibits, the Bicentennial Council created a subgroup called the Circle of Tribal Advisors (COTA). Its leadership included Pinkham, Conner, Amy Mossett (Mandan, Hidatsa, Arikara), Chris Powell (Pawnee), Robert J. Miller (Eastern Shawnee), Daphne Richards-Cook (Oglala Sioux), Dark Rain Thom (Ohio River Tribes), George Heavy Runner (Blackfeet), and Greg Pitcher (Shawnee). COTA convened gatherings of Native people to have frank discussions about the benefits and drawbacks of participating in commemorative events. COTA thus worked as a complement to Baker's efforts within the NPS and ensured that tribal participation in the bicentennial was Native-led and not government-directed.[51]

COTA membership was open to all Indigenous nations with ancestral homelands along the Corps of Discovery's route. Within several years, around forty nations, representing two-thirds of tribes documented by Lewis and Clark, became active members of COTA. COTA also had a federal representative from the Bureau of Indian Affairs (BIA), Ed Hall, who was the BIA's tourism coordinator and an enrolled member of the Mandan, Hidatsa, and Arikara Nation.[52] COTA became a forum in which tribes could share their plans, opinions, and concerns regarding the bicentennial. Its leaders described the group as "an historic coalition that viewed the Lewis and Clark Bicentennial as an opportunity to preserve and celebrate what tribes have left of their lands, cultures and languages; present tribal perspectives about the expedition and its aftermath; honor their ancestors' legacies; enhance their children's future; teach the public about American Indians today; and collaborate with non-Indian neighbors to realize mutual goals and benefits. COTA helped elevate cross-cultural dialogue to impart a more nuanced and complete telling of our shared American history."[53]

COTA meetings took place in conjunction with Bicentennial Council meetings. Pinkham led COTA for several years and placed a high value on all tribes having a chance to air their concerns and feel heard. Because of this, COTA meetings were rarely short, in order to allow everyone a chance to speak.[54] Despite their length, COTA members remember the meetings fondly, as a place to get to know members of other tribes, express their tribes' priorities, and hear those of other tribes.[55]

COTA leaders utilized the bicentennial as a venue to draw attention to and garner funding for critical issues in reservation communities, such as "language revitalization, cultural resource protection, elder services, education, health care, safety, or infrastructure."[56] One of COTA's primary goals was to remind tourists that tribes were not a fixture of the past but modern, functioning communities with concerns and hopes like any other community.[57] In 2002, COTA adopted two resolutions that advocated for (1) federal recognition of all tribes along the expedition route, and (2) "protection of tribal cultural resource areas, burial grounds, and sacred sites" after the bicentennial.[58] COTA worked with tribes

A meeting of Bicentennial Council and COTA board members. On the near side of the table, from left to right, Daphne Richards-Cook, Chris Howell, Karen Goering. On the far side, Bobbie Conner, Bob Miller, and Robert Archibald, 2003. Courtesy of the Lewis and Clark NHT.

across the country to prepare for increased visitation, both by ameliorating negative impacts that could come with greater numbers of tourists and harnessing new revenue that those guests might bring.[59]

The NPS funded tribal participation in the bicentennial largely through Challenge Cost Share (CCS) grants, a federal matching-funds grants program for entities that partnered with land management agencies.[60] CCS funding to the Lewis and Clark NHT ballooned during the bicentennial: from 1995 to 2006, the grants funded 768 projects totaling over $25 million.[61] No other NPS site had received even close to this much money in operations funding, let alone grant monies to distribute to partners. The CCS funds paid for Indigenous speakers in the Tent of Many Voices and supported many projects initiated by tribes, including visitor center or other infrastructure planning, cultural preservation projects, interpretation projects, bicentennial planning, and educational projects.[62]

The Lewis and Clark Bicentennial in Retrospect

COTA initiated several programs as enduring legacies of the bicentennial. One program was the Native Voices Endowment, which is now housed within Yale University's Endangered Language Fund.[63] Another enduring impact of the bicentennial was the recording (with consent) of presentations in the Tent of

Many Voices, which were made available online through a website called the "Lewis & Clark Trail—Tribal Legacy Project," made possible through an NPS partnership with the University of Montana.[64]

Bicentennial grants from federal agencies and private foundations drove local-level cultural and educational projects, as well as tourism-centered businesses. It was noteworthy and precedent setting that tribes shared in this economic development.[65] Pinkham explained that, looking back on the bicentennial, "Indian people called it a success," because they were an important part of the decision-making process of how to disperse millions of federal dollars, and Native nations were able to benefit from these funds.[66] In addition to cultural and tourism projects, bicentennial grants funded publications by Indigenous poets, historians, language specialists, and storytellers, as well as by non-Native authors, which lived on after the commemorations.[67]

Another important legacy of the bicentennial is a book created by COTA entitled *Enough Good People*. The book serves as a guide for meaningful inclusion of Native people in future commemorative events. Recommendations range from the profound (inclusion should "not be about blame, shame or guilt but about moving forward from where you are") to the practical ("include a budget for gifting").[68] Like the Tribal Legacy Project, the book is available to the public online.

COTA Communications Coordinator Sammye Meadows called the Lewis and Clark Bicentennial a turning point, one that ushered in a new era in which "American history is being told by American Indians."[69] Pinkham and Hall argued that the bicentennial established a new model of commemorative events, in which Native people could freely claim and share their stories and the issues important to them.[70] Hall recounted, "It was so rewarding to see people start off defiant in telling that story and then being proud and assertive and confident in that story. I think that, to me, was so important because we can now take that forward to countless other events that are coming up, or to other public lands that have a place for us to work with and get that integrated. And use this as an example of why it works."[71]

The bicentennial also helped Native and non-Native communities develop new relationships with one another. Baker recalled having had, during the bicentennial, invited several Sioux elders to a town meeting in a mostly white town. Despite initial wariness by both parties, "By the end of the day, they're all joking and having a good time. Sharing coffee. And I said that's it. That's it. We did it. Nothing else for that day, anyway. And to me, that's the main difference. If nothing else, if they start waving to each other, we had success. Even to this day. If we still wave at each other, we had success. Open the door a little bit. Might disagree. But as long as they know you're a human being and I'm a human being."[72]

Like Baker, Halfmoon noted positive changes in relations between Native and non-Native neighbors near his home on the Nez Perce Reservation, which he attributed to cooperation during the bicentennial:

They started opening up a dialog within the community. We started making friends with these people that hated us. And that hatred was not so much—I mean, it's ominous hate, but a lot of it was ignorance. They know about those Indians down there. But they didn't know us. We played football against them. Played basketball against them. But they didn't know us. Same as us toward them. So the doors were opening. Some of the barriers were being destroyed. And that was a good thing. That was a good thing to watch some of these things being worked out with the communities. That was a beautiful sight.[73]

This legacy of cooperation and collaboration has faded since the bicentennial. Lewis and Clark NHT American Indian Liaison Dick Basch explained that once the funding and opportunity for collaboration ran out, those relationships faded. Basch expressed concern about the difficulty of conveying to new NPS staff the importance of collaborating with tribes and sustaining strong relationships: "I mean . . . when they throw all the components in the pot to stir it up, that they make sure and throw the tribes in that same pot so everything gets figured out appropriately that includes tribes. And so you don't have to go back and say, oh, we forgot something! And then have a shakeup."[74]

Baker agreed with Basch's assessment about the lasting impact of the bicentennial:

But the only thing I disagree with the park service, in this instance, is that it turned out to be just like any other program. . . . Meaning when the bicentennial's over, it's over. There's no afterlife. And that's what I disagree with, with any kind of federal organization, is that when it's over, they close the books on that one. Put it on a shelf and look for something else. They don't continue that, you know? And I think they should. . . . I think for future programs, or future superintendencies, I think they need to look at how they can continue that going. And the question would be, or should be, does the National Park Service have people in place to continue those partnerships and to continue to open these dialogs with tribes?[75]

Baker urged the NPS to consider funding a group like COTA for the NPS Centennial in 2016, but the agency did not create such a group. Some of the ideas from COTA made their way into a NPS group called the Council for Indigenous, Relevance, Communication, Leadership and Excellence (CIRCLE), which Otis Halfmoon co-created.[76]

The Lewis and Clark Bicentennial opened a door for the start of a much overdue dialogue among tribes, rural communities, and the nation as a whole. However, it did not fundamentally change the relationship between Native people and the NPS. The NPS failure to sustain funding, staffing, and prioritization of meaningful collaboration in the following decades contributed to the bicentennial's powerful but limited lasted legacies.

Notes

1. Department of the Interior (DOI), NPS, "Columbus Quincentennial Projects: A Directory" (Washington, DC: NPS, [1991]), 51.
2. Richard Williams, interview by Emily Greenwald, March 2, 2017, Omaha, Nebraska.
3. Sammye Meadows, interview by Jackie Gonzales, January 30, 2017, Gunnison, Colorado; Robert J. Miller, interview by Jackie Gonzales, February 2, 2017, Chandler, Arizona.; James Brooke, "Indians in Protest Against Columbus," *New York Times* (October 13, 1992). http://www.nytimes.com/1992/10/13/world/indians-in-protest-against-columbus.html.
4. Richard N. Williams, Coordinator, LCNHT, NPS, to Jerry Garrett, April 14, 1992, Drawer A—Administration, Folder: Bicentennial Council 1993, LCNHT Central Files.
5. For more on the history of the Lewis and Clark Trail Heritage Foundation, see Gonzales, Jackie and Greenwald, Emily. *Commemoration and Collaboration: An Administrative History of the Lewis and Clark National Historic Trail* (National Park Service, 2018), see especially chapters 2 and 3.
6. Jerry Garrett, Chair, Lewis and Clark Bicentennial Celebration Committee, to Members, Lewis and Clark Celebration Committee, April 1, 1993, Drawer A—Administration, Folder: Bicentennial Council 1993, LCNHT Central Files; LCTHF, "Bicentennial Committee, Year ending June 30, 1992," 1992(?), Drawer A—Administration, Folder: Bicentennial Council 1993, LCNHT Central Files; Bicentennial Committee, Lewis and Clark Trail Heritage Foundation (LCTHF), "Internal Mission Statement," August 1991, Drawer A—Administration, Folder: Bicentennial Council 1993, LCNHT Central Files.
7. LCTHF, "Minutes of Bicentennial Committee Meeting, Collinsville, IL," August 2, 1993, Drawer A—Administration, Folder: Bicentennial Council 1993, LCNHT Central Files; LCNHT, "A Summary Administrative and Interpretive History of The 'Corps of Discovery II: 200 Years to the Future,' A Project of the Lewis and Clark Bicentennial 1994–2006," (September 2008), 13.
8. An Act to provide for the establishment of a Commission on the Bicentennial of the Constitution, September 29, 1983, 97 Stat. 719 (P.L. 98-101).
9. Harry Hubbard, Chairman, Bicentennial Committee, LCTHF, to the Bicentennial Committee, October 11, 1993, Jerry Garrett, Chair, Lewis and Clark Bicentennial Celebration Committee, to Members, Lewis and Clark Celebration Committee, April 1, 1993, and Harry Hubbard, Chairman, Bicentennial Committee, LCTHF, to Stuart E. Knapp, President, LCTHF, August 20, 1993, in Drawer A—Administration, Folder: Bicentennial Council 1993, LCNHT Central Files; Williams, interview.
10. LCNHT, "A Summary Administrative and Interpretive History of The 'Corps of Discovery II,'" 3.

11. Thomas D. Thiessen, Archeologist, Midwest Archeological Center, NPS, to Chief, Midwest Archeological Center, NPS, memorandum, May 11, 1994, Drawer L cont'd—end, Folder: L6017 Lewis and Clark NHT Bicentennial Celebration, LCNHT Central Files.
12. Thomas L. Gilbert, Manager, Ice Age, North Country, and Lewis and Clark National Trails, NPS, to Tom Thiessen, Archeologist, Midwest Archeological Center, NPS, list of invitees attached to memorandum, April 6, 1994, Drawer L—L6015, Folder: L6017 Lewis and Clark NHT [1993–1994] Bicentennial Celebration, LCNHT Central Files; LCNHT, "A Summary Administrative and Interpretive History of The 'Corps of Discovery II,'" 3.
13. Circle of Tribal Advisors (COTA), NLCBC, *Enough Good People: Reflections on Tribal Involvements and Inter-Cultural Collaboration 2003–2006* (Gunnison, CO: 2009), 91.
14. Allen V. Pinkham, Sr., interview by Jackie Gonzales, February 24, 2017, Lapwai, Idaho.
15. NLCBC, "Post-Celebration Wish List," March 5, 1995, Drawer A—Administration, Folder: Bicentennial Council, Inc., LCNHT Central Files.
16. COTA, *Enough Good People*, 92; Harry Hubbard, President, Lewis and Clark Bicentennial Council, to Friends [form letter], November 17, 1995, LCTHF Organizational Records, Series VI, Box 5, Folder: Box 46 Folder 1—Foundation Headquarters—Nat. Council of L&C Bicentennial 1995, William P. Sherman Library and Archives, Lewis and Clark Trail Heritage Foundation, Great Falls, MT.
17. Pinkham, interview.
18. COTA, *Enough Good People*, 92; Meadows, interview; Miller, interview.
19. "Lewis and Clark Planning Meeting—Ft. Osage, MO," September 9, 2001, Drawer A–Administration. Folder: [no label] (A43?), LCNHT Central Files; Williams, interview.
20. Stephen Ambrose, *Undaunted Courage: Meriwether Lewis, Thomas Jefferson, and the Opening of the American West* (New York: Simon & Schuster, 1996); Duncan and Burns, *Lewis and Clark: The Journey of the Corps of Discovery*, film, directed by Ken Burns (Public Broadcasting Corporation, 1997); "Best Sellers Plus," *New York Times* (September 20, 1998); Gary R. Edgerton, *Ken Burns's America: Packaging the Past for Television* (New York: Palgrave, 2001), 176.
21. Tom Kenworthy, "Lewis and Clark Fever Catches On," *USA Today* (June 9, 2003); Timothy Egan, "Recalling a Storied Trek to Parts Unknown," *New York Times* (January 18, 2003); Otis Halfmoon, interview by Jackie Gonzales, February 1, 2017, Santa Fe, New Mexico; Williams, interview.
22. A resolution to support the commemoration of the bicentennial of the Lewis and Clark Expedition, S. Res. 57, 105th Cong. (1997).
23. 146 Cong. Rec. H9507 (daily ed., September 23, 1998); US Senate Lewis and Clark Expedition Caucus, member list, updated May 11, 2000, Drawer H-History—K3023 Interp., Folder: Caucus, LCNHT Central Files; DOI, NPS, "Bicentennial Commemoration of the Lewis and Clark Expedition,"

briefing statement, undated (2001?), Drawer A46—C-Concessions, Folder: A6423 LECL NHT Internal Control, LCNHT Central Files; Goering, interview.
24. Gorski, interview; Michael L. Lawson, *Dammed Indians: The Pick-Sloan Plan and the Missouri River Sioux, 1944–1980* (Norman: University of Oklahoma Press, 1994), 156.
25. Gerard Baker, interview by Jackie Gonzales, February 21, 2017, Miles City, Montana.
26. "Federal Lewis and Clark Interagency Update for the Lewis and Clark Congressional Caucus," July 21, 2000, Drawer A—Administration, Folder: A3815 LECL NHT Public Relations With Federal, State, and Local Agencies, LCNHT Central Files.
27. NPS, JNEM, "Lewis and Clark Corps of Discovery II: 200 Years to the Future, Lewis and Clark Bicentennial Program" (September 1998), Drawer A—Administration, Folder: Corps of Discovery II c.1998, LCNHT Central Files.
28. Ken Schaefer, Assistant Superintendent, for Gary W. Easton, Superintendent, JNEM, to Bill Schenk, Midwest Regional Director, NPS, January 29, 1998, 1–3, Drawer A—Administration, Folder: Corps of Discovery II c.1998, LCNHT Central Files.
29. Regional Director, Midwest Region, to Regional Directors, NPS, "Lewis and Clark Bicentennial Project," memorandum, December 9, 1998, Drawer D—6215, Folder: A82 LECL NHT Special Events OPENING Corps II, LCNHT Central Files.
30. Cal Calabrese to Suzy Hubbell, Kim Prill, Dick Williams, Tom Ross, and Margaret Gorski, January 31, 1999, Drawer A—Administration, Folder: [no label], LCNHT Central Files; Calabrese, interview.
31. DOI, NPS, to Cal Calabrese, Superintendent, LCNHT, "Lewis and Clark National Historic Trail, Federal Interagency Lewis and Clark Initiatives/Issues," briefing statement, April 5, 1999, Drawer A46—C-Concessions, Folder: A6423 LECL NHT Internal Control, LCNHT Central Files; "Briefing on Lewis and Clark Tribal Consultations," July 7, 1999, Drawer A–Administration, Folder: [no label], LCNHT Central Files.
32. "A Report to the National Park Service: A Summary of Issues and Recommendations From the Consultation with American Indian Tribes Regarding The Lewis and Clark Bi-centennial, April 15, 16, 1999, Lewiston, Idaho," April 15–16, 1999, Drawer [no label, drawer 2 of 24], Folder: COTA '93–'99, LCNHT Central Files; "Briefing on Lewis and Clark Tribal Consultations," July 7, 1999, Drawer A–Administration, Folder: [no label], LCNHT Central Files.
33. COTA, *Enough Good People*, 38.
34. Roberta Conner, interview by Jackie Gonzales, February 22, 2017, Pendleton, Oregon; Meadows, interview; Pinkham, interview.
35. Conner, interview.
36. Conner.

37. Many interviewees for this project and Indigenous speakers during the bicentennial used this phrase, but we have been unable to track its source.
38. Baker, interview; James Brooke, "Controversy Over Memorial to Winners at Little Bighorn," *New York Times* (August 24, 1997).
39. Baker, interview.
40. Baker; Halfmoon, interview.
41. Conner, interview.
42. Baker, interview.
43. Halfmoon, interview.
44. Richard Basch, interview by Jackie Gonzales, May 1, 2017, Astoria, Oregon.; Baker, interview; Halfmoon, interview.
45. Lewis and Clark Bicentennial Corps of Discovery II: 200 Years to the Future Project Meeting Notes, Washington, DC, December 14, 2000, Drawer A—Administration, Folder: A44 Interagency Agree. MOU Group, LCNHT Central Files.
46. Steve Adams, interview by Jackie Gonzales, February 3, 2017, Oro Valley, Arizona; Margaret Gorski, interview by Emily Greenwald, February 23, 2017, Missoula, Montana; Robert J. Miller, interview by Jackie Gonzales, February 2, 2017, Chandler, Arizona; Meadows, interview.
47. "Lewis & Clark Expedition Bicentennial, 2003–2006, The Tent of Many Voices," (2002), Drawer A–Administration. Folder; [no label], LCNHT Central Files.
48. Conner, interview.
49. Karen Goering, interview by Jackie Gonzales, February 18, 2017, St. Louis, Missouri.
50. Baker, interview.
51. COTA, *Enough Good People*, 6–7, 67, 93; DOI, NPS, "Bicentennial Commemoration of the Lewis and Clark Expedition," briefing statement, undated (2001?), Drawer A46—C-Concessions, Folder: A6423 LECL NHT Internal Control, LCNHT Central Files; Meadows, interview; Conner, interview; Lewis & Clark Trail—Tribal Legacy Project, "About the Circle of Tribal Advisors." https://cms.lc-triballegacy.org/cota-about (accessed January 18, 2017).
52. COTA, *Enough Good People*, 93; Lewis & Clark Trail—Tribal Legacy Project, "About the Circle of Tribal Advisors"; "Lewis and Clark Planning Meeting—Ft. Osage, MO," September 9, 2001, Drawer A–Administration. Folder: [no label] (A43?), LCNHT Central Files.
53. Lewis & Clark Trail—Tribal Legacy Project, "About the Circle of Tribal Advisors."
54. Pinkham, interview; Chris Howell, interview by Jackie Gonzales, February 23, 2017, Spokane, Washington.
55. Meadows, interview; Conner, interview.
56. COTA, *Enough Good People*, 72.
57. "Notes from August 16–17, 2001," August 16–17, 2001, Drawer A46—C-Concessions, Folder: D18 Briefing Statements (Many re: CII), LCNHT Central Files; Conner, interview.
58. COTA, *Enough Good People*, 94.

59. DOI, NPS, "Bicentennial Commemoration of the Lewis and Clark Expedition," briefing statement, undated (2001?), Drawer A46—C-Concessions, Folder: A6423 LECL NHT Internal Control, LCNHT Central Files.
60. The Federal Grant and Cooperative Agreements Act of 1977 provided authority for such partnerships, and the BLM issued its first CCS grants in 1985 for resource management projects. 31 USC. 6301-6308; BLM, "Challenge Cost Share," 1991.
61. LCNHT, "A Summary Administrative and Interpretive History of The 'Corps of Discovery II," 11–12.
62. Gerard Baker to Midwest Regional Director, "Superintendent's 2003 Annual Report," memorandum, February 10, 2004, LCNHT Digital Files, 2; Stephen E. Adams, Superintendent, LCNHT, to Midwest Regional Director, "Fiscal Year 2004 Annual Narrative Report of the Superintendent," memorandum, February 28, 2005, LCNHT Digital Files, 8; Stephen E. Adams to Midwest Regional Director, "Fiscal Year 2005 Superintendent's Annual Report," memorandum, March 20, 2006, LCNHT Digital Files, 3–4.
63. Conner, interview; Meadows, interview; Goering, interview.
64. Basch, interview; Jones, interview; Conner, interview; Meadows, interview; COTA, *Enough Good People*, 76; Lewis & Clark—Tribal Legacy Project, "Site Credits." https://cms.lc-triballegacy.org/credits (accessed September 22, 2017).
65. Pinkham, interview; Conner, interview; Baker, interview; Meadows, interview.
66. Pinkham, interview.
67. COTA, *Enough Good People*, 77; Miller; interview.
68. COTA, *Enough Good People*, 130–33; Goering, interview; Conner, interview; Meadows, interview.
69. Meadows, interview.
70. Pinkham, interview; Hall interview.
71. Hall.
72. Baker, interview.
73. Halfmoon, interview.
74. Basch, interview.
75. Baker, interview.
76. CIRCLE provides guidance and recommendations to the NPS on hiring, retaining, and improving visibility of American Indian, Alaska Native, and Native Hawaiian NPS employees. Halfmoon, interview; National Park Service, Office of Relevancy, Diversity, and Inclusion, "Employee Resource Groups." https://www.nps.gov/orgs/1244/ergs.htm (accessed October 30, 2017).

SEVEN | **After the Opening**
*Shared Authority and Multivocality at
the Sand Creek Massacre National Historic Site*

ARI KELMAN

AT DAYBREAK ON NOVEMBER 29, 1864, more than seven hundred soldiers from the 1st and 3rd Colorado Regiments descended upon an encampment of Arapaho and Cheyenne people located in the southeastern portion of the territory, near the Kansas border. The soldiers ignored signals that they were approaching a peace camp comprised of Native people friendly to the United States. Chief Black Kettle, who for many years had sought amicable relations between his followers and federal authorities, flew an American and a white flag over his lodge. Nevertheless, the volunteer troops, commanded by Colonel John Chivington, poured rifle and artillery fire—including shot from a so-called mountain howitzer, the only time such a weapon was ever used in Colorado—indiscriminately into the settlement throughout the day and evening. The assault killed perhaps two hundred Native Americans, the vast majority of whom were women, children, or the elderly. During the carnage, Chivington's men committed horrifying atrocities: murdering pregnant women, infants, and other helpless Arapaho and Cheyenne people. In the wake of the carnage, the soldiers combed the bloody ground for gruesome trophies, hacking scalps and genitalia from their victims' bodies. The incident would come to be known as the Sand Creek massacre.[1]

Nearly a century and a half later, on April 27, 2007, the National Park Service (NPS) co-opened its 391st unit—the Sand Creek Massacre National Historic Site—with great fanfare and some controversy. Elected officials, park service administrators, and descendants of Sand Creek's victims and survivors spoke to share their sense of what memorializing Sand Creek could mean. The site's creation, some speakers suggested, represented an effort at cross-cultural cooperation in service of healing. They celebrated the fact that descendants of Native people killed by federal soldiers had cooperated with park service officials—representatives of the same government culpable in their ancestors' slaughter—to find and protect the field upon which they died. Battles over competing administrative priorities, disparate methodologies for understanding history, and incommensurable narratives of the past punctuated their labors. Nevertheless, the descendants worked with their park service counterparts in service of a common goal: preserving Sand Creek's memory. For some observers, then, the historic site's opening in 2007 represented a high-water mark in modern federal-tribal relations. For other onlookers, though, the memorialization project seemed like a troubling effort to erase enduring mistreatment of Native nations.[2]

In the years since the site's establishment, conflict over how best to interpret the historical record for visitors has lingered. The park service, guided by an increasingly pluralistic vision, a desire to represent the diversity of the American people's experiences, and details of the site's enabling legislation, has continued working closely with Sand Creek descendants in these years, embracing practices that public historians call "shared authority." The concept of sharing authority has roots in the Works Progress Administration's Federal Writers' Project, which gathered and archived the stories of formerly enslaved people. This was accomplished through the scholarship of so-called New Social Historians, who included bottom-up narratives informed by the experiences of workers, women, and people of color, as they recounted more fully realized stories of the nation's past, and in the writing of scholars like Michael Frisch, who suggested that practitioners of public history should not elevate themselves above the members of the communities with which they hope to engage. Rather than policing boundaries or relying on elite interpretations of the past that are couched in professional hierarchies, Frisch suggested that administrators at monuments, museums, and other historic sites should work to build more inclusive and collaborative relationships with visitors. In this way, consumers of history can sometimes become producers as well.[3]

Sharing authority and the related goal of multivocality—featuring multiple voices, sometimes clashing rather than in concert, within a single interpretive landscape—has not always been easy at the Sand Creek Massacre National Historic Site. The descendants have their own aspirations for the memorialization project and their own sense of what the site can mean: not so much what it can accomplish for the United States but instead for their own nations. They view the historic site's creation as an act of redemption, a reclaiming and repurposing of colonized land, as well as a powerful expression of tribal sovereignty and persistence. The Sand Creek site for them is an emblem of what Native scholar Gerald Vizenor has called "survivance." Vizenor writes that "survivance is an active sense of presence, the continuance of native stories, not a mere reaction," adding, "Native survivance stories are renunciations of dominance, tragedy and victimry." Informed by sentiments like Vizenor's, the tribal descendants were never passive during the memorialization effort, and they have not been in the years since the site opened. They have always fought to have their views of the past represented at the Sand Creek memorial, using it as an example of successful tribal historic preservation efforts, and as a springboard from which to launch spiritual healing runs and other efforts to protect traditional tribal practices.[4]

And so, while the theory of shared authority pivots on radical inclusivity, its practice at the site since 2007 has been plagued by questions of whose views of history should shape interpretive choices. The descendants have bristled when asked to share authority over history they consider sacred and theirs; the park service, even when it has tried to share authority, has not always known how to do so. Power struggles between federal authorities and Native peoples over how best to remember Sand Creek—disputes that in some cases date back to the era of the massacre, and in others emerge out of more recent controversies surrounding the politics of commemoration—have echoed throughout the process of memorializing the violence. Park service interpreters, no matter how cutting edge their methods, no matter how deep their engagement with the documentary record, sometimes have found themselves awash in meta-narratives of US history that rely on unexamined assumptions of American exceptionalism. Little room exists within such storytelling frameworks, many of which are shaped by materials housed within imperial archives, to grapple with the bloody and tortuous process of empire-building in the trans-Mississippi West, especially not the rapacious and violent logic of settler colonialism. The descendants, the tribal peoples most invested in the historic site's day-to-day operations, especially the contours of its interpretive landscape, have little patience for triumphal stories of American greatness or innocence. The result has been intermittent conflict, albeit in the context of a strategic collaboration.

Enabling legislation hardwired cooperation, sometimes strained, between tribal peoples and federal authorities into the Sand Creek site. Senator Ben Nighthorse Campbell—the only Native person serving in Congress and a member of the Council of Forty-Four Chiefs, the traditional civilian governance body of the Northern and Southern Cheyenne tribes—sponsored hearings in 1998 to purchase the Sand Creek site from private landowners and establish a unit of the national parks system. The descendants, though, pleased by Senator Campbell's interest in protecting the Sand Creek site, grew frustrated when NPS experts testified that before the massacre could be memorialized, it first had to be found. Native elders and activists insisted that they knew the hallowed ground's location: a remote ranch located in Southeastern Colorado, where for many years their kin had traveled to venerate their ancestors and perform sacred rituals. The park service, the descendants implored, should allow them to interpret episodes from their own past. Steve Brady, Headman of a Cheyenne soldier society and director of the Northern Cheyenne Sand Creek office, insisted after the Capitol

Hill hearings that "the federal government refuses to respect Indian people, even when it comes to understanding Indian history."[5]

Senator Campbell responded by including provisions within his Sand Creek Massacre National Historic Site Study Act that bound the park service to the descendants. Tribal peoples and federal officials would have to work collaboratively, Campbell's legislation made clear, to find, protect, and memorialize the massacre site. Although the descendants remained frustrated that representatives of the park service had challenged their cultural authority during the Congressional hearings, ignoring their insistence that the Sand Creek site had never gone missing, they still supported Campbell's legislation. They focused on what they recognized as important victories: after more than a hundred years of struggles over nomenclature, Sand Creek would definitively be labeled "a massacre" rather than "a battle" at the historic site, and Campbell's act would guarantee their people prerogatives during the search process and beyond. Members of the affected tribes would always have "the right of open access to visit the site and rights of cultural and historical observance" there. On October 6, 1998, President Clinton signed Senator Campbell's Sand Creek Act, making it federal law and starting a hunt for the site.[6]

Over the next eighteen months, the descendants and the park service worked together, uneasy partners who occasionally clashed over how to balance the authority Senator Campbell's legislation forced them to share. Disputes over conflicting approaches to history and memory, over competing methodologies and epistemologies, sometimes threatened to derail the search process. At one juncture, park service officials celebrated a "triumph." Relying on archival records generated by soldiers who had participated in the massacre, historians working on the site search arrived at a tentative conclusion about where the violence had taken place. Led by battlefield archeologists, the search team went into the field to test the theory. Armed with metal detectors and shovels, they unearthed a plume of period-correct artifacts, including bullets and fragments from a mountain howitzer's shot. Their "discovery" seemed to point definitively—offering "mute testimony," in the words of one of the researchers—to the massacre's location: less than a mile away from the spot that the descendants, using their own ways of understanding the past, called the "traditional site." But the distance separating the two places stretched wide enough to divide the Arapahos and Cheyennes from the historians, archeologists, and anthropologists on the government's payroll—well-meaning scholars who nevertheless seemed to be recapitulating imperial inequities that marred federal-tribal relations throughout the nation's history.[7]

The descendants were outraged, just as they had been during Senator Campbell's Sand Creek hearing, when it appeared that the federal government would "not allow Indian people control over Indian history." The Cheyenne representatives to the search were particularly upset that the park service chose to rely upon historical documents generated by the soldiers who had butchered their ancestors.

Those records were held in government archives, the descendants noted, suggesting that they were part of a settler-colonial project that had nearly wiped out their people. "Why," Chief Laird Cometsevah asked, "would the government ignore Indian people who knew that place, knew that land, knew that history," focusing instead on the experiences of "Chivington's men," soldiers who "had committed murder"? Some of the descendants pointed to what they perceived as callous reactions during the archeological reconnaissance—"park service folks jumping around and shouting on top of our family members' remains"—as evidence that federal officials had insufficient regard for how to steward such "a sacred place." Consequently, rather than accepting the park service's conclusions, rooted as they were in suspect methods and evidence, the descendants threatened to splinter the search process. Eventually, they generated their own map of the killing field, placing its location exactly at the "traditional site."[8]

In the end, the park service, though initially wrongfooted by the search controversy and the descendants' dissent, floated an elegant compromise that embodied principles of shared authority and multivocality. The Sand Creek Massacre National Historic Site would feature expansive boundaries, capacious enough to encompass multiple interpretations of the massacre's history and memory. There would be room for the descendants' perspective, informed by traditional ways of understanding the past, including the transmission of stories from one generation of Arapahos and Cheyennes to the next, and the NPS's "scientific findings," built as they were upon scholarly methods and practices drawn from fields like archeology, anthropology, and history. These were radically different perspectives—not just incompatible narratives of where the bloodshed at Sand Creek had taken place, but more fundamental clashes over how to grapple with the uncomfortable relationship between past and present and even the production of knowledge. Eventually, though, after years of additional wrangling and countless painful twists and turns in the planning process, the NPS and the descendants decided that their competing visions could coexist within a single commemorative landscape.[9]

In the years since the historic site's opening, sharing authority at Sand Creek has remained challenging, yielding uneven results for the park service and the descendants. Alexa Roberts learned many lessons working with Navajo people early in her career as an anthropologist, and still more during the site search, when she led efforts to collect ethnographies from Arapaho and Cheyenne descendants. Roberts believed that federal authorities had a responsibility to embrace what scholars call "decolonized methodologies" informed by traditional tribal protocols when collaborating with Native peoples. Although bound by the structures of the park service's unwieldy bureaucracy, she allowed the descendants to make strategic methodological decisions about handling oral histories. She explained that she "never lost sight of [her] outsider status," which, she suggested, provided her "at least some understanding" of the descendants' relationship with a dominant settler-colonial society. Roberts hoped to capture "the perspective of the tribal people, who," she said, "understood more about the lived history of Sand Creek than anyone else ever could." Roberts later would become the Sand Creek site's first superintendent.[10]

Convinced that the act of memorializing Sand Creek had the power to reshape broader discussions of American empire and studies of genocide—in both national and transnational contexts—Roberts hoped to use the historic site as a lever to realize social and cultural change. She understood that such a lofty goal would necessarily remain out of reach without a genuine collaboration between NPS officials and the descendants, a partnership that could only be cemented by confronting the source of the ill will that lingered following the site search: the federal government's longstanding mistreatment of and disrespect for Native peoples, even when engaged in cross-cultural collaborations. Roberts vowed, consequently, that she would operate the Sand Creek site as both a federal and an Indigenous landscape, embracing multivocality, no matter how discomfiting, as a way of confronting visitors with details of one of the darkest chapters from the American past. Put another way, she viewed the site's potential through a utopian lens, embracing work that scholars of education Paulo Freire and Ira Shor have labeled "a pedagogy for liberation"—wrought in this case through commemoration and shared authority.[11]

Even before the site opened its doors to the public, Roberts, working with Steve Brady and his brother, Otto Braided Hair, considered how to educate people about Sand Creek's history. Informed by fallout from the NPS's decision to rely on historical documents generated by Sand Creek's perpetrators rather than its victims, Roberts collected oral histories to serve as an evidentiary counterweight. At that time, she hatched plans for a Sand Creek research center—a postcolonial archive that would place tribal sources, including family stories, on equal footing with materials associated with non-tribal people. She, Brady, and Braided Hair discussed a nonprofit entity independent of the park service. In 2007, they crafted a proposal, which, absent funding, languished. But then, in 2010 the United Methodist Church chose to grapple with its culpability in the Sand Creek Massacre. Colonel John Chivington, the "Fighting Parson," had been a Methodist minister. John Evans, Colorado's territorial governor in 1864, had been a church elder. The Methodist hierarchy hoped to engage in a process of "active repentance," first confronting and then making restitution for the violence at Sand Creek. The church sought exculpation in part by helping to fund the research center. A repository of tribal and non-tribal documents, it would be a place where people could study past wrongs and contemplate a more just future.[12]

With the Methodists' gift serving as a kind of proof of concept, the Interim Director of the park service's Intermountain Region, Mary Gibson-Scott, suggested that the research center should be part of the historic site. Roberts, who thought the archive could become a model for sharing authority, agreed. The park service would provide additional funding for renovations and an operational budget for the facility, which would be housed in a historic structure in Eads, Colorado. Gateway to the Sand Creek site, Eads, as with small towns scattered across Colorado's plains, required economic development projects to keep young people who otherwise fled to live in the Front Range's booming cities. In 2012, as planning for the research center gathered momentum, the United Methodist Church pledged another gift to the facility. Five years after that, Roberts, Braided Hair, and Karen Wilde, the Sand Creek site's tribal liaison, compiled names for a board of directors and another of scholarly advisors. In 2019, the Sand Creek Massacre Foundation, the "official philanthropic partner of the Sand Creek Massacre National Historic Site," incorporated as a nonprofit organization. The research center opened its doors.[13]

The Sand Creek Massacre Foundation's mission pivots on the belief that remembrance promotes healing for Native and non-Native people. Its work, though, is not entirely retrospective. "By promoting initiatives to understand the relevance of the Sand Creek Massacre in the contemporary world," the foundation and research center not only "honor the legacy of those lost at Sand Creek" but also "assist in minimizing the chances of similar atrocities in the future." Roberts implores visitors to "learn, remember, and heal." The foundation's board of directors and scholarly advisors are models of shared authority, featuring Arapaho and Cheyenne elders, NPS officials, museum professionals, activists, representatives from the United Methodist church, scholars of Native American and Indigenous Studies, and local politicians. As Roberts says, "We put a group together that would be broadly representative, keeping our work grounded in the communities most affected by Sand Creek while also helping us to share the massacre's history." She goes on to explain, "We wanted to make sure that Native voices would guide us, because our goal is to ensure that nothing like Sand Creek ever happens again."[14]

While Roberts made plans for the research center and foundation, the park service wrestled with the practicalities of sharing authority and featuring multivocality at the site. In one fraught case, undergraduates from Colorado College visited the memorial on October 3, 2017. Having spent the previous month in a small seminar titled "Power, Place, and Protest in the West," they were interested in the construction of historical knowledge, emphasizing the experiences of Native peoples. The class read extensively about violent encounters in the West, including at Sand Creek. They studied theories of settler colonialism, federal Indian policy, and representations of Native cultures. A day before traveling to the historic site, the class attended a lecture given by Norma Gorneau, a Northern Cheyenne descendant. Gorneau discussed the political currents swirling around the massacre and its memorialization. The students believed that the region in which they lived had a history of violence and dispossession that could only be understood by hearing from multiple voices. They were primed to test the limits of the park service's efforts.[15]

When the seminar disembarked from a tour bus at the historic site, an NPS employee began lecturing about the massacre. One student recounted that the guide employed antiquated terminology and analytical framing, describing "Arapaho and Cheyenne peoples as 'nomads'" while "suggesting that they d[id] not have systems of governments and fail[ed] to engage in diplomatic relations with other Indigenous peoples." Stunned by what she perceived as cultural insensitivity, the student noted that it seemed like the park service's "narrative of history is framed from the colonizer's perspective." Another student agreed, recalling that the upsetting encounter with the NPS guide underscored the importance of "the descendants maintain[ing] control over the memory" of the massacre. By contrast, interpretive signage scattered throughout the memorial featured "[I]ndigenous voices," suggesting that the park service, even if some its employees echoed "master narratives" of regional history and "perpetuated white supremacy," nevertheless highlighted multiple perspectives, including those of descendants.[16]

After the students walked the site throughout the morning, Alexa Roberts hosted them for lunch. She discussed the challenge of navigating treacherous interpretative terrain at the site. The students shared their experiences with the guide, expressing frustration with the limits of her presentation and wondering why she had not done better. Roberts defended her colleague, noting that "even scholars who spend years studying Sand Creek have a hard time coming to terms with its horrors," and suggested that the problem was structural. The park service, she explained, had no mechanisms for providing special training for employees at a unit like Sand Creek, no methods for deepening cultural literacy despite the site's subject matter. She promised that feedback from the students would inform future management decisions. She shared authority, allowing site visitors to help determine how history would be presented there. One of the students later remarked, "It is important to note, however, that the National Park Service cannot be generalized into one collective unit. As Alexa Roberts demonstrated," it is actually a diverse organization that includes "individuals who do not always agree on every controversial issue."[17]

Roberts made good on her promise to the students, formulating a new training program for interpreters at the site. Designed to field-test the efficacy of multivocality, "we made the decision to bring in speakers who would give a public lecture and then work with our interpreters, highlighting different ways of understanding history." Those speakers, Roberts hoped, would help the staff at the historic site to "move beyond any single, unified viewpoint of the American past and focus instead on how different groups of people have different ways of understanding what happened in Colorado and throughout the region during the era of Westward expansion." A group of scholars and Native leaders, she believed, would introduce newcomers to the history of Sand Creek with "foundational perspectives on American Indian experiences, including the impact the massacre had on Arapaho, Cheyenne, and other Indigenous peoples." As Roberts explained, guides at the site "mean well. And they want to do well for every visitor, no matter how educated they may be." She noted that "our people always want to be thoughtful. They want to be sensitive. We just have to give them the tools to do their job. We don't always do that. We sometimes set them up to fail." Linked to the general management planning process for the site, the speaker series would generate materials that she hoped to include in future interpretive training.[18]

Beginning almost exactly a year to the day after the students from Colorado College visited the Sand Creek site, Roberts brought in ten speakers over eight months, "including historians, educators, scholars, tribal representatives, and current and former NPS employees." The program presented "to park staff, volunteers, and members of the public various perspectives on the understanding of history and the implications of these perspectives for how the stories of the Sand Creek Massacre are interpreted to visitors." The massacre, a planning document noted, happened "on a single day," but interpreters at the historic site needed to understand and "convey [that] the Sand Creek Massacre [w]as an atrocity that never ended and is embedded in the lives and cultural identities of entire tribal nations to this day." Site interpreters needed to grapple with how the massacre remained living and lived history. Speakers included Rick Williams, former CEO of the American Indian College Fund; Ladonna Brown, Director of Research and Cultural Interpretation, Heritage Preservation, Department of Culture and Humanities, the Chickasaw Nation; and Henrietta Mann, founding President of the Cheyenne and Arapaho Tribal College.[19]

As Roberts considered the possible impact of the speaker series, she remarked that her primary goal remained the site's "core mission . . . to inspire visitors to think more seriously about the legacy of past injustices and to work to ensure that events like the massacre never happen again." She suggested that current events indicated that the site was achieving that goal. On the massacre's 150th anniversary, for instance, Colorado Governor John Hickenlooper issued a formal apology for the violence at Sand Creek. Speaking on the steps of the state capitol, surrounded by a huge crowd, including Arapahos and Cheyennes who had just completed a three-day spiritual healing run from the massacre site to Denver, Hickenlooper spoke "to all Indigenous people . . . on behalf of the loving people of Colorado. I want to say I am sorry for the atrocities of our government that were visited on your ancestors." He did not offer the apology alone; he first consulted with all of Colorado's living governors. Otto Braided Hair, who attended the ceremony, "encourage[d] people to visit the Sand Creek National Historic site and learn about the events of that day." The descendants hoped that experience would help build a "deeper understanding and brighter future." The site, in this view, could heal wounds suffered from historical violence.[20]

Hickenlooper's remarks were unsparing yet hopeful, creating space for cross-cultural reconciliation. He recounted the "deep moral failure" of one of his predecessors, Governor John Evans, and the perfidy of John Chivington. But then Hickenlooper read from a letter composed by one of Chivington's subordinates, Captain Silas Soule, who had refused to commit the Colorado volunteers who served under him to the slaughter. Soule later corresponded with well-placed connections, who spread word of Sand Creek to officials in Washington, DC. Those efforts resulted in a series of federal investigations into the event, all of which labeled the violence a bad act, and which, Steve Brady suggested, seeded the ground for the park service to memorialize not just the massacre, but also the United States' culpability. As Brady noted, "It's one thing when an Indian talks about terrible things from our history. White people say, 'Well, Indians complain all the time.' But it's something else again when an American soldier, a white man like Silas Soule, says Sand Creek was a massacre." Before running their final leg to the capitol to hear Hickenlooper's speech, the Arapahos and Cheyennes had stopped at Riverside Cemetery in Denver, where they performed graveside ceremonies honoring Soule's memory.[21]

In another instance, the Sand Creek site's impact on public memory manifested itself in Denver's response to the Black Lives Matter movement in 2020. As protesters around the nation considered the origins and power of commemorative landscapes, arguing that white supremacists had inscribed racial hierarchies into civic spaces, activists in Denver focused on a Civil War memorial on the state capitol steps—the spot from which Governor Hickenlooper had issued his apology in 2014. In 1909, the Colorado Pioneers Association commissioned a statue of a Union cavalrymen facing west, toward the Rocky Mountain, with a plaque at its base cataloging "battles" in which Coloradoans had fought during the war. Sand Creek was among them, a depiction that whitewashed the actions of Chivington's men. That rhetorical move made sense at the time. A wave of memorialization swept over the United States as men who fought the Civil War reached the end of their lives. Commemorators stocked archives, wrote books, and built statues, preserving a heroic vision of the war. When the Pioneers Association unveiled its statue, thousands of onlookers, including veterans from the 1st and 3rd Colorado Regiments, looked on as a "hush of patriotic awe" fell over the scene. Coloradoans had cast Sand Creek within a deracinated narrative of the Civil War, erasing the massacre's violent repercussions for Native people.[22]

Their consciousness raised by Senator Campbell's Sand Creek Act, state lawmakers were ready in 2002 to reappraise the Civil War memorial. Legislators first pushed to have Sand Creek removed from the honor roll at the statue's base, suggesting that its inclusion represented an "insult to the memory" of the "Native Americans who were killed at Sand Creek," and also to the "Colorado Civil war veterans who fought and died in the actual Civil War battles that are listed on the memorial." But then the descendants, working with Colorado Chief Historian David Halaas, said that the plaque should be reinterpreted rather than erased. Laird Cometsevah "appreciated that those Colorado politicians finally understood that Sand Creek was a massacre and not a battle," but he thought "it was silly to fight to remember Sand Creek in one location and forget about it in another." Cometsevah "respectfully request[ed] that the words 'Sand Creek' presently engraved on the Civil War memorial be retained." He then suggested that "signage be placed around the Civil War statue that would inform and educate the public about the holocaust of Sand Creek." On November 29, the state unveiled a new plaque contextualizing the list of Civil War "battles," noting: "Protests led by Native Americans and others throughout the twentieth century have since led to the widespread recognition of the tragedy as the Sand Creek Massacre."[23]

Seventeen years later, on June 25, 2020, protestors tore down the statue and spray-painted the words "No Justice, No Peace" on its plinth. In the month following the lynching of George Floyd, monuments to white supremacy had fallen around the United States. A person who helped topple Colorado's Civil War memorial explained his comrades' motivation: "We figured what better way to get rid of a statue that represents racism." An eyewitness said, "I know that [soldier] is one of many men who were part of the Sand Creek Massacre and many other genocidal acts that happened throughout Colorado's early history." Governor Jared Polis responded with "outrage at the damage to a statue that commemorates the Union heroes of the Civil War who fought and lost their lives to end slavery." He suggested that "those responsible for the damage" may have been "hooligans, white supremacists, Confederate sympathizers, or drunk teenagers." He did not allow for the possibility that activists had expressed their fury at the murder of people of color, including the massacre of Arapahos and Cheyennes at Sand Creek, by engaging in acts of symbolic violence. Governor Polis overlooked an irony that punctuated Western history: that regional settlers could simultaneously fight for Lincoln and liberty, while also dispossessing and exterminating Native peoples. That disjuncture loomed over efforts at the historic site to interpret an event that for many visitors—and, in some instances, also for the park service—remained incompatible with threads of American exceptionalism and innocence imbricated within the national tapestry.[24]

In advance of the massacre's anniversary in 2020, Colorado's legislature chose to revise Denver's commemorative landscape, replacing the toppled statue with a memorial to the victims of Sand Creek. The new figure would be a Native woman in mourning, explained artist Harvey Phillip Pratt, a Sand Creek descendant who previously had designed the Smithsonian's National Native American Veteran's Memorial. As for the Union soldier, the statue would travel to History Colorado, the state historical society. It would stand as part of an exhibit titled, "This Is What Democracy Looks Like," focused on "differences in how various groups have interpreted its meaning, including tribal anger that the same cavalry units memorialized by the statue for heroism in the Civil War also perpetrated the Sand Creek massacre two years later." A museum curator noted, "We view this as a teachable moment. That's how we'd present it—not as an erasure or reinstallation, but as a chance to consider monuments and how we value them." Referring to the power of cultural positioning, he promised: "We take on the work of displaying this monument humbly and understand that it holds different meanings to different people." He also suggested that "we know some of the stakeholders we're interested in working with are military veterans and their families, tribal representatives of those victimized in the Sand Creek massacre and their descendants, and those advocating for more social justice today." Sharing authority and embracing multivocality, as at the Sand Creek historic site, would remain a complex task.[25]

A bit more than a year after the fall of the Civil War memorial, Governor Polis took further action, demonstrating again that the Sand Creek site had the power to shape interwoven strands of public memory and public policy. After more than a century and a half, he rescinded an order to capture and kill Colorado's Native Americans. On June 27, 1864, following the slaughter of a family of settlers near Denver, John Evans issued a proclamation to the "friendly Indians of the Plains." He asked them to come to "places of safety," military installations where authorities would "protect" them. But violence kept escalating, and Evans issued a second proclamation on August 11, urging "all citizens of Colorado, either individually or in such parties as they may organize, to go in pursuit of all hostile Indians on the plains." He asked these state-sanctioned vigilante mobs to spare peaceful Native people but offered no guidance on how to differentiate between hostile and friendly Indians. Regardless, "all good citizens," he implored, "are called upon to do their duty for the defense of their homes and families." The next day, the War Department authorized Evans to raise a regiment, the 3rd Colorado, to "pursue, kill, and destroy all hostile Indians." Those volunteer soldiers would perpetrate the Sand Creek massacre.[26]

For 157 years, that order remained in place, a grim reminder of one of the bloodiest chapters in Colorado's history. On August 17, 2021, though, Governor Polis signed his own executive order, nullifying Governor Evans's proclamations. Polis suggested that by confronting the legacy of Sand Creek, the state might begin making amends for "the sins of the past." He acknowledged that "we can't change the past," but added that at least "we can honor the memories of those who we lost by recognizing their sacrifice and vowing to do better." Reggie Wassana, an official in the Cheyenne and Arapaho Tribes, suggested that restitution needed to precede reconciliation: "We would like to see all those wrongs that were done all those years ago come back to right." Rick Williams, a member of the Lakota and Cheyenne Tribes, suggested that Polis's order marked the "end of the Colorado-Indian wars." Press coverage connected the event to the Sand Creek site, sometimes drawing on materials archived in the research center and mentioning that the memorial's creation had spurred a reassessment of the state's collective memory. Alexa Roberts hoped that "work the park service did with the descendants, really led by the descendants, was a starting point. There's more work to be done," she said, "more sites of violence that have been lost, erased, or misinterpreted. We've only taken the first steps of a long journey."[27]

It is difficult to predict where that journey might lead. But even as the nation continues struggling with racial violence—grim echoes of Sand Creek—the federal government grows more inclusive, boasting an increasing number of Native leaders. On December 16, 2021, Ben Nighthorse Campbell, acting as

Honorary Chair of the Sand Creek Massacre Foundation's Board of Directors, sent out a press release celebrating the park service's new director, Charles F. Sams, a member of the Confederated Tribes of the Umatilla Indian Reservation. Sams, Campbell noted, was the first Native person to head the Service in its 105-year history. Campbell went on to connect Sams's appointment with that of Secretary of the Interior Deb Halaand, the first Native woman to serve in the United States cabinet, calling both "historic steps," part of an effort "to return Native representation to our national story." Campbell hoped that Sams and Halaand would "visit the Sand Creek Massacre National Historic Site," where they could "join us in our work to promote initiatives to understand the relevance of the Sand Creek Massacre in the contemporary world, honor the legacy of those lost at Sand Creek, and assist in minimizing the chances of similar atrocities in the future." Campbell wanted more voices to join a commemorative chorus, to share authority so that connections between past and present would be more legible.[28]

Notes

1. For further reading on the massacre, please see: Stan Hoig, *The Sand Creek Massacre* (Norman: University of Oklahoma Press, 1974); Gary L. Roberts, "Sand Creek: Tragedy and Symbol," unpublished PhD dissertation (University of Oklahoma, 1984); Elliott West, *The Contested Plains: Indians, Goldseekers, and the Rush to Colorado* (Lawrence: University Press of Kansas, 2000); Ari Kelman, *A Misplaced Massacre: Struggling over the Memory of Sand Creek* (Cambridge, MA: Harvard University Press, 2013).
2. Kelman, *Misplaced Massacre*, 1–43.
3. Michael H. Frisch, *A Shared Authority: Essays on the Craft and Meaning of Oral and Public History* (Albany: State University of New York Press, 1990), 179–264.
4. Quotes from Gerald Vizenor, *Manifest Manners: Narratives on Postindian Survivance* (Lincoln: University of Nebraska Press, 1999), vii.
5. Quotes from Steve Brady, Headman, Crazy Dogs Society, Northern Cheyenne Tribe, interview by author, August 29, 2004, transcription held by National Park Service, Western Archeological and Conservation Center (NPS-WACC), Tucson, AZ. See also Kelman, *Misplaced Massacre*, 65–67.
6. Quotes from *Public Law 105-243*, 105th Congress (1998). See also Kelman, *Misplaced Massacre*, 67–70.
7. "Triumph" from Doug Scott, chief archeologist, National Park Service Midwest Archeological Center, interview by author, October 3, 2003, transcription held by NPS-WACC. "Discovery" from Jerry Greene research historian, National Park Service, interview by author, May 27, 2003, transcription held by NPS-WACC. "Mute testimony" and "nearly unequivocal" from National Park Service, Intermountain Region, *Sand Creek Massacre Project, Vol. 1: Site Location Study* (Denver: National Park Service, Intermountain Region, 2000),

132. "Traditional site" from Laird Cometsevah, Chief, Southern Cheyenne Tribe, interview by author, May 12, 2003, transcription held by NPS-WACC. See also Jerome A. Greene and Douglas D. Scott, *Finding Sand Creek: History, Archeology, and the 1864 Massacre Site* (Norman: University of Oklahoma Press, 2004), 30–33, appendices A–D.

8. "Not allow Indian people any control . . ." and "Park Service folks . . ." from Steve Brady, Headman, Crazy Dogs Society, Northern Cheyenne Tribe, interview by author, August 29, 2004, transcription held by NPS-WACC. "Why would the government ignore Indian people . . ." and "traditional site" from Laird Cometsevah, Chief, Southern Cheyenne Tribe, interview by author, May 12, 2003, transcription held by NPS-WACC.
9. Quote from Doug Scott, chief archeologist, National Park Service Midwest Archeological Center, interview by author, October 3, 2003, transcription held by National Park Service, Western Archeological and Conservation Center (NPS-WACC), Tucson, AZ. See also Kelman, *Misplaced Massacre,* 135–79.
10. "Never lost site of [her] outsider status . . ." from Alexa Roberts, Site Superintendent, Sand Creek Massacre National Historic Site, interview by author, April 29, 2003, transcription held by NPS-WACC. For more on decolonized methodologies, see: Linda Tuhiwai Smith, *Decolonizing Methodologies: Research and Indigenous Peoples* (London: Zed Books, 1999).
11. Quote from Ira Shor and Paolo Freire, *A Pedagogy for Liberation: Dialogues on Transforming Education* (Westport, CT: Bergin and Garvey, 1987). See also Alexa Roberts, Site Superintendent, Sand Creek Massacre National Historic Site, interview by author, April 29, 2003, transcription held by NPS-WACC.
12. "Active repentance" from Alexa Roberts to Ari Kelman, e-mail, November 23, 2016, in NPS-WACC. See also "RESOLUTION: United Methodist Responses to the Sand Creek Massacre," *Advance Daily Christian Advocate,* Volume 2, Section 3; Gary L. Roberts, "Remembering the Sand Creek Massacre: A Historical Review of Methodist Involvement, Influence, and Response," Authorized by the Commission on the General Conference of the United Methodist Church, 2016; Sam Hodges, "GC2016 recalls, laments Sand Creek Massacre," *UM News,* May 18, 2016.
13. Quote from "Sand Creek Massacre Foundation." https://www.sandcreekmassacrefoundation.org. See also Alexa Roberts to Ari Kelman, e-mails, July 15, 2019, September 22, 2020, and November 4, 2021, in NPS-WACC and "Kiowa County Economic Development Foundation." http://www.kcedfonline.org.
14. Quotes from "Sand Creek Massacre Foundation." https://www.sandcreekmassacrefoundation.org; and Alexa Roberts to Ari Kelman, e-mails, September 22, 2020, and November 4, 2021, in NPS-WACC.
15. Amy Kohout to Ari Kelman, e-mails, August 3, September 20, and October 10, 2017, in NPS-WACC; Alexa Roberts, Site Superintendent, Sand Creek Massacre National Historic Site, interview by author, November 28, 2017, transcription held by NPS-WACC); Norma Gourneau, Deputy Superintendent, Department of the Interior, Bureau of Indian Affairs, interview by author, October 2, 1017, transcription held by NPS-WACC.

16. Anonymized student comments held by Amy Kohout, Professor, Colorado College.
17. Quotes from Alexa Roberts, Site Superintendent, Sand Creek Massacre National Historic Site, interview by author, November 28, 2017, transcription held by NPS-WACC and anonymized student comments held by Amy Kohout, Professor, Colorado College.
18. Quotes from Alexa Roberts to Ari Kelman, e-mails, July 15, 2019, September 22, 2020, and November 4, 2021, in NPS-WACC.
19. Quotes from Alexa Roberts to Ari Kelman, e-mails, July 15, 2019, September 22, 2020, and November 4, 2021, in NPS-WACC and "The Sand Creek Massacre Speakers Series: Supplement to the Long Range Interpretive Plan," in uncatalogued files of the Sand Creek Massacre National Historic Site, Center for Sand Creek Massacre Studies, Eads, CO.
20. Quotes from Alexa Roberts to Ari Kelman, e-mail, and November 30, 2014, in NPS-WACC and Bente Birkeland, "In Commemorating the 150th Anniversary of Sand Creek, Governor Hickenlooper Apologizes," Colorado Public Radio (December 4, 2014). See also Megan Verlee, "Hickenlooper Offers Apology for Sand Creek Massacre on 150th Anniversary," Colorado Public Radio (December 4, 2014).
21. Quotes from Patricia Calhoun, "Sand Creek Massacre: Governor John Hickenlooper's Apology, Story Behind It," *Westword* (December 9, 2014), and Steve Brady, Headman, Crazy Dogs Society, Northern Cheyenne Tribe, interview by author, August 29, 2004, transcription held by NPS-WACC. See also Megan Verlee, "150 Years Later, A Formal Apology for The Sand Creek Massacre," *All Things Considered* (December 15, 2014).
22. Quote from "Shaft to Civil War Martyrs of State Unveiled with Pomp," *Denver Daily News* (July 25, 1909). See also David Blight, *Race and Reunion: The Civil War in American Memory* (Cambridge, MA: Belknap Press of Harvard University Press, 2001), 1–5; Michael Kammen, *Mystic Chords of Memory: Transformations of Tradition in American Society* (New York: Vintage, 1993), 101–39; Gaines M. Foster, *Ghosts of the Confederacy: Defeat, the Lost Cause and the Emergence of the New South, 1865–1913* (Oxford: Oxford University Press, 1988), 4–8, 23–67.
23. "Insult to the memory …" from Colorado Senate Joint Resolution 98-034, found in File 6–10, "Civil War Monument, 2002," in History Colorado, Denver, CO. "Appreciated that those Colorado politicians …" from Laird Cometsevah, Chief, Southern Cheyenne Tribe, interview by author, May 12, 2003, transcription currently held by National Park Service, Western Archeological and Conservation Center (NPS- WACC), Tucson, AZ. "Respectfully request[ing] …" and "signage be placed …" from Brady and Cometsevah to Senate and House of Representatives of the State of Colorado, July 25, 1998, found in File 6–10, "Civil War Monument, 2002," in History Colorado, Denver, CO. "Protests led by Native Americans …" found in File 6- 10, "Civil War Monument, 2002," in History Colorado, Denver, CO.
24. Quotes from Rick Sallinger, "Civil War Statue In Front Of Colorado State Capitol Pulled Down," *Denver CBS* (June 25, 2020). See also Evan Ochsner

and John Frank, "Civil War Monument at Colorado Capitol Torn Down and Marred by Graffiti," *Colorado Sun* (June 25, 2020).

25. Quotes from Caroline Goldstein, "Colorado Will Replace a Statue Honoring a Civil War Soldier, Toppled This Past Summer, with One of a Native American Woman," *artnet news* (November 25, 2020); and Kevin Simpson, "When the Union Soldier Fell at the Colorado Capitol, It May Have Started a Chain Reaction," *Colorado Sun* (September 3, 2020).

26. "Friendly Indians of the plains" and "places of safety" from *Condition of the Indian Tribes. Report of the Special Joint Committee, Appointed under Joint Resolution of March 3, 1865. With an Appendix* (Washington, DC: Government Printing Office, 1867), 55. "Pursue, kill, and destroy . . ." from *Rocky Mountain News* (August 13, 1864). All other quotes from "Proclamation of Governor Evans of Colorado Territory," in "Massacre of Cheyenne Indians," in *Report of the Joint Committee on Conduct on War, at the Second Session, Thirty-Eighth Congress* (Washington, DC: Government Printing Office, 1865), 47.

27. Quotes from Jonathan Edwards, "For 157 Years, a Colorado Governor's Order to Kill Native Americans Remained on the Books. Not Anymore," *Washington Post* (August 20, 2021); Kyle Cook, "Governor Polis Officially Rescinds John Evans' Proclamation That Led to Sand Creek Massacre," *Rocky Mountain PBS* (August 17, 2021); Paolo Zialcita, "The Proclamations Used To Incite The Sand Creek Massacre Have Been Officially Rescinded, 157 Years Later," *CPR News* (August 17, 2021); Alexa Roberts to Ari Kelman, e-mail, September 4, 2021, in uncatalogued files of the Sand Creek Massacre National Historic Site, Center for Sand Creek Massacre Studies, Eads, CO. See also Patty Nieberg, "Colorado Governor Voids an 1864 Order to Kill Native Americans," *Associated Press* (August 18, 2021).

28. Ben Nighthorse Campbell e-mail, December 16, 2021, in uncatalogued files of the Sand Creek Massacre National Historic Site, Center for Sand Creek Massacre Studies, Eads, CO.

PART THREE | **SUSTAINED COLLABORATIONS**
Maintaining Agreements, Successful Co-management

Interview: Lance Michael Foster

LANCE MICHAEL FOSTER is a member of the Ioway Tribe of Kansas and Nebraska. He has been the THPO for the Ioway Tribe since 2013 and is currently the tribal vice-chairman. He is one of the few members of his community who still speaks the Ioway language. He has a bachelor's of science in anthropology with a minor in Native American Studies from the University of Montana in Missoula and a master's degree in anthropology from Iowa State University. He has conducted archeology for the National Forest Service and worked as a historic landscape architect for the National Park Service (NPS). The following is adapted from an interview with Christina Gish Hill on September 27, 2021. This interview reflects on the protocols that Foster and others have developed to regulate collaboration, with the goal of sustaining relationships between Native nations and the Park Service. He discusses his own work building collaborations to reassert tribal control over federal lands at Effigy Mounds, Blood Run National Historic Landmark, and Good Earth Tribal National Park, laying out the limits of establishing traditional cultural properties (TCP) for protecting Native landscapes. Foster ends by considering the impacts of creating a tribal national park and the maintenance of Indigenous sovereignty.

Christina Gish Hill (CGH): Could you reflect about the projects you have worked on with national parks? When have they worked well, and when haven't they worked so well? We are especially interested in reflections on Effigy Mounds and the Good Earth site. Maybe start with Effigy Mounds. Were you THPO when all that was going on?

Lance Foster (LF): No, actually, Alan Kelly was THPO. Tom Munson was the previous superintendent who started in the '60s. Back then they had people's remains on display there. And Maria Pearson said, "I understand that we need to

183

have a talk. You need to repatriate those."[1] Because actually, Iowa had a landmark burial law, a state burial law before the whole NAGPRA thing came in. So that first kicked in about 1990. Around the same time, Munson worked with one of his employees, Sharon Greener, to load a bunch of boxes of those remains into his car. He went off and hid them in his garage. He assumed that if there weren't any remains, they could keep their stuff—you know, all the pots and [spear] points. Then the next superintendent was the one that got in trouble for not following section 106.

CGH: What happened specifically? What did that person do?

LF: Phyllis [Ewing] had gone through the process to be an interpretive ranger. And the park service was looking for people to diversify the workforce—to find somebody who could be trained for superintendency. She was interested. She was really into maintenance, into park building, putting in ADA ramps and all that kind of stuff. That was the lens that she saw things through. You have to build a good road and mow everywhere and put the flowers out—that kind of thing. Effigy Mounds is not that kind of a park, unfortunately. But she got through training, and she was selected to be the superintendent there. People had been asking where all these human remains were for a decade before Ewing even got there. We (the Ioway Tribe) were working so we could find them.

When Ewing got there [Effigy Mounds], she immediately set to building the park the way she wanted it. She thought all these government regulations are a bunch of foolishness. Even though she had been trained that they're not foolishness. She worked with her maintenance guy, saying we'll build a big bridge and a big walkway. They damaged mounds just because they wanted a nice, pretty trail that people could go through. It's just the wrong park for that. It's an archaeological park and it's a Native American park. Anyway, there was an ex-employee who saw the huge bridge and started asking questions. He was getting stonewalled, so he finally sent [a message] to the inspector general's office to figure out what was going on. They found out about the whole big mess. Eventually, after a long period, they reassigned her to the office in Omaha to do other kinds of work until she could retire.

Luckily, they sent Jim Nepstad [to Effigy Mounds as superintendent]. Jim got there and he found out what the report indicated [about the lost remains]. He talked to David Barland-Liles from the Inspector General's office to figure out if he had found all the remains by that point. All the forces were coming together saying that there's something wrong and that it has to do with Munson. At their first big meeting [of tribal representatives], when they were going to talk about how the park violated section 106, Jim had just learned that the remains had been hidden. He had to tell all the tribes. He was a new superintendent. And he had to step in cold as the new representative of NPS. Of course, people were shocked and mad.

It's been a long period of healing. Since then, Jim has been superb. Sharon [Greener] had been covering up this thing for a long time. She had to leave; she got booted out and they had a new museum person take her place—Albert LeBeau. He's a Lakota guy that had been a THPO himself. He started trying to heal all this and bring things together. They took the heat from the tribes, and they followed it all the way through to the end. They got a lot of the remains recovered [with the help of] David Barland-Liles. It was just last year that we reburied the last of the remains in the park. That was a kind of closure for many of us.

Alan Kelly was the [THPO] at that first [Effigy Mounds] meeting in 2012. For a while we had Pat Murphy, who was one of our NAGPRA coordinators, attending some of the meetings. I took over in 2014. My first meeting [at Effigy Mounds] was in 2013. I've consistently kept an eye on it.

Another good thing we've done in my eight years is that we developed Ioway Tribal National Park. I asked if Effigy Mounds would like to be a sister park, because they have those for other nations. And this would be a good way to move forward for all of us. I'm trying to get that going. This stuff takes a long time. And then I just found out in a meeting two weeks ago. . . .

Are you also aware of the Dickson mounds situation in Illinois?

CGH: Just a little bit. I haven't heard what's happening now.

LF: Okay, but you kind of know the story. All those people on the surface, right?

CGH: Yeah, they had all those uncovered burials on display. And it was opened to tourists in like the '40s or the '50s?

LF: It might have been in the '20s or '30s. He was a chiropractor or something and he had this family farm. He cut into the mound and made it a tourist attraction for a while. I think it was back in the '80s, AIM had big protests there and everything.[2] So. . . .

CGH: Yeah.

LF: Of course, local people want to keep it open, and Natives want to shut it down. So, it's been kind of vampirized by the state, taking away a lot of their funding over the years until they have, ironically, one might say a "skeleton crew." I think there's two people at the desk and maybe one other person walking around. Huge museum. I knew they were trying to work on some NAGPRA issues there. I am one of the consulting parties for that. The Osage are also [consulting]. And the Peoria. A number of other folks are as well—the Potawatomi. The week before last, we had a meeting to see if we can get things going again. Just like poor Jim who had to tell us about that situation [at Effigy

Mounds]—they had to tell us that there was some woman who broke open one of the cases, stuck her hand in, and stole some artifacts.

CGH: Oh no!

LF: They've been trying to find her, but it's been hard. We asked, "What kind of cases are these?" Then they told us how few people were there. So, we said, "Well, you can get your people to go on tours." They don't have enough people to go on tours. So, we said, "Shut the exhibits down. The security's not there." And then they said, "Well, okay. But then we have all the people in that room." And we said, "What people?"

All those people that were laying around on the surface are still laying around on the surface. They're still there. Instead of burying them with dirt, they're covered with a black cloth. So sometime in the fall I'm going to have to go down there, to see for ourselves what the situation is.

It's really hard when you can't even protect. . . . It's like saying, you're worried about your hangnail when somebody cuts your head off. It's just ridiculous. You get really cynical, but it's hard not to be.

CGH: Yeah. Wow. . . . So, you can't use NAGPRA to force the reburial at Dickson Mounds?

LF: No, [the law] is about inventory. It's about repatriation. Reburial happens if the person is repatriated to a particular Indian tribe or collection of tribes. Then they can do the burial.

CGH: Would that involve removing the remains?

LF: We always prefer in situ. Because they were buried there in particular. But unfortunately, the museum is built over that part now. The ideal thing would be to remove that part of the building, then put them back and re-cover them. But they don't have any money to disassemble a big part of the museum to do that. So, the best you can do, they say, is dig everybody up and move them to a different site. Because the museum's the important thing, right? So, this is a big unholy mess. We were just wrapping up the last chapters of the Effigy Mounds situation. Now we've got a new one.

CGH: Yeah.

LF: Of course, we also had some issues at Good Earth that we are still going through. A big part of the problem is that land is a quilt of ownership and easements. Blood Run [the site that Good Earth is a part of] is a National Historic Landmark. If you consider the Mississippian period, there's upper, middle, and lower Mississippian. North is upper. Middle is central. And southern is lower Mississippian. So, Cahokia is middle Mississippian. It was a multiethnic community. We know that the Osage and Omaha were involved with it to some extent. The upper Mississippians were the Oneota, the Iowa, and the Ho-chunk. We weren't the overall empire, but we shared ideas and culture and ideology.

If Cahokia is like the New York of that period, Blood Run is like the Chicago. It was a major site [with a population of] five thousand people. Ten thousand some say. It was on the Big Sioux [River]. If you go farther up the Big Sioux, you get to Pipestone. Blood Run seems to be a central trading area. You get buffalo hides coming from the west. Then you get pipestone from the north. And obsidian. Blood Run National Historic Landmark is on both sides of the river, the South Dakota side and the Iowa side. There's a huge, pecked boulder—it was a pretty significant site, occupied starting in the 1500s. By the early 1700s, the Sioux were getting pushed south by the Ojibwe. And that's when the ones who were there last—Iowa, Otto, Omaha, and Ponca—were getting push down into that area.

The governor of South Dakota wanted to have a legacy project for people to remember him by. There were golf courses and housing developments expanding on the site, so he declared [Good Earth] as a state park. Originally, they were going to use a Sioux term like the *Pte Oyate*, the buffalo nation. But it's not really a Sioux site. The Sioux were there afterwards. But that particular period was not Sioux. We all argued for a while about what it should be named. I will say that I was the one that came up with a name that can be translated into anybody's language.

Blood Run wasn't good because nobody knows where that term came from. They always assume that every Indian site is some kind of battlefield. With Blood Run, they really jumped to assume that, but it wasn't. It was a trading center. Run is an old word [used to] name a creek. And blood, nobody can come up with where that came from. Some people say it was a settler family. But there's no evidence of that. One other option that's more likely is that Sioux quartzite comes to the surface there. There may have been creeks that looked red like blood because of the Sioux quartzite, which is very red in color. Nobody knows for sure.

We had a story that that was the origin place where the pipe dance was exchanged between the Arikara, Iowa, Omaha, Otoe, Cheyenne, a bunch of different nations. You give the pipe to each other and adopt each other into your own group. The term for that is *Byownway*, or they sing. But it also means to make peace. To make peace in our languages is *maya pihi*. *Maya* is the earth. *Pi* is good. And *hi* is to cause something to be that way. When you when you go to war, you make the earth bad. *Maya pihi sh'gunikey.* Our term, "to make peace there," comes from the idea that this was the site where they exchanged the pipe dance. So, the peaceful earth. The good earth. That's where that term came from. The good thing about Good Earth is that it can be translated to any of our languages, Lakota or Omaha or whatever.

CGH: Nice. That's beautiful. I'm also interested in hearing about the Ioway Tribal National Park. How did that come to be? That's pretty unique.

LF: Yeah. I'd worked for the national parks, even though I knew there were problems with it, like how they came to push some people out of their land, like the Blackfeet at Glacier. But I knew it was also a symbol of one of the things that's good with America, which is to try to preserve places that are special, as best we can. The Leary Site National Historic Landmark was a village of our people from about 1200 to 1400. It was sort of like Blood Run on the other side of the river, but a little bit smaller. With the same kind of purpose as a trading area with the Pawnee, instead of the Cheyenne and Arikara. And yet people were always farming it and trying to collect from it, so it has suffered a lot of damage over the years. It has mounds from the Hopewell area. It's a significant site, but it hasn't really been recognized. So, when I first came here in 2013, I had to fight to protect it [from] two different projects. One was a bridge and one was trying to re-terrace the hill. I stopped them from doing that.

In the 1980s, a guy named Ray Shulenberg deeded over about 284 acres of his land here on the Ioway reservation to the Nature Conservancy. He started to try to do prairie restoration, trying to find old prairie plants and replant those. They call it the Reuleaux Bluffs Preserve. Then the Conservancy added another chunk of land. It added up to about 444 acres, I think.

Over the years, they've had burns there, and have tried to do a lot of different activities. But it's far away from their headquarters up in Nebraska. They haven't been able to get down here very often. So, at a certain point they asked Ioway tribal management to help with some of the burns. They wondered if we wanted to take it on. Alan, when he was the vice chair, was able to take on the part of that property that didn't have so many conservation restrictions on it. That way we could use it for grazing or whatever.

But we didn't want to take the other piece of the property because it had a conservation clause on the deed. We couldn't drive mechanized vehicles, we couldn't hunt, we couldn't do all the stuff that farmers like to do. We are farmers. That's what we do. The tribe didn't want it, so that part didn't come back to us. The first part came back to us, I think in 2016. It was in 2019, when I got in office, that I said, let's go ahead and try to do that. We'll come up with some kind of cool way to preserve it. [The tribal council] was more open to it at that point. So, I got it moved through in 2019. And then the pandemic hit. The casino shut down for three months. They closed the buffet and closed a lot of the stuff. And everybody was really upset. You remember?

CGH: Yeah.

LF: I mean, you experienced it. Everybody was worried about what was going to happen next. And I'm trying to think about how to preserve these places for the long term. I said, different parks have different units. What if we had a tribal national park that had a Leary unit and a Reuleaux bluffs unit. It's not very big compared to US national parks. But if you do that, you have to go through Congress. But if you call something a refuge, people just do what they want to do anyway.

CGH: Yeah.

LF: That's the great thing about the term national park. If you call it a tribal park, people think you just go out there to go on the swings and stuff. I argued that [the park] is all about our historical connection to the Leary site, as well as the biologically unique landscape that includes endangered and threatened species. I was thinking about the Nebraska side in the Reuleaux bluffs area, which had all this preservation. I brought it up to [the council]. I said, how about if we do a tribal national park. Then we might get more people coming in. I know economic development is the important thing.

So, we established Ioway Tribal National Park in 2020. Then I saw that there's a chunk of land right next to it. It was one of our family allotments. It had another monument—the iron boundary monument. The Kansas Nebraska Act came in at that particular point. It was the start of bloody Kansas. They were divided into the free state of Nebraska versus Kansas. And I said, let's include that too. And they finally agreed to that. In the meantime, we were also getting our mission back—Ioway Sac and Fox Presbyterian Mission—that was part of the boarding school experience here.

So, I looked around to see if we could call it a Tribal National Park. I saw that the Red Cliff Ojibwe had already denoted Frog Bay Tribal National Park. I said, that's perfect; I don't have to be the first one. If someone argues with me, I can say, it's already been done. So that's what we did. We're larger than they are at this point. But they're also on the edge of another park, which is huge. And other places—the Navajo and the Utes and other people—have either tribal parks or tribal refuges. But I knew the importance of that term, national park.

We're going to have control over visitation. It's more about connecting our own people, and then bringing in guests as we see fit. So that's the story of the origins of Ioway Tribal National Park.

CGH: Wow, that's cool. And so, it's not under the national or state park system at all. It's fully under tribal. . . .

LF: Sovereignty.

CGH: Yeah.

LF: That's the whole point, right?

CGH: Yeah, for sure. It's a really cool idea. That's a good transition to talk about your experiences using traditional cultural properties (TCP) to protect Indigenous lands.

LF: It's important to realize that TCP isn't a standalone concept. When federal agencies try to make a site, they give it multiple separate locations, and they can wreck the parts in between. Landscape, by definition, is interconnected. It could even be a travel corridor hundreds of miles long, like the salt pilgrimage. So, landscape is a concept that is not looked on with favor by these agencies.

They don't mind if it's a cabin with trees around it. That's what they think of as landscape. But something that has connecting places like Petroglyphs National Monument in New Mexico. . . . When I was doing a study there, I walked with this Zuni guy. We were all focusing on the petroglyphs that have been pecked into the rock. He said, the importance of this place is that all this lava came out [of the Earth] in this one place. It's like a wound where all the blood of the earth came out and then hardened over time. It's like an earth scab.

The Earth is a living thing, and it has veins and arteries. That's how places connect, and the earth can suffer. When I was in the hospital, they blew out one of my veins for an IV, but then new ones connected in different ways. As long as you don't lose the whole hand. But we're totally destroying entire veins and arteries [of the earth].

Those places are telling stories; they're creating power connections. And then he said, you see over there across where Albuquerque is? Over by Albuquerque, there are these mountains called the Sandia Peaks. And Sandia is Spanish for watermelon. When the sun sets behind you, the reddish rays go on the Sandias and all the tiny pine trees look like watermelon seeds. There is a connection between the petroglyphs and the Sandias. It's a spirit trail—the spirits travel between there.

I did a lot of landscape work with the park service. They have four kinds: historic sites, ethnographic landscapes, vernacular landscapes, and design landscapes. Design landscape is like Meridian Hill Park [in Washington, DC]. Professional, white landscape architects have designed alleys of views and all that. Vernacular landscape is how a landscape naturally develops with people living their lives in circulation. A place might include docks and people go fishing out there and up here [on the shore] is the orchard. That's a vernacular landscape. A historic landscape is where a battle happened or some important event, especially with a famous person. Ethnographic landscape is a catch all for everything else. They say, it could be the Swedes. But mostly it's the Indians and Mexicans and Asians. All those "other" guys.

I was in the cultural landscape program, working on that kind of stuff for the Park Service for a total of four years. First in the inner mountain region and then in Alaska. The National Historic Preservation Act has bulletins on things like how to nominate something to the register, or how to know why cemeteries may or may not go on the register. Then Patricia Parker and Thomas King came out with something about traditional cultural properties.[3] That was to address the situation with the Go Road and the San Francisco Peaks. Non-Indians were saying, "Hey, there's no archaeology site here. There are no buildings here. This is just a bunch of belief, somebody's religion. It's not really a real place." So, they came up with a way to evaluate these kinds of places, so that there could be a chance for national registry eligibility. And that's what a TCP is—traditional cultural place.

They used to call them properties, but a lot of people don't like the word property, so they say place. When I got into my [THPO] position in 2013, I started hearing a lot of Native people getting excited about TCP's, especially with the [DAPL] pipeline, saying this is a traditional cultural place. They also didn't understand that it's a process law. TCPs are usually historic districts. So, there are historic sites and historic districts. The law says how things get defined. When you deal with a district, you're arguing about boundaries. They want to shrink the boundaries as much as you want to enlarge them.

CGH: Yeah.

LF: (gesturing to the building he is in) This is a building that we built as part of our WPA CTC Indian division in the 1930s and '40s. I worked on it, so I have the experience of going through the entire nomination process. It took about a year and a half, and we got it on [the registry]. It's through a multiple property nomination, through a thematic nomination, not a standalone one, but buildings of the Depression era. And that's good. It gave me an understanding of the nomination process. A TCP is just another term that someone can use as part of the evaluation process for, say, a district. It's not a magic pill at all.

So, a TCP has become a bone of contention between the people that think of it as something that protects something that's a Native place. But it's not just Native. There are TCPs that are Filipino and TCPs that are Hispanic. It just means a traditional cultural place. It can be a plaza; it can be almost anything. And as far as I know, in the Midwest, here, the only ones that I'm really aware of that have been nominated or are even on the register are the Stomp Dance grounds down in Oklahoma.

The argument is critical with anything, whether it's a TCP or anything else is. You cannot evaluate the significance of something without knowing *why* it's significant. There's the core criteria, but you still have to know the history of a place and what connects it to the significance. Then they'll ask, does it have integrity. And they will try to bully you into the idea that there's nothing left. That the integrity is really poor. But that's condition. Condition is different from integrity. Integrity asks, can you tell the story of why it's significant based on what's physically there?

A good example is a mine. You know what head frames are, right? They are those big things you go down. Imagine that there's two sites. One site has a nice, beautifully preserved head frame. But all around it there are [modern] stores and houses. So that [site] has one element of the landscape in excellent condition. On the other hand, you'll go out in the woods, and you'll find a tramway collapse, maybe some rusty bottles in a pile over there, a falling in cabin. And you got a couple of tunnels collapsed and a few logs. They'll try to convince you it's got really poor integrity. No, it's got poor condition, but it's got good integrity, because it tells all those stories.

CGH: Oh, that's the difference!

LF: It's the people who don't know, don't take the time to learn the law. And I need a refresher every once in a while. It changes all the time, and case law changes that sometimes too.

CGH: Have you ever done work on creating shared governance arrangements when it comes to specific landscapes?

LF: At this point, no, and that's because the only landscape to be managed is ours. We have been consulting for some projects like Good Earth and Effigy Mounds, but nope, no management. Most tribes are not staffed to the point of being able to respond to all these people that want stuff all the time. There's [just] me here. Alan started working here a few months ago, and he's really been invaluable to get any kind of compliance through. But most tribes only have one or two people. You know, we were in nine different states precontact. And then there's HUD and FEMA and BIA and NPS and FAA and FCC and all these other agencies. We get stacks of projects every week. These agencies gripe about their staffing situation. They have no clue.

CGH: What does that mean for consultation?

LF: It's sort of like the old show, M*A*S*H with the helicopters coming in. You gotta triage. Let's compare some examples. There's a project at Effigy Mounds where they're going to change the ground where we know there's a site. We would consult on that. There are certain sacred sites or known occupation areas where we lived. And then there's the location of, say, an FAA tower on a building in downtown Des Moines. So, realistically, the first two are the ones we're going to pay most attention to. If we even get to any of the others. We just don't have the people. It's a matter of where you're going to be able to do the most good. The other thing is, we are mandated by our agreements to do the work on our reservations. We are not mandated to do off the reservation. Those are [additional] opportunities.

CGH: That makes a lot of sense. I was also thinking about how several of these locations—Effigy Mounds, Dickson Mounds—are connected to several tribal nations. I was wondering if you could speak a little bit about how that works?

LF: For the most part, the approach I take is multi-vocal, which means we all have our own story. People always say, Indian versus white man stories. But every tribe has its own version of history, about where we came from and where our lands are.

There was a situation over in Trenton, Missouri, which was near one of our villages, and we just didn't have the staff to monitor out there when they were going to put a tower in. With only me and sometimes Alan, I just can't leave here, especially now that I'm also the vice chairman. So, the Arapaho claimed it. I said, I don't have a problem [with that], just let us know if you find something. For me, it's about being pragmatic. I'm not going to try to tell some other tribe they can't do something. I will share what history I will with them. They will do the same with me. And we'll try to figure out if there's some commonality.

I don't have an ego about it—that it's got to be done my way. If you want to ask me, I'm not going to wrap [a person who needs reburial] in a prettier cloth, because that's White Man's Cloth. I'm going to put them back in the earth where we took them from exactly the way they were. That's what I do. And I don't have to [do it]. I'm not the one that dug them up. I don't have to try to fix that. I'm just the facilitator.

CGH: Could you reflect on what these processes mean for Native sovereignty?

LF: My father talks about this. He said, they took our language, they took our land, they even took a big chunk of our people. There was a lot of genocide. Acculturation was a big thing, assimilation was much more, but we're alive. And the limited sovereignty that we have, we must express it. If you do not express your sovereignty whenever you can, you surrender it. So, we will continue to do that.

CGH: Yeah, and the Ioway Tribal National Park is a profound way to express your sovereignty.

LF: Honestly, if they let it go, then it's up to them. I feel more like Benjamin Franklin, when he said, we gave them a democracy, if they can keep it. So, I feel we gave them a tribal national park, if they can keep it. All I can do is try.

CGH: That's powerful. So, can you reflect a little bit about how park staff and researchers could best support a tribal nation's efforts to restore those sovereign relations with Native landscapes?

LF: A lot of it is personal relationships. Some tribes have had such bad experiences that they have left the field. Others are going through their own challenges with staffing. So, [researchers need to] realize tribes may not have the staff to answer you right away. I would say have patience. I would say personal relationships are number one. There are some cultural resource managers that have been in that job for twenty years, and other people are in there for six months or a year. That's something that cripples us with the NPS. At the same time, tribes go through election cycles. And like everything else, THPOs or other cultural advisors are subject to the politics on the reservation too. So, you need to have a phone conversation at least every year, if not more often than that, just to be in touch. That's how things come together in the best way.

CGH: Yeah, maintain those personal relationships. Any advice on that? What can we do beyond a phone conversation?

LF: When in doubt, [visit] face to face for a day or two. You might also go to some meetings held in your park or at the tribe. You'll see each other at trainings—like a climate training. That's how you get to know people. I've made good relationships with people at the park service and in the Corps of Engineers and other places because we interact a lot. The Iowa DOT (Department of Transportation) has a tribal summit every few years. They bring together the DOT folks with the tribes of interest in Iowa for a couple of days. Those are always fruitful.

CGH: Any thoughts on sovereign relations in the future? Are there relationships or activities that might improve those relationships?

LF: You know, we've been here—depends on what clock you want to use. We've been here for thousands of years. Ten thousand. Twenty thousand. The United States has been here for two hundred years, and it's shaking a little bit as it is. So, I imagine that there will always be change.

Sovereignty exists as long as you hold it. Even when you're a prisoner, and someone has taken everything else from you. As long as you don't surrender your sovereignty. Because it can only be surrendered or given. It can never be taken. You may not be able to practice it. You may not have an army or a monetary system. But you still have it. You better study sovereignty—the deep parts of it. Because your soul, as long as you haven't given that away, that's your sovereign state.

CGH: Yeah. Yeah. So, what are your thoughts on the future potential of collaborative work between tribal nations and the park service or public lands? Stretching from the kind of collaboration that you're talking about—consultation—all the way through to the potential to create tribal national parks.

LF: You gotta do the right thing while you're on Earth. And while you're able to act. If there's an opportunity to develop co-management or to try to preserve a place, I say we gotta do it. Gotta do it. Because hope is in the act itself. More than whatever the future might bring.

CGH: Yeah, that's powerful. I really appreciate you giving me this time.

LF: Thank you. I know in some ways it's a depressing topic. But thank you for the opportunity to have some of this in writing for those who might go through this stuff down the road.

CGH: Yeah, that's the goal.

Notes

1. Maria Pearson began fighting to protect Native American burials in Iowa in the 1970s, advocating for the repatriation of Native remains and grave goods. She pioneered new legislation in Iowa to protect graves, the first of its kind in the nation, and spearheaded the passage of the federal Native American Graves Protection and Repatriation Act (NAGPRA). For more, see Lora Starr, "Protecting the Past: Finding Common Ground in the Native American Repatriation Movement," *Women Leading Change: Case Studies on Women, Gender, and Feminism* 3, no. 2 (2018).
2. For more, see June Camille Bush Raines, "One Is Missing: Native American Graves Protection and Repatriation Act: An Overview and Analysis," *Native American Cultural and Religious Freedoms* (2014): 309–34.
3. Parker and King published National Park Service Bulletin 38 defining Traditional Cultural Properties. Parker was a cultural anthropologist and archeologist in the National Park Service's Interagency Resources Division at the time, and would go on to become the head of the National Park Service's American Indian Tribal Liaison Office. King was Senior Archeologist and Director of the Office of Program Review and Education in the Advisory Council on Historic Preservation. For more, see Thomas F. King, "What Are Traditional Cultural Properties," *Applied Anthropologist* 25, no. 2 (2005): 125–30.

EIGHT | # Indigenous Agency and Protected Spaces of Nature
Three Case Studies of Collaboration in North America

RANI-HENRIK ANDERSSON

IN 1841 THE FAMOUS WESTERN ARTIST George Catlin proposed the establishment of a "Nation's Park" that would display Native Americans and wildlife.[1] "What a beautiful and thrilling specimen for America to preserve and hold up to the view of her refined citizens and the world, in future ages! A Nation's Park, containing man and beast, in all the wild and freshness of their nature's beauty!" wrote Catlin.[2] While his idea did not lead to the establishment of such of a park, it is illustrative of nineteenth- (and twentieth-) century Euro-American thinking regarding nature conservation and Indigenous people in which the worldviews of Indigenous peoples were pushed aside. Indigenous peoples suffered from dispossession, treaty violations of hunting and fishing rights, and the loss of sacred places at the hands of national parks and other protected natural spaces. The original owners of the land appeared in this debate only as a curiosity, a romantic stereotype of a people forgotten in the past. Native Americans, their homelands, sacred places, and stories became the "other" within the bordered spaces of national parks, "America's best idea." Only very recently have attempts to understand Indigenous concepts of nature become incorporated into political and legal debates, but there is still a long way to go.[3]

National parks and other protected spaces of nature have become symbols of nature protection and are valuable sites for global cultural heritage. Sometimes they have even been harnessed to promote political, patriotic, and nationalistic agendas.

At the same time, they are colonial constructs that to the Indigenous people who previously inhabited these now bordered spaces of nature can represent loss of traditional homelands and cultural heritage.[4] This situation has resulted in the near silencing of Indigenous voices, practices, and values related to the natural world.

While trying to preserve a "pristine wilderness," most national parks and protected areas allow tourism, even mass tourism, but the original inhabitants—Indigenous peoples—are removed from these designated areas. The narrative of pristine wilderness is a paradox, as human presence has been continuous in most of these places for thousands of years. This has resulted in many Indigenous communities having tense, even antagonistic relations with government-protected natural spaces, most of which nation-states had carved out of Indigenous homelands. In Finland, the Malla Nature Preserve does not allow the Sámi to herd reindeer within its perimeters for fear that this practice will degrade its "unspoiled environment," as if it had been untouched by human practices. In reality, the Sámi have herded reindeer there for generations.[5]

While the Sámi example captures an old problem that plagues Indigenous peoples, in other parts of the world, Native communities and practitioners have restored access to culturally important sites within protected spaces of nature. As the historian Joshua L. Reid (Snohomish) has noted, there are cases in which newly found cooperation strengthens the relationship between Indigenous people and settler-colonial states. Through access to culturally significant sites, this cooperation also strengthens both Indigenous identity and sovereignty.[6] This article highlights what can be gained from the inclusion of Indigenous perspectives when they become active partners in managing natural spaces of conservation and wilderness preservation.[7]

The political and economic consequences of ignoring Indigenous perspectives have been recorded over the past century, and in recent years new studies have discussed the processes affecting protected areas and Indigenous people, but few actually investigate the conflicting worldviews of Indigenous people and those promoting the "Western," mostly Euro-American, conservation narrative.[8] For example, Stan Stevens' groundbreaking study, *Indigenous Peoples, National Parks, and Protected Areas: A New Paradigm Linking Conservation, Culture and Rights* (2014), makes a major contribution in classifying the many ways in which Indigenous peoples have suffered from the creation of protected areas.[9] Stevens summarizes the various forms of displacement and marginalization as follows: 1) spatial and physical, including forced relocation and lack of access to traditional territories; 2) economic effects, including restrictions or bans on land and marine use, loss of livelihood, loss of access to food security, water, shelter etc., and lack of benefits from revenues from protected areas; 3) political effects, including loss of territorial control and self-governance and loss of authority over cultural sites; and 4) cultural effects, including loss of shared life in homelands, loss of care for homelands, loss of access to cultural sites and resources, and lack of respect for cultural practices, livelihoods and customary law and governance.[10]

Other scholarly works have concluded that allowing Indigenous presence in certain protected areas has actually helped the conservation effort by reintroducing traditional, Indigenous, place-based knowledge. This knowledge had been ignored or lost when settler-colonial states developed their environmental policies and management practices. Ethnobotanist Julianne Cordero-Lamb, a member of the Coastal Band of the Chumash Nation of California, has noted that Native practices, such as prescribed burning, have for thousands of years affected California's natural environment. The famous environmentalist John Muir failed to realize that the Garden of Eden he saw in his beloved Yosemite Valley had been molded by thousands of years of human presence.[11]

This article will bring these differing concepts of nature to the forefront of discussion on the environment, sustainability, and nature protection in the context of North America. It will bring the "other," that is, Native Americans, from the margins of the discourse back to the center by introducing three case studies emphasizing Native voices, ontologies, agency, and belonging: the Wind Cave National Park (South Dakota), the Channel Islands National Park and Marine Sanctuary (California), and the Gwaii Haanas National Park (Haida Gwaii, Canada).[12] While this volume focuses on the United States, I also want to set our gaze north of the border, where the Haida people and Parks Canada have established a unique management model that truly highlights Haida agency, priorities, and goals. The Gwaii Haanas National Park serves as an example of a collaborative model that can allow for further inclusion of Indigenous perspectives in the management of national parks in the United States as well. These three parks provide us with a glimpse into what I call a model of re-Indigenization of national parks.[13]

I will employ the methodological approaches mapped out by Māori intellectual Linda Tuhiwai Smith, who urges scholars to pursue research projects in collaboration with Indigenous communities and in a way that supports Native priorities and needs. Additionally, this article will build on emerging scholarship on Indigenous peoples, preservation, and conservation.[14] Stan Stevens notes that the old paradigm that Indigenous peoples are excluded from the conservation and protection of natural areas is gradually changing. The new paradigm calls for the incorporation of Indigenous voices; the case studies I include in this article illustrate such a shift. They represent different stages of collaboration, ranging from mere inclusion of Indigenous perspectives to the park's interpretation at Wind Cave National Park, to comprehensive strategical collaboration at Channel Islands National Park, to a more complete case of shared management at Gwaii Haanas National Park.[15] This article is wrapped around themes and research questions such as: what forms of cooperation have been developed or are currently in place? And how can Indigenous ontologies and understanding of places and their knowledge better be represented and included in the conservation, protection, and interpretation of these spaces?

While acknowledging the continued problems of settler-colonialism, this article will focus on three comparative instances of Indigenous agency in maintaining culturally relevant practices of sustainability even within the context of limited access to power in nation-states.[16]

Worldviews and Nature Conservation

The romantic stereotype of Indigenous peoples being magically connected to nature has in recent years been replaced by a more nuanced understanding and respect for what many call an "Indigenous way of being." This specific relationship with the environment is rooted in kinship and meaning. That meaning could be sacred, practical, or both. On a fundamental level, Indigenous peoples do not separate themselves from nature and the environment; rather, they are part of them. This relationality based in kinship is sometimes referred to as "kincentric ecology."[17] According to Chumash educators Alicia Cordero and Luhui Isha, settler-colonial cultures have "developed a different relationship with the land, waters, and living things based on a fundamentally different type of connection and concept of belonging."[18]

For many Indigenous peoples, time and place are linked through the connection to lands and waters, to places they hunt and fish and to where the ancestors have lived and been buried. It is not only the visible world but also the invisible, spiritual world that manifests itself through and in nature. One could argue that Indigenous peoples study nature from an ecological perspective and their knowledge of the ecosystem is interconnected in their belief systems.[19]

National parks are constructed spaces of nature, with specific boundaries and sets of rules and regulations that are aimed at guiding how people are supposed to be in that place. In creating protected spaces of nature, nation-states have built their management strategies on Western notions of wilderness preservation. Thus, "the way of being" is based on Euro-American worldviews. Professor Donal Carbaugh has noted: "Such ways of being-in-place are based upon what we each understand about place, nature, land, animals, people, and history. In order to help visitors understand and conduct themselves properly, the National Park Service relies upon policy, interpretation, and other knowledgeable visitors. With this shared knowledge, people more reliably do what best serves the place, wildlife, waters, wind, and our common good."[20] As Carbaugh further explains, "There are different ways of seeing, being in, and understanding a place. One can see, hear, and feel not only the physical presence of such 'objects' or 'things,' but along with it, more deeply, spirituality, an enlivened spirited co-presence."[21]

Oníya Ošóka, or Wind Cave National Park:
Toward a New Interpretation

Long before humans were born, different powers, spirits, and creatures fought for dominion over the world. Eventually, the godlike creatures grew tired of each other and sent *Iktómi* (trickster) to find people. At that time people lived underground with the buffalo in a state of chaos. According to some versions of the story, the people and the buffalo emerged from beneath the earth together. That is why the people were called *Pté oyáte,* the Buffalo people.[22]

The Lakota, or the western branch of the Sioux Nation, made the Black Hills area of today's South Dakota their home in the late 1770s. In a short time, the Ȟesápa became so central to the Lakotas that the stories of Lakota and Dakota origin in the wooded areas east of the Missouri and subsequent migrations were, if not replaced, at least supplemented by the story of *Iktómi* and the *Pté Oyáte.* Thus, Lakota mythology takes the Lakotas to the Black Hills and explains Lakota origins and their relationship with the universe. These stories connect the Lakotas to the land, the environment surrounding them, and to the sacred, *wakȟáŋ*. The foundation for Lakota belief is a general, spiritual force or energy that manifests itself in nature in the visible and the invisible worlds. This all-encompassing spirit force is known as *Wakȟáŋ Tȟáŋka*, sometimes translated as Great Spirit or Great Mystery. While *Wakȟáŋ Tȟáŋka* can be considered as a godlike or divine being or energy, it is more complicated. On a fundamental level, *wakȟáŋ* is everything. Above all things is *Wakȟȟáŋ Tȟáŋka,* which encompasses everything *wakȟáŋ*. *Wakȟáŋ* also reflects kinship networks, comprised of human-human relationships, human-nonhuman relationships, and human-sacred relationships.

Throughout the nineteenth century the Black Hills gained importance as white encroachment on Lakota lands diminished Indigenous people's living space. As Lakota land base was disappearing, so did the buffalo, which had become the major source of sustenance for the Lakota. The Black Hills, which teemed with other wildlife, became even more important. They started to call the hills *Wagmúŋka Óǧnaka Ičháŋte*—the "Heart of Everything That Is."[23] In addition to being a food source, the Black Hills held tremendous spiritual power. The famous Lakota holy man Black Elk said that the hills were the center of the universe, a place where spirits came and connected him to the sacred, to *Wakȟáŋ Tȟáŋka*. When gold was found in the Hills in the 1870s, major wars were fought over the ownership of the land. The Lakotas were forced to relinquish this sacred land. This event of dispossession continues to reverberate through Lakota communities, affecting their sense of belonging, identity, and sovereignty.[24]

For contemporary Lakotas the Black Hills remain a source of power and identity. They have been dispossessed from the area, but they still consider the mountains as *Wakȟáŋ*.[25] While most of the Black Hills area has been developed either for housing or corporate gold mining, small enclaves of protected spaces of nature do exist, the most famous being Mount Rushmore National Memorial, which is explored more in chapter 6. Within the Black Hills area, there are also several caves protected as national parks. At one of these caves, a tourist can wander to a small opening in the limestone wall and listen to the wind howl within the huge cave. This is Wind Cave National Park, or the cave in which *Iktómi* long ago found the Buffalo people. For the Lakota, this cave, *Oníya Ošóka,* is the place where their people were born.[26] It does not matter if others believe this story or not; what matters is its significance to the Lakota people, and what it means to their sense of who they are as a people.[27]

In 1903, Wind Cave was designated by President Theodore Roosevelt as the seventh national park, making it the first cave with that status. In 1912, the American Bison Society hoped to reestablish the bison in the Black Hills. A national game preserve was established next to Wind Cave, which had excellent prairie habitat for the bison. The preserve was initially managed by the US Biological Survey, and in 1935, the game preserve was included in the Wind Cave National Park.[28]

From the start, the park service put forward a narrative that ignored Lakota presence in the park. Tourists were introduced to the park through the first white men, Jesse and Tom Bingham, who "discovered" the cave in 1881. Wind Cave is now visited by one hundred thousand tourists every year. The park, including its visitor center and webpage, tells a story of discovery and geological miracles. The park's webpage advertises it as *"A hidden world beneath the prairie."*[29]

Bison, elk, and other wildlife roam the rolling prairie grasslands and forested hillsides of one of America's oldest national parks. Below the remnant island of intact prairie sits Wind Cave, one of the longest and most complex caves in the world. Named for barometric winds at its entrance, this maze of passages is home to boxwork, a unique formation rarely found elsewhere.[30]

The Wind Cave is one of the world's longest caves, with 237.72 km of explored passageways. Much more remains uncharted. While the boxwork and frostwork formations are fascinating and important natural phenomena, and the story of exploration fits the national narrative of settlement and pioneer spirit, they reflect only the settler-colonial stories of the park and its vicinity.

When viewed from Lakota cultural perspectives, something essential was missing. Until very recently the Lakotas could be found on the park's webpage only if one opened a link to an article discussing the bison and how the Lakotas hunted there *in the past*.[31] However, a welcome change has taken place at Wind Cave following the broader NPS efforts to include Indigenous voices and ontologies into the twenty-first century national parks experience. At Wind Cave, one can now read about Lakota origin stories and the park's webpage introduces the story told by park ranger Sina Bear Eagle, a member of the Oglala Lakota.[32]

Since the early 2000s, the park has paid much more attention to Lakota perspectives. Thomas Farrell, the Chief of Interpretation at Wind Cave, reflects on how the park first approached Lakota tribal councils through a letter inviting them to work with the park service. This resulted in a round of meetings, where people got to know and trust each other.[33]

Oglala Basil Brave Heart was one of the Lakota elders whom the park service approached. He immediately understood the importance of this suggestion and saw it as an opportunity to make a difference and promote Lakota agency in the park. Mr. Brave Heart contacted other tribal elders, all of whom were positively inclined to work with the park service. The initial discussions were followed by meetings amongst Lakota elders, tribal council representatives, and *wičháša wakȟáŋ*, or holy men. After they agreed on the goals, a series of meetings with the park service was organized.[34]

Based on these meetings, Mr. Brave Heart took the lead in drafting plans on how to incorporate Lakota perspectives. A completely new plan was introduced that now seeks to include Lakota voices in all aspects of interpretation in the park. The park, for example, invited native artists to contribute to the park's story, and today the visitor is greeted by a statue and a "winter count" describing the Lakota emergence story.[35]

The goal of the cooperation between the park and the Lakotas has not necessarily been to seek full co-management practices, but rather to change the interpretation of the park. To achieve this there have been several exhibits focusing on Lakota history and culture. The ultimate goal, according to Thomas Farrell, is to make sure that each visitor leaves the park with an understanding of its significance and sacredness to the Lakota. Yet, he says, it is not an easy task to find a balance that satisfies Native needs, tourism, conservation, and nature protection goals. While much has been done to achieve a more balanced interpretation, there are, as Sina Bear Eagle has noted, many practical and political obstacles that need to be resolved.[36]

Basil Brave Heart agrees that much progress has been made, and he is satisfied with the results for the moment. The Lakotas are still contemplating how to add more traditional knowledge into the park's interpretation. There are certain rules and restrictions as to how much of that knowledge can and should be shared with the outside world. Medicine men and tribal elders continue to discuss the ways in which some of this sacred knowledge could be made public, or whether it should be kept among the Lakota people.[37]

In addition to the Lakota, there are more than twenty tribal nations that have affiliations with the Wind Cave area. The NPS is required to consult these nations in matters relating to sacred or otherwise significant spaces. Even so, the fact remains that the NPS operates within the settler-colonial state, and it is not obligated to follow the suggestions and needs expressed by Indigenous people. At Wind Cave, as in many other places, the long histories of colonialism and dispossession cannot and should not be erased. By acknowledging continued Lakota presence and the cave's importance to their culture, Wind Cave has added a valuable piece of history to the tourist experience without forgetting the existing wealth of information on the geology, exploration, and natural world of the park. Acknowledging Lakota understanding of the environment and the connectedness of human-to-non-human dimensions brings about a more nuanced interpretation of the area below and above the surface of the Wind Cave. Wind Cave is a place of great significance to the Lakota people, and the challenge will be understanding and interpreting it as a Native place with relational significance instead of simply a bordered and protected public space.

The collaboration at Wind Cave National Park has resulted in changing narratives and interpretation of the park. As such it represents a first stage toward a more inclusive model for shared management.[38]

Wishtoyo: *Building a Bridge toward Co-Management*

A long time ago, the Chumash people lived only on the islands we now call the Channel Islands. The islands became too crowded, so Kakunupmawa (the Mystery Behind the Sun) decided that it was healthier for the islands and their inhabitants to have some people move to the Big Land. Hutash (the spirit of the Earth) and Kakunupmawa made a Rainbow Bridge for the people to cross over. Some of the people looked down from the rainbow bridge and fell into the sparkling ocean. Kakunupmawa saved them and made them into dolphins. Chumash people tell this story to remind us that the dolphins are very close relatives of humans.[39]

The Chumash have deep respect for and connections to the islands and their surrounding waters in the Santa Barbara Channel just off the coast of Southern California. The Chumash believe their responsibility is to care for the environment, to understand and respect it, and to maintain a balance. Their ancestors lived off the bounty of the land and the sea, but like the story above informs us, they were a part of that environment in a balanced, sustainable way. As Alicia Cordero and Luhui Isha (Coastal Chumash) explain, "The Chumash peoples, including Chumash culture, values, cosmology, lifeways, epistemologies, and languages have thus emerged specifically from the lands and waters of the Santa Barbara Channel and have continued to develop and change in relationship with them."[40]

The Santa Barbara Channel is one of the world's richest marine environments, and since 1980 a part of the waters has been protected as Channel Islands National Marine Sanctuary (CINMS). Surrounded by the marine sanctuary are the Channel Islands: *Limuw* (Santa Cruz), *Tuqan* (San Miguel), *Wi'ma* (Santa Rosa), *'Anyapakh* (Anacapa), and Santa Barbara. The Chumash have lived on these islands for thousands of years. On Santa Cruz Island alone, more than ten villages existed thirteen thousand years ago, and the oldest human remains in North America, known as the Arlington Springs Man, were discovered on the Santa Rosa Island.[41] The Chumash, then, are the true keepers of the land and waters, but due to centuries of colonization by the Spaniards, Mexicans, and Americans, they were completely dispossessed from their homelands by the 1830s.[42]

By the mid-nineteenth century, white farmers and ranchers had taken hold of the islands, greatly altering the environment that had previously been carefully cultivated by the Indigenous people. The newcomers did not tend to the natural world as the previous owners did, and drastic changes took place within this delicate environment. After more than one hundred years of exploitation, the United States began recognizing the unique island environment. In 1936, President Franklin D. Roosevelt designated Santa Barbara and Anacapa as national monuments, which would protect "the fossils of Pleistocene elephants and ancient trees, and furnish noteworthy examples of ancient volcanism, deposition, and active sea erosion."[43] Roosevelt failed to recognize the original inhabitants of the islands. Finally, in 1980, the Channel Islands National Park was established. Although the charter did not mention the Chumash, it included the protection of sites of "archeological and cultural" value.[44] Despite the detrimental environmental effects of farming and overgrazing, several species of endemic plants and animals remain on the islands.[45]

There is no doubt that the creation of the Channel Islands National Park and, later, the CINMS has helped the islands' recovery from years of sheep and cattle raising and restored the Santa Barbara Channel's diverse marine environment. The NPS and the National Oceanic and Atmospheric Administration (NOAA) in charge of Marine Protected Areas take great pride in this success, and rightly so. The invasive pigs and sheep have been removed and endemic animals and plants are recovering. Furthermore, these places are truly stunning and represent the NPS's conservation ideals perfectly. The outside visitor is well taken care of, the diversity of the environment, geology, and history is well explained, and the long cultural presence of the Chumash is emphasized by, for example, promoting the huge cave with Chumash ancestral petroglyphs.[46]

However, there is another element to the story of these islands: The Nature Conservancy, a private organization that owns approximately half of Limuw or Santa Cruz Island. Much of this area is restricted, and tourists have no access to the area. The University of California Nature Reserve System has a field station there and researchers can apply for a permit. This side of the island holds several ancient Chumash villages. The Chumash have only had access to this part of the island for a few decades; some of their elders visited their old village sites for the first time in the early twenty-first century. According to Director Lyndal Laughrin, the Chumash will always have access to their cultural sites, but they too must apply for permission.[47]

The Chumash may need permission to visit the Nature Conservancy side, but they have been actively participating in the discourse of nature protection on the islands and the surrounding waters. According to Cordero and Isha, "The CINMS waters and the National Park Service and The Nature Conservancy islands, although regarded as distinct regions by public and private interests, are, in fact, physically and conceptually inseparable in terms of ecology as well as culture, spirituality, and history."[48]

The Chumash have been vocal and successful in their attempts to seek cooperation with government institutions that have overseen these areas. Through nonprofit organizations, such as Wishtoyo Chumash Foundation and Chumash Maritime Association, they have developed a relationship in which the Chumash actually have a voice. One of their successes includes the establishment of the Chumash seat of the CINMS advisory council. This brings the Chumash and the park closer to shared management of the area than at Wind Cave, where the goal is a change in the interpretation rather than co-management. Chumash elder Roberta Cordero was the first Chumash person in the council, which really is a council of stakeholders. Because there are no federally recognized coastal Chumash bands, the Sanctuary was not required to provide anything other than a stakeholder status. According to the 2009 Management Plan, The Sanctuary Advisory Council's Chumash Community, as well as the Chumash Community Working Group, includes representatives of the various Chumash bands living in the area. But because the Santa Ynez Band of Chumash is a federally recognized tribe, the CINMS consults with them on a government-to-government basis regarding regulatory matters whenever "tribal implications exist." Roberta Cordero noted that this status has caused some concerns, especially at the beginning of the collaboration when it was not yet official. "I was a public-at-large member, which made it really hard for me to identify my constituency. I lobbied for a dedicated Chumash Community seat and alternate, which the Sanctuary eventually adopted as I was ending my term. Since then, several Chumash have filled the seat."[49]

Officially, the Advisory Council's Chumash members and the Chumash Community Working Group give advice and make recommendations to the Sanctuary superintendent about Chumash community-related issues, activities, or interests regarding the Channel Islands.[50] The Chumash have been actively involved in other environmental protection activities, such as the proposal of the Chumash Heritage National Marine Protected Area, north of the Channel Islands, education programs, the development of the white paper "Tribal Marine Protected Areas: Protecting Maritime Ways and Practice," and the Chumash Eyes on the Water program, which focuses on bringing science directly to the communities. Roberta Cordero notes that "there is meaningful tribal participation in several of California's Marine Protected Areas (MPA), but no true tribal co-management of which I am aware. [This is] also true for the federal MPAs. Also in the Chumash area, there is one MPA with a traditional place name, *Kashtayit* (place of the willows), and we have been able to participate in the design for the signage interpretations, but not much else."[51] According to Cordero, Wishtoyo is the most active in anything approaching co-management with the State Marine Protected areas. Through Wishtoyo, the Chumash have developed the California Naturalist Certification Program and brought lawsuits that seek to protect the channel from offshore fracking. Their environmental efforts also protect culturally significant endangered species like humpback whales and steelhead trout.[52]

While the successes above are important, there is also an equally, if not more, important story of spirituality, identity, and belonging that plays out within the context of environmental protection.[53] One aspect of belonging is the revival of traditional Chumash maritime culture. For generations the Chumash people traveled, traded, and harvested the waters along the California coast and the islands, making long journeys with traditional tomols (redwood plank canoes). Canoe construction ended in the early 1800s because of Spanish colonization, and with that, a central element of identity and belonging was lost. Not until 1976 was a tomol built and a modern "Brotherhood of the Tomol" was born. The tomol took the Chumash back to the sea and back to *Limuw* and the other islands of origin. In 1976, the tomol *Helek* (Peregrine Falcon) was built and made a historic journey to circumnavigate the islands of *Tuqan*, *Wi'ma*, and *Limuw*, the first time since the early 1800s. It was not until 2001 that Chumash people returned when the tomol *'Elye'wun* (Swordfish) was paddled from the mainland to *Limuw*, there to be celebrated by some two hundred Chumash people and friends. This return was so significant that, with even more tomols, the crossing and gathering now comprise an annual homecoming event.[54]

Roberta Cordero explains, "The Channel Islands National Marine Sanctuary (NOAA) was proactive in reaching out to the Chumash community.... They (NOAA) were the grantors for the funds that went to building our tomol, *'Elye'wun*, completed in 1997. Sanctuary leadership and staff have continued to be wonderful and consistent partners for all the tomol crossings since 2001, providing technical guidance and on-the-water support, including making their own vessels available as support platforms."[55]

The Chumash Maritime Association led by Roberta Cordero and Julie Cordero-Lamb was in the beginning chiefly responsible for organizing, building, outreach, and coordination with the sanctuary and a little later with initiating a similar partnership with the Channel Islands National Park. As for the practical aspects of the collaboration, Roberta Cordero relates, "Park personnel have supplied on-the-ground assistance at the campground as well as providing the camp for free. They have also accommodated our need for a sacred fire—not otherwise allowed on the Island—and group kitchen facilities. They have gone way beyond the course of duty in transporting tents, Coleman stoves, and elders and others who would not otherwise be able to participate, from the landing to the campground."[56]

The symbolism of the tomol construction and returning to the sea cannot be overestimated. Coupled with celebrations and ceremonies on *Limuw*, the Chumash have come almost full circle. Obviously, the circle is not complete before they have free access to their island home and a full voice in the management of the protected natural spaces known now as Channel Islands and the surrounding marine sanctuary. They are still an integral part of the narrative and the landscape. Alicia Cordero and Luhui Isha elaborate on this: "Even though the Chumash have been dispossessed of their islands and surrounding waters, they always have been and will always be there. They are there in the ecosystems shaped by untold generations of Chumash traditional tending. They are there as protectors of the buried ancestors and villages. And they are there through the prayers of people longing for reconnection with their home.... The Chumash are the islands and the waters."[57]

By tirelessly explaining and teaching their worldviews, traditional knowledge and practices, the Chumash have established a working cooperation with government and other agencies and are seeking fuller inclusion in the (hi)story and management of these sacred Chumash places. In 2021, the Chumash filed an official petition to the State of California entitled "Renaming the Northern Channel Islands: Honoring Indigenous Ancestors" to change the names of the islands back to their original Chumash names. The original keepers of the lands and waters are gradually finding their place at the center of the story of the islands despite centuries of dispossession and "othering" by various people, who are actually the "others" to the area.

Gwaii Haanas: *The Way Forward?*

The Wind Cave and the Channel Islands National Park and Marine Sanctuary represent different stages of cooperation with Indigenous peoples, with varying levels of success. Regardless of the ongoing problems and the context of settler-colonialism, these two cases represent significant steps forward. Across the border with Canada, there is a case where this cooperation has been taken much further.

Haida Gwaii (*Xaayda Gwaay*), or The Islands of the People or Queen Charlotte Islands, off the coast of British Columbia, is the traditional home of the Haida Nation. These seafaring people have inhabited these islands since the time Raven released human beings from a giant seashell. The Raven was born from the Foam Woman, who then turned into a rock that even now sits on one of the secluded beaches on the northernmost island. Haida Gwaii consists of hundreds of islands, the largest being Graham, or the North Island (*Kiis Gwaay*), and Moresby, or the South Island (*Gwaay Haanas*)—the "island of beauty." These islands are an ecological treasure, sometimes referred to as the Galapagos of the North. Several endemic species of plants and animals, like the Haida Gwaii Black Bear (*Ursus Americanus Carlottae*), live on the islands, and the surrounding waters teem with life.

The first Europeans arrived on the islands in 1774, and during the early nineteenth century, fur trade brought increasing numbers of outsiders to the islands. The fur trade was eventually replaced by mining, logging, and whaling enterprises. These brought rapid and devastating ecological and environmental changes to the area, causing significant economic and cultural damage to the Haida. Smallpox and other diseases wreaked havoc, reducing their population from tens of thousands to approximately six hundred in only one hundred years. This continuing devastation led the Haida people to seek cooperation with Parks Canada in the 1970s to protect the southernmost part of the South Island, which included several old Haida villages. In 1981, a Haida Gwaii Watchmen Program was established and after a series of protests against the logging industry, the Haida nation established a Haida Heritage Site in 1985. In cooperation with the Government of Canada, the "South Moresby Memorandum of Understanding" was signed in 1987, and the "South Moresby Agreement" in 1988. In 1993, the "Gwaii Haanas Agreement" set forth an agenda of mutual understanding and co-management of the area.[58]

Gwaii Haanas and the protected waters surrounding it are still a remote place for outside visitors. The islands can only be reached by seaplanes or boats. This has helped the conservation efforts as the number of tourists seldom exceeds more than fifteen thousand per year.[59] This seclusion has helped the unique ecosystem to recover from the exploitation of the past two hundred years. Like the environment surrounding them, the Haida are recovering from the effects of dispossession and colonization. The Haida Watchmen take tourists to the park, offering unique insights into the environment, Haida traditions, and contemporary way of life. The Watchmen, traditionally important guardians of the Haida people, now guide tourists to culturally significant sites that for the outsiders can seem unassuming, such as rivers, beaches, intertidal zones, and forests. The Haida place-based knowledge is shared in a manner that respects the Haida way of life and Haida priorities. Outside the protected area, on the North Island, the Haida Heritage Center at Kay Llnagaay displays a culture that has been connected to the land and sea for thousands of years.[60]

From the beginning of the cooperation between the Haida Nation and the Canadian government, it was important for the government to acknowledge that the proposed park was situated on Haida ancestral homelands. The area included several Haida villages, some of them now recognized as UNESCO World Heritage Sites. Similar to Grand Portage, discussed by Tim Cochrane in this volume, establishing protocols was challenging. There were economic issues relating to forestry and fishing that needed to be solved. After negotiations, a set of common goals and ideals were set in an interim management plan in 2010. Gwaii Haanas National Park Reserve, National Marine Conservation Area Reserve, and Haida Heritage Site were established. Equally important was the creation of the Archipelago Management Board (AMB), which consists of members of the Haida Nation and representatives of the Canadian government and Parks Canada.[61]

According to Parks Canada, "The Gwaii Haanas *Gina 'Waadluxan KilGulGa* (Talking about Everything) Land-Sea-People plan is the first management plan of its kind in Canada, if not the world." It lays out several themes for inclusive, respectful, and sustainable management practices. These guiding principles "are based in Haida law and include *yahguudang* (respect), *gina 'waadluxan gud ad kwaagid* (interconnectedness), *'laa guu ga kanhllns* (responsibility), *giid tll'juus* (balance), *gina k'aadang.nga gii uu tll k'anguudang* (seeking wise counsel), and *isda ad dii gii isda* (giving and receiving)." According to the management plan, they "align with principles of ecosystem-based management," including themes and measures like precautionary approach, integrated and adaptive management, sustainable use, and equitable sharing, and they are inclusive and participatory."[62]

One key aspect of the management of the park is called "zoning," which means dividing certain areas of both land and water so that sets of guidelines define what is allowed in each area. According to the management plan, zoning "is driven by key ecological and cultural targets . . . informed by the best available information, including Haida traditional knowledge." Indigenous traditional ecological knowledge (TEK) is included in the planning, management, and implementation of all aspects of the park's operations. Zoning also allows the AMB to respond quickly and effectively both to ecological and cultural issues as they arise.[63]

In addition to these major themes, the plan addresses a plethora of ways in which Gwaii Haanas and the marine sanctuary will move toward a future that acknowledges different ways of being, seeing, and understanding this unique Haida place. For the Haida, Gwaii Haanas is a place where they gather traditional foods and medicines, where spirits and ancestors live on and below the surface, and where their ceremonies are alive. As the 2018 management plan states, Haida culture is "intertwined with all of creation in the land, sea, air and spirit worlds of Haida Gwaii. Humans exist between the undersea and sky worlds, shared with other creatures and supernatural beings. . . . Connecting Haida to the past, present and future of Gwaii Haanas results in improved stewardship and a greater sense of place and belonging."[64] Gwaii Haanas demonstrates that an Indigenous place colonized for two hundred years can be re-indigenized if there is mutual political will, ability to seek respectful cultural understanding, and, most importantly, common goals. At Gwaii Haanas the common goals of nature protection and cultural survival/revitalization have brought people with different worldviews into a working relationship that represents a significant advancement in nature conservation and protection. All this was initiated by the Haida and achieved under Haida terms, the "other" emerging as an equal partner with Parks Canada.

Stages of Strategic Collaboration

These three examples demonstrate the vitality of including Indigenous perspectives and voices in the management of protected natural spaces. They highlight Indigenous agency, goals, and perspectives, each in their own way. It needs to be realized and accepted that full co-management might be difficult, even impossible, to achieve—and it is not always even necessary. Like Basil Brave Heart noted, the Lakotas are currently satisfied with the outcomes of the collaboration and the change in the interpretation of the park. This is what they set out to achieve, and for the moment this is sufficient. Since their relationship has now been established, it is easier to consider next steps. The Chumash represent a next step in a more in-depth collaborative model, in which the Chumash have actively pushed their agenda and have formed a long-term meaningful relationship with various administrative agencies. The Haida and Gwaii Haanas cases highlight what can be achieved with a full co-management model. The Haida took the initiative from the start and the Canadian government has been a willing partner. At Gwaii Haanas, Indigenous voices, ontologies, and practices are truly at the heart of all aspects of the park's operations.

By making Indigenous peoples central to their operations, these national parks pave the way forward. Granted, as settler-colonial nation-states, the United States and Canada are still the main decision-makers, but Indigenous nations like the Chumash and Haida have emerged as equal partners. Setting up practices for co-management does not happen without problems, however. The historian Brad Coombes (Maori) has noted that in the case of Te Urewera National Park in New Zealand, co-management and the ultimate return of the park's land and handing full management over to the local Tuhoe Maori has presented serious problems. Coombes argues that "redressing a colonial history of national parks requires a rethinking of conservation and development," but collaborative management is often, in fact, promoted as a reconciliation process that will "calm Indigenous protests, allowing for the perpetuation of national parks. Its motivation to pursue co-management is, therefore, a disguised and sometimes contradictory case of biocentrism." This is especially true when Indigenous rights are mixed with the concept of rights of nature, which brings about echoes of the noble savage, he further argues.[65]

This article highlighted the important work being done by Indigenous peoples in the United States and Canada as they seek to maintain and/or reclaim management opportunities in national parks and similar protected spaces. This article has demonstrated that national parks services and institutions worldwide need to renegotiate and reevaluate their relationships with Indigenous communities. This article approached the topic from a cultural standpoint, highlighting Indigenous agency, decolonization, and re-indigenization to investigate examples of successful collaborations between Indigenous peoples and non-Native stakeholders of protected natural spaces. These examples could guide nation-states to develop more humane and inclusive policies with Indigenous communities as they collaboratively seek new ways to conserve, preserve, and manage the environment. They could also spark new ways of thinking about the discourse between nature conservation and protection and Indigenous worldviews. I hope this will have real impact and value to Indigenous communities as they continue to navigate their relationships with human and non-human partners and seek to strengthen—even restore—access to their homelands and waters.

Notes

1. Thank you to: Roberta Cordero, Julie Cordero-Lamb, Alicia Cordero, Teresa Romero and Luhui Isha (Coastal Chumash), Sina Bear Eagle, Robert Brave Heart Sr., Basil Brave Heart, Lula Red Cloud, LaDonna Brave Bull Allard and Waste Win Young (Lakota/Dakota Nations), and the Archipelago Management Board, Haida Gwaii; Hilary Thorpe of Parks Canada, Gwaii Haanas NP, Chief of Interpretation Thomas Farrell and Earl Perez-Foust, US National Park Service, Wind Cave NP; Donal Carbaugh, Boyd Cothran, Brad Coombes, Saara Kekki and Joshua L. Reid.

2. George Catlin, *Letters and Notes on the Manners, Customs, and Condition of the North American Indians* (New York: Wiley and Putnam, 1841), 261–62, https://archive.org/details/lettersandnotes002catlrich/page/192.
3. Shepard Krech III, *Ecological Indian: Myth and History* (New York: W. W. Norton, 2000); Anne Ross et al., *Indigenous Peoples and the Collaborative Stewardship of Nature: Knowledge Binds and Institutional Conflicts* (New York: Routledge, 2018).
4. Mark David Spence, *Dispossessing the Wilderness: Indian Removal and the Making of the National Parks* (Oxford: Oxford University Press, 1999).
5. Päivi Magga and Eija Ojanlatva, *Ealli biras—Elävä ympäristö* [Ealli biras—Living Environment], Saamelaismuseosäätiön julkaisuja (2015), 9; Aslak Paltto, "The Role of Mass Media in Conflicts: Sámi Reindeer Herders Balancing between Traditional Law and State Law in a Predator Dispute against Officials in Finland," unpublished Master's Thesis in Indigenous Journalism, Sámi University of Applied Sciences (2017).
6. Joshua Reid, "Beyond Dispossession: Indigenous Peoples & Nationally Protected Spaces of Nature," keynote at the "Bridging Cultural Concepts of Nature: A Transnational Symposium of Indigenous Places and Public Spaces of Nature" (Helsinki, Finland, September 20, 2018).
7. Rani-Henrik Andersson, "Re-Indigenizing National Parks: Toward a Theoretical Model of Re-Indigenization," *Dutkansearvvi Journal of Sami Studies* 3(2) (2019): 65–82; Rani-Henrik Andersson, Boyd Cothran, and Saara Kekki, "Traditional Indigenous Knowledge and Nature Protection: Collaboration and Changing Paradigms," in *Bridging Cultural Concepts of Nature: Indigenous People and Protected Spaces of Nature* (Helsinki: Helsinki University Press 2021).
8. Carbaugh Donal and Lisa Rudnick, "Which Place, What Story? Cultural Discourses at the Border of Blackfeet Reservation and Glacier National Park," *Great Plains Quarterly* (Summer 2006): 167–84.
9. Stan Stevens, *Indigenous Peoples, National Parks, and Protected Areas: A New Paradigm Linking Conservation, Culture and Rights* (Tucson: University of Arizona Press, 2014); Robert H. Keller and Michael F. Turek, *American Indians & National Parks* (Tucson: University of Arizona Press, 1998); Peter Nabokov and Lawrence Loendorf, *Restoring a Presence: American Indians and Yellowstone National Park* (Norman: University of Oklahoma Press, 2004).
10. Stevens, *Indigenous Peoples*, 38.
11. Alicia Cordero et al., *Chumash Ecosystem Services Assessment* (Chumash Women's Elders Council, 2018), 1–20 (used with the permission of the authors); discussion with Julianne Cordero-Lamb, Helsinki, Finland, September 22, 2018. See Ross, *Indigenous Peoples*; Melissa K. Nelson and Daniel Shilling, *Traditional Ecological Knowledge: Learning from Indigenous Practices for Environmental Sustainability* (Cambridge: Cambridge University Press, 2018).
12. John A. Powell and Stephen Menendian, "The Problem of Othering: Towards Inclusiveness and Belonging," *Othering and Belonging: Expanding the Circle of Human Concern* 1 (2016): 14–49; Karen Barkey, "Contemporary Cases of Shared Sacred Sites: Forms of Othering or Belonging?" *Othering and Belonging: Expanding the Circle of Human Concern* 3 (2018): 30–49.

13. Andersson, "Re-Indigenizing National Parks."
14. Tuhiwai Smith, Linda, *Decolonizing Methodologies: Research and Indigenous Peoples* (London: Zed Books, 2012). See also Clint Carroll, "Native Enclosures: Tribal National Parks and the Progressive Politics of Environmental Stewardship in Indian Country." *Geoforum* 53 (2014): 31–40.
15. Andersson, "Re-Indigenizing National Parks."
16. Andersson, "Re-Indigenizing National Parks"; Andersson, "Traditional Indigenous Knowledge."
17. Aileen M. Moreton-Robinson, "Relationality: A Key Presupposition of an Indigenous Social Research Paradigm," in Chris Andersen & Jeani O'Brien, eds., *Sources and Methods in Indigenous Studies* (New York: Routledge, 69–77); Enrique Salmón, "Kincentric Ecology: Indigenous Perceptions of the Human-Nature Relationship," *Ecological Applications* 10, no. 5 (2000): 1327–32.
18. Cordero, *Chumash Ecosystem Services Assessment*, 2.
19. Robin Wall Kimmerer, *Gathering Moss: A Natural and Cultural History of Mosses* (Corvallis: Oregon State University Press, 2003); Robin Wall Kimmerer, *Braiding Sweetgrass: Indigenous Wisdom, Scientific Knowledge and the Teachings of Plants* (Minneapolis: Milkweed Editions, 2015).
20. Donal Carbaugh, "Two Different Ways of Knowing the Glacier Area," in J. Thompson and A. Houseal, eds., *America's Largest Classroom: What We Learn from our National Parks* (Berkeley: University of California Press, 2018), 36.
21. Rising Wolf as quoted in Carbaugh, 39–45. See also Carbaugh and Rudnick, "Which Place, What Story?" 170–81.
22. James R. Walker, *Lakota Myth*, ed. Elaine A. Jahner (Lincoln: University of Nebraska Press, 2006).
23. Sina Bear Eagle, "Oníya Ošóka: The Interpretation of Oglála Lakȟóta Continuing and Historical Relational Connections at Wind Cave National Park," master's thesis (UCLA, 2018), 1.
24. See Jeffrey Ostler, *The Lakotas and the Black Hills: The Struggle for Sacred Ground* (New York: Penguin Books, 2010); and for the Black Hills as a sacred place, see Raymond J. DeMallie, ed., *The Sixth Grandfather* (Lincoln: University of Nebraska Press, 1986).
25. Matthew J. Hill in this volume and Bear Eagle, "Oníya Ošóka."
26. Lakotas have various names for the cave and the surrounding country. According to Sina Bear Eagle, *Oníya Ošóka* or heavy breath is the oldest name, and others include *Makȟá Oníye*, breathing earth, *Oníya Ohlóka*, breathing cave, and *Makȟóčhe Ohlóka*, cave (home)land. Bear Eagle, "Oníya Ošóka," 24.
27. Bear Eagle.
28. National Park Service, "Wind Cave National Park Time Line," Wind Cave National Park (2019). https://www.nps.gov/wica/learn/historyculture/wica-time-line.htm (accessed February 14, 2019).
29. Jim Kent, "Wind Cave Numbers Highest in 40 Years," SDPB Radio (January 19, 2016). https://listen.sdpb.org/post/wind-cave-numbers-highest-40-years.
30. National Park Service, "Wind Cave," Wind Cave National Park (2020). https://www.nps.gov/wica/index.htm (accessed October 31, 2020).

31. See Patricia C. Albers, "The Home of the Bison: An Ethnographic and Ethnohistorical Study of Traditional Cultural Affiliations to Wind Cave National Park," US National Park Service and Department of American Indian Studies (University of Minnesota, 2003), https://home.nps.gov/wica/learn/historyculture/the-home-of-the-bison-title-page.htm.
32. National Park Service, "The Lakota Emergence Story," Wind Cave National Park (2020), https://www.nps.gov/wica/learn/historyculture/the-lakota-emergence-story.htm (accessed modified November 7, 2020).
33. Thomas Farrell, Chief of Interpretation, Wind Cave National Park, discussion, February 22, 2019.
34. Basil Brave Heart, Oglala elder, personal communication, August 7, 2020; Robert Brave Heart, Vice Director of Red Cloud Indian School, personal communication, August 24, 2019; Thomas Farrell, personal communication, August 21 and September 21, 2019.
35. Basil Brave Heart, personal communication, August 7, 2020; Lula Red Cloud, Oglala elder, personal communication, May 24, 2018 and September 2019.
36. Bear Eagle, "Oníya Ošóka," 100–103; Thomas Farrell, personal communication, February 22, 2019 and August 21, 2019; Wind Cave National Park, Official Brochure 2018.
37. Basil Brave Heart, personal communication, August 7, 2020.
38. Andersson, "Re-Indigenizing National Parks."
39. Hulmesmu' hil Wishtoyo (The Rainbow Bridge), Chumash origin story Cordero, *Chumash Ecosystem Services Assessment*, 6.
40. Cordero, 2–3; See also Mati Waiya, "Chumash Values." https://www.wishtoyo.org/cp-chumash-values (accessed March 1, 2021).
41. See Jeanne E. Arnold, ed., *The Origins of a Pacific Coast Chiefdom: The Chumash of the Channel Islands* (Salt Lake City: University of Utah Press, 2001); Lynn H. Gamble, *The Chumash World at European Contact: Power, Trade, and Feasting Among Complex Hunter-Gatherers* (Berkeley: University of California Press, 2008); Phil C. Orr, "Arlington Springs Man," *Science* 135 (3499) (1962): 219.
42. Cordero Reyes and Roberta & Alicia Cordero (in collaboration with the Chumash Wishtoyo Foundation), "The Chumash People of California: An Overview," article manuscript; See also Wishtoyo Chumash Foundation, "Chumash History." http://www.wishtoyo.org/cp-chumash-history/ (accessed March 1, 2021).
43. Theodore Roosevelt as quoted in National Park Service, "Establishing Channel Islands National Park," Channel Islands National Park (2020). https://www.nps.gov/chis/learn/historyculture/park-history.htm (accessed August 3, 2020).
44. *Public Law 96–199,* March 5, 1980.
45. Frederic Caire Chiles, *California's Channel Islands: A History* (Norman: University of Oklahoma Press, 2015); Dolan H. Eargle Jr., *Native California: An Introductory Guide to the Original Peoples from Earliest to Modern Time* (n.p.: Trees Company Press, 2017), 234–36; Kent G. Lightfoot and Otis Parrish,

California Indians and Their Environment: An Introduction (Berkeley: University of California Press, 2009).

46. National Park rangers and tour guides, personal communications, fall 2016 and fall 2017. See National Park Service, "Close to the California Mainland . . . Yet Worlds Apart," Channel Islands National Park (2020). https://www.nps.gov/chis/index.htm (accessed July 1, 2020); for the Marine Sanctuary, see National Ocean Service, "Channel Islands National Marine Sanctuary." https://channelislands.noaa.gov/marineres/welcome.html (accessed March 1, 2021).

47. Lyndal Laughrin, Director of the University of California Field Station, personal communication, November 23, 2017; The Nature Conservancy, "Places We Protect: Santa Cruz Island, California," https://www.nature.org/en-us/get-involved/how-to-help/places-we-protect/santa-cruz-island-california/ (accessed March 1, 2021). See Natural Reserve System, University of California, "Santa Cruz Island Reserve," https://ucnrs.org/reserves/santa-cruz-island-reserve (accessed March 1, 2021).

48. Cordero, *Chumash Ecosystem Services Assessment*, 4–5.

49. CINMS Management Plan 2009, 46–47; Roberta Cordero, personal correspondence, February 2019. For the current members, see https://channelislands.noaa.gov/sac/members_alternates.html (accessed February 26, 2021).

50. CINMS Management Plan 2009, 46–47.

51. Roberta Cordero, personal correspondence, February 2019.

52. Cordero, *Chumash Ecosystem Services Assessment*, 12; Cordero and Cordero, n.d. a, 6. See Michael Vincent McGinnis and Roberta R. Cordero, "Tribal Marine Protected Areas: Protecting Maritime Ways and Cultural Practices," *A Special White Paper for Wishtoyo Foundation*, https://static1.squarespace.com/static/5459dd35e4b0eb18b9b5599b/t/56bb76be859fd0422da8978d/1455126215937/TribalMPAsWhitePaper.pdf (accessed March 1, 2021); Chumash Marine Sanctuary. https://chumashsanctuary.com (accessed March 1, 2021); Roberta Cordero, personal correspondence, February 2019.

53. I want to acknowledge that terms like "spiritual" and "sacred site" can, at worst, be understood as settler-colonial terms that do injustice to Indigenous worldviews and concepts, and I would suggest the reader keep that in mind.

54. Cordero, n.d. b, manuscript used with permission of author; Roberta Cordero, personal communication, December 3, 2017; Teresa Romero and Julie Cordero-Lamb, personal communications, September 18–22, 2018; Teresa Romero, "Collaboration—Paths to Land Restoration and Recovery," in "Bridging Cultural Concepts of Nature: A Transnational Symposium of Indigenous Places and Public Spaces of Nature" (presentation) (Helsinki, Finland, September 20–21, 2018); Julie Cordero-Lamb, "Tending to our Families: The Syuxtun Plant Mentorship Collective and the Return of Food and Medicine Sovereignty among the Coastal Chumash," in "Bridging Cultural Concepts of Nature"; Roberta R. Cordero, "Our Ancestors' Gift across Time: A Story of Indigenous Maritime Culture Resurgence," *News from Native California* 11 (3) (1998): 4–6; Julie Cordero-Lamb, "Families Gathered at Limuw." *News from*

Native California 21 (2) (2001); Roberta R. Cordero and Georgiana Valoyce Sanchez, "Full Circle: We Return to Swaxil," *News from Native California* (2004); Roberta R. Cordero, "Full Circle Chumash Cross Channel in Tomol to Santa Cruz Island." https://channelislands.noaa.gov/maritime/chumash1.html (accessed March 1, 2021); Roberta R. Cordero, "Anacapa," Manuscript.
55. Roberta Cordero, personal correspondence, February 2019.
56. Cordero.
57. Cordero, *Chumash Ecosystem Services Assessment*, 16–17.
58. Parks Canada, "Gwaii Haanas Gina 'Waadluxan KilGuhlGa Land-Sea-People Management Plan 2018," Gwaii Haanas National Park Reserve, National Marine Conservation Area Reserve and Haida Heritage Site (2020). https://www.pc.gc.ca/en/pn-np/bc/gwaiihaanas/info/consultations (accessed June 30, 2020). See Daryl W. Fedje and Rolf W. Mathewes, eds., *Haida Gwaii: Human History and Environment from the Time of Loon to the Time of the Iron People* (Vancouver: University of British Columbia Press, 2006); Dennis Horwood, *Haida Gwaii: A Guide to BC's Islands of the People* (Seattle: University of Washington Press, 2016); Haida Heritage Center. https://haidaheritagecentre.com/ (accessed March 1, 2021); and Parks Canada, "Gwaii Haanas National Park Reserve, National Marine Conservation Area Reserve, and Haida Heritage Site" (2020). https://www.pc.gc.ca/en/pn-np/bc/gwaiihaanas/visit (accessed August 18, 2020).
59. The number of annual visitors between 1995–2015 has increased steadily from approximately 1,000 in 1995 to approximately 15,000 in 2015. *Haida Gwaii Observer*, "Summer Tourism Keeps on Growing" (September 16, 2016). https://www.haidagwaiiobserver.com/news/summer-tourism-keeps-on-growing.
60. Haida Heritage Center.
61. For developing the joint management plan, see Parks Canada, "Gwaii Haanas Gina 'Waadluxan KilGuhlGa Land-Sea-People Management Plan 2018."
62. Parks Canada, "Gwaii Haanas National Park Reserve, National Marine Conservation Area Reserve, and Haida Heritage Site," 7.
63. Parks Canada, 27–30, appendix A.
64. Parks Canada, 7–9.
65. Brad Coombes, "PERSONifying Indigenous Rights in Nature? Treaty Settlement and Comanagement in Te Urewera," in Rani-Henrik Andersson, Boyd Cothran, and Saara Kekki, eds., *Bridging Cultural Concepts of Nature: Indigenous People and Protected Spaces of Nature* (Helsinki: Helsinki University Press, 2021).

NINE | **Returning to Gather**
Cherokee Medicine Keepers, the National Park Service, and the Making of a Plant-Gathering Agreement at Buffalo National River

RICHARD W. STOFFLE, MICHAEL J. EVANS, AND CLINT CARROLL

[Being] in this park—it is like being back home in the east where we lived, before we were relocated to Oklahoma. It is like being home again. I can hardly wait until the spring when we will return to gather.

—Cherokee Elder and Medicine Keeper,
Buffalo National River, May 2017

IN 2019, THE CHEROKEE NATION and the National Park Service (NPS) at Buffalo National River (henceforth Buffalo NR) in Arkansas established an historic agreement that enacts a federal rule allowing tribes to gather plants within US national parks to which they have traditional connections. Members of the Cherokee Medicine Keepers—a small group of elders who advise the Cherokee Nation Secretary of Natural Resources—partnered with a team of university researchers (including authors Stoffle and Carroll) and lent their ethnobotanical expertise to provide the basis for this landmark agreement. Stretching 153 miles, the Buffalo River is one of the last wild rivers in a region of manmade dams and lakes. The national park encloses a dense natural forest surrounded by thousands of acres of farmland (Figures 9.1 and 9.2). Established in 1972, the park marked the first designation of a national river by US Congress, with 135 miles of the river's length under the NPS's control. Gathering within Buffalo NR

Figure 9.1. Researchers looking over Wild Buffalo River and Dense Park Forest. Courtesy of the authors.

offers Cherokee people a way to continue their sustainable use and stewardship of plants impacted by climate change in eastern Oklahoma, and to reestablish their connection to the park lands as a collective source of sustenance, cultural knowledge, and health.

Each of us (Carroll, Evans, and Stoffle) contributed to the development of the Cherokee-Buffalo NR gathering agreement. This chapter represents our shared assessment of this work and its broader significance. As co-authors, we approach this essay from distinct, yet complementary, positions. Richard Stoffle is a full research professor in the Bureau of Applied Research in Anthropology at the University of Arizona and led the research team as principal investigator for the project. Michael Evans is a regional cultural anthropologist for the NPS and helped facilitate the agreement process and communication with park staff. Clint Carroll is a Cherokee Nation citizen and associate professor in the Department of Ethnic Studies at the University of Colorado Boulder. Carroll has worked with the Cherokee Medicine Keepers since their inception in 2008 and served as a liaison between the elders, tribal staff, and the research team. All of us worked collaboratively to initiate the research project and shepherd the agreement in partnership with Cherokee elders, tribal staff and officials, and NPS staff and administrators.

As the epigraph illustrates, Cherokee elders viewed their experience in this project as akin to returning home to what they call ᏨᏯᎯ ᎠᏝᎵ ᎤᏬᎩ, the

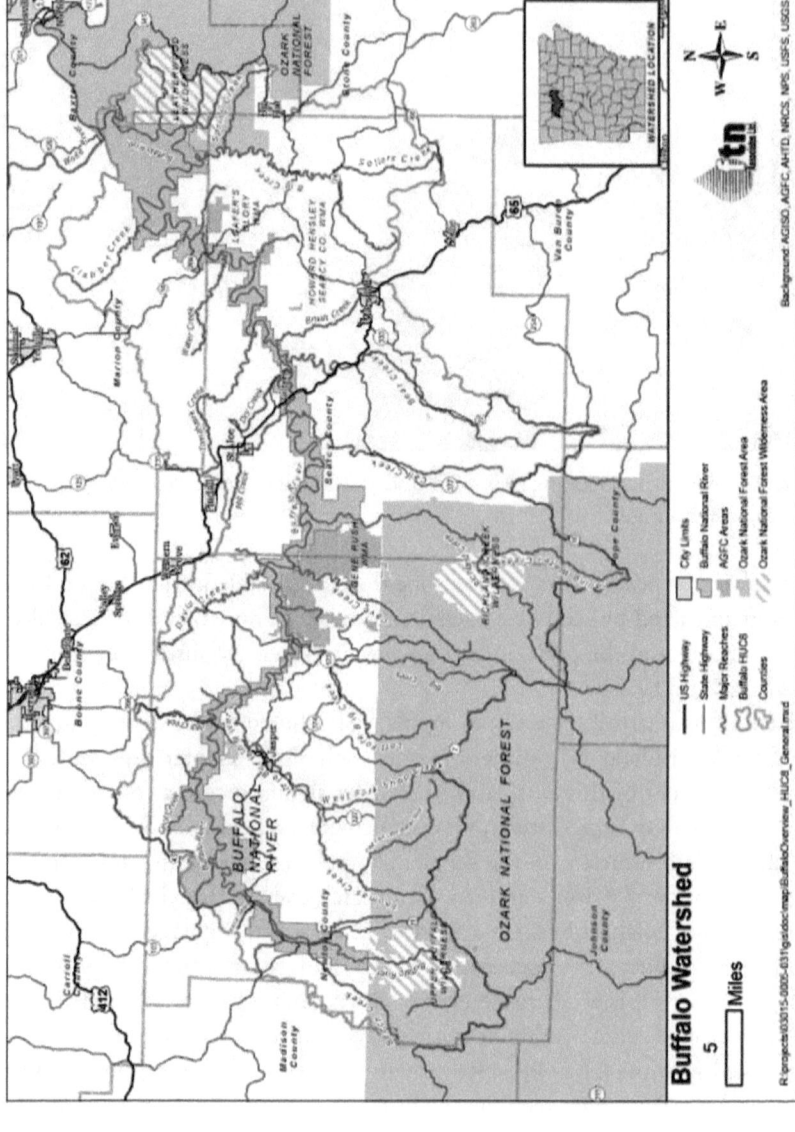

Figure 9.2. Map of Buffalo River watershed in northern Arkansas. Courtesy of the National Park Service.

Old Cherokee Nation in the southern Appalachian Mountains.[1] To varying degrees, Oklahoma Cherokees maintain their relationships with their aboriginal homelands, most often through their participation in joint programs between the three federally-recognized Cherokee tribes—one of which is headquartered in Cherokee, North Carolina, and is the governing body for the descendants of Cherokee people who remained in the east despite the Indian Removal Policy of the 1830s.[2] And yet, the homelands are roughly nine hundred miles away from the current reservation in eastern Oklahoma, which makes such trips infrequent and dependent upon tribal funding and programming. By contrast, Buffalo NR is a relatively short three-hour drive from Tahlequah (the tribal capital city) and is situated deep within the Ozark Highlands.

To the elders and knowledge keepers who participated in this project, the rolling hills and oak-hickory woodlands of the park landscape bore topographical, ecological, and botanical familiarity. As another elder remarked, "To me, when I entered this place, it was just like I was back in our traditional home in the east again. Now, that is the way I felt, and I still feel the same way. And if we can take medicine from here, it would be a blessing. This area is just like some places in North Carolina that we have seen. It is almost like being in North Carolina." This sense of familiarity with the park lands is not as removed from Cherokee experience as it may seem. Although the history of Cherokee relocation along the Trail of Tears is widely known, as we discuss below, Buffalo NR sits within an historical treaty boundary in which a faction of Cherokee migrants lived prior to the forced march of most Cherokee people from their homelands in the winter of 1838–39. Thus, the elements mentioned above demonstrate numerous layers of meaning for this project, including Indigenous reconnection with traditionally associated lands, climate change adaptation strategies, the dynamics of federal-tribal partnerships, and Indigenous cultural and political resurgence.

We assess the project's broader significance through two conceptual lenses: *strategic engagement* and *relational continuity*. By establishing a gathering agreement with the NPS, Cherokee people are strategically engaging in a federal partnership opportunity to regain access to lands they historically inhabited. This strategy entails taking advantage of openings like the federal gathering rule that seek to reconcile the troubled history of Indigenous dispossession and exclusion from traditional lands enacted by the US conservation movement throughout the late nineteenth and early twentieth centuries.[3] Through strategic engagement, Cherokees are acknowledging this history while forging partnerships that can support the continuation of land-based practices and cultural knowledge transmission. Relatedly, the project exemplifies what co-author Carroll has termed *relational continuity*, or "the persistence of ethically and culturally grounded relationships with the land and nonhumans despite social and spatial change."[4] Due to the ecological similarities between the Cherokee homelands and the lands within Buffalo NR, Cherokees are continuing their relational obligations with communities of plants and animals they regard as central to their cultural identity through the plant-gathering agreement. Such obligations entail taking care of the land through sustainable gathering practices and other forms of Indigenous land management that are now widely regarded as ecologically beneficial, including by the federal government.[5]

In what follows, we first describe and contextualize the NPS Plant-Gathering Rule, followed by a discussion of Cherokee ancestral connections to the Buffalo River and leading up to the contemporary relevance of the project. We then consider the process of conducting the ethnobotanical study and the role of trust-building, time, and pre-established relationships in the finalized agreement with the NPS. Lastly, we discuss the broad significance of the project and the Plant-Gathering Rule for the Cherokee and other Indigenous nations.

The NPS Plant-Gathering Rule

In 2016, following years of discussions, drafting, and public comments, the NPS issued a rule that permits tribal members from culturally associated Native American tribes to gather culturally important plants from traditional lands that are part of NPS units.[6] The rule, titled "Gathering of Certain Plants or Plant Parts by Federally Recognized Indian Tribes for Traditional Purposes" (Code of Federal Regulations, title 32, sec. 2.6, 2016), centers on the establishment of an agreement between a requesting tribe and a park with which the tribe is culturally associated.

The first step in developing an agreement is to document *cultural association* with lands that are currently the congressionally mandated responsibility of a federal park. This can be accomplished several ways, including the tribe providing information that demonstrates the cultural connections, conducting a general ethnographic overview and assessment (a baseline document for parks), or conducting a traditional use study.[7]

After cultural association is established, further *ethnobotanical research* is conducted to accomplish six goals: (1) to identify the tribe's traditional use plants that now grow in the park; (2) to establish which of these plants are of contemporary interest to tribal members; (3) to assess how much of the plant is being sought; (4) to determine how the plant will be gathered; (5) to assess what time of year gathering will occur; and (6) to verify that the plants will be used for traditional purposes after being gathered.[8]

Field visits to the park by tribal members are essential to identify and confirm the location of the plants and thus establish where the tribe would prefer to gather. Subsequently, the park must conduct an *environmental assessment* (EA) of the proposed plants to be gathered and places where gathering would occur before the agreement can be finalized. The agreement calls for production of an annual *special use permit* that describes how the tribe will select persons to gather, determine how they will be identified at the time of gathering, and describe ways the tribe will participate in an annual review of the environmental impacts of their gathering.

While not required by the Plant-Gathering Rule, it is recommended that the ethnobotanical study document the tribe's ecological knowledge of plants and which practices they may have traditionally used to conserve the broader ecosystem. Such information provides an understanding of the tribe's cultural commitment to the plants and reveals that sustainable uses are a mutual goal of both the park and the tribe. In general, a research team can be employed by the park, the tribe, or through a third-party contract.

For this project, a team of applied cultural anthropologists conducted and produced the study. Stoffle led the ethnobotany study with an applied cultural anthropology research team from the School of Anthropology at the University of Arizona and the support of Carroll. The study was funded by the NPS and designed by Evans, regional cultural anthropologist for Interior Regions 3, 4, and 5. Earlier, while the Plant-Gathering Rule was being developed, Evans designed and procured funding for a precursor ethnobotany study involving three Odawa Tribes and Sleeping Bear Dunes National Lakeshore in Michigan.[9] That Odawa study, also conducted by Stoffle and a university research team, was designed as a model way forward towards an agreement and ultimately referenced as such in the official publication of the Plant-Gathering Rule.[10] Evans is also a co-author of the final Plant-Gathering Rule.

The Cherokee-Buffalo NR study was strategically proposed by Evans to explore a type of cultural association situation in which an Indigenous nation has historical and cultural association with a park, but the park lands do not comprise their aboriginal homelands. Stoffle contacted Carroll to consult on the project based on his then ten years of work with Cherokee people in Oklahoma, and to serve as a liaison between the research team, Cherokee Nation administrative staff, and tribal elders. The proposed study was presented to the Cherokee Medicine Keepers—the tribe's formally constituted body of knowledge-keepers whose mission is to perpetuate Cherokee ecological knowledge.[11] They agreed to proceed, noting the alignment of the gathering agreement with their mission, the proximity of the park to the Cherokee reservation in northeastern Oklahoma, and the fact that the park encompasses an area that includes Cherokee historical treaty territory and numerous culturally significant plant species.

Cherokee Relationships with the Buffalo River

Like many Indigenous nations, Cherokees have faced displacement from their ancestral homelands in the Carolinas, Tennessee, Georgia, and Alabama. Although the Indian Removal policy of the US government during the 1830s marked a devastating period in Cherokee history, over time Cherokee people developed cultural connections to new lands. Even before the forced relocation, many Cherokee communities voluntarily reestablished themselves in the Ozark

Mountains, which contain dramatic hills and valleys and a climate similar to the southern Appalachian Mountains.[12] Relocation placed them in the westernmost extent of the Ozark Highlands, which were significantly less biodiverse than their homelands but still contained numerous familiar food and medicine plants.[13]

Cherokee people began migrating in the 1700s across the Mississippi River into what was once French territory (1673–1764), then Spanish (1764–1773), and then French again (1773–1803). They migrated into lands that now make up the state of Arkansas to escape threats and pressures from both US settlers and political leadership. This area included the homelands of the Caddo, Tunica-Biloxi, and Osage nations.

Cherokee people who crossed into the French and Spanish Louisiana colony were permitted to safely settle and farm in areas that were not being used by Spanish or French traders/trading communities. According to historian Kent Blansett, "Within the Mississippi River region the French practiced *frontier inclusion*, choosing to create trade ties with Native people but refusing to establish settlement within Native communities."[14] Large French settlements on the outer rim of the Ozarks were at ports such as St. Louis and Cape Girardeau. French settlements were centered along the main rivers, so the Ozark Plateau hinterlands and its smaller rivers, like the White River, were open for Cherokee settlement.

Historical accounts document Cherokee people occupying the Buffalo River region and making use of the natural resources at the same time as the Osage.[15] During the Spanish Louisiana period, the Viceroyalty encouraged the Delaware and Shawnee to migrate into the eastern Ozarks to help create a buffer zone against the Osage (who were hostile to the Spanish), and to serve as a buffer against US citizens establishing settlements in the region.[16] There were enough Cherokee people already in the region to be a party to such a significant alliance. According to Blansett, "By the late 1700s one of the first migrant tribes to relocate to the Ozarks was the Old settler Cherokee under Chief Toquo, or Turkey. Some of these Cherokee represented a particular band called the Chickamauga, who had allied with the British during the American Revolution (1776–1784). They established settlements between the St. Francis and White rivers in the Arkansas Ozarks. By the early 1800s they were officially recognized through treaty with the US as the Western Cherokee Nation and supported a population between fifteen hundred and three thousand."[17]

By 1808, the Cherokee population in this region was considerable, leading them to file a legal petition for the formal recognition of the land as Cherokee territory. The US government granted this petition in 1817, recognizing lands that included Buffalo River and its associated tributaries as belonging to the Cherokee people. However, stemming from the Louisiana Purchase in 1803, Euro-American settlers began to relocate across the Mississippi River. They arrived in the Ozark Mountains, including the Buffalo River area in the early 1800s.[18] Due to this encroachment, Native American groups began to lose their traditional historic homelands and were pushed into new territories. In 1828,

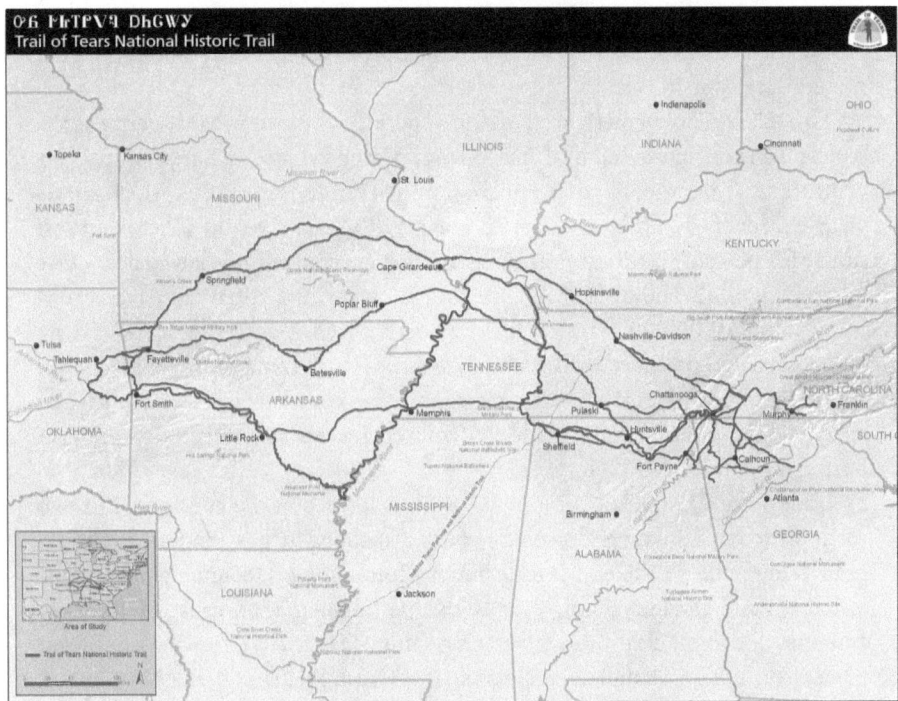

Figure 9.3. Trail of Tears National Historic Trail Map (NPS). Courtesy of the National Park Service.

another treaty with the Western Cherokee overturned the Arkansas land allotment that was granted to them in 1817.[19]

US citizens were eager to expand their land holdings to increase agriculture and trade productivity, as well as to support the growing population.[20] The Indian Removal Act, passed in 1830, granted money and land even farther west to Native Americans in exchange for their lands in the South. Tensions ensued, and subsequent land treaties were increasingly abusive of Indigenous rights.[21] In 1835, the Treaty of New Echota prescribed forced removal of Cherokee people then living throughout the US South and Midwest, including those people living across the Mississippi River in the Buffalo River area. All Cherokee people were then forcibly removed to the Indian Territory (present-day eastern Oklahoma) along what is known as the Trail of Tears.[22] The relocation involved more than thirteen thousand Cherokee people over the course of nine months in 1838–39. The journey is approximately nine hundred miles; however, there were multiple routes of slightly varying distances. Some scholars estimate that four thousand Cherokee people died from various diseases and weather conditions during those nine months.[23] Russell Thornton argues that eight thousand people died leading up to and immediately after the forced march. Relocation to Tahlequah, Indian Territory (now Oklahoma) from Cherokee aboriginal territory followed a trail that passed north of Buffalo River and south of the Missouri border.[24] Figure 9.3 highlights where the trail was located, approximately twenty miles north of present-day Buffalo NR.

Cherokee people experienced extended periods of peace and prosperity in the Indian Territory post-Removal Act, but soon they suffered the crippling effects of the federal allotment and assimilation policies of the late 1800s. These effects were worsened by Oklahoma statehood in 1907. As a result, Cherokees lost nearly 98 percent of tribal lands to encroachment and surplus land sales. Once comprising 4.42 million acres in fee simple ownership, tribal trust lands now number only 100,000 acres in scattered and checkerboarded parcels.[25] These land losses, compounded by the assimilatory effects of Indian Boarding Schools, threatened cultural practices and environmental knowledge tied to land-based ways of life. The Cherokee people now faced increasing pressures to preserve both their culture and their lands.

Today, the Cherokee Nation reservation is located at the confluence of two vastly different climate and ecology zones. To the west is a semi-arid tallgrass prairie zone and to the east is a deciduous forest zone. Documented and projected climate changes, along with landscape fragmentation caused by human activities like forest clearing and cattle ranching, have and are creating significant stresses on native plant habitats across the Great Plains and the Southeast.[26] These forces threaten the health of plant communities supported by eastern deciduous forests, which Cherokee people continue to rely on for medicine, food, crafts, and other cultural and economic purposes. The resulting species loss and the shifting ranges of species further inhibit Cherokee people's access to these plants. The Plant-Gathering Agreement with Buffalo NR, in addition to recognizing ancestral and political relationships to the lands within the park (through inhabitance and treaty-making), offers Cherokee people a way to continue their relationship responsibilities with cultural use plants that in many cases are more plentiful and healthier within the park boundaries than those growing on tribal trust lands in Oklahoma.

The Cherokee-Buffalo National River Ethnobotanical Study

The ethnobotanical study makes up the foundation of the Cherokee-Buffalo NR Plant-Gathering Agreement and directly informs critical policy procedures and requirements. However, the completion of this foundational component required careful attention to context, relationships, and process. This section details the dynamics of this federal-tribal-university partnership and the measures the research team took to ensure its success.

Considering Cherokee experiences with forced removal, land theft, and broken treaties, foremost among our concerns was building trust. Indeed, most tribes and pueblos have very little trust in the US federal government, including the NPS. Tribes are keenly aware that national parks occupy their lands, and that the establishment of the parks effectively severed their intricate relationships to them. However, the Plant-Gathering Agreement is now an important and positive vehicle for recognizing this history and taking steps to mend the severed relationships. This process requires patience and persistence. Despite the professional experience of all participants, the Cherokee-Buffalo NR case required five years of constant work. Over time, as more plant-gathering agreements are successfully established, mutual trust in the process should increase and will require less time.

One aspect of the project that contributed to building trust was the collaborative effort between Cherokee Nation and researchers in planning research. Carroll, a citizen of the Cherokee Nation and professor of Indigenous studies, became a member of the research team and contributed to the design, execution, and write-up of the study. Having an Indigenous consultant on the project who had established relationships with the community contributed significantly to its success. Collaboration continued when researchers traveled to Tahlequah, Oklahoma in December 2015 to meet with the Cherokee Medicine Keepers and tribal administrative staff to discuss aspects of the project and listen to expressed interests by potential participants. Mr. Pat Gwin, tribal biologist and senior director of environmental resources for the Cherokee Nation, contributed significantly to these discussions and to the project as a whole. Mr. Gwin also serves as a tribal administrative liaison to the Cherokee Medicine Keepers, and has co-facilitated their activities with Carroll since their inception in 2008.

The next research phase entailed the development of a Cherokee traditional plant inventory for Buffalo NR by comparing plant species recognized as currently growing within the park with those recognized as being traditional Cherokee use plants. We consulted five previously published ethnobotany studies that span from 1932 to 2009 to track the types of traditional plants continuously used by Cherokee communities. Cherokee plant uses documented in previous studies provided a foundation for understanding the addition of new uses and similar plants. We used this information to develop a plant recording instrument that aided our collection of ethnobotanical data with Cherokee tribal representatives in the field. The park has documented 1,780 different species of plants within Buffalo NR. The tribal plant database identified that Cherokee people traditionally used 281 of these.

The next phase of the project entailed a scoping trip and ethnographic fieldwork with tribally appointed representatives to document specific aspects of plant-gathering knowledge. In January 2017, the research team, along with Michael Evans and Pat Gwin, traveled to Buffalo NR and spent three days visiting the park to determine possible site locations for the first field session with Cherokee Medicine Keepers. Two sites were selected for field visits due to ease of access, amenities (such as toilets, benches, and shading), and variations in plant life. The group also met with NPS staff to discuss the project, including a field activity plan for the coming spring.

Figure 9.4. Gathering study participants from tribe, park, and university. Courtesy of the authors.

In May 2017, Cherokee Medicine Keepers and other representatives from the Cherokee Nation visited the park with researchers for a field session (Figures 9.4 and 9.5). During this trip, researchers and NPS staff accompanied the Cherokee Medicine Keepers to provide site-specific information and record both ethnobotanical and gathering data. Cherokee representatives participated in two meetings before the site visits in the park occurred; the first took place exclusively between the research team and Cherokee representatives. This meeting was essential for discussing the schedule for the field session, introducing the plant recording form, and answering questions from the elders. This meeting helped familiarize the group with the study design and schedule. The second meeting occurred at the Buffalo NR offices and involved Cherokee representatives and NPS staff members who met and discussed the process of establishing a Plant-Gathering Agreement.

Four Cherokee Medicine Keepers and five helpers who assisted them were accompanied by the research team in the field. Participating Cherokee Medicine Keepers were tribally appointed consultants, each of whom was accompanied by a research team member. Helpers were made up of Cherokee Nation staff and family members. They assisted with recording information on the plant-gathering form (Figure 9.6) and provided ethnobotanical insights into the uses of the plants. Pat Gwin, a trained biologist, hiked each area in advance and marked specific cultural use plants with orange flagging tape to aid in plant identification for the interviews with the elders.

Following the field session, researchers drafted the ethnobotany report.[27] A total of seventy-six plants in Buffalo River NR were identified as being both

Figure 9.5. Medicine keepers and university researchers in a group sharing event. Courtesy of the authors.

traditionally used and of contemporary interest to the Cherokee Nation. We established "traditional use" as a category by cross-referencing plants known to exist within the park and plants recorded as being used by Cherokees at some point in the past. We established the category of contemporary interest through the field visits to the park and from an official booklet produced by the tribe regarding contemporary use plants.

The Cherokee plant-gathering form includes information regarding the traditional uses that these plants served and the culturally appropriate methods for gathering them. We observed that fifty-three of the seventy-six recorded plants are gathered for medicinal purposes and thirty-five are collected for food. Plant data recorded on a form and on tape were considered formal data-sharing events. Informal data-sharing events included any data that did not fit well on the Cherokee plant-gathering form. These were generally participant-guided conversations that covered a range of topics, including history, geography, geology, culture, and general ecology. In all, eighty-eight data sharing events occurred.

Stoffle and Evans have documented through previous studies that Indigenous people commonly use plants for multiple purposes.[28] Therefore, categories of use, such as food, craft, or medicine should not be viewed as mutually exclusive. The Buffalo NR ethnobotany study recorded that Cherokee people had more than one use for individual plant species. Of the twenty-three identified multi-use plants, 74 percent were identified as used for medicine and food.

Plant gathering is a seasonally specific activity. Cherokee tradition dictates the correct times to gather plants and plant parts based on long-standing traditional

Buffalo National River Ethnobotany: Cherokee Plant Gathering Form

Ethnographer:		Tape:	
Representative:		Location:	

Plant Name

Common:	
Scientific:	
Cherokee:	

Photograph

Camera:	
Time:	
Title:	

Contemporary Use

Med	Food	Craft	Const.	Other

Season Collected / Who

Sp	Sum	Fall	Win	M	F

Amount Collected per Visit

A.	Handful
B.	Bucketful
C.	Bushel Basket
D.	More

Plant Parts

- A. Flower
- B. Fruit/Seed
- C. Leaf
- D. Stem/Trunk
- E. Root

What Tools would be used to gather this plant?

What would you need to gather this plant here?

How would Cherokee People have gathered this plant so it would always be there in the future?

Figure 9.6. Plant gathering form. Courtesy of the National Park Service.

use of these plant resources over seasonal cycles. This seasonal gathering is a tradition that promotes sustainable practices that balance maximum yield with plant regrowth and reproduction. This is an important component of gathering practices based on traditional ecological knowledge. Cherokee representatives were asked to provide seasonal gathering information for the seventy-six traditional plants. The preferred seasons for collecting are the fall and spring.

The agreement hinges in part on the desired volume for each plant as identified per person and place (for gathering). We based volume measures on a scale developed by the research team during previous work at Sleeping Bear Dunes National Lakeshore, Michigan.[29] These categories include: (1) a handful or less; (2) a bucket full; (3) a bushel basket; and (4) more. Over half of the identified plants, totaling forty-one, were selected as only needing the smallest quantity during collection. A handful constitutes as much as one can carry without the use of containers or other apparatuses. The second most selected amount was a bucketful, with a total of twenty-two identified ethnobotanical resources, or 29 percent. Amounts equaling a bushel or more were less common. Only eight identified plants were selected as needing to gather a bushel, and seven plants were selected as needing to gather more. Tools necessary for gathering were also recorded, demonstrating that most of the plants can be gathered by hand, with a few necessitating the use of a small spade or clippers. The NPS regulation requires exclusive gathering by hand and using human-powered tools.

Sustainability is a deeply rooted feature of Cherokee plant-gathering practices. This philosophy is expressed in the discussion of almost every category of the plants identified in the Cherokee plant-gathering form. Cherokee representatives highlighted the concept of *plant sustainability* in the following statements:

> When beginning to gather you ask the creator to protect the plant and to have them always be there for us to use. You never ever collect more than what you need and you always leave some.
> Leave every other one. You might want to do annual prescribed burn on some plants.
> And you do not touch it or nothing until you say your prayer to the creator and keeper of the medicine. And then you have tell the plant your name. If it's a medicinal plant you tell what you want that medicine for, and who you're getting it for to cure.
> But even collecting a plant that is not a medicinal plant, we were taught to tell it our full Cherokee name, what clan we are from, and we pray to collect the plant and let it [know]. But we do not take it all. We just take a little bit, you know? In that way, it can keep growing.

These responses characterize the sustainable use approach of Cherokee plant gathering. Cherokee people create an environment where they build relationships with the plant community; relationships in which the plants they gather and depend on are symbiotically supported and physically encouraged by their gathering activities.

Stories have been passed down from generation to generation to teach practices of sustainable plant gathering.[30] These stories often include plant-collection methods, such as the removal of specific plant parts. For example, when removing a plant from the ground, Cherokee people are taught to replant the severed roots so that the plant can continue to grow.[31] Plant removal can also entail spreading the seeds by hand.[32]

In summary, Cherokee plant interviews indicated that they know about the traditional uses of at least seventy-six plants in the park, most of which are for medicine and ceremonial foods. They gather small amounts of most plants and use their hands and small tools to ensure the flourishing of these plants and their ecosystems.

Environmental Assessment and Agreement

Cherokee cultural proscriptions for plant gathering and use were an important component of the study. Upon approval by the Medicine Keepers, the technical report was submitted to Buffalo NR so that park staff could begin to conduct an environmental assessment (EA) of the potential impacts of proposed Cherokee gathering of seventy-six plants in two designated areas. That EA agreed with the Medicine Keepers that there would be no overall adverse impacts on park ecosystems and plants. A few plants, however, were highlighted as requiring closer monitoring after gathering begins. Careful analysis of the Cherokee request led the park superintendent to suggest two additional areas (now a total of four) be added to the agreement to provide more access and to further mitigate the effects of gathering. The EA was posted for a ninety-day public review period after it was reviewed by both the Cherokee Nation and the NPS.

During the summer of 2018, the Plant-Gathering Agreement was drafted and for a year continued to be reviewed by both the Cherokee Nation and the NPS at the park, regional, and national levels. The final document, dated June 11, 2019, was officially termed a Memorandum of Agreement (MOA), and it states: "This Memorandum of Agreement ("MOA") is entered into by and between the National Park Service (hereinafter referred to as NPS or "the Park"), United States Department of the Interior, acting through the Superintendent of Buffalo NR, and the Cherokee Nation for the purpose of establishing a mutual framework governing the respective responsibilities of the parties in managing the gathering of plants and plant parts from the Park for traditional purposes, in accordance with the regulation at 36 CFR 2.6." Further, the agreement defined the Cherokee Nation's eligibility based on its

> traditional association to the Buffalo River [which] dates back to the early eighteenth century when Cherokee people were migrating westward

due to increasing encroachments upon their southeastern homelands by Euro-Americans. This group of Cherokees, often referred to as the Old Settlers, sought to avoid conflict with Euro-American people by establishing new settlements west of the Mississippi River. During this time, Cherokees continued ways of life that included the use of wild plants for food, tools, utilities, and medicine. Due to the similarity of the Ozarks to their southeastern homelands, Cherokee people were able to use many of the same plants they had previously known and cherished. Today, Cherokee people use these plants to sustain our connection to the land and to perpetuate cultural lifeways that are inseparable from the natural world. These uses include food from wild greens, nuts, and berries; crafts from bushes, trees, and cane; and medicine from the many leaves, barks, and roots of the forests and fields.

In addition to articulating the scope and agreement specifics (e.g., which plant species are allowed to be taken and designated gathering locations), the MOA outlines responsibilities of each party to uphold the agreement. These include the responsibility of the park to convene an annual meeting, maintain the confidentiality of the attendees, and to facilitate access to gathering areas for citizens of the Cherokee Nation. The responsibilities of the Cherokee Nation include attending the annual meeting (through a principal representative), establishing parameters for authorizing individuals approved to gather, and establishing a method for the proper identification of authorized gatherers. Notably, the MOA combined legal language for establishing the Plant-Gathering Agreement with findings from the ethnobotany study.

Discussion

Plant-Gathering Agreements offer opportunities for the establishment and renewal of relationships between tribes, the NPS, researchers, and the park lands. This relational process offers many mutual benefits. Access to park lands for plant-gathering provides tribes with increased opportunities to perpetuate land-based knowledge and practices. When elders return to gather and teach their youth about traditional ecosystem management, both park staff and tribes benefit through opportunities for knowledge sharing. These practices, in turn, promote the cooperative and mutually beneficial stewardship of plants on the park lands. Additionally, revised park interpretations that result from such collaborations can authoritatively reflect the voice of Native people. Such mutual benefits achieved through relational processes bring us back to our initial framing of this essay through the lenses of Indigenous *strategic engagement* and *relational continuity*.

By engaging in the agreement process, Cherokee people saw several opportunities to advance the interrelated and urgent projects of: a) traditional knowledge and language perpetuation; b) access to suitable land on which to carry out these activities; and c) climate change adaptation. Although the tribe is actively working to develop conservation areas within its territory, there are few tribal lands that support the biodiversity necessary for gathering and educational opportunities, and land reacquisition is a slow and expensive process. Further, as we noted earlier, climate change threatens many cultural use plants within the current Cherokee Nation reservation, which straddles vastly different ecoregions and is subject to ongoing assaults by development and habitat fragmentation like cattle grazing. This situation calls for multifaceted approaches to ensure that Cherokee people can sustain their land-based cultural knowledge and practices. The agreement represents part of a multipronged strategy to enhance and enable cultural revitalization work by anticipating climate change and securing plant-gathering rights from locations further east of the reservation. The Medicine Keepers have expressed their observations of changing landscapes that have led to many plants becoming scarce in Oklahoma, with one elder stating, "When you see the plants here [Buffalo NR], some of them are more [abundant] and bigger than they are at home on our reservation in Oklahoma. And I am thinking, our plants are disappearing from Oklahoma? It would be nice if we could really come here and get what we need."

The Plant-Gathering Agreement thus represents one way that Cherokee people are planning for uncertain futures by centering the continuation of land-based knowledge, relationships, and practices. We might view this as an "eco-cultural insurance policy" or otherwise employing a strategy of *environmental multiplicity*.[33] This perspective aligns with other work in Indigenous environmental studies on *collective continuance* and *bio-cultural sovereignty*. Potawatomie scholar Kyle Whyte describes collective continuance as "an Indigenous community's capacity to adapt in ways sufficient for its members' livelihoods to flourish into the future."[34] For Hupa/Yurok/Karuk scholar Cutcha Risling Baldy, biocultural sovereignty signals the ability of Indigenous nations to continue enacting their responsibilities to the land in ways that promote ancestral cultures and traditions.[35]

The agreement is also a method by which Cherokee people are asserting a broader ethical stance of *relational continuity*.[36] Like many relocated Indigenous nations, Cherokee people have maintained their ethically and culturally grounded relationships with the land and nonhumans despite social and spatial change. Doing so requires continuing the practices that are inextricably linked to traditional environmental knowledge, including sustainable gathering. In another project carried out with the Medicine Keepers, the elders stressed that if the people do not use the plants the Creator will take them away.[37] This philosophy assumes that proper, respectful use of plants contributes to the well-being of plant communities themselves. Furthermore, many Cherokee people feel a profound obligation to caretake lands in Oklahoma while maintaining their relationships to their original homelands in the east. As one elder put it, Cherokees have a sacred responsibility to "honor the spirit of this land" and therefore to uphold their relationships with the nonhuman world and the Creator.[38] Through the Plant-Gathering Agreement, this responsibility extends beyond the reservation to include the historically inhabited lands in Arkansas. To honor the spirit of the land is to acknowledge and act on the relational responsibilities that come with being Indigenous despite colonial displacement.

The Medicine Keepers are actively conveying Cherokee environmental stewardship ethics and knowledge to younger generations through a program called the Cherokee Environmental Leadership Program, directed by co-author Carroll and funded by the National Science Foundation and the Indian Land Tenure Foundation.[39] Along with a staff of tribal biologists, they are working with a cohort of Cherokee students to train them in Cherokee knowledge and language, botany, biology, and tribal natural resource management strategies. This land-based education project aims to build a cohort of tribal environmental leaders that can creatively address future issues from culturally grounded perspectives. Significantly, the first plant-gathering activity under the MOA was planned to include the tribal students during a three-day visit to the park, so they can participate in the fulfillment of this landmark agreement while learning how to identify and properly gather cultural-use plants. Further, as a part of the project, tribal students seek to transport seeds and plant these in a designated plot of tribal land in the hopes of reestablishing them in current Cherokee Nation territory and developing a culturally based community conservation initiative.[40] These and other efforts by the Cherokee Nation assure an informed and culturally sustaining engagement with Buffalo NR for generations to come.

Conclusion

Native American peoples have been internally relocated within North America, causing cultural damage and challenges to their persistence as peoples. Relocation often occurred because they occupied homelands containing natural resources desired by white settlers. National parks and protected areas often removed traditional people who were perceived as threats to nature or barriers to the commodification of alluring natural resources, as seen in the histories of Zion Canyon in Utah and Yellowstone Hot Springs in Wyoming.[41] Cultural impacts occur whether the relocations are near or distant; thus, the desire and problems of returning to homelands are strong and complex for most Native Americans. In this essay, we have sought to illuminate how the impacts of relocation can be mitigated by homeland (re)connections through the new NPS Plant-Gathering Rule.

To be sure, the process of establishing a Plant-Gathering Agreement has its challenges. For one, it requires resources that not all tribes have access to. It is time-consuming and entails an onerous bureaucratic process. For these and other reasons, it may not be the pathway chosen by all tribes.[42] But for some, it represents one way to regain access to traditionally associated lands and influence the park land management via sustainable stewardship practices, which have not been a part of park service management until now. It offers an opportunity for enacting such practices within protected areas that, despite their troubled history, have ensured that those lands remain relatively untouched from the detrimental effects of development and environmental contamination that plague many tribal lands today. Plant-gathering agreements also give the NPS an opportunity to account for past injustices and to unsettle the very idea of the park itself as a Euro-Western enclosure mechanism that artificially separates humans from nature.

By describing how Cherokee people entered a collaborative relationship with university researchers and NPS staff, we have intended to illuminate the elements that made this project successful, although the process was far from simple. The development of the ethnobotany study that led to the agreement required time, patience, trust, and care to ensure the success of the project for all involved. The study revealed that despite forced relocation and continued assaults on their territory and culture, Cherokee people have retained their knowledge of—and relationships to—the land and seek to continue their practices that uphold them. We see the work to develop this Plant-Gathering Agreement as ensuring the ability of future generations to continue in this path.

Notes

1. Jalagihi ayehli uweti, or more simply, ᏣᎳᎩ ᎠᏰᎵ ᎤᏪᏘ / jalag uwet ("old Cherokee").
2. The three federally recognized Cherokee tribes are the Cherokee Nation (Oklahoma), the United Keetoowah Band of Cherokee Indians (Oklahoma), and the Eastern Band of Cherokee Indians (North Carolina).
3. See, e.g., Mark D. Spence, *Dispossessing the Wilderness: Indian Removal and the Making of the National Parks* (New York: Oxford University Press, 1999); Karl Jacoby, *Crimes against Nature: Squatters, Poachers, Thieves, and the Hidden History of American Conservation* (Berkeley: University of California Press, 2001).
4. Clint Carroll, "Fauna and Flux on the Plains' Edge: Animal Kinship, Place Making, and Cherokee Relational Continuity," in Brian Frehner and Kathleen A. Brosnan, eds., *The Greater Plains: Rethinking a Region's Environmental Histories* (Lincoln: University of Nebraska Press, 2021), 114–37.
5. White House Office of Science & Technology Policy and Council on Environmental Quality, "Joint Memorandum on Indigenous Traditional Ecological Knowledge and Federal Decision Making" (November 15, 2021). https://www.whitehouse.gov/ceq/news-updates/2021/11/15/white-house-commits-to-elevating-indigenous-knowledge-in-federal-policy-decisions (accessed March 23, 2022).
6. As stated in the *Federal Register*, the Plant-Gathering Rule "limits gathering and removal of plants or plant parts to members of an Indian tribe or Alaska Native tribe, band, nation, pueblo, village, or community that the Secretary of the Interior acknowledges to exist as an Indian tribe under the

Federally Recognized Tribe List Act of 1994, 25 U.S.C. 479a. This requirement limits gathering and removal to members of Indian tribes with which the United States has a government-to-government relationship. Other groups that may be traditionally associated with park areas, including non-federally recognized tribes and Native Hawaiian groups, do not have the same legal and political relationship with the United States and therefore this rule does not extend to such groups" (*Federal Register*, Vol. 81, No. 133, 45026). See also National Park Service, "Tribal Leaders Guide to the National Park Service Plant Gathering Regulation." US Department of the Interior, National Park Service, American Indian Liaison Office (2017). https://www.nps.gov/history/tribes/Documents/Public_NPSPlantGathering_Guide_July2017.pdf (accessed March 23, 2022).
7. Traditional use studies generally apply to Alaska Native contexts, but are applicable in cases when a tribe uses park lands through treaty, statute, or other regulations.
8. The regulation requires gathering by hand or hand tools only, and the plants must be used for traditional purposes and not commercial use. The ethnobotany work has so far been conducted a couple of different ways, from producing detailed inventories and creating habitat models to address sustainability of gathering specific species (Wind Cave Nat. Park), to compilations of species lists with abbreviated use information (Sleeping Bear Dunes National Lakeshore, Buffalo National River, and Indiana Dunes National Park), and to focusing on a single species in detail (Saguaro National Park and Great Smoky National Park). Which of these approaches is to be used depends on the individual circumstances of the tribe's request, the park, and the species.
9. Richard Stoffle et al., "Climate Change Impacts on Odawa Contemporary Use Plants and Culture at Sleeping Bear Dunes National Lakeshore," report to National Park Service (Tucson: Bureau of Applied Research in Anthropology, University of Arizona, 2015).
10. *Federal Register*, Vol. 81, No. 133 (2016): 45026.
11. Clint Carroll, *Roots of Our Renewal: Ethnobotany and Cherokee Environmental Governance* (Minneapolis: University of Minnesota Press, 2015); Clint Carroll, Eva Garroutte, Carolyn Noonan, and Dedra Buchwald, "Using PhotoVoice to Promote Land Conservation and Indigenous Well-Being in Oklahoma," *EcoHealth* 15 (2018): 450–46; Clint Carroll, "Cherokee Relationships to Land: Reflections on a Historic Plant Gathering Agreement between Buffalo National River and the Cherokee Nation," *Parks Stewardship Forum* 36(1) (2020): 154–58.
12. Carroll, *Roots of Our Renewal*.
13. R. Alfred Vick, "Cherokee Adaptation to the Landscape of the West and Overcoming the Loss of Culturally Significant Plants," *American Indian Quarterly* 35(3) (2011): 394–417.
14. Kent Blansett, "Intertribalism in the Ozarks, 1800–1865," *American Indian Quarterly* 34(4) (2010): 475–97.
15. Maria Zedeño and Nicholas Laluk, *Cultural Affiliation Statement: Buffalo National River, Arkansas, Final Report,* Report to National Park Service (Tucson:

Bureau of Applied Research in Anthropology, University of Arizona, 2008). Between 1800 and 1801 Osage people were devastated by a smallpox epidemic, and their population dropped below four thousand. Thus, the large population of Osage people who effectively controlled a vast territory was significantly diminished due to disease and conflict. This decline in population by the early 1800s led to the Osage losing control of their aboriginal lands. In 1808 and 1818, treaties were signed, and the Osage people were relocated to present-day Oklahoma. NPS, *Environmental Factors—Buffalo National River.* http://www.nps.gov/buff/learn/nature/environmentlafactors.htm (accessed October 17, 2015).

16. Blansett, "Intertribalism in the Ozarks," p. 478.
17. Blansett, p. 477.
18. NPS, *Environmental Factors—Buffalo National River.*
19. NPS.
20. Marion Blackburn, "Return to the Trail of Tears," *Archaeology* 65(2) (2012): 53–64.
21. Blackburn.
22. Ronald Satz, "The Cherokee Trail of Tears: A Sesquicentennial Perspective," *The Georgia Historical Quarterly* 73(3) (1989): 431–66.
23. Blackburn, "Return to the Trail of Tears."
24. Russell Thornton, "Cherokee Population Losses During Trail of Tears: A New Perspective and New Estimate," *Ethnohistory* 31 (1984): 289–300; Russell Thornton, "American Indian Holocaust and Survival: A Population History Since 1492," *Journal of American History* 75(4) (1987): 1288–89; Zedeño and Laluk, *Cultural Affiliation Statement.*
25. Clint Carroll, "Shaping New Homelands: Environmental Production, Natural Resource Management, and the Dynamics of Indigenous State Practice in the Cherokee Nation," *Ethnohistory* 61(1) (2014): 123–47.
26. Lynne M. Carter et al., "Chapter 17: Southeast," in Jerry M. Melillo, Terese C. Richmond, and Gary W. Yohe, eds., *Climate Change Impacts in the United States: The Third National Climate Assessment,* US Global Change Research Program (2014), 396–417; Mark Shafer et al., "Chapter 19: Great Plains." in *Climate Change Impacts in the United States,* 441–61.
27. Richard Stoffle et al., "Ethnobotany and Traditional Ecological Knowledge at Buffalo National River, Arkansas," report to National Park Service (Tucson: University of Arizona, 2019).
28. Richard W. Stoffle et al., "Calculating the Cultural Significance of American Indian Plants: Paiute and Shoshone Ethnobotany at Yucca Mountain, Nevada," *American Anthropologist* 92(2) (1990): 416–32; David Halmo, Richard Stoffle, and Michael Evans, "Paitu Nanasuagaindu Pahonupi (Three Sacred Valleys): Cultural Significance of Gosiute, Paiute, and Ute Plants," *Human Organization* 52(2) (1993): 142–50; Richard W. Stoffle, David B. Halmo, and Michael J. Evans, "Puchuxwavaats Uapi (To Know About Plants): Traditional Knowledge and the Cultural Significance of Southern Paiute Plants," *Human Organization* 58(4) (1999): 416–29.
29. Stoffle et al., *Climate Change Impacts on Odawa Contemporary Use Plants.*

30. Barbara Duncan, "Living with the Plants and the Earth," in Barbara Duncan, ed., *The Origin of the Milky Way and Other Living Stories of the Cherokee* (Chapel Hill: University of North Carolina Press, 2008), 51–52.
31. Duncan, 52.
32. Duncan, 52.
33. Richard Stoffle and Jessica Minnis, "Resilience at Risk: Epistemological and Social Construction Barriers to Risk Communication," *Journal of Risk Research* 11(1–2) (2008): 55–68.
34. Kyle Whyte, "What do Indigenous Knowledges Do for Indigenous Peoples?" in Melissa K. Nelson and Dan Shilling, eds., *Keepers of the Green World: Traditional Ecological Knowledge and Sustainability* (Cambridge: Cambridge University Press, 2018), 57–81.
35. Cutcha Risling Baldy, "Why We Gather: Traditional Gathering in Native Northwest California and the Future of Bio-Cultural Sovereignty," *Ecological Processes* 2(1) (2013): 1–10.
36. Carroll, "Fauna and Flux."
37. Carroll et al., "Using PhotoVoice."
38. Carroll, *Roots of Our Renewal,* 140.
39. For project details, see http://knowingtheland.edublogs.org.
40. This visit was scheduled to occur in the spring of 2020, however, due to the Covid-19 pandemic, the inaugural event has been postponed for a later date.
41. Richard Stoffle et al., "Cant of Reconquest and the Struggle for Restoring Sustainability of the Southern Paiutes," in Marie-Theres Albert, Francesco Bandarin, and Ana Pereira Roders, eds., *Going Beyond: Perceptions of Sustainability in Heritage Studies* (Berlin: Walter De Gruyter, 2017), 231–46.
42. For a discussion of challenges and critiques of this process, see Rochelle Bloom and Douglas Deur, "'Through a Forest Wilderness': Native American Environmental Management at Yosemite and Contested Conservation Values in America's National Parks," in Kathleen M. Sullivan and James H. McDonald, eds., *Public Lands in the Western US: Place and Politics in the Clash between Public and Private* (Blue Ridge Summit, PA: Lexington Books, 2020), 151–73.

TEN

Making the Tribal Self-Governance Act Work at Grand Portage

TIMOTHY COCHRANE

ELEMENTARY STUDENT NORMAN DESCHAMPE JR.'S 1960s drawing of Grand Portage National Monument, in northeastern Minnesota, is true to the scene. It shows an ability for detail and abstraction, providing a bird's-eye view of "the fort" and even the vessel *Wenonah*, which was used to transport visitors to Isle Royale. Norman, his siblings, his friend Mel Gagnon, and others used to sneak into the stockade at night and play hide-and-seek, hiding behind the Great Hall and the few other buildings. Norman would go on to be the tribal chairman at Grand Portage, and Mel (Bun) Gagnon would become the maintenance foreman during the Tribal Self-Governance Act (TSGA) era at Grand Portage. Norman was the architect of the TSGA at Grand Portage and Bun was the tribe's senior employee on the ground.[1] Both families had long associations with the monument. Norman Deschampe Sr. and Mel's grandfather and mother had briefly worked there.[2] That association continued with Norman Jr.'s family members, who had worked at the monument in various jobs. A number of Grand Portage elders had worked at the monument creating craft objects for sale.

The Grand Portage, or Gichi Onigaming, is both an ancient and historic trail. The Anishinaabeg band and monument are named after it, but the monument essentially cut the village in two. The portage that linked vast portions of the North American continent by canoe travel, which became important in the international fur trade, ran through the center of the reservation.[3] Tribal Chairman Norman Deschampe quietly led efforts to create the longest, largest, most diverse, and ever-expanding Tribal Self-Governance Act agreement in the nation.[4] The Tribal Self-Governance Act is a law building upon earlier legislation

Norman Deschampe Jr.'s childhood drawing of Grand Portage National Monument. Courtesy of the Norman Deschampe family.

to shift some governance and self-determination from federal to tribal jurisdiction. The agreement between the tribe and the monument led to sustained collaboration on topics within the agreement or, more broadly, for the greater good. The Grand Portage people are present—in a literal and symbolic sense—in virtually everything the monument staff does. This agreement with the tribe and our collective actions demonstrate that a national park unit and a federally recognized tribe can work together to operate a park in an efficient, thoughtful, and fully representational way. Natural resources are better understood and protected. Cultural resources are democratically celebrated, protected, and interpreted. Park visitors learn, in great depth, about the role of Grand Portage people, past and present—a story intrinsic to the monument. In the years of this agreement maturing, we found ourselves regularly pursuing mutually beneficial objectives and tasks. We better understood each other and were willing to make hard decisions for the betterment of our collective goals.

We—Norman and I—conversed a lot, the joke being that I had a second office at the Reservation Tribal Council (RTC) Office. He had a great gift for reading people, including me, while often disarmingly swapping stories with me about fishing, hunting, or our kids. He was humble and reticent to tout his and the band's successes. The agreement is in its twenty-third consecutive year at Grand Portage. It is not only the oldest such agreement—it is one of the few that integrate tribal and National Park Service (NPS) staff. Other agreements have failed elsewhere and still others have been discussed and tribes chose not to proceed.[5] Indeed, "both" staff work together on a daily basis: they share offices, computer systems, and the responsibility of responding to visitors and utilizing monument resources. Most other TSGA agreements do not merge or blend staff, relying on separate systems and equipment (computers, offices, phones, vehicles, boats). If a TSGA tribe is performing a distinct project, there is little need to share operations. But the Grand Portage agreement was designed to address the daily tasks that make a park run. It grew to include projects and project funds and administration for over three hundred projects. The agreement has also been expanded to include projects at two national park units: over two dozen at Isle Royale and two at Voyageurs.[6] In one sense, the agreement between the NPS and the Grand Portage Band is just a part of Norman Deschampe's tribal self-determination legacy—Norman being the impetus for agreements with the Bureau of Indian Affairs (BIA), Indian Health Service, EPA, Department of Justice, and even a similar agreement with Minnesota state at Grand Portage State Park.[7] This relatively small band is a strategic innovator in utilizing government tools like TSGA to their advantage.

The Preconditions That Led Up to Tribal Self-Governance at Grand Portage

There were few well-paying jobs in Grand Portage for the first two-thirds of the twentieth century. Several band members left (some following government programs) to seek employment in cities. But there was an underutilized asset in hand—Grand Portage, a site of national importance, which was the location of the North West Company's inland headquarters. It was one of the largest business firms in the so-called New World. While headquartered at Grand Portage (1784–1803), the North West Company was larger than the Hudson Bay Company. This branch of the fur trade sponsored exploration of a third of North America.

During the 1930s, to combat hunger a lack of jobs, and due to a growing interest in state history, Depression-era programs led by the WPA, Indian CCC, and Minnesota Historical Society began efforts to reconstruct the North West Company post, beginning with archeological efforts.[8] A Great Hall was constructed (shown in Norman's sketch) and furnished with objects made by Grand Portage band members in these programs. But only a Great Hall was built, and tourism languished, even during a period in the 1950s when the Grand Portage band managed the site. In the twentieth century, white elites in the Upper Midwest became enamored with the fur trade and canoeing in the North Country, which engendered state pride and identity. The Boundary Waters Canoe Area had already been established, but its storied capital of the fur trade, Grand Portage, had not been fully recognized. The same elites turned to Grand Portage in the 1950s and initiated congressional interest in establishing the national monument.

The enabling terms of the national monument were hashed out between elites like conservationist author Sigurd Olson and Judge C. R. Magney, the Grand Portage band, the Minnesota Chippewa Tribe (of which Grand Portage is a constituent band), and the NPS. The Grand Portage Tribal Council passed a resolution supporting the monument's creation, although a few residents disagreed. Grand Portage National Monument was established in 1958. The Grand Portage band and the Minnesota Chippewa Tribe donated roughly half of the land to make up the 710-acre park unit. In return, the enabling legislation provided for a tribal hiring preference and other unique provisions.[9] Regardless, fewer jobs were created than had been hoped. NPS officials also verbally promised that a visitor center, museum, and more reconstructed North West Company buildings would be built.[10] Most of these promises were not kept for decades.

NPS managers at Grand Portage faced an uphill battle trying to convince superiors to provide further investment at the site. Eventually, after a lightning strike burned down the original Great Hall and all its precious objects, the NPS reconstructed the Great Hall, a kitchen, and a canoe warehouse. However, more than a dozen other North West Company buildings remained unbuilt. A rigid NPS policy that opposed reconstructions made embarking on more work difficult.[11] NPS also neglected to build a visitor center or museum, viewing Grand Portage as a second- or third-class park unit among those that garnered more attention and money.

As a stop-gap measure, park headquarters were established in leased buildings in Grand Marais, thirty-seven miles away. The separation of senior staff from Grand Portage exacerbated communication problems, removed staff from informal interactions with band residents and created hard feelings. Personal and informal communications were vital to tackling problems in Grand Portage, such as the unfulfilled promises at the monument. Norman knew this and suggested that headquarters move to Grand Portage. This idea made good sense for many reasons, but could we make it happen? I had learned from my work with tribal communities near Glacier Bay and Katmai National Parks in Alaska never to promise anything that I couldn't deliver.

Notwithstanding the monument's location on the reservation, the NPS continued to tell an "elite white man" story, although they added the French-Canadian voyageurs to the interpretive focus. For example, NPS interpretation focused on North West Company partners and individuals, such as Alexander McKenzie, a North Wester and the first white man to cross the North American continent, eleven years before Lewis and Clark. As Gonzales notes in her chapter, earlier interpretations of Western expansion, like those at the Lewis and Clark trail, focused on white men, not Indigenous men or women. At Grand Portage, the role of the trappers (Anishinaabeg) and local residents (Grand Portage people) were less commonly discussed. The idea that Native Americans were essential and coequals with white traders in the "golden age" of the fur trade had not yet been significantly represented despite the location of the park within a Native American community.

The opening of a modestly sized Grand Portage casino provided the resources for numerous jobs at the lodge and casino and the growth of tribal government. The Grand Portage Band went into action: buying back reservation lands and putting them in trust, building a community center and their own school, greatly expanding their natural resources work, and eventually buying the marina used by vessels to go to and from Isle Royale National Park. They could now afford to retain attorneys and lobbyists in St. Paul that would amplify their effectiveness. Norman Deschampe worked with the Minnesota Land Trust and the state Department of Natural Resources (DNR) to acquire land for Grand Portage State Park and ensure it would be managed by band members.

How Did It Happen?

The Grand Portage Band's frustration with the direction of the monument, lack of meaningful communications with monument staff, lack of job growth, and lack of NPS infrastructure development led Norman Deschampe and others on the Reservation Tribal Council to turn to the new 1994 TSGA amendment to the 1975 Indian Self-Determination Act.[12] Mark David Spence explores the amendment further in his chapter in this volume. This frustration, coupled with a strong pride in the Grand Portage community and how it was "represented" to outsiders, also compelled the tribal council and community interest in a TSGA agreement.[13] Title IV of the amendment contains provisions for federally recognized tribes with a "special geographic, historical, or cultural significance" to assume "functions, programs, and services" of protected area lands and resources managed by non–BIA/Department of the Interior (DOI) agencies. TSGA sought to maximize tribal control and involvement over Indian trust property and assets, while at the same time reducing federal bureaucracy by inserting tribal methods of accomplishing the same tasks.[14]

Grand Portage band was an early tribe to apply for and receive a Tribal Self-Governance Act demonstration grant in 1995. The grant helped the band articulate their TSGA interests and hire attorney James Hamilton to begin negotiations with the NPS. In 1996, the band formally approached the NPS about their wish for a TSGA agreement at Grand Portage. At the onset of negotiations, Hamilton knew much more about TSGA than anyone on the NPS side, but his understanding was legal and abstract rather than about how it would be specifically applied to conditions at Grand Portage. Negotiations quickly got hung up on minutia—"standards" such as the length of the grass to be mowed and how often. The band put together an extensive and detailed notebook on maintenance activities they were already successfully doing at their lodge and casino. NPS interests often lingered on "what to do if there is a failure," creating a negative tone for negotiations. Due to lack of trust and the NPS's initial skepticism about a TSGA agreement (and their worry that it might "spread" elsewhere), negotiations stalled. I arrived at Grand Portage in 1997 as a first-time superintendent and was able to participate in discussions that led to the first agreement in 1998 and implementation the next year. Our negotiating "team" was made up of a DOI solicitor named Al Kashinski, a contracting officer and associate regional director from the Midwest Region Office, and myself. The band was led by Norman Deschampe, Jim Hamilton, and tribal council members Gilbert Caribou, Kenneth Sherer, Tony LeSage, and John Morrin.

The Grand Portage Band's negotiating strategy was to be firm, patient, and "get their foot in the door" in terms of the scope of the agreement. Above all, the band wanted negotiations to succeed, to increase their voice and stake in monument management, and to create more jobs.[15] In one negotiating session, Norman stated: "He wanted the monument to be the best little park in the country." This statement was a balm to a few reluctant NPS managers who were worried the band would "take over" the park and care less for the American public visiting the monument. Norman's tactic of working incrementally was prescient and gave the NPS more time to adapt to the idea and specifics of the agreement.[16] The agreement was complicated because the NPS and tribal representatives sought to integrate band and NPS staff in daily operations. A few other tribes and parks tried TSGA agreements, but the agreements were defined by discrete projects. We were attempting to work together to blend communication systems, to compete for project funding in the NPS system, and to be collectively responsive to change on a daily basis.

We reached our first TSGA agreement in 1998, but a congressional moratorium on new agreements in 1999 temporarily halted the start of our agreement (and planned festivities celebrating the agreement with dignitaries like Senator Paul Wellstone). After some deliberations among the NPS, solicitors, and the band, we reached a decision that our agreement was not "new," since it had been signed before the moratorium was put in place; therefore, we decided to proceed. DOI solicitors agreed with our plan, but it was clear that local officials would be held responsible if something went awry.

The NPS never really articulated their endgame in negotiations. Arriving on the scene, I pointedly asked my boss, the regional director, what he would like to see done at Grand Portage (with the TSGA agreement). I was told, "Ask me again in nine months and we'll talk about it." Those nine months came and went twenty-three years ago. Thus, I was in a peculiar position of being a new superintendent, having little direction from senior managers. I had been left to my own devices—with, of course, DOI solicitor Al Kashinski and regional team members working alongside me. Furthermore, we were negotiating without the TSGA regulations that would be published in December 2000. Or, as the attorney Jim Hamilton stated, we were "not negotiating the Grand Portage AFA (annual funding agreement)," but rather, the "Self-Governance Act" because we were setting a national precedent.[17] While I was under-advised, I was given full

Refurbished Grand Portage sign and two Band employees, Jerry Waha and Bob Walker. Courtesy of the Grand Portage National Monument, NPS.

reign to represent the NPS after running our ideas by Washington solicitors and a few senior managers. However, since very few people in the DOI and outside of the BIA understood the TSGA, they provided little input. In retrospect, that freedom (because TSGA was outside of what NPS managers knew) gave us the latitude to be creative in how we approached an agreement. Once our agreement was in place, this tradition of finding our own way became a tradition in how we collectively administered it.

The Grand Portage negotiators, both the band and the NPS, made a habit of focusing on "shared interest" rather than differences or intractable problems. Still, the negotiators struggled with a number of legal issues and the lengthy review of DOI solicitors.[18] A number of the problems were never fully "solved." For example, the 1994 amendment does not spell out what an "inherently federal function" is, other than it can't be "transferred" to a tribe in a TSGA agreement.[19] Also, the law is extremely clumsy on what should happen to federal employees who, once an agreement is put into place, are effectively replaced by tribal employees. This was a scary part of the law for local NPS employees who might lose their jobs. Initially, Grand Portage sought to assume responsibilities for maintenance at the monument, a significant part of park operations. However, there was also an assumption that the agreement might grow and "go into" other divisions, particularly interpretation (another large part of the monument staff). And, in our case, a couple of employees transferred to different parks out of the fear that they might lose their positions.[20] In another case, we were able to assist a tribal member who had many years of federal service and thus wanted to retire with federal benefits—part of an Intergovernmental Personal Act agreement in which he was supervised by the band but remained a federal employee. Unfortunately, the DOI only allowed this arrangement for four years; after that we had to be creative again.

The negotiations were mostly held in St. Paul, where the group could focus on the topics at hand and not be disrupted by day-to-day issues in Grand Portage. We agreed that TSGA appeared to be a good fit for Grand Portage, but a few critical points were more difficult to resolve. Thus, we would discuss topics, get a sense of where both parties stood (and hopefully agreed), and follow that up with draft agreement language. The attorneys then took the lead on writing the agreement, and they would bounce back and forth on email with suggestions, corrections, and comments. Perhaps fifteen draft versions were exchanged. The first agreement and all that followed were exactly fifteen pages long. DOI solicitor Al Kashinski took the lead composing the draft agreements. Background information on TSGA was shared among the negotiators. As park superintendent, I made a point of providing full transparency on NPS documents, budgets, and everything but personnel files to the band. We were determined to negotiate in good faith, and holding information back was clearly antithetical to developing trust, negotiations, and a workable agreement. On the band side, prior to signing the agreement, the Tribal Council would review the document one last time and take a formal vote on a resolution supporting it. The first resolution and all that followed were passed unanimously. The first agreement was signed by Norman, me, and a contracting officer at the Midwest Region Office on August 17, 1998.[21] In the ensuing years, the agreement language has changed very little, despite multiple legal reviews.

During negotiations Norman and I contacted our congressional delegation and convinced them that TSGA was a positive move for all of us. Senator Paul Wellstone and Congressman Jim Oberstar were enthusiastic supporters. We also talked with the county commissioners, who largely had a hands-off relationship with the band, and they also agreed it was the right thing to do. The monument's support group, Friends of Grand Portage, made up largely of white elites from the Twin Cities, had been struggling to win funds for a visitor center for years. Some of their members initially were not enthusiastic supporters. They were skeptical of the band's interest and of shifting the park story to include a more Indigenous perspective on the fur trade. But soon the group's support increased. While the subsequent 2000 TSGA regulations required public input, we thought it was the right thing to do.[22] The most reluctant group to support TSGA at Grand Portage were "traditionalists in the park service"—those who favored NPS control of all aspects of park management.[23] TSGA agreements threaten park superintendents who enjoy great control and ultimately question the hierarchical conceptual model of the NPS.

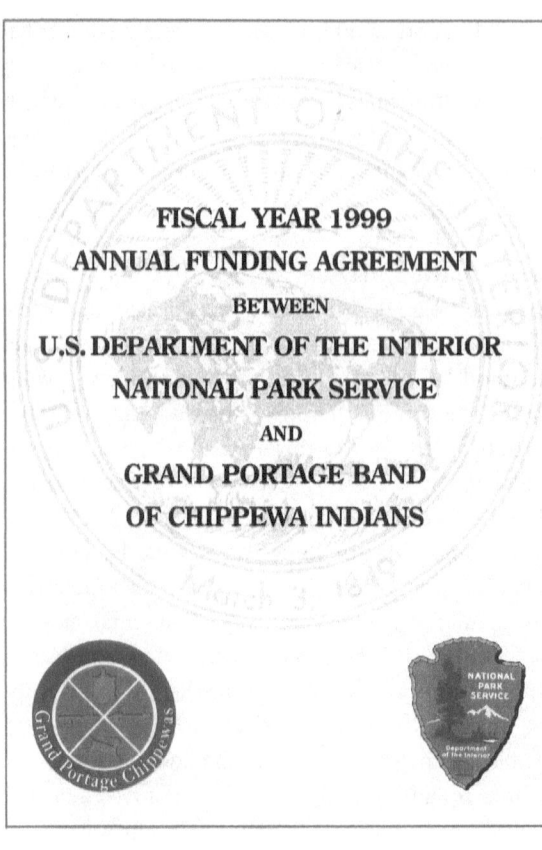

Cover of first annual funding agreement, or our "activating" Tribal Self Governance Act document. Courtesy of the Grand Portage National Monument, NPS.

Slowly, the NPS warmed up to the idea of TSGA at Grand Portage (and potentially elsewhere) as evidenced by their willingness to find additional "base" monies to fund contract support costs called for in the TSGA.[24] The problem emerged because agencies within the DOI budget differently, and the authors of the law were familiar with BIA budgets and not those of other bureaus.[25] To raise these funds, there were two options: "grow" the money from a congressional budget increase, or "take it" from another park function. Since taking it from the park would have meant "hurting" the administrative capabilities of the park (and the band employee in that job), we sought a base increase. Within two weeks of submitting our paperwork, a small base increase was added to Grand Portage National Monument budget.[26] A few more senior NPS managers had finally gotten on board.

Meanwhile, the maintenance staff—predominantly band members who became band employees—immediately appreciated the advantages of the agreement. Two positive results stood out. First, they could now receive a benefit package from the band that NPS seasonal employees do not receive. Second, instead of being limited to the maximum number of hours of work permitted by federal regulations as a seasonal employee, band maintenance employees could work longer, including project work in the colder months.[27] Within a couple of years, the agreement became routine. By 2002, the band did not renew the retainer of their lawyer, James Hamilton, for TSGA legal advice. The band believed the agreement was stable and there was enough trust established with the NPS that they no longer needed Jim Hamilton's services.[28] The NPS, on the other hand, was not so comfortable and continued to have a solicitor look at the document prior to formal acceptance for ten more years. NPS regional office managers initially assumed the agreement should be reviewed by a contracting officer and solicitor as any contract would be. While on the local level there was growing trust in the agreement and candid communications, concern from the regional office and interest from DOI attorneys meant continued oversight. They reviewed each agreement document despite their increasingly formulaic nature. The NPS/DOI felt oversight was necessary but did not contribute to a collective trust. The band, as was customary, graciously overlooked my inability to do much about this.

Overcoming Headaches with Creativity and Trust

The cumbersome federal budgeting process, especially continuing resolutions, shutdowns, and delayed federal appropriations, created problems not foreseen by the TSGA law. Quite often it required creative Band-Aids and risk-taking during the financially awkward "in-between" period after a fiscal year ended but before there was a new fiscal year budget. In particular, since the visitor season at Grand Portage extended beyond the federal budget year (end of September), if a new fiscal year's appropriations were delayed, there were no appropriations to cover costs for maintenance at the monument from October onward, to the next fiscal year. Norman and the band "solved" this problem by using funding in the band's bank account for project funding not yet spent to "hold its crew over" until that fiscal year funding became available. Sometimes this would be months later, but the band accepted this financial risk.

We never did fully resolve the problem of indirect costs (largely administrative costs shouldered by the band to manage and pay their employees). And yet we were deeply committed to providing the same amount of funding the NPS would provide to the band to complete a project or service. The law is clear that indirect costs are part of any annual funding agreement. Instead of truly solving the problem, we developed "workarounds." For example, the NPS normally includes monies for profit in their project or construction funding, assuming a company would do the job. Instead of using it as profit, the band could use it to partially pay for indirect costs or administrative costs. Other "workarounds" were found, but we were largely left at the local or monument level to find them. We quickly realized that because we were a small park, the NPS budgeting process was not going to change for us, despite what the law said.[29] The only permanent and structural solution was the one-time "base" increase in 1999—meaning annual funding added to the monument's overall budget. The band did not press the monument for indirect costs, realizing that NPS budgeting was not easily changed. The band came to this realization early, as the NPS administrative officer was a band member and was encouraged to be absolutely transparent regarding the monument's financial situation if asked. Here, and elsewhere, trust, transparency, and willingness to adapt increased our comfort levels and ability to mutually solve problems.

Another common hiccup in our work together was the occasional implementation of new NPS policy, known as "Director's Orders." These "changes" invariably came after our agreement was reached and thus could not be anticipated in the negotiation or agreement language. Without thinking about it, NPS Region and Washington Office officials assumed these orders would be followed by all, including the band. TSGA calls for following all laws and regulations (that are not waived), but it does not mean following agency policies or orders, as ultimately NPS policies have no standing in tribal sovereignty. Thus, when NPS policy decisions were made, often midyear after our agreement was in place and legally binding, the unanticipated policy did not have to be followed by the band—which NPS senior managers elsewhere did not understand and on occasion were upset about, as this was a "surprise" to them. In one instance, following an NPS–wide safety-lockout protocol banning NPS employees from using off-road vehicles (ORVs) after an accident, the band's reaction was generous to monument staff put in a difficult spot. The band tribal council made the important point that they did not have to follow "new" NPS policy, but then they graciously volunteered to do so even though most of the maintenance work in the park was done with ORV. The band could see the bind the monument would be put in if they declined to agree to it. Norman told me later, "He didn't want to get me in trouble" or cause extra scrutiny of our agreement by angry, senior NPS managers.

NPS or sometimes even federal government business practices did not neatly fit into our agreement. Monument base funding (the primary funding source for a park unit) grew in the early 2000s, but only after we found a "workaround" to a problem in how the money was allocated, which was based on the number of NPS employees. In other words, the band employees did not "count" in this formula, which decreased the overall allocation to the monument. Fortunately, the NPS region comptroller, Marty Sutherland, worked with us to get the base dollars we were due as co-managers. Another rough patch was getting security clearance for band employees to use computers tied to the NPS/federal system after 9/11. The band's maintenance foreman needed to be on the NPS system to learn about project funding criteria, surplus equipment, and general trends among his NPS peers. Since he was not a federal employee, the blanket security measures made it difficult for him to get access. And since the NPS system requires that completed projects must have a narrative reporting on its completion in order to receive new funding, it was imperative that he be able to log in to complete reports. Eventually, we were able to get select band members access to NPS computers and

Grand Portage "patch" worn by Band employees on their uniform. Courtesy of the Grand Portage National Monument, NPS.

access to buildings, bolstering the realization among NPS personnel elsewhere that band members were integral to Grand Portage operations.

Perhaps the greatest disconnect between the intention of the TSGA law and the reality on the ground is enmeshed in how the NPS does business. The law presumes that "service, functions and activities" can be fully described, its costs estimated, and that it will have a beginning and end, before a fiscal year begins. But project funding, for example, a significant portion of a park's overall budget, is often not ready until a few months after a fiscal year begins. Most projects cannot be legally included in the annual funding agreement for each year (which would be breaking the Antideficiency Act for committing funds before they are authorized). For example, project funding for an ethnohistorical study of the post–1854 Treaty village site was not available until months after the fiscal year began. However, an amendment was made to the agreement, allowing projects or functions to be completed later in the fiscal year. This flexibility regarding when an agreement could be made meant it could take effect when a project was available, which is a great administrative advantage. More philosophically, TSGA law as it applies to agencies like the NPS never reconciles the fact that this law was passed with the intent of Native self-governance while the NPS Organic Act presumes parks should be conserved for all Americans, including future generations.[30]

What We Accomplished Together in Twenty-Two Years of Successive Agreements

The success of the agreement—as assessed by both the NPS and the band—has meant a huge expansion in the scope, size, and number of projects. We have developed additional projects beyond "maintenance," such as cultural and natural resource projects, that have ranged from million-dollar projects to much smaller ones. We often manage two to three dozen a year. We were particularly interested in projects that were of mutual benefit; for example, a project proposed by Isle Royale, which the band was deeply interested in because it addressed the threat of aquatic invasive species in the ballast water of large, Lake Superior–plying vessels. Grand Portage inhabitants are people of the lake and "fish people," subsisting on lake trout and whitefish. Protecting these species by killing aquatic invasive species is important to Portagers who regularly catch and eat these native species. Norman's commitment to the Great Lakes genetic archive of lake trout at Isle Royale—nonexistent elsewhere—meshed with NPS stewardship interests. This and other Isle Royale projects deepened the integration of the band's voice in park management.[31] Where once Isle Royale management rarely communicated with Grand Portage, it now does so regularly, both formally and informally. Indeed, being mindful of the band's traditional territory in northeastern Minnesota and over to Isle Royale, the TSGA now bridges two states.[32] In the span of successive TSGA agreements at Grand Portage, the maintenance budget has more than doubled as their responsibilities and assets have grown (new Heritage Center, new dorm, new maintenance shop, new Mount Rose Trail, etc.). And while their responsibilities have grown, their quality has not wavered—Grand Portage is routinely given a 99 or 100 percent visitor satisfaction rating.

A common misconception was that our agreement was only for "maintenance." While maintenance was always at the core of the agreement, before long we added natural and cultural resource management and research projects, interpretation, and construction. Projects are wide-ranging, from geographic information system (GIS) analysis to protecting the community sewer system. One advantage we had (which was missing from the TSGA attempts at the National Bison Range, for example) was that Grand Portage had its own construction company. Cost savings were possible working with the Grand Portage Construction Company (rather than having a contractor mobilizing equipment and paying per diem and housing for employees). It was easy to see the Grand Portage construction workers' pride in their work. For example, band member and heavy equipment operator Jim Corcoran meticulously removed rocks from the Heritage Center basement. Furthermore, if Grand Portage could complete a project with the same or higher quality than the NPS and there was money left over, that remaining money would remain with the band, according to TSGA. Hence there was an incentive for the band to complete projects with a great deal of fiscal responsibility, which was the intention of the law. TSGA was formulated, in great part, to reduce bureaucracy and ensure that a greater proportion of federal dollars would get to tribes rather than be intercepted and used by agencies such as the BIA.

Cumbersome NPS bureaucracy was sometimes a boon to us. Within the NPS, most projects are awarded competitively—parks compete with one another for projects. But through the unique structure of TSGA, we were able to dramatically increase the rate of projects coming to Grand Portage. As projects in other Midwestern parks were scrubbed or the contracting phase of projects could not be completed within the fiscal year, regional project managers turned to Grand Portage and its backlog of unfunded projects. We were quickly able to negotiate receiving the funds that could not be used within the region because of timing for Grand Portage projects and to complete an amendment with the band within a compressed time frame. Suddenly, we were able to accelerate the rate of addressing and completing languishing infrastructure projects. A significant increase in funding came to Grand Portage this way, permitting us to complete many of the three hundred–plus projects. Much good work was completed in an accelerated time frame.

Grand Portage is the closest mainland to Isle Royale. Today, with two marinas on Lake Superior, Grand Portage remains a traditional gateway to Isle Royale, and adding the park to the agreement underscored that historic relationship. The addition of Isle Royale also dramatically increased the scale of funding in the agreement (where project funding would often dwarf funding for park operations at Grand Portage). Wanting to simplify negotiations between the band and the two parks' staffs (and sometimes with dozens of projects), the Midwest Region Director signed a memorandum that the Grand Portage Superintendent would take the lead and negotiate with the band for both parks. This made logistical sense because the monument office and band tribal council office are literally a couple hundred yards apart, while Isle Royale headquarters is miles across the fickle and sometimes dangerous Lake Superior.[33] The addition of Isle Royale, a higher status park, meant that more people in the NPS had really begun to appreciate the agreement, not just tolerate it.

Not long after Isle Royale was added to the agreement, other park managers asked to join it. The law is clear about which tribe, after meeting eligibility criteria, can approach a specific park or protected area. We were also protective of our agreement in the sense that projects that were of high risk and low reward for the band were earmarked. I would talk with Norman about questionable projects and together we would agree to say "no thank you." For a TSGA agreement, a tribe must have a special geographic, historical, or cultural nexus with a park. Usually, this legal clause is understood in a geographical or historical sense. But we did add one culturally significant project—removing invasive cattails from wild rice beds at a "new park," Voyageurs National Park, because wild rice is such an important and sacred food for Anishinaabe people. The Midwest Region Office has also requested projects be run through our agreement if they pertain to our area. Even with projects devised elsewhere, the band has veto power on whether they would commit to it, thus asserting their strategic vision to choose which projects they were involved with.

The three hundred–plus projects completed through TSGA are highly varied; some projects are small and reoccurring, and others are one of a kind. For example, the band built a "platinum" LEED-certified solar powered dormitory. Other projects solved chronic problems at the monument, such as a new and fully equipped maintenance shop that permitted us to remove the old and mostly unheated shop built on top of the Grand Portage trail—the very resource the park was established to celebrate and protect. Some projects are part of nationally significant endeavors, although the band's role in them is not always called out. For example, the band assisted Isle Royale with the recent reintroduction of wolves through the agreement. Some projects combine the documentary skills of the NPS with the cultural conservation interests of the band. For example, NPS authors completed a traditional cultural property nomination for *all* of Minong and nearby waters, underscoring Grand Portage's historic and contemporary connections to Isle Royale.[34]

Our "Best Practices" to Make TSGA Work at Grand Portage

While working together we developed informal rules. First, a commitment to a shared future—better or worse. We did this by retaining the same proportion of maintenance funding through the years. Thus, one quarter of the budget went to the band for maintenance; monies to the band fluctuate depending on the funding the monument receives as a whole—we share the satisfaction or misery of budget fluctuations equally. Second, while we worked together on a daily basis, we were also deferential of respective personnel boundaries. Each entity, the band or the monument, handled any personnel problem without meddling by the other. For example, Norman would not second-guess NPS personnel decisions, even though many monument employees were band members. Third, we required a mutual commitment to transparency beyond what TSGA calls for or indeed presumes. For example, if I asked, the band would inform me on the budget status of a project, which they were not legally required to do. But if I needed to advocate for supplemental project funds, which was rare, I was better equipped to do so if I really knew what was going on.

As a result, there have been several mutually beneficial byproducts of the agreement. As our comfort has grown, each party has been willing to risk solving problems, sometimes beyond the scope of the agreement. For example, the band agreed to lease lands to the monument for a new maintenance shop and dorm. They had to do some difficult work to find a good location on monument grounds that did not have heritage resources related to band history, wetlands, or rock. Furthermore, we developed a tradition of mutual assistance that extended beyond our TSGA agreement, such as the monument providing the band assistance to achieve compliance with the National Historic Preservation Act regarding timber sales. Another example is that the monument can temporarily take care of precious cultural objects on loan in a professional museum facility.

The platform of goodwill established by the TSGA means that disagreements between the band and NPS do not derail our relationship. The band can advocate

Photo of Norman Deschampe Jr., Senator Amy Klobuchar, and Tim Cochrane, 2013. Courtesy of the Grand Portage National Monument, NPS.

for the monument and Isle Royale. When Senator Klobuchar came to visit the band, Norman brought her to the Heritage Center to learn about monument issues and conditions. Having a US senator understand a small national park unit and its importance to an innovative tribe is rare and extremely helpful. Or, returning the favor, the NPS adds its voice to affirm band capabilities in language preservation grants. Another mutually beneficial byproduct is training and employment. The NPS provides a mentorship program for Grand Portage youth. The band and NPS working together has meant an increase in band employees (in senior and entry-level positions) at the monument. Some years the band members exceed 50 percent of the NPS staff.

Can TSGA Work at Other Parks?

Yes, but it will not be easy. Tribes have tried it at Redwood, Bering Land Bridge, and Sitka. Tribes have investigated implementing TSGA at River Raisin, as mentioned in chapter 5, Sleeping Bear Dunes, and Chickasaw. It is much easier for a tribe to use TSGA as the instrument to do distinct project(s), large or small. It is harder to make TSGA work when it is integrated into the day-to-day functions of a park. What would it take? A precondition is that a tribe is already a TSGA tribe and has a geographic, cultural, or historical nexus to a park. Since so many parks share boundaries (and histories) with tribes, many tribes easily fit this legal precondition. Another precondition is stability in tribal council members and senior members of a park staff. It takes time to negotiate, develop trust, and find ways to address differences. A park manager must delay a promotional move (often in three-to-four-year cycles) and the regional office must support such a "stay." But there are few institutional rewards for doing so. There must be stability in the makeup of tribal personnel and overall intent of the tribe as well. In our case the financial "reward" for the tribe was modest, certainly not a windfall. But a TSGA agreement was more about a win in adding the tribe's perspective, talents, and presence to park management. In short, there must be a deep mutual commitment to wanting to make it work.

A commitment to transparency is also helpful. Without this, problems persist, trust does not develop, and thus failure becomes more probable. There must be a willingness to frequently engage with each other and to ramp up informal and formal communications to make it work well. The TSGA provides a pathway for tribes to use NPS functions, activities, and services. But the model of how this is done presumes it is done separately to affirm tribal sovereignty and self-governance. However, park operations are highly integrated, making such idealized separation untenable in the long run.

Until there is a structural change in how the NPS creates its budgets, including a line item for indirect costs (costs to administer an agreement), tribes will have to (sadly) accept more modest indirect fees in the near-term. In the current NPS budgeting process, high indirect costs create friction and result in less conceptual support for such agreements by NPS staff working elsewhere (as it appears to "take" monies from other parks or even regional offices). The NPS will have to reconcile the demands of the law with its budgetary process. TSGA agreements are really a merger of two bureaucratic systems (tribal and NPS) that will inevitably demand compromise. In order to really work well, however, such a merger requires commitment to looking out for one another. On the NPS side of things, the primary actor should be the park superintendent, not staff from the regional office or Washington. The "on-the-ground" specifics that matter for a TSGA agreement should be tailored to such conditions; thus, the park superintendent must lead. Tribes need to respect this arrangement too, rather than going over the superintendent's head to get a better result. This maneuver might work in the short term, but it dooms the ability to solve problems quickly, locally, and with immediate conditions in mind. A TSGA agreement will work best with park staff who are adaptable and can quickly adjust to a different way of doing things, beyond orthodox park management. It is fundamentally different than how a park normally runs. It is more a marriage of equals than being a captain of a merged crew ship.

The NPS needs a nudge from its leadership, or DOI leadership, to inspire nascent interest in agreements. After two unsuccessful tries at the National Bison Range, the Confederated Salish Kootenai tribe's efforts resulted in federal legislation in which the Fish and Wildlife Refuge moved to BIA management. This made the land more accessible to the tribe through TSGA or other means.[35] The road was difficult and required great effort, but it is now an alternative model of how a tribe can fundamentally change who manages DOI lands. Knowing the outcome, this example might spur on greater response from DOI agencies.

Unless TSGA is seen by local park officials as mutually beneficial, there will always be a disincentive to embark on such an agreement. Park staff must see it as an asset and the right thing to do rather than an aberration in park management. Thus, staff must come to grips with the fear of losing personnel (replaced by tribal employees) in a large-scale TSGA agreement. This will be harder to achieve at a large park than a small one. Furthermore, park managers will avoid TSGA if it is not "career enhancing." Since park managers are often seeking some big development to occur under their tenure, if TSGA is seen more widely as a positive outcome, it might be more attractive to senior managers. All these concerns and caveats aside, a highly functioning TSGA agreement is terrific for both parties and gives participants a sense that they are making history and seeing parks in a wider context.

Why Did It Work at Grand Portage?

Both sides had a deep commitment to make it work, knowing that it was critical to community pride, the local economy, and the future of the park. The commitment involved extra effort and time, some compromises on both sides, and a strong belief that it was the right change to make. Second, our TSGA had national implications. While still in the negotiation phase, Norman and I understood that we had to be most responsive to the agreement—not, in my case, to the regional office or others in Washington. Because Norman was obviously the "captain" of the agreement, and I had little interference from afar, we came to realize that we were both responsible—the power was localized. We knew the on-the-ground situation better than others and were able to solve problems that were tailored to our situation.[36]

This was not a result of "consultation" as it is legally or even professionally understood. It was made of *many* informal conversations—I went to the Tribal Council Office a few times a week to speak with officers there, and Norman called me on the phone (often while traveling). Formal "consultation" is often about "getting information" in an unequal decision-making relationship. Information is haltingly exchanged, often in the most politicized contexts. It is rarely geared towards problem-solving or risk-taking by either party. Through a gamut of communications methods (including seeing each other at football games or in the grocery store), we often learned specific information from each other that gave us a more complete picture to inform our decisions. Brian Upton, the lead tribal self-governance attorney for the Confederated Salish Kootenai Tribe and student of our agreement, said it worked at Grand Portage because of individual personalities and leadership.[37] For me, it was an appropriate merger of our fortunes (the monument and to a lesser degree the NPS and the Grand Portage band), seeing our commonalities, and often working toward goals that were mutually beneficial. The band demonstrated, as the law intended, that they would reduce bureaucracy while getting the same level of work done. Band maintenance workers were used to making do with what they had—the ingenuity they used to complete some projects was striking to behold. Their ingenuity in getting things done was mirrored in actions taken by the RTC leadership.

Our agreement worked, in part, because of the consistency in the players. Norman, Melvin Gagnon, and I stuck with it for twenty years. Norman's position as tribal chairman for twenty-seven years, Mel Gagnon as the maintenance foreman for almost the entire length of the agreement, and my twenty-year tenure as superintendent provided institutional knowledge, the benefits of deep trust, and a zeal to nurture the agreement.[38] There were times we had to fight for it within internal NPS discussions, but it was most often NPS misunderstanding of the agreement that was the root cause of our disagreements. To paraphrase what one observer said, the NPS employees I most often dealt with did not see TSGA as an aberration in public land policy (if they thought about it at all). Rather, they were unaware that the NPS had a role in Indian self-determination and federal Indian policy.[39] The flip side of a dearth of basic knowledge of TSGA outside of Grand Portage and Isle Royale is that this "gap" in the bureaucracy permitted creativity on our part. Indeed, the NPS ambiguity in understanding TSGA provided room for innovation and possibilities outside of the typical confines of NPS business methods.

Today, the TSGA agreement is a platform for a mutually beneficial relationship. It is how business is done in Grand Portage. Or, as Norman once said to me, "It doesn't matter who does it, the band or the NPS. What does matter is what is being done is of value to the community, that it is important."[40] The NPS regard for the TSGA is captured in the monument's new "Foundation" document. The "relationship with [the] Grand Portage band" is deemed a "fundamental resource" akin to a physical resource, such as the Grand Portage Trail itself.[41] In other parks, that would translate as: tribal relationships are as important to Grand Portage as Old Faithful is to Yellowstone, or Cliff Palace is to Mesa Verde.

Following the lead of Norman and the Grand Portage band, we often flew under the radar, not seeking publicity about what we were doing. This gave us "space" to problem-solve and develop trust outside of a public spotlight. But even so, some would ask or ponder, were we co-managing at Grand Portage? Certainly, there were ingredients of co-management: mutual problem solving, financial and power sharing, trust, outsiders agreeing it was a good thing and not often meddling, frequent communications, and willingness to reach beyond tribal or NPS self-interest. Other commentators, stunned by the number of collaborative projects, wondered if we were only "contracting." But these projects were, at minimum, an extension of mutually beneficial work. The agreement was a community asset because it became a means to address the lag in infrastructure and research at the monument. It would sometimes amplify the park budget by two or threefold. It meant we were outcompeting other parks with "orthodox" staff by winning a lion's share of projects. But we also had a real restraint on capacity in what we could collectively do and manage; both the monument and band are relatively small in terms of numbers and thus limited in capacity. As only approximately eight hundred people live on the Grand Portage reservation, and virtually all are employed through the lodge/casino or tribal government, we could only "grow" our agreement in select ways. Thus, Norman's comment about not caring who did a project as long as it was for the community's benefit makes great sense. Remember, too, that many projects continued to be done by the NPS. For example, the NPS spearheaded the first ever park movie, with band members fully participating throughout and offering the narration in the Grand Portage dialect of Anishinaabemowin. Another "ingredient" of co-management is obvious: governance. Because there was more room for local, mutual self-governance, I believe our results were more mixed here. We were very comfortable working together locally. However, it was also clear that the lesson of "mutuality" of tribal self-governance at Grand Portage was only accepted, or even known about, among a small circle within the NPS. Some NPS managers knew it was working well, but few knew of its details. And certainly, the TSGA law did not have enough sway to modify NPS business practices.

As far as I can recount, we did not "aim" for co-management of the monument—an idealized goal for many (who are generally distant from the process). What we aimed for was giving the band an equal voice in monument operations because it was the right thing to do, and it would make the monument better and get the community involved. We aimed for jobs, responsiveness of the monument to the people of Grand Portage (and others), and for the monument being an integral asset to the community, as the enabling law intended. We realized we had to understand each other's business practices and did so, despite the intent of TSGA. In hindsight, we wanted to seamlessly blend the best historic preservation and interpretive capabilities of the NPS with the cultural conservation (voice, representation, and honor) and economic interests of the band. Co-management was a wonderful byproduct of these efforts. A better measure of what we did together is what Grand Portage elder (and remarkable knowledge-bearer) Ellen Olson remarked on during her first visit to the new Heritage Center. Walking through the doors, looking up at the towering mural by Anishinaabe artist Carl Gawboy, and then sitting by the fireplace made of Grand Portage stone, she quietly observed, "This feels like home."

Notes

1. Grand Portage Reservation Tribal Council, and indeed, both recent tribal chairpersons, Elizabeth Drost and the current chair, Robert Deschampe, support this effort to describe "the Grand Portage agreement history." Both have

requested that this history be made available to band members, hence, this is written with two different audiences in mind.
2. Personal communication with Mel Gagnon, retired maintenance foreman, Grand Portage, November 14, 2021. Mel Gagnon's grandfather, Jerome Montfferrand, had been the first maintenance foreman at the newly established park.
3. Anishinaabeg bands are often named after their geographic location. Grand Portage Anishinaabe band is named after the ancient trail, Gichi Onigaming1.
4. Tribal Self-Governance Act of 1994, Pub. L. 103-413.
5. The Grand Portage agreement language has been borrowed by the Yukon Flats Refuge in Alaska and Redwood National Park. Our agreement was often compared with the failure of an "operational" TSGA agreement at the National Bison Range Refuge in Montana. However, recently, the Confederated Salish Kootenai Tribe has found a legislative answer to being stymied by a TSGA agreement with the Fish and Wildlife Service.
6. Tribal Self-Governance Act agreement files, Grand Portage National Monument, Grand Portage.
7. When I use "I" in this document, I mean, my former role as superintendent. When I use "we" I mean both the band and the NPS.
8. Carolyn Gilman, *The Grand Portage Story* (St. Paul: Minnesota Historical Society Press, 1992), 128.
9. "An Act to provide for the establishment of Grand Portage National Monument in the State of Minnesota, and for other purposes, approved September 2, 1958 (72 Stat. 1751)."
10. Melissa Hendricks, "A Turnaround at Grand Portage," *National Parks* (Spring 2008): 55.
11. The NPS only justified reconstructions when explicit details are documented about any "missing" buildings. With only three of sixteen building being reconstructed, the grounds of Grand Portage do not create an atmosphere akin to when the North West Company was in operation. Instead, the interior of the picket stockade is mostly empty. The lack of further reconstructions (and jobs they might entail) was and is a further point of contention between the band and the NPS. The same can be said for not having a full scale Anishinaabeg village.
12. Indian Self-Determination and Education Assistance Act, Pub. L. 93-638.
13. Personal communication with Mel Gagnon, retired Maintenance Foreman, Grand Portage, October 12, 2020.
14. In addition to federally recognized tribes having a demonstrable connection to DOI administered lands and resources, tribes also had to pass a three year audit to prove fiscal responsibility to be eligible for a TSGA compact and Annual Funding Agreement. Technically there are three tiered legal documents to our agreement. The first is a compact between the US government and the Grand Portage band—an umbrella agreement that sets the conditions under which all TSGA agreements are executed. The second is called an Annual Funding Agreement, which sets the specific terms for monies, projects, and services agreed upon each year. The third are the amendments that we added specifying the terms of additional projects, funds, and services.

15. Anon, "Tribal Profile: Grand Portage Band of Chippewa," *Sovereign Nations: Newsletter of Tribal Self-Governance* (November–December 1998): 4.
16. I believe engendering trust in this way was a key to reaching an agreement a. However, this took some courage on Norman's part as the rhetoric of some tribes engaging in TSGA negotiations was to "take over" a park or refuge. The goal was to reach an agreement for all the elements of a park or refuge that were transferrable. Norman went his own way here. Later, he used to joke with me "they were still going to take over the monument. . . ."
17. Mary Ann King, "Co-management or Contracting? Agreements Between Native American Tribes and the US National Park Service Pursuant to the 1994 Tribal Self-Governance Act," *Harvard Environmental Law Review* 31 (2007): 520.
18. "Tribal Profile: Grand Portage band of Chippewa," *Sovereign Nations* (November–December 1998): 4.
19. For many years, Tribes and the non-BIA DOI Agencies disagreed about what "inherently federal function" meant on the ground, or who might be impacted. The few who thought about it in the NPS defined as inherently federal function as: overall federal decision making (superintendent), fiscal authority (administrative officer), and federal law enforcement (law enforcement rangers). While this "take away" was never stated this succinctly or widely known, it was the operative view of the NPS.
20. Few full time Monument employees were interested in converting to band employees, primarily because they had a vested interest in the federal retirement program.
21. "Fiscal Year 1999 Annual Funding Agreement between US Department of the Interior, National Park Service and Grand Portage band of Chippewa Indians," Tribal Self-Governance Act files, Grand Portage National Monument. It was technically unnecessary for a contracting officer to co-sign the Annual Funding Agreement, but the NPS felt some assurance that someone 'outside' of Grand Portage would sign it. After the original negotiations, the regional contracting officer never attended negotiations for Annual Funding Agreements. Still, the contracting officer was a signature party for ten plus years.
22. "Final Rule—DOI, Office of the Assistant Secretary—Indian Affairs, Tribal Self-Governance," *Federal Register*, Friday, December 15, 2000.
23. Robyn Dalzen, "Historic Agreement at Grand Portage National Monument," *Cultural Survival Quarterly* (Winter 1999): 5.
24. I believe the NPS eventually warmed to TSGA not because they philosophically "adopted" TSGA tenets, but because it didn't become a "problem" at Grand Portage or other parks. Its advantages became readily apparent to senior NPS managers, as they could see the Monument and band working cohesively to get many projects done. Politically the NPS wanted to do the right thing and Grand Portage was an isolated place for the experiment.
25. The Bureau of Indian Affairs has an identified line item in their annual appropriations for "Contract Support Costs" called out in TSGA and regulations. This line item is part of the "Operation of Indian Programs" in federal appropriations. No other DOI agencies, including the NPS, have such a

budget line item to draw upon. Hence, while transferring funds from the BIA to tribes for contract support costs is relatively easy, other agencies struggle.

26. Pat Parker in Washington and myself advocated for a line-item budget increase, which happened in record time. Tribal Self-Governance Act files, Grand Portage National Monument, Grand Portage. That the NPS supported and "found" base funding for indirect costs in two weeks was miraculous. In my thirty years of federal service, I never witnessed such speed for a base increase.
27. The limit is 1,034 hours in a year for a seasonal employee, or roughly six months' employment.
28. Personal communication with John Morrin, Grand Portage tribal council member, October 13, 2020.
29. One comptroller in the region office understood the dilemma and helped us. A subsequent comptroller was not sympathetic, adding extra tasks for us—one way NPS management elsewhere can slow parts of the agreement.
30. "The Organic Act" is the 1916 law (39 Stat. 535) that created the National Park Service as an organization.
31. Perhaps the best example of this is when I retired in January 2018, the Midwest Region Director, permitted Norman Deschampe to play an instrumental role in choosing my successor.
32. Timothy Cochrane, *Minong—the Good Place: Ojibwe and Isle Royale* (East Lansing: Michigan State University Press, 2009), 14–15.
33. Summer headquarters is on Mott Island on the northeast end of Isle Royale, more than 80 miles by water from Grand Portage. The winter headquarters is at Houghton, Michigan, further distant.
34. Ashley Brown and Timothy Cochrane, "Minong," Traditional Cultural Property, National Register of Historic Places, National Park Service, US Department of Interior, 2019. The NPS and the band held a ceremony and feast celebrating the TCP at Windigo Ranger Station, Isle Royale, July 23, 2019 and again with the raising of Grand Portage flag at Isle Royale on August 17, 2021.
35. https://www.mtpr.org/post/feds-begin-transfer-national-bison-range-confederated-salish-and-kootenai-tribes. In the time the Confederate Salish Kootenai Tribe have managed the Bison Range they have added wonderful interpretation to the visitor center, including cultural heritage about the animals, the range, and the region.
36. At Norman Deschampe's funeral service, band member Billy Blackwell in his remarks called Norman "the captain" of Grand Portage. These remarks are apt because Norman was a quintessential leader and marshalled Grand Portage into a new era of employment, infrastructure, and self-determination.
37. Brian Upton, "Returning to a Tribal Self-Governance Partnership at the National Bison Range Complex: Historical, Legal, and Global Perspectives," *Public Land and Resources Law Review* 35 (2014): 106–7.
38. I believe I was hired because I had a passing knowledge of Tribal Self-Governance at a time when almost no one in the NPS had much TSGA experience at that time. Although being committed to making our TSGA work through time was not a great career enhancing stratagem, it was acceptable to me as I had no hankering to "advance" to another park.

39. King, "Co-management or Contracting?" 480.
40. Norman Deschampe made a similar statement to Mary Ann King for her research on Tribal Self-Governance Act agreements within non-BIA, Department of Interior bureaus. King, "Co-management or Contracting?" 522.
41. "Foundation Document Overview: Grand Portage National Monument," National Park Service, US Department of Interior, 2018.

Epilogue

IN JUNE 2022, after years of political vacillation and uncertainty, the US Interior Department finalized a co-management agreement for Bears Ears National Monument with five tribal nations that have deep ties to the region. The event garnered national attention, with headlines in the *Washington Post* and the *New York Times* flagging the agreement as a groundbreaking and unique model for tribal and federal collaboration.[1] This historic moment has highlighted how Native peoples can strategically engage with the federal government on their own terms. The Bears Ears Inter-Tribal Coalition, a partnership of the Hopi Tribe, the Navajo Nation, the Ute Mountain Ute Tribe, the Pueblo of Zuni, and the Ute Indian Tribe, was the driving force behind advocating for the creation of Bears Ears National Monument.[2] These tribal nations have collaborated in order to gain recognition by the United States of their sovereign rights to steward this important cultural landscape. Now that these nations are formal co-management partners with the federal government, they have released their own land management plan.[3] We celebrate these developments at Bears Ears as a notable example of the collaborative work being done between tribal nations and US national parks.

We believe that this book offers valuable context not only for the Bears Ears co-management agreement but for the wide range of collaborations happening today, and it provides evidence of the long-standing and varied efforts by tribal nations and the National Park Service (NPS) to work together in more meaningful ways. Indeed, the case studies in this volume showcase the diverse approaches to and possibilities for strategic collaboration. They highlight the challenges and the mutual benefits of collaborative work between Native peoples and national parks. Under some conditions the collaborations have led to persistent connections, partnerships, and even co-management (see Cochrane, Spence, Kelman, Andersson, Stoffle et al., this volume). These collaborations allow NPS sites to complicate one-sided histories, recognize the diversity of connections to park landscapes, and develop more culturally sensitive ways of managing natural resources and cultural heritage. They also offer opportunities for tribal nations to advocate for their interests on US public lands.

While the Bears Ears case provides an example of a more collaborative framework for management of US public lands, it also shows how the recognition of Native sovereign relationships with federal lands is often hard won. Similarly, the case studies in this volume reveal that the NPS has often struggled to acknowledge Native concerns. Hill and Gish Hill both highlight the erasure of Native voices at Mount Rushmore, and several other chapters illustrate the fraught relations underlying any collaboration between tribal nations and NPS. Over time, however, many of parks discussed in this volume have worked with the nations connected to the lands they manage to change these relationships. When they do, the collaborations that have emerged demonstrate the power of ongoing dialogue around contested sites and the value of sharing authority over how to come to terms with the erasure of Native cultures and histories. Both parties have been enriched from engaging with Native protocols and creating new interpretative frameworks that include Native voices. Several case studies also show the potential of these collaborations to support Native sovereignty through shared governance. The volume as a whole highlights the benefits that emerge when Native partners and the NPS are on a more equal footing.

The Bears Ears co-management plan illustrates how tribal nations and federal land agencies can engage strategically to align their interests and find common ground. Similarly, this volume demonstrates that Native efforts have created strategic engagement with the NPS, whether through asserting sovereign relationships with lands, articulating a sovereign relationship with the NPS as an arm of the US government, accessing culturally essential resources, or establishing dialogue and representation on their own terms. In some cases, this strategic engagement has led to the strengthening of Native sovereignty. In this volume, Spence describes such an engagement when discussing the reconciliation between the US and Canadian Wyandot Native communities and the recovery of part of their historic land base. Furthermore, Gonzales, Cochrane, Neely, and Myhal all describe the establishment of tribal leadership roles in managing operations within national parks. Bears Ears National Monument is now the fourth national park site to establish a co-management agreement with tribal nations. This agreement was preceded by Canyon de Chelly National Monument, Glacier Bay National Park, Big Cypress National Preserve, and Grand Portage National Monument. In this volume, Cochrane, the superintendent of Grand Portage at the time of their co-management agreement, describes the processes involved in establishing such a groundbreaking collaboration.

While this new era of federal-tribal land management increasingly recognizes that NPS lands are, and always have been, Indigenous lands, many parks remain contested spaces. As Hill and Gish Hill point out in this volume, national parks like Mount Rushmore continue to present celebratory narratives about the conquest of Native lands. Parks like Yellowstone or Devil's Tower reflect such narratives as well, while continuing to exclude Native peoples from fully articulating their historical, cultural, and spiritual relationship with these traditional territories. As historians Adrian Howkins, Jared Orsi, and Mark Fiege have demonstrated, national parks work to celebrate the conquest of lands and people and to forge national cultures.[4] On the other hand, the national claim to these spaces has also turned them into sites of contestation, what historian Ann McGrath refers to as "elastic signifiers of the sacred."[5] While our volume overwhelmingly explores the collaborative outcomes of partnerships between tribal nations and NPS, the parks discussed here remain sites of contestation, sacred to both the nation state and the tribal nations who have maintained their relationships with these lands since time immemorial.

One striking but hard-won acknowledgment came in June 2021, when the federal government fully transferred management of the National Bison Range, formerly managed by the US Fish and Wildlife Service, to the Confederated Salish and Kootenai Tribes.[6] In the spring of 2022, the US Congress held an unprecedented hearing to discuss tribal co-management of public lands.[7] By the fall of 2022, the new NPS director, Charles Sams III, introduced policy guidance for the parks that set a formal priority to co-steward public lands held by NPS with tribal nations.[8] The guidance calls on park units to go beyond traditional consultation with tribes, and instead to build more long-lasting and substantive collaborative relationships with tribal partners.[9] All of this points to a new era in US federal public land management, one in which tribal sovereignty and Native connections to historic lands are more fully recognized and integrated into federal policies and practices. This volume seeks to contribute to this conversation, exploring the pitfalls and successes of recent collaborative efforts.

Ultimately, if the US government is prepared to honor the Native sovereignty recognized through the treaty process, the goal of all tribal-federal collaborations should be to restore Indigenous sovereign relationships to these landscapes. This is a point Native peoples have continued to assert and reassert over time, even when this fact has been ignored or denied by non-Natives. Historically, the pathways to such collaborative efforts have been complicated in practice and have not always lived up to this ideal. While this volume seeks to illuminate the ways that these collaborations uphold Native sovereignty, we have also highlighted the limits that having to negotiate with NPS has placed on that sovereignty. Many of the contributors acknowledge that specific personalities within tribal governance and NPS, as well as the right environment, have led to the collaborations discussed here. Hill, Gish Hill, and Gonzales reflect on the profound difficulties of building collaborative relationships when many national parks work to celebrate conquest. At Mount Rushmore and the Lewis and Clark Trail, just creating space for Native guidance has been a challenge. On the other hand, the national claim to these spaces has also turned them into sites of contestation over Indigenous and non-Indigenous sovereignty.[10] In this contestation, opportunities arise for collaboration and recognition of Native sovereignty.

Looking ahead, we see growing interest and investment in co-stewardship and meaningful collaboration between Native peoples and national parks. As Native nations gain the economic freedom to purchase lands and create their own monuments and even tribal national parks, it is time to acknowledge the importance of Native relationships with their historic landscapes. In this volume, Lance Foster describes the challenges of creating the Ioway Tribal National Park. It is the second park of this kind in the nation after Frog Bay Tribal National Park on the Red Cliff Reservation. As Native nations return to managing their historic landscapes through diverse means, including purchasing land and creating parks, NPS has had to reevaluate its relationship with tribal nations. Yet building true collaborative relationships requires reassessing standard practices, establishing new protocols, and reimagining agendas and ideals.

In fact, the United States has been quite late to rethink the national park ideal in relationship to Native claims. As Howkins, Orsi, and Fiege note, Australia, New Zealand, and Latin America recognized Indigenous claims to the land much earlier than the US and have incorporated Indigenous perspectives in their preservation efforts.[11] Even in South Africa, where national parks functioned as apartheid institutions into the 1990s, Carruthers shows they are being redefined in some fascinating ways under the new democratic government. Howkins, Orsi, and Fiege argue that as these elastic spaces evolve to be more inclusive, we may come to see the dispossessive tendencies of early US national park history as the exception rather than the rule.[12] Therefore, for NPS to continue to reflect the narrative of the US as an aspirational democracy, it must expand the kinds of collaborative relationships discussed in this volume. For this work to be most effective and long-lasting, however, we would argue that building collaboration must involve consistent and persistent outreach, deep listening, and flexibility to adjust course along the way. To accomplish such a shift, these collaborations must recognize Native relationships with the land and work toward supporting Native goals while relinquishing authority to Native leadership.

Notes

1. Alex Traub, "In a Return to the Land, Tribes Will Jointly Manage a National Monument," *New York Times* (June 20, 2022), https://www.nytimes.com/2022/06/20/us/bears-ears-native-american-tribes-management.html. Maxine Joselow, "Native American Tribes to Co-manage National Monument for First Time," *Washington Post* (June 20, 2022), https://www.washingtonpost.com/climate-environment/2022/06/20/bears-ears-national-monument-tribes.
2. Bears Ears Inter-tribal Coalition, https://www.bearsearscoalition.org.

3. "Bears Ears Inter-tribal Coalition Releases Land Management Plan for the Bears Ears National Monument," https://www.bearsearscoalition.org/beitc-land-management-plan-2.
4. Adrian Howkins, Jared Orsi, and Mark Fiege, *National Parks Beyond the Nation: Global Perspectives on "America's Best Idea"* (Norman: University of Oklahoma Press, 2016).
5. Ann McGrath, "Conquering Sacred Ground? Climbing Uluru and Devils Tower," in Howkins, Orsi, and Fiege, *National Parks Beyond the Nation.*
6. *MTN News*, "National Bison Range Transferred to BIA in Trust for CSKT," https://www.kpax.com/news/western-montana-news/interior-transfers-national-bison-range-lands-in-trust-for-cskt.
7. *High Country News*, "Congress Meets with Native Leaders to Discuss Co-management of Federal Lands," https://www.hcn.org/articles/indigenous-affairs-national-park-service-congress-meets-with-native-leaders-to-discuss-co-management-of-federal-lands.
8. National Park Service, "National Park Service Issues New Policy Guidance to Strengthen Tribal Co-stewardship of National Park Lands and Waters," https://www.nps.gov/orgs/1207/national-park-service-issues-new-policy-guidance-to-strengthen-tribal-co-stewardship-of-national-park-lands-and-waters.htm.
9. National Park Service.
10. McGrath, "Conquering Sacred Ground."
11. Howkins, Orsi, and Fiege, *National Parks Beyond the Nation.*
12. Howkins, Orsi, and Fiege.

CONTRIBUTORS

Clint Carroll is an associate professor of Native American and Indigenous studies in the Department of Ethnic Studies at the University of Colorado Boulder. He received his doctorate from the University of California Berkeley in Environmental Science, Policy, and Management. A citizen of the Cherokee Nation, he works closely with Cherokee people in Oklahoma on issues of land conservation and the perpetuation of land-based knowledge and ways of life.

Tim Cochrane worked for the National Park Service as a fire lookout, backcountry ranger, historian, regional cultural anthropologist, and retired as superintendent at Grand Portage National Monument. At the Monument he worked closely with the Grand Portage Band of Anishinaabeg. His books include: *Minong: The Good Place—Ojibwe and Isle Royale* (Michigan State University Press); *A Good Boat Speaks for Itself: Isle Royale Fishermen and Their Boats*; *Gichi Bitobig, Grand Marais: Early Accounts of the Anishinaabeg and the North Shore Fur Trade*; and most recently *Making the Carry: The Lives of John and Tchi-Ki-Wis Linklater* (the last three published by the University of Minnesota Press).

Michael J. Evans is the Regional Cultural Anthropologist and program lead for Cultural Anthropology and NAGPRA for the Midwest Region of the National Park Service. He has worked with over a hundred Native American tribes on cultural resource management, resource access and use, and traditional ecological knowledge. He has also worked on historic preservation program development in the Federated States of Micronesia (Pohnpei, Chuuk, Kosrae, and Yap), the Republic of Palau, and the Republic of the Marshall Islands.

Jackie Gonzales, PhD, is an historian with Historical Research Associates, Inc (HRA). She has written numerous administrative histories and other history studies for the National Park Service (NPS). Before HRA, Jackie worked for the NPS at several different sites. Her chapter stems from her administrative history of the Lewis and Clark National Historic Trail, co-written with Emily Greenwald, PhD.

Rani Henrik-Andersson served as the interim McDonnell Douglas Chair, Professor of American Studies at the University of Helsinki Finland during 2014–16. In 2017, he was appointed a CORE Fellow at the Helsinki Collegium for Advanced Studies and a Senior University Lecturer of North American Studies at the University of Helsinki. He is the author or editor of ten books, including the *Lakota Ghost Dance of 1890* (University of Nebraska Press, 2008), *A Whirlwind Passed Through Our Country: Lakota Voices of the Ghost Dance* (University of Oklahoma Press, 2018) and *Bridging Cultural Concepts of Nature: Indigenous People and Protected Spaces of Nature*, edited with Boyd Cothran and Saara Kekki (Helsinki University Press 2021). His newest book *Lakȟóta: An Indigenous History* was published by the University of Oklahoma Press in 2022.

Christina Gish Hill is an associate professor in the World Languages and Cultures department at Iowa State University, focusing on Native cultures of the Northern Plains and Midwest. Her research explores how social relations impact cultural expressions of Native relationships with their landscapes in the face of colonial forces working to disrupt these relationships. She is the author of *Webs of Kinship: Family in Northern Cheyenne Nationhood* (University of Oklahoma Press, 2016). She currently studies the history of Native agriculture in North America, the US policies that led to its decline, and the efforts of communities to reverse that process today. She is now working on a book entitled *Three Sisters Gardening: An Ethnohistory of Indigenous Agricultural Survivance in Midwestern Native American Nations*.

Matthew J. Hill is a cultural and applied anthropologist and an independent scholar. He has consulted extensively with the National Park Service, serving as Principal Investigator on sponsored research projects seeking to improve ties between National Parks and Native Peoples. Recent projects include an ethnohistorical study of the legacy of treaty-making at Fort Stanwix in upstate New York, and an ethnographic study of Native perspective on Mount Rushmore in the context of the Black Hills. He also directs Matthew J. Hill Consulting, an organizational development and capacity-building consultancy for mission-driven organizations facing complex social challenges. He formerly conducted research on UNESCO World Heritage sites in Cuba and the Spanish-speaking Caribbean.

Ari Kelman is Chancellor's Leadership Professor of History at the University of California, Davis. He is the author of *Battle Lines: A Graphic History of the Civil War* (Hill and Wang, 2015), *A Misplaced Massacre: Struggling Over the Memory of Sand Creek* (Harvard University Press, 2013), and *A River and Its City: The Nature of Landscape in New Orleans* (University of California Press, 2003). Kelman's essays have appeared in *The Journal of American History*, *The Journal of Urban History*, *The Nation*, *Slate*, *The Times Literary Supplement*, and many others. He is now working on a book titled *For Liberty and Empire: How the Civil War Bled into the Indian Wars* and editing the journal *Reviews in American History*.

Natasha Myhal is a Provost's Tenure-Track Fellow at The Ohio State University in the School of Environment and Natural Resources and will join the department as an Assistant Professor in 2025. She received her doctorate in Ethnic Studies from the University of Colorado Boulder. A citizen of the Sault Ste. Marie Tribe of Chippewa Indians, she works closely with Anishinaabe Nations in the Great Lakes on issues pertaining to ecological restoration and climate change adaptation.

Brooke Neely is research faculty at the Center of the American West and a faculty affiliate of the Center for Native American and Indigenous Studies at the University of Colorado Boulder. She has worked and written at the nexus of US national parks and tribal nations for nearly two decades. She is the author of "Social Geographies of Race: Connecting Race and Space" with Michelle Samura in *Ethnic and Racial Studies*. She holds a PhD in sociology from the University of California, Santa Barbara. Her interdisciplinary research and teaching focuses on public history, community engagement, and belonging in the western United States.

Mark David Spence (Métis) ended a brief but rewarding career as an Associate Professor of History and Chair of American Studies at Knox College in Illinois in 2004, where his scholarship and teaching focused on comparative and cross-disciplinary approaches to US environmental, western, American Indian, and Latin American subject areas. After leaving Knox College, he has since crafted a new career as a public historian, consultant, and visiting professor in the Oregon University System. For the past several years, his writing has involved historical studies for the National Park Service with a primary focus on Indigenous nations of the Americas.

Richard W. Stoffle is a professor and research team director in the Bureau of Applied Research in Anthropology in the School of Anthropology, University of Arizona, Tucson. He is an applied cultural anthropologist who has worked with a number of culturally different people in the United States, and in the Caribbean in Barbados, Antigua, St. Lucia, and the Dominican Republic. His work with rural people in North America involved the upper South and Mississippi. He has facilitated the heritage goals of more than a hundred Native American tribes, including the Cherokee Nation of Oklahoma.

INDEX

Italicized references indicate illustrations.

acknowledgement: of shameful histories, 7, 45, 47, 51–52, 54–55, 58, 123, 175, 219; of tribal knowledge contributors, 55–56, 57, 202, 209, 233, 265; of tribal sovereignty, 6, 17–19, 28n11. *See also* taking responsibility
activism, 17–19, 143–44, 173–74
Agate Fossil Beds National Monument, 24
Albers, Patricia C., 123, 130
Alcatraz, 17
Alfred, Taiaiake, 54
Alliance of Tribal Tourism Advocates (ATTA), 135
American Indian Movement, 17, 121n2, 185
American Indian Religious Freedom Act (AIRFA; 1978), 17, 23
American Indian Studies, 21
animal protection projects, 25, 258n5, 260n35. *See also* ecology restoration work; nature conservation
Apsáalooke, 24
Arapaho, 35, 36, 41, 43–59, 164
Archeological Resources Protection Act (1979), 23
Archibald, Robert, *156*
Arikara, 187
Arlington Springs Man, 203
Awa-Di-ghick-hoo, 106

Babbitt, Bruce, 23
Badlands National Monument, 16

Badlands National Park, 16, 24
Baker, Gerard, 47, 62, 105–21, 123–24, 135, 149–54
Baldy, Cutcha Risling, 232
Barland-Liles, David, 184, 185
Basch, Dick, 151, 158
Battle of Little Big Horn, 136
Battles of River Raisin, 83–86
Bay Mills Indian Community, 101n31
Bear, Max, 35–42, 49, 56, 67
Bear Butte, 24
Bear Butte State Park, 137
Bear Chum, Wallace, 46, 51, 52
Bear Eagle, Sina, 201
Bear Lodge Multiple Use Association v. Babbitt, 23
Bear Lodge Multiple Use Foundation, 23, 30n29
Bears Ears Inter-Tribal Coalition, 262–63
Bears Ears National Monument, 3, 262–63
Bentley, Scott, 89, 92
Big Cypress National Preserve, 263
Bighorn Canyon National Recreation Area, 24
Big Sioux River, 187
Big Spring Reserve, 81
Bison Range Refuge, 258n5, 260n35
Bissonette, Doug, 128
Black Elk, Ben, 26, 136
Black Elk, Charlotte, 126, 129, 130, 133
Black Elk, Nicholas, 16–17, 126

271

Blackfeet Nation, 27n6, 188
Black Hills, 16, 24, 43–59, 122–38
Black Hills National Forest, 137
Black Hills State University (BHSU), 137
Black Kettle, Chief, 164
Black Lives Matter, 173, 174
Blansett, Kent, 222
Blood Run National Historic Landmark, 11, 183, 186, 187
Bodéwadmi, 78
Borglum, Gutzon, 123, 125, 126, 127, 136, 137
Boundary Waters Canoe Area, 240
Brady, Steve, 166, 169, 173
Braided Hair, Otto, 169, 170, 172
Brave Heart, Basil, 127, 130, 134, 138, 201–2
Brown, Ladonna, 172
Buckner, Matt, *146*
Buffalo Gap, 16
Buffalo Home Buttes, 24
Buffalo National River, 11, 216–34
Bureau of Indian Affairs (BIA), 71, 155, 240, 259n25
Burns, Ken, 113, 146–47
Byownway, 187

Cahokia, 187
Calabrese, Francis, 148
California State Parks (organization), 25
Campbell, Ben Nighthorse, 166–67, 173, 175–76
Canyon de Chelly National Monument, 263
Carbaugh, Donal, 199
Caribou, Gilbert, 243
Carroll, Clint, 217
Catlin, George, 196
Cave Hills, 24
cell phone towers, 35–36
Center for Native American and Indigenous Studies (CNAIS), 61, 63
Center of the American West (CAW), 61, 63
ceremonial sites. See *names of specific places*
Challenge Cost Share (CCS) grants, 156
Channel Islands, 203–7
Channel Islands National Marine Sanctuary (CINMS), 198, 203–7
Channel Islands National Park, 11, 198, 204–7

Cherokee, 216–34
Cherokee-Buffalo NR Plant-Gathering Agreement, 220–34. *See also* Buffalo National River; Cherokee
Cheyenne, 35, 36, 41, 43–59, 164, 167–68, 187
Cheyenne River Sioux, 135–36
Chippewa Tribe, 241
Chivington, John, 164, 169, 172
Chumash, 198, 199, 203–7
Chumash Eyes on the Water program, 205
Chumash Heritage Marine Protected Area, 205
Chumash Maritime Association, 204, 206
Chun, Wendy Hui Kyong, 54
Circle of Tribal Advisors (COTA), 155–56
Civilian Conservation Corps (CCC), 15
Clearwater National Forest, 144
climbing, 21–23, 30n25, 30n28
Clinton, Bill, 13n15, 17–18, 23, 26, 30n29, 167
Cochrane, Tim, *253*, 263
collaborations, 7–10, 196–99; at Bears Ears, 262–63; Channel Islands and, 203–7; Haida Gwaii and, 207–9; Max Bear on, 35–42; partnership principles of, 19–21; reciprocal respect and, 43–59; Rocky Mountain NP project, 61–75; stages of, 209–10; Wind Cave and, 207–9
Colorado Pioneers Association, 173
Columbus Quincentennial, 143–44
Cometsevah, Laird, 168, 173–74
condor, 25
Confederated Salish Kootenai, 254, 255, 258n5
Conner, Bobbie, 148–49, 150, 153, 155, *156*
consultation work, 35–42
Cook, John E., 23
Coombes, Brad, 210
Cordero, Alicia, 199, 203
Cordero, Roberta, 205–6
Cordero-Lamb, Julianne, 198, 206
Council for Indigenous, Relevance, Communication, Leadership and Excellence (CIRCLE), 158, 163n76
Council of Forty-Four Chiefs, 166
Crazy Horse, 16

Crazy Horse Memorial, 128. *See also* Mount Rushmore National Memorial
Creation, 24, 31n35, 132–33, 203
Crow Indian Reservation, 107
cultural insensitivity, 148–49
cultural *vs.* natural resources, 37–38
Culver, David, 98n22
Custer, George A., 16, 88, 123
Custer Battlefield Associates, 109, 116

DeCory, Jace, 125, 126, 127–28, 129, 134
deep listening, 52–54, 57, 109–11, 113, 265
Deloria, Vine, Jr., 47
Deschampe, Norman, Jr., 238, *239,* 242, *253,* 256, 260n31, 260n36
Deschampe, Norman, Sr., 238
Detroit River International Wildlife Refuge, 80–81, 91
Devils Tower National Monument, 16, 21–23, 24, 26
Dickson Mounds, 193
Doctrine of Discovery, 127
dolphins, 203
Dorgan, Byron L., 147
Douville, Victor, 128, 131, 135, 139n21
Dry, Debbie, 88
Dull Knife College, 43, 46

ecology restoration work, 25–26. *See also* animal protection projects; nature conservation
Eder, Jeanne, 144–45
Effigy Mounds, 11, 183, 186, 192, 193
endangered animals, 25
Endangered Language Fund, 156
Enough Good People (publication), 157
environmental assessment (EA), 230
erasure of Indigenous people, 2, 51, 133–36, 263
ethnographic overview and assessment (EOA), 43, 57, 122, 136
Ethnography in the Parks program, 2
Evans, John, 169, 175
Evans, Michael, 217, 225
Evans, Mike, 50
Ewing, Phyllis, 184
Executive Order 13175, 18, 19

Farrell, Thomas, 202
Feast of Souls, 90
federal recognition, 17–19. *See also* acknowledgement
Federal Writers' Project, 165
Fiege, Mark, 264, 265
Final Climbing Management Plan (FCMP), 22, 23
Finland, 197
FireCloud, Dorothy, 23, 31n30
fisher, 25
Five Villages, 106
FLETC (Federal Law Enforcement Training Center), 120
Floyd, George, 174
food rituals and diet, 25–26
forest restoration, 25. *See also* ecology restoration work
Fort Berthold Reservation, 105
Fort Laramie Treaty (1868), 136
Fort Malden, 78
Fort Meigs, 86
Fort Robinson, 24
Fort Union Trading Post National Historic Site, 24, 108
Foster, Lance Michael, 183–95, 265
Friend, Chief Billy, 99n22
Friends of Grand Portage, 245
Frog Bay Tribal National Park, 189, 265

Gagnon, Melvin (Bun), 238, 256, 258n2
"Gathering of Certain Plants or Plant Parts by Federally Recognized Indian Tribes for Traditional Purposes" (federal code), 220, 234n6, 235n8. *See also* plant gathering
Gawboy, Carl, 257
genocide, 122, 127, 169, 193
Gibson-Scott, Mary, 169
Gichi Onigaming, 238–39. *See also* Grand Portage National Monument
Glacier Bay National Park (Alaska), 241, 263
Glacier National Park (Montana/Canada), 2, 62, 133, 188
Goering, Karen, 153, *156*
Golub, Alex, 55
Good Earth Tribal National Park, 11, 183, 186
Gorneau, Norma, 170

government-to-government relationship, 17–18
Grand Canyon National Park, 62
Grand Portage (tribe), 238–57
Grand Portage National Monument, 8, 11, 53, 145, 238–57, 263
Grand Portage Reservation Tribal Council, 239, 241, 242, 245, 248, 251, 254, 255, 257
Grand Portage State Park, 240, 242
Grand Traverse Band of Ottawa and Chippewa Indians, 101n31
Great Sioux Nation, 16
Greener, Sharon, 184, 185
Gwaii Haanas National Park, 11, 198, 207–9
Gwin, Pat, 225

Haaland, Deb, 1–2, 3, 40, 114, 176
Haida Gwaii, 207–9
Haida Gwaii Watchmen Program, 207–9
Haida Heritage Site, 207, 208
Halaas, David, 173
Halfmoon, Otis, 151, *152*, 158
Hall, Ed, 155
Hamilton, Bobbi, 52
Hamilton, James, 242–43, 247
Hannahville Indian Community, 101n31
heart, as metaphor, 130
"the heart of everything that is *(Wamaka Og'naka I'Cante)*," 130, 200
Heavy Runner, George, 155
Hehaka Sapa, 16–17
Hells Angels, 129
Hickenlooper, John, 172
hiking trails, 24–25
Hill, Christina Gish, 123, 124, 183, 263
Hill, Matthew J., 43
Historical Research Associates, 21
History Colorado, 174
Hohag, Anna, 25
Hopewell mound site, 188
Hopi, 262
Howell, Chris, *156*
Howkins, Adrian, 264, 265
Hubbard, Harry, 144
Hudson Bay Company, 240
human remains, 36, 148–49, 183–85. *See also* Native American Graves Protection and Repatriation Act (NAGPRA; 1990)
Humboldt marten, 25
Humbug Marsh, 90
Hyde, Anne, 122

Indian Removal Act (1830), 223, 224
Indian Self-Determination Act (1975), 242
Indian Self-Determination and Education Assistance Act (1974), 17
Indigenous Connections project, 62–74
Indigenous nationhood, 6, 17–19, 28n11, 77–94. *See also* self-determination; *names of specific tribal groups and persons*
Indigenous people: activism by, 17–19, 143–44; Creation stories of, 24, 31n35, 132–33, 203; erasure of, 2, 51, 133–36; interpretive storytelling by, 108–10, 150–54; –national parks relationship overview, 1–3; –NPS collaborations, 35–42, 196–210; reciprocal respect with, 43–59; self-determination of, 17, 74, 100n31, 239, 240, 256, 260n36; self-governance of, 238–57; on *Wamaka Og'naka I'Cante*, 16–17. *See also names of specific tribal groups and persons*
Indigenous Peoples, National Parks, and Protected Areas (Stevens), 197
Indigenous Women Hike group, 24–25, 32nn36–37
Ingold, Tim, 130
Inyan Kara Mountain, 133
Iowa Department of Transportation (DOT), 194
Iowa Tribe, 187
Ioway language, 183
Ioway Sac and Fox Presbyterian Mission, 189
Ioway Tribal National Park, 185, 188–89, 193, 265
Ioway Tribe, 183–84, 188
Isha, Luhui, 199, 203

Jandreau, Jim, 129, 137
Jefferson, Thomas, 128. *See also* Mount Rushmore National Memorial
John Muir Trail, 24–25, 26

Kansas Nebraska Act, 189
Kashinski, Al, 243, 245
Katmai National Park, 241
Keepers of the Great Council Fire, 81, 85, 94
Kelly, Alan, 183, 185
Kelman, Ari, 62
Kennedy, Roger G., 23
Keweenaw Bay Indian Community, 101n31
King, Mary Ann, 18
King, Thomas, 191, 195n3
Klamath River, 25–26
Klobuchar, Amy, 253
Knife River Indian Villages National Historic Site, 24, 108, 115–16, 119–20, 143
Ku Klux Klan, 126
Kukpwski, Judy, 99n22

Lac Vieux Desert Band of Lake Superior Chippewa Indians, 101n31
Lakota, 16, 27n6, 46, 122–38. *See also* Black Hills
Lakota, Nakota, and Dakota Heritage Village, 124, 134
Lakota land claim, 136, 141n68, 200
Lame Deer, 122
#LandBack movement, 74
La Pointe, Ernie, 125–26
Laughrin, Lyndal, 204
Leary Site National Historic Landmark, 188
LeBeau, Albert, 185
LeSage, Tony, 243
Lewis and Clark Bicentennial, 142–59
Lewis and Clark National Historic Trail, 149–54, 241, 264
Lewis & Clark: The Journey of the Corps of Discovery (PBS miniseries), 146–47
Lewis and Clark Trail Heritage Foundation (LCTHF), 144
"Lewis & Clark Trail—Tribal Legacy Project" (website), 156–57
Liggett, Deborah, 22, 23
Lincoln, Abraham, 128. *See also* Mount Rushmore National Memorial
listening. *See* deep listening
Little Bear, Richard, 46, 57–58
Little Bighorn Battlefield National Monument, 36, 62, 107, 108–10

Little River Band of Ottawa Indians, 101n31
Little Thunder, Karen, 125
Little Traverse Bay Bands of Odawa Indians, 101n31
Llnagaay, Kay, 208
logging, 207–9
Lowler, Danielle, 99n22
Lowler, Tom, 98n22

Magney, C. R., 241
Maka Oniye, 24. *See also* Wind Cave National Park
Mako Sica, 16
Malla Nature Preserve, 197
Mandan-Hidatsa, 106
Mann, Henrietta, 172
Martin, Darrell, 151
Match-e-be-nash-she-wish Band of Pottawatomi Indians of Michigan, 101n31
Mato Paha, 24
Mato Tipila, 16, 21–23, 24, 26, 30nn24–25
maya pihi, 187
Maya pihi sh'gunikey, 187
McKenzie, Alexander, 241
Meadows, Sammye, 157
Means, Russell, 117–18
Mearhoff, Sarah, 141n59
Memorandum of Agreement (MOA), 230–31
Mesa Verde National Park, 256
Miller, Robert J., 155, *156*
Mississippian period, 186–87
Missouri River, 24
Mnisose, 24
Morrin, John, 243
Mossett, Amy, 155
Mountain at the Center Where He Comes, 126
Mountains of History Teachers Institute, 135
Mountain States Legal Foundation, 22, 23
Mount Rushmore National Memorial, 24, 44–59, 111–12, 121n1, 121n3, 122–38, 139n21. *See also* Crazy Horse Memorial
Mount Rushmore Society, 107, 116, 125
Mount Whitney, 25
Muir, John, 198

Munson, Tom, 183
Murphy, Pat, 185
Myeerah, 78

NAGPRA. *See* Native American Graves Protection and Repatriation Act (NAGPRA; 1990)
National Bison Range, 254
National Historic Preservation Act (1966), 35, 190, 252
National Native American Veteran's Memorial, 174
National Oceanic and Atmospheric Administration (NOAA), 204, 206
national parks and monuments. See *names of specific places*
National Park Service (NPS): as agency, 6, 15–16, 18–19; Bears Ears and, 262–63; Channel Islands and, 203–7; collaboration projects of, 7–10, 40; first Native director of, 1; Grand Portage policies of, 241–54, 258n11, 259n19; Haida Gwaii and, 207–9; –Indigenous people, overview of relationship, 1–3; Mount Rushmore and, 43–59; partnership principles of, 19–21; Plant Gathering Rule of, 220–34; –SRL partnership, 25; Wind Cave and, 199–203
National Park System, 15–16, 89
Native American Free Exercise of Religion Act (1994), 17
Native American Graves Protection and Repatriation Act (NAGPRA; 1990), 3–4, 13n15, 17, 19–20, 65, 185–86, 195n1
Native groups. See *names of specific tribal groups*
Native people. *See* Indigenous people
natural *vs.* cultural resources, 37–38
Nature Conservancy, 188, 204
nature conservation, 196–99. *See also* animal protection projects; ecology restoration work
Navajo, 189, 262
Nepstad, Jim, 184–85
New Holy, 130–31, 140n40
Nez Perce Reservation, 157–58
Niitsitapii, 27n6

Northern Cheyenne Reservation, 43
North West Company, 240–41
NPS. *See* National Park Service (NPS)
Nüümü group, 24–25, 32nn36–37
Nüümü Poyo (The People's Trail), 24–25, 26

Oberstar, Jim, 245
Oceti Sakowin, 16
Očhéthi Šakówiŋ, 27n6
Oglala Lakota College and Sinte Gleska University, 137
Oglala Sioux, 128, 135
Oglala Sioux Tribal Council, 128
Ojibwe, 187
Olekwo'l (Yurok), 25–26
Olson, Ellen, 257
Olson, Sigurd, 241
Omaha (tribe), 187
Oníya Ošóka, 24, 133, 199–203. *See also* Wind Cave National Park
Opaha Ta I, 126
Organization of American Historians (OAH), 20
Orsi, Jared, 264, 265
Osage, 185
Ostler, Jeffrey, 122
Otoe, 187
Otto (tribe), 187

Paha Sapa. See Black Hills
Parker, Patricia, 191, 195n3, 260n26
partnerships. *See* collaborations
Pearson, Maria, 183–84, 195n1
Petefish, Andy, 22, 23
Petroglyphs National Monument, 190
Pine Ridge Historical Society, 136
Pine Ridge Reservation, 17
Pinkham, Allen V., Sr., 144–46, 155, 157
Pitcher, Greg, 155
plant gathering, 11, 216–34, 235n8
Pleiades, 126–27, 132, 138n20
Pokagon Band of Potawatomi Indians, 101n31
Polis, Jared, 174, 175
Ponca, 187
poverty, 135
Powell, Chris, 155
Pratt, Harvey Phillip, 174

Presidential Memorandum for the Heads of Executive Departments and Agencies (1994), 17–18, 23
proprietary jurisdiction, 23–24, 31n33
Pte Kinapapi, 16
Pte Oyate, 187, 200
Public Lands History Center, 21

Quechuan Nation, 29n21

reciprocal respect, 43–59
recognition. *See* acknowledgement
Red Cliff Ojibwe, 189
Red Cliff Reservation, 265
Red Cloud, Darrell, 137
Red Cloud Agency National Landmark, 24
Red Power Movement, 17
Redwood National Park, 25, 258n5
Redwoods Rising, 25
Redwood State Park, 25
Reid, Joshua L., 197
religious freedom, 17, 22–23
Religious Freedom Restoration Act (1993), 17
"Renaming the Northern Channel Islands" (petition; 2021), 207
repatriation, 17, 36, 183–84. *See also* Native American Graves Protection and Repatriation Act (NAGPRA; 1990)
research methods and protocol, 47–50
Reuleaux Bluffs Preserve, 188–89
Richards-Cook, Daphne, 135, 155, *156*
Ritchie, Virginia, 46, 47, 57
River Raisin National Battlefield Park, 77–94
la Rivière Aux Raisins, 78. *See also* River Raisin National Battlefield Park
Roberts, Alexa, 168–69, 170, 171, 175
Robinson, Reed, 23
rock climbing, 21–23, 30n25, 30n28
Rocky Mountain National Park (RMNP), 36, 39, 61–75
Roll, Brenda, 98n22
Roll, Ted, 86–87, 90
Roosevelt, Franklin D., 203–4
Roosevelt, Theodore, 128, 201. *See also* Theodore Roosevelt National Park
Rosebud Sioux Tribe, 23

sacred site, as term, 214n53
Saginaw Chippewa Indian Tribe of Michigan, 101n31
Sámi, 197
Sams, Charles "Chuck," III, 1–2, 3, 114, 176, 264
Sand Creek Act (1998), 167
Sand Creek massacre (1864), 164, 166–67, 169, 170, 172–74, 175
Sand Creek Massacre National Historic Site, 7, 62, 164–76
Sault Ste. Marie Tribe of Chippewa Indians, 101n31
Save the Redwoods League (SRL), 25, 26
Scotts Bluff National Monument, 24
self-determination, 17, 74, 100n31, 239, 240, 256, 260n36
self-governance, 18, 238–57
Sherer, Kenneth, 243
Shulenberg, Ray, 188
Sierra Nevada Mountains, 24–25
Sioux, 16, 23, 125, 128, 187
Six Grandfathers of Creation *(Tunkasila Sakpe Paha),* 16, 24, 126, 132–33. *See also* Mount Rushmore National Memorial
Sixty Years' War for the Great Lakes, 93
slavery, 128
smallpox, 115–16
Smith, Linda Tuhiwai, 47, 198
Soule, Silas, 172–73
Southern Ute Indian Tribe, 61, 65, 66, 69, 70–73
Spence, Mark David, 242
spiritual, as term, 214n53
spiritual poverty, 135
Sprague, Donovin, 136
Standing Rock protest, 74
Stayeghtha, 78
Stevens, Stan, 197, 198
St. Lawrence River Basin, 89
storytelling, 108–10, 150–54, 165–66
strategic collaboration. *See* collaborations
Sun Dance, 46, 129, 131
Sundstrom, Linea, 24
surrendering power, 54–56
survivance, 165–66

taking responsibility, 47–50. *See also* acknowledgement
Tamástslikt Cultural Institution, 148
Tammaro, D'Arcy, 98n22
Tent of Many Voices, 152–54
Te Urewera National Park, 210
Thasuŋke Witko, 16
Theodore Roosevelt National Park, 20, 106. *See also* Roosevelt, Theodore
Thom, Dark Rain, 155
Thornton, Russell, 223
Timbisha Shoshone Homeland Act (2000), 12n8
Tolowa Dee-ni' Nation, 25–26
tomol, 205–6
tourism, 16, 47, 78, 134–35, 141n59, 142
traditional cultural properties (TCP), 183, 190–91, 195n3
traditional ecological knowledge (TEK), 208–9
Trail of Tears, 219, 223
Treaty of New Echota (1835), 223
Tribal Historic Preservation Office (THPO), 2, 35–42, 44, 48–49
Tribal Legacy Project (website), 156–57
"Tribal Marine Protected Areas" (publication), 205
tribal national parks, 11, 183, 185, 188, 189, 193, 194, 265
Tribal Self-Governance Act (TSGA), 18, 238–57, 260n26, 260n38
tribal sovereignty, 6, 17–19, 28n11. *See also* Indigenous nationhood; Indigenous people; self-determination; *names of specific tribal groups and persons*
Tumanguya, 25
Tunkasila Sakpe Paha, 16, 24, 126. *See also* Mount Rushmore National Memorial

Undaunted Courage (Ambrose), 146–47
UNESCO World Heritage Sites, 208
United States v. Sioux Nation of Indians, 136
University of Colorado (CU) Boulder, 61, 62, 66
Upper Sandusky Reservation, 81
US Army Corps of Engineers, 147
US Biological Survey, 201

US-Dakota War (1862), 128
US Department of the Interior, 1, 40, 242–46, 254–55, 259n19, 259n21
US Fish and Wildlife Refuge, 254–55
US Fish and Wildlife Service, 85, 264
Ute Indian Tribe, 189, 262
Ute Mountain Ute Tribe, 61, 65, 66, 69, 70–73, 262
Ute Tribal Historic Preservation Office, 71
Ute Tribe of Uintah and Ouray, 61, 65, 66, 69, 70–73, 189

violence against Indigenous people, 7, 10, 69, 71, 81, 125. *See also* Sand Creek massacre (1864)
Vizenor, Gerald, 165–66
Voyageurs National Park, 251

Waha, Jerry, *244*
Wakhaŋ Tháŋka, 200
Walker, Bob, *244*
Wamaka Og'naka I'Cante, 16–17, 130
War of 1812, 78, 80, 81–83, 85, 89, 93–94
Warrow, Charles Oscar, 83
Washington, George, 128, 139n28. *See also* Mount Rushmore National Memorial
Watkins, Joe, 123, 124
Wellstone, Paul, 243
westward expansion, 57–58
Wetsit, Lawrence, 144
White, Susan, 91
White Face, Charmaine, 125
White Man, Chester, 51
Whyte, Kyle, 232
Wild Buffalo River and Dense Park Forest. *See* Buffalo National River
Wilde, Karen, 170
Williams, Richard, 143–44, 172
Wind Cave *(Maka Oniye/Oníya Ošóka)*, 24, 133, 200
Wind Cave National Monument, 43
Wind Cave National Park, 11, 16, 17, 24, 123, 198, 199–203
Wishtoyo, 203–7
Wishtoyo Chumash Foundation, 204
Woodard, Sandra, 126, 127, 129, 130, 131, 133–34, 140n45

Works Progress Administration, 165
Wounded Knee, 17
Wright, Deryl, 88
Wyandotte of Anderdon Nation, 77–94, 95n6, 100n31, 263

Yellowstone National Park, 2, 62, 256

Yellowstone National Park Protection Act (1872), 31n32
Yosemite National Park, 2, 62
Yukon Flats Refuge, 258n5
Yurok Nation, 25–26

Zuni, 190, 262

www.ingramcontent.com/pod-product-compliance
Lightning Source LLC
Chambersburg PA
CBHW020943230426
43666CB00005B/149